SEVENTH
EDITION

Criminal Investigation
Basic Perspectives

PAUL B. WESTON
Professor Emeritus
Criminal Justice
California State University
Sacramento

KENNETH M. WELLS, J.D.

Prentice Hall
Upper Saddle River, New Jersey 07458

Library of Congress Cataloging–in–Publication Data

Weston, Paul B.
  Criminal investigation : basic perspectives / Paul B. Weston,
Kenneth M. Wells.—7th ed.
    p.   cm.
  Includes bibliographical references and index.
  ISBN 0–13–569013–7
  1. Criminal investigation—United States.   I. Wells, Kenneth M.
II. Title.
HV8073.W44 1997
363.2'5'0973—dc20

96-7975
CIP

Acquisitions editor: Neil Marquardt
Editorial assistant: Rosemary Florio
Managing editor: Mary Carnis
Editorial/production supervision: Linda Pawelchak
Copy editor: Karen Verde
Cover design: Jayne Conte
Proofreader: Maria McColligan
Manufacturing buyer: Ed O'Dougherty

 ©1997, 1994, 1990, 1986, 1980, 1974, 1970 by Prentice-Hall, Inc.
Simon & Schuster/A Viacom Company
Upper Saddle River, New Jersey 07458

Printed in the United States of America
10 9 8 7 6 5 4 3 2 1

ISBN   0-13-569013-7

Prentice-Hall International (UK) Limited, *London*
Prentice-Hall of Australia Pty. Limited, *Sydney*
Prentice-Hall Canada Inc., *Toronto*
Prentice-Hall Hispanoamericana, S.A., *Mexico*
Prentice-Hall of India Private Limited, *New Delhi*
Prentice-Hall of Japan, Inc., *Tokyo*
Simon & Schuster Asia Pte. Ltd., *Singapore*
Editora Prentice-Hall do Brasil, Ltda., *Rio de Janeiro*

For

Gerry Wolcott (1936–1994)

An achiever in motion
an inveterate learner
a student-friendly professor

1959	Appointed deputy sheriff, Sacramento (CA)
1965	Promoted to sheriff's sergeant B.A., Public Administration (Specialization in Police Science), California State College—Sacramento Earl Warren award
1967	Promoted to sheriff's lieutenant
1968	M.A., Social Science, California State College—Sacramento
1969	Appointed Assistant Professor, Cal State McGeorge School of Law, University of the Pacific, Stockton California—Earned Bancroft-Whitney award
1972	Promoted to Associate Professor, Cal State Graduated McGeorge School of Law, with Distinction
1973	Admitted to California Bar
1974	Opened part-time law office, courthouse area
1978	Promoted to Professor, Cal State
1993	Retired

Thirty-four years in California criminal justice
a world-class resource on law and what happens to it in the courts
a long-time role model for many of his students

Contents

Preface

This seventh edition was researched and written in a year of fast-breaking change in crime investigation. Police conduct at crimes scenes and the work of forensic scientists in crime laboratories were examined and reexamined during the O. J. Simpson trial. It was an educational experience that resulted in a heightened awareness as to how best to revise this text.

Initially, three chapters were deleted; Chapter 13 (Report Writing) was moved forward and combined with Chapter 4 (Recording the Crime Scene); and two old chapters covering interrogation and interviewing were combined into one chapter: Interviewing Witnesses and Interrogating Suspects.

Additional material on criminal law was added to the opening segments of each of the chapters in Part III—Investigating Major Crimes.

Eight major chapter segments were added to various chapters:

Classification of crime laboratories (Chapter 6, Laboratory and Technical Services)

Videotaping of suspects (Chapter 9, interviewing Witnesses and Interrogating Suspects)

Stalkers (Chapter 15, Homicides and Assaults)

Community threat groups (Hate Crimes) Chapter 20, Terrorist Activity)

Search warrants—drug cases (Chapter 21, Dangerous Drugs and Narcotics Cases)

Overcoming apathy and indifference of investigators assigned to investigate burglaries (Chapter 23, Burglary)

ATM fraud (Chapter 24, Fraud)

Computer Fraud (Chapter 24, Fraud)

Eight new illustrations, five additional case studies, a four-segment appendix, and a glossary have all been added to this edition, along with two new and timely chapters: Chapter 25, Carjacking, and Chapter 26, Violent Crime, and Kids with guns.

The seventh edition of *Criminal Investigation: Basic Perspectives* ia a bigger and better book, in part because of the helpful suggestions of the following reviewers: Paula M. Broussard, Louisiana State University–Baton Rouge; and Larry R. Phillips, Arizona Institute of Business and Technology.

I also want to acknowledge the meaningful contributions of the following in the development and preparation of this edition: Marlene Hertoghe, an attorney and co-author of *Criminal Evidence for Police*, reviewed the copy on criminal; Charles Lushbaugh, a lieutenant in the Sacramento Sheriff's Department and former U.S. Postal Inspector provided professional advice based on his years of experience and study; Robin Baliszewski, former Criminal Justice editor at Prentice Hall requested this revision and obtained justice educators as reviewers; Rosemary Florio, executive assistant to the criminal justice editor provided prompt and useful responses to telephone calls and letters; Joseph Nekola, former captain in the New York City Police Department and commanding office of the Bronx District Attorney's Detective Squad—now retired and director of security for Rockefeller University in downtown New York—provided professional advice on crime investigation; Kathleen Quinn, Bureau of Justice Statistics Clearinghouse, U.S. Department of Justice skillfully probed the database of the National Criminal Justice Reference Service; Kathryn A. King, Interlibrary Loan Supervisor, California State University, Sacramento help find books and periodicals in a vast network of libraries; Mary Ellen Fraley, my daughter and school psychologist provided insightful comments and helpful suggestions; and Erin Fraley, my granddaughter shared her unique knowledge of teenagers and was willing to talk about this new and important world in crime investigation.

P.B.W.

CHAPTER

1

The Criminal Investigation Function of Police

Criminal investigation is a lawful search for people and things useful in reconstructing the circumstances of an illegal act or omission and the mental state accompanying it. It is a probing from the known to the unknown, backward in time, and its goal is to determine truth as far as it can be discovered in any post-factum inquiry.

Successful investigations are based on fidelity, accuracy, and sincerity in lawfully searching for the facts of an event under investigation and on an equal faithfulness, exactness, and probity in reporting the results of an investigation. Investigators are persons who stick to the truth and are absolutely clear about the time and place of an event and the measurable aspects of evidence. They work throughout their investigation fully recognizing that even a minor contradiction or error may destroy confidence in their investigation.

Some people believe successful police investigations result from intuition or some flash of inspiration or imagination, as in the tradition of Sherlock Holmes. On the other hand, students exposed to old-school detectives are led to believe that police investigations are routine, plodding legwork requiring little imagination and no inspiration. A belief has developed among many persons both in and out of the field of criminal justice that all problems of criminal investigation can be solved quite simply by microscopic examination and laboratory analyses. The truth lies somewhere among the three viewpoints. Criminal investigation involves a close relationship between innovative thinking and diligence and between the investigator in the field and the investigator in the laboratory—the police scientist. Investigators and police scientists work together as a team, reacting to and extending one another's theories and findings, both working patiently and thoroughly to reconstruct a crime from their investigative discoveries.

The joining of science with traditional criminal investigation techniques offers new horizons of efficiency in criminal investigation. New perspectives in investigation bypass a total or major reliance on informers and custodial interrogation and instead increasingly utilize a skilled scanning of the crime scene for physical evidence and a search for as many witnesses as possible. Mute evidence tells its own story in court, either by its own demonstrativeness or through the testimony of an expert witness involved in its scientific testing. Such evidence may serve in lieu of, or as a corroboration of, informers, custodial interrogation, and testimonial evidence of witnesses found and interviewed by police in an extension of their responsibility to seek out the truth of all the circumstances of a crime. An increasing certainty in solving crimes is possible and will contribute to the major deterrent of crime—the certainty that a criminal will be discovered, arrested, prosecuted, and convicted.

Hans Gross (1847–1915) was the earliest advocate of criminal investigation as a science. Gross was a native of Austria, born in Graz. Educated in law, he became interested in investigation while serving as an examining magistrate. He became a professor of criminology at the University of Vienna. Perhaps it was the legal training, or the education in rational theory that is joined with the study of law, that made Magistrate Gross unhappy with the lack of science in police investigation. In any event, he deserves credit for developing a system of investigation. His *System der Kriminalistik*, translated into English and published in 1906, is a classic text in this field.[1]

Gross strongly supported scrupulous accuracy and high ethics in criminal investigation. His greatest contribution to the introduction of science in criminal investigation was the advocacy of a parallel system of inquiry based on the crime scene.

The nature of the crime and the relationship between the time of the occurrence and the time of apprehending the perpetrator determine whether or not the event will be promptly investigated in any depth. When the perpetrator is promptly arrested at or near the scene of the crime, the limits of a preliminary investigation may be extended. If an extensive search for and interview of witnesses is needed, or if an extensive search of the crime scene for physical evidence is necessary, a continuing investigation may begin immediately. Homicides, felonious assaults, "bunco" frauds, drug, and vice cases are prime examples of this type of case. Some criminal acts require detection. They normally would go undiscovered and unreported, except for an alert investigator seeking knowledge of clandestine criminal operations. The preliminary and continuing investigations merge in detecting and investigating such cases as arson, the racketeering activities of organized crime operations, and suspicious deaths. To ensure adequate available personnel with specialized knowledge and abilities for in-depth investigations, as well as the time that is necessary for this work, police agencies usually designate a "detective bureau" or an "investigation division" as the organizational segment responsible for criminal investigation. In medium-sized and large police agencies this segment generally is divided into functional units such as a property crimes unit (burglaries and larcenies) and a violent crime unit (homicides, assaults, robberies, and rapes).

A reasonable period of time in which to expect an apprehension varies with the seriousness and complexity of the case. Assigned investigators often encounter temporary setbacks in a continuing investigation and must distinguish between these blocks and real dead ends. When an investigator believes that work on the case has exhausted all promising leads, it is within his or her duty to recommend that the case be suspended or closed.

The investigator is responsible for bringing an investigation to a successful conclusion, for exonerating innocent persons involved in the case, and for focusing the investigation on the guilty person(s). The responsibility for developing evidence that will further the investigation, lead to the identification and apprehension of the offender(s), and assist in the prosecution is placed on the assigned investigator. In effect, it is a command responsibility in that it is ultimate.

In many police agencies the follow-up work involved in a continuing investigation is segmented, so that individual leads, rather than the entire case, are assigned to an investigator. The assignment is considered complete when the basic inquiries along avenues suggested by the lead are completed and a report of work done is filed by the investigator. Of course, if this inquiry led to the perpetrator of the crime, the case would be closed by an arrest made either by the investigator whose inquiry disclosed the perpetrator or by another person.

THE LEGAL SIGNIFICANCE OF EVIDENCE

Evidence is the only means of satisfying the triers-of-fact of the truth or untruth of allegations and accusations made by the parties in their pleadings. Inasmuch as investigators must collect all the evidence, and prosecutors and the court must weigh the significance of any evidence in relation to its possible presentation in court, the first item of importance is whether the evidence is admissible. All investigators must have a working knowledge of the rules for the admissibility of evidence in order to ensure that the evidence will be admissible in court. Admissibility usually depends on the evidence being relevant, material, and competent.

The legal significance of evidence rests in its influence on the judge or juror. Once evidence has passed the test of admissibility and is part of the court record, it has a potential for influencing the outcome of the trial. Any piece of evidence, either alone or in combination with other evidence, must be persuasive to the triers-of-fact. This is the impact energy of an item of evidence.

Investigators must learn the difference between evidence and facts to avoid confusion in evaluating evidence in its role as proof. Evidence is not synonymous with fact. Evidence may be ambiguous—that is, subject to different interpretations. It may be false—exaggerated, planted, or perjured. It may be modified by forgetfulness, inattention, or silence. On the other hand, a fact is the truth (insofar as the truth can be determined by the triers-of-fact in a criminal trial). A fact (in this sense of the term) is the effect of evidence, and it is dependent upon evidence. A fact is established from a very personal evaluation of the evidence presented in a particular case by the trier-of-fact. Evidence may tend to prove a fact, or may be sufficiently strong to compel a conclusion of fact, or may be just strong enough to create a reasonable doubt.

The American system of justice presumes the defendant to be innocent and requires the prosecution to prove the case against the defendant beyond a reasonable doubt—to a moral certainty. These legal principles of the adversary system of justice have a simple reality factor—accusations of crime must be supported in court by legally significant evidence.

A knowledge of evidence and its legal significance is essential to success as an investigator. The investigator must know what evidence is required on the issue of guilt or innocence; whether such evidence indicates guilt or innocence; and, when guilt is apparent, whether such evidence—in total—is likely to prove guilt beyond a reasonable doubt. In the final analysis, the success of an investigation depends on the evidence collected and its legal significance.

QUALIFICATIONS OF AN INVESTIGATOR

An investigator must have outstanding qualifications. He or she must be quick thinking and unusually keen of mind. The following personal attributes contribute to a successful career in the detection of crime:

1. An unusual capability for observation, objective perception, and recall.
2. The power of deliberation and deduction—unhurried, rational thinking.
3. An extensive knowledge of criminal law, rules of evidence, investigative concepts and techniques, scientific aids and laboratory services, and knowledge about the people who commit crimes and of the *modus operandi* of criminals.
4. The power of an intellectually controlled constructive imagination or some "native" awareness of the mental processes of criminals, and—sometimes—of their victims.
5. The capacity to work and cooperate with fellow investigators, to share knowledge and crime information with them, and to accept and give constructive criticism.
6. The ability to offer some indication of the development of a personal ethical philosophy that likely will cope adequately with the confusion, ambiguity, and compromise not uncommon while conducting criminal investigations.
7. Apparent potential for mastering job skills and work dimensions of crime investigation and developing as an investigator-trainer (instructing and supervising less experienced investigators).
8. Past history of physical fitness and emotional stability, and no apparent ongoing problems in these areas.

Most police managers and supervisors believe that a review of job performance as a patrol officer is the best indicator of future potential as an investigator. In turn, assignment to work on major cases usually depends on job performance as an investigator.[2]

SELECTING AND TRAINING INVESTIGATORS

There is always room for improving the method of selecting investigators. Matching people to the function of criminal investigation requires a complex review of past accomplishments, present capacity, and future promise. Ideally, the persons selected will prove to be men and women with an extra ounce of ability, judgment, integrity, initiative, and industry—individuals who can meet the unexpected and handle events as they arise.

In New York City, many years ago, the selection method for detectives (investigators) was at the complete discretion of the police commissioner. It still is. So is the policy of rewarding unusually good arrests or beyond-the-line-of-duty courage with press-conference promotion to detective. However, over the years, the chief of detectives in New York City has emerged as the dominant factor in this selection process, and recent chiefs have utilized an advisory board of superior officers within this division to screen candidates and make recommendations.

At one time, it was not unusual for a board member to receive a "hook," which is an off-the-record call by a "very important person" about an applicant. Today, however, such calls are of limited value.[3] Legal restraints and antidiscrimination procedures are merged with great care in identifying detective applicants who can do the work.

Selection of personnel through a civil service system requires a written test of proven validity and reliability that is reasonably job-related (and will not lead to lawsuits). An agency other than the employing police department should be used and a contract negotiated that will: (1) allow for the design and preparation of a job-related written examination of short answer or short essay questions with easy-to-defend "key" answers; (2) keep this examination confidential (and safe from theft or unauthorized scanning) prior to testing; (3) utilize a confidential coding system so that examiners grading answer sheets see only numbers, rather than the names, of applicants; (4) grade each test, establish a "pass" grade, prepare a list of successful applicants, and deliver that list to the chief of police. In addition, the contractor should establish a no-excuse policy for applicants who claim they are unable to appear at the time and date of the test—or at least allow a surgery-only excuse.

Civil service tests also require adequate notice of the testing, a full-text job description, and related information such as the "weight" or value of the written test as part of the overall examination.

If the decision makers in the police department want a nonpartisan, nonpolitical overall test, they need to ask the contractor to develop a test that measures judgment and decision making, for example, ascertaining how certain the applicant is of his or her response to questions (a. agree; b. strongly agree;

c. disagree; d. strongly disagree), and have the "strong" responses carry a reward.

In the nonpartisan/nonpolitical test, the written test carries a high "weight"—90 percent. The remaining 10 percent is usually allocated to seniority in the patrol force, departmental awards, or disciplinary penalties.

This type of testing is useful because the qualities of an investigator spelled out earlier in this chapter are a "wish list," but an applicant's potential as an investigator can be identified by using state-of-the-art selection techniques designed to test for desired characteristics.[4]

New investigators usually begin training with a few days or weeks in a vestibule school (a new assignment) and complete it after a short period of on-the-job training under the guidance of an investigator-trainer. The entry-level classes orient the new women and men to life on the street without a uniform, including what to expect and what is expected of them. The on-the-job trainer is viewed as a mentor rather than a supervisor—a co-worker who identifies a new investigator's mistakes as "ours" and discusses corrective actions as options. The objective of this training is keep as many new detectives on staff as possible.

An emerging need is the addition to this training of a hands-on course in forensic science (criminalistics) that will upgrade the skills of the new men and women in recognizing and collecting physical evidence at crime scenes. Ideally, the investigator-trainer would be assigned to complete this training along with his or her "rookie."

CRIMINAL INVESTIGATION AS ART OR SCIENCE?

Sometimes, a nagging fear enters the minds of senior and command investigators regarding whether crime investigation can be taught. It usually follows a huge mistake by an investigator who should not have bungled any case—a man or woman with extensive experience. Excuses fail to fully explain these situations.

In England, a top-drawer chief constable responded to this disturbing problem in a paper presented at a conference of high-level British police officials concerned with criminal investigation. His position was that crime investigation can be taught, if the selection of new investigators discovers women and men who have the basic qualifications and they are taught by the best available teachers.[5]

Selected References

1. HANS G. A. GROSS, *Criminal Investigation,* 5th ed., trans. John Adam and J. Collyer Adam, rev. by R. L. Jackson (London: Sweet & Maxwell Ltd., 1962).
2. BARBARA GELB. *On the Track of Murder: Behind the Scenes with a Homicide Commando Squad* (New York: William Morrow & Company, 1975), pp. 16–23.
3. E. W. COUNT, *Cop Talk—True Detective Stories from the NYPD* (New York: Pocket Books—Simon and Schuster, 1994), pp. 2–4.

4. Bernard Cohen and Jan Chaiken, *Investigators Who Perform Well* (Washington, D.C.: Department of Justice, 1995), p. 55.

5. ———, *Crime Investigation—Art or Science,* edited by Alistair R. Brownlie, SSC (Edinburgh and London: Scottish Academic Press, 1984), pp. 48–53.

Chapter Review

Discussion Questions

1. Define criminal investigation.
2. Explain the legal significance of evidence.
3. What personal attributes of a man or woman are likely to be most important to investigators?
4. Compare the New York City method of selecting investigators with the civil service method.
5. Can investigation of crime be taught? During an in-class discussion session, would you choose to support or disagree with the British writer?

Library Assignment

Locate at least five books or articles related to the criminal-investigation function of police and list them under the names of the authors as a selected bibliography.

CHAPTER

2

Ethical Awareness

> The best evidence in the world will not stand up in court if the jurors have doubts about its integrity.
>
> —*Los Angeles Times*

Ethics is used as a euphemism for corruption and crime in U.S. police and law enforcement agencies. A *euphemism* is a substitution of an inoffensive word for others that might offend or suggest something unpleasant.

A twenty-page article in a recent issue of the *Journal of Criminal Justice Education* suggested using ethical dilemmas involving in-service police students as in-class discussion topics. However, the dilemmas cited concerned arresting elderly individuals for minor crimes, waving off relatives for traffic infractions, and accepting meals without payment—a great article, but . . .[1]

Currently, police officers are accused of or have pled guilty to murder during an armed robbery (New Orleans); forging a judge's name on an arrest warrant (Los Angeles); and—in a group of about fifteen—robbing drug dealers of money and illegal drugs (New York City). The result is that the police officers involved—men and women—are likely to serve many years in prison.

Add to the list of ethical problems perjury, racism, police brutality, "planting" and tampering with evidence, and there is no doubt that unethical law enforcement personnel exist. And there is no doubt that all right-thinking people need to know that *police officers are "clean" at hiring time. What is it then that turns some of them into "dirty cops"?*

If the major ethical problem is criminal conduct by working police officers, are discussion sessions keyed to common ethical philosophies relevant or meaningful? If not, eliminate them and deal directly with the problem of criminal behavior by working police officers—from wrongful death and other felonious acts to less serious misconduct.

Dealing with these concerns can be called *ethical awareness,* as this term deals with some of the influences likely to cause criminal behavior and gets all the issues out on the table.

Ethical awareness, even at average levels, warns a person that criminal behavior is "wrong" as well as unlawful, and that misconduct on the job is "wrong" and substandard conduct. Similarly, there are inner indications that it is not "right" for criminal investigators to use the wrong means to gain a desired result, the right means to achieve a wrong end, or to act out anything that is immoral or unprincipled.

In the last few years, "street" detectives have become aware of a change from the good old days, when witnesses were not reluctant or unwilling to talk to investigating officers. They have identified this unfriendliness as a general mistrust of police, that simply blaming a "few bad apples" in the department could not erase all of its recent transgressions. There's also a bitter awareness that the term *jury nullification* is becoming more common in the courthouses of America: The jury's not-guilty verdict is influenced by mistrust of police witnesses.

Let us hope that there is an awareness in the criminal justice academic community of a need to begin "focusing attention on ethical issues that go to the heart of policing." This is the message of a full-page advertisement in the *Police Chief* of August 1995, announcing a new Center for Law Enforcement Ethics by the Southwestern Law Enforcement Institute on the campus of the University of Texas at Dallas.

Since this announcement was made in the official publication of the International Association of Chiefs of Police (IACP) a month before its annual convention, it is reasonable to assume that it was aimed at IACP members. They are an appropriate audience because they are all men and women likely to understand that "ethics" means no misconduct, no corruption, and no criminal behavior.

ETHICAL AWARENESS AND MORALITY

Morally decent persons develop an awareness of moral goodness and a feeling of obligation to obey their inner sense or conscience. Conscience is a self-policing phenomenon alerting an individual to the moral goodness of contemplated action.

James Q. Wilson's book, *The Moral Sense,* is about morality and conscience and people. In its preface he writes: "I wrote this book to help people recover the confidence with which they once spoke about virtue and morality." It is a hopeful book that could help police executives now confronted with an aggressive and hostile community trying to understand the scandals in police departments across the country, and for fellow officers seeking the same understanding.[2]

PRE-EMPLOYMENT ASSESSMENT

Entrance-level hiring procedures in police agencies usually precede an appointment as an investigator, because hiring is at the uniformed police officer level. In other law enforcement agencies the screening of job applicants for the position of special agent or investigator occurs just prior to hiring.

A law enforcement agency assigns investigators to inquire into the character and reputation of job applicants and reject any applicant found to be unfit because of want of character or integrity, or the existence of habits making the applicant unfit to assume on-the-job duties. This background examination scans the past-life history of applicants for about 15 years, depending on age. References, co-workers, and neighbors are among those interviewed and questioned as to the character, reputation, and job suitability of an applicant.

Psychological tests and lie-detector examinations have been used to supplement background investigations, but the major reliance has long been on this past-life probing and prying. Character assessment based on past performances is tricky, but it is a proven valid and reliable means for forecasting future behavior.

CRIME AND OUTRAGEOUS CONDUCT

There is a rich history of corrupt conduct in America's police establishment. Years ago the locus of this corruption was vice and gambling, with the madams, bookmakers, and other gambling-game operators paying police officers on vice squads for "protection" each month to avoid arrests. Today, the money tree includes narcotics and drug dealers and the thing of value is money—big money.

Outrageous behavior is detailed in the complaints of citizens against police officers and the litigation and settlements made upon these claims.

However, the real-world dimensions of police crime and outrageous behavior were never disclosed until the Fuhrman tapes were played at the O. J. Simpson trial and were aired on prime-time television.

IMPACT ON CRIMINAL INVESTIGATION

A major result of these disclosures is that the labor pool of men and women who want to become police officers will decrease and the most desirable candidates will not apply. Recruitment of working police officers will become more difficult as many applicants may now have records of prior misconduct.

A secondary problem may be keeping detectives from contamination before remedial action corrects the problem.

Because it is vital to their work, detective squad bosses are likely to be active participants in future discussion and decision-making sessions aimed at solving the problem of criminal and outrageous behavior by police officers.*

STANDARDS FOR INVESTIGATORS OF CRIME

Investigators have obligations that derive from common membership in the community of investigators. There is a basic responsibility to conform to prevailing practices and an accountability when behavior is strange and unusual. In general, the behavior expected is that of a reasonable person exercising care and prudence, self-discipline and judgment in his or her work.

Reasonable care—in its legal definition—is care fairly and properly taken in response to the circumstances of a situation—such care as an ordinary prudent person would take in the same time frame, conditions, and act(s).

Self-discipline and *judgment* mean jump-starting an inner moral sense in decisions on the moral quality of actions and discriminating between right and wrong.

Conforming to professional standards of conduct and having an appreciation of the ethical viewpoint of a reasonable person presents a profile of an investigator who is conscientious, reliable, and responsible without regard for varying situations. It also describes a person who can justify, warrant, or excuse his or her conduct.

Selected References

1. JOCELYN M. POLLOCK and RONALD F. BECKER, "Law Enforcement Ethics. Using Officer's Dilemmas as a Teaching Tool," *Journal of Criminal Justice Education*, 6, No. 1 (Spring 1995), pp. 1–20.
2. JAMES Q. WILSON, *The Moral Sense* (New York, The Free Press, 1993), p. vii.

Chapter Review

CASE STUDY: THE SPECIAL CRIME SQUAD* _____

The scene and the characters in this case are the standard ones in U.S. criminal trials. The scene is a courtroom, and the participants are judge and jury; prosecutor and defense counsel; prosecution witness and defendant. The unusual nature of this case, however, is that both the witness and the defendant are police officers.

*See Department of Justice Document 1 in Appendix C.
*This is the first of the case studies. The content of case studies relates to chapters in which they appear. The story line of the event is true; facts are from police or public records. Names and places have sometimes been changed to ensure anonymity.

The testimony reported here details the essential elements of the process of the corruption of a police officer. The crime charged is unstated, and the defendant is identified only as "Bob," but it is apparent that the witness being questioned is a police officer exposing police dishonesty and corruption. The testimony presents a very unpleasant picture: the corruption of almost an entire police unit. This is a unit known as "The Organized Crime Suppression Squad," or "OCSS," which is staffed with two lieutenants and fifteen detectives who specialized—at least that was their assigned function—in developing intelligence about organized crime.

Cast of Characters

Judge	Anonymous
Defense Counsel	Anonymous
Assistant District Attorney	Anonymous
Defendant	Bob (not otherwise identified)
Prosecution Witness	Detective Sergeant Daniel Costello

SCENE 1: *A courtroom. There is a high judicial bench, an adjacent witness stand and chair, and a table and two chairs in front of the bench and witness stand. As the scene opens, the judge is seated on the bench, the two chairs are occupied by the defendant and his counsel, the witness chair is empty, and the Assistant District Attorney is standing in front of it.*

ASSISTANT DISTRICT ATTORNEY: I would like to call my first witness: Detective Sergeant Daniel Costello. *(Sergeant Costello appears and sits down in witness chair.)*

JUDGE: Have you been sworn in?

DETECTIVE COSTELLO: Yes, your Honor.

(Assistant District Attorney walks toward witness stand and begins questioning Detective Costello.)

ASSISTANT DISTRICT ATTORNEY: What is your name and occupation?

DETECTIVE COSTELLO: Daniel Costello—I am a sergeant of detectives—all detectives are sergeants—and I work for the police force of this city.

ASSISTANT DISTRICT ATTORNEY: How long have you been in this occupation and rank?

DETECTIVE COSTELLO: Ten years in the police department, four years in the rank.

ASSISTANT DISTRICT ATTORNEY: About two years ago, I understand you were assigned to this new unit, the Organized Crime Suppression Squad, and that within a few days of working in your new job you visited a high official of your police force. Do you recall this event?

DETECTIVE COSTELLO: Yes, I do.

ASSISTANT DISTRICT ATTORNEY: When was it and who was involved?

DETECTIVE COSTELLO: It was just after St. Patrick's Day, March 18th, of this year. It was about ten in the morning, and the person involved was Captain Richard Jones of the Police Academy.

ASSISTANT DISTRICT ATTORNEY: Tell us in your own words what happened on this occasion.

DETECTIVE COSTELLO: I knew Captain Jones from the Academy—he was my instructor. He was a lieutenant, and I was a recruit. I told him I thought the OCSS, the whole group, was infiltrated or penetrated by the mob, the hoodlums, and narco pushers. He listened—I talked. His advice was to take it up with higher authorities in the department. He made a phone call arranging a meeting for me, and I thanked him, and left the office.

ASSISTANT DISTRICT ATTORNEY: What happened next in direct relation to this talk?

DETECTIVE COSTELLO: I met a captain from the Internal Security Division that night, at a few minutes after ten, in the parking lot of the golf course— the city one.

ASSISTANT DISTRICT ATTORNEY: Would you please identify this man and tell us, again in your own words, what happened at this meeting.

DETECTIVE COSTELLO: His name is Captain John Behan—he works directly under the chief. He came over to my car, and I told him substantially what I had told Captain Jones. He told me that I had no specific evidence that he could use, but that if I was willing to work with him, I could get the evidence. Captain Behan gave me his home phone number, and told me to call him. He said we would meet again where we were, in the golf course parking lot. That was for when I had something to tell him. We shook hands and split.

ASSISTANT DISTRICT ATTORNEY: Did you meet the captain again in this golf course parking lot? That is, Captain Behan?

DETECTIVE COSTELLO: Yes, I did. All told, I met with him about seven or eight times.

ASSISTANT DISTRICT ATTORNEY: At any of these meetings did Captain Behan spell out in any way what your job was in this new arrangement with him?

DETECTIVE COSTELLO: Yes, he did. Thoroughly. I was to work undercover, for him and the chief. I was to act as if nothing was out of order, and to come up with some specific evidence of what I had said about dishonesty.

ASSISTANT DISTRICT ATTORNEY: In this new role, did you know the defendant?

DETECTIVE COSTELLO: Yes, he was one of my associates, another detective sergeant—a member of OCSS.

ASSISTANT DISTRICT ATTORNEY: During this time of your association with the defendant, did you at any time participate with the defendant in any event which led you to make a report about him to Captain Behan?

DETECTIVE COSTELLO: Yes, and it was on the Monday after I first met Captain Behan. That would be March 21st, of this year.

ASSISTANT DISTRICT ATTORNEY: Tell us, in your own words, what happened at this time—on this occasion.

DETECTIVE COSTELLO: I met the defendant, Bob, in the Nitro Bar and Grill, on Seventh and Main Streets. It was about 11:00 A.M. He had a hoodlum with him that I knew as Big Bart, Bart Nino, and he introduced us. Nino took some money from his pocket right away and handed some bills to me. I said, "What's that for?" Nino said, "Get yourself a hat." I said, "I don't wear a hat," and gave him back the money.

ASSISTANT DISTRICT ATTORNEY: Do you know the amount of money?

DETECTIVE COSTELLO: No, I don't. Several bills, folded up. No, I do not.

ASSISTANT DISTRICT ATTORNEY: What happened next?

DETECTIVE COSTELLO: Nino shrugged his shoulders and gave the money to Bob—the defendant. Then, Nino talked a little bit about nothing much, ball games and girls, and he left. I asked Bob, "What's he buying?" He said, "Not much." Then I said something like, "Why me?" He said, "Why not, you don't use money?" Then he told me that Nino wanted to get some records taken out of our squad files about his brother—his younger brother. Bob said the kid was trying to go legit, and our records were bugging him in getting a job. I heard him out, then left and went back to the office.

ASSISTANT DISTRICT ATTORNEY: Did you do anything in relation to this conversation?

DETECTIVE COSTELLO: Yes, I did. I went to our files—everyone was out to lunch. I got young Nino's file folder out, looked at it, found he was wanted for suspicion of receiving stolen property and for suspicion of homicide in another case. I xeroxed the file papers, and I put the xerox copies in my desk drawer—which I locked—put the record file back in our filing cabinet, and then I went out to lunch myself.

ASSISTANT DISTRICT ATTORNEY: Now—at any future date, did you have anything to do with this record again?

DETECTIVE COSTELLO: Yes. It was the following Saturday, that's March 26th, this year. I went into the office early, went to our files and looked for young Nino's record. I took it out and examined it, and I found that the photo had been changed—Big Bart's photo was substituted for his brother's picture, and the wanted cards were missing.

ASSISTANT DISTRICT ATTORNEY: I show you folder marked "Nino, Alberto," and I ask you do you recognize it?

DETECTIVE COSTELLO: *(Reading)* Yes, it's the fixed-up, tampered-with folder.

ASSISTANT DISTRICT ATTORNEY: In relation to this xerox copy of the original folder in your squad files about this young Nino—what happened to that?

DETECTIVE COSTELLO: I have that here *(showing file folder)* with me now.

ASSISTANT DISTRICT ATTORNEY: Your Honor, can I have both these files marked for identification? Thank you. Your witness *(to defense counsel)*, counselor.

(Defense Counsel stands, and begins cross-examination.)

DEFENSE COUNSEL: Are most of your fellow police officers honest?

DETECTIVE COSTELLO: Yes, most of them are honest—and hard working.

DEFENSE COUNSEL: How many officers, in your knowledge, entered the police department for the purpose of becoming dishonest?

DETECTIVE COSTELLO: None, to my knowledge—not to my knowledge.

DEFENSE COUNSEL: I gather, from your prompt answers, that you know a great deal about your fellow police officers, is that true?

DETECTIVE COSTELLO: Well—I guess I do. They're my co-workers. Why not?

DEFENSE COUNSEL: Now—Tell the court if any conduct of yours has bothered or upset your fellow co-workers.

DETECTIVE COSTELLO: I don't—I don't understand the question.

DEFENSE COUNSEL: It's a simple question, but let me withdraw it, and phrase it in this fashion: To your knowledge has any of your conduct upset your fellow police officers?

DETECTIVE COSTELLO: Oh sure! That's a different thing. Sure, yes.

DEFENSE COUNSEL: Tell us of such an incident that you consider important.

DETECTIVE COSTELLO: Well—When I was transferred out of uniform, from patrol to the OCSS in plainclothes, I grew a beard *(puts hand to face, indicating beard)* and wore some clothes; well—the kind of clothes I only used to wear on my day off, kind of sharp, I suppose. The guys in the squad used to tell me, "What a disguise!"

DEFENSE COUNSEL: And that upset you, bothered you—emotionally disturbed you?

DETECTIVE COSTELLO: Well, I don't know all that. You asked the question. Say it bugged me a bit.

DEFENSE COUNSEL: Why? Why would this remark bother you—this "Quite a disguise"?

DETECTIVE COSTELLO: It wasn't any makeup, really a disguise. It was just the clothes I liked. That's why it bothered me.

DEFENSE COUNSEL: Oh, I'm beginning to understand. Now—Tell me this: In relation to the charges of dishonesty against my client, your fellow police officer, did you ever get any feedback from him about yourself as a person, or as a police officer?

DETECTIVE COSTELLO: Yes, a few times, mostly about—or along the lines of—something like: "Why don't you go along with the guys?" or, "Why do you have to be different?"

DEFENSE COUNSEL: This was in relation to your manner of dress, your appearance?

DETECTIVE COSTELLO: No, it wasn't. It was in relation to the money he was making, and that I didn't want to take—like from Nino.

DEFENSE COUNSEL: Your Honor, would you direct the witness just to answer the question.

JUDGE: No, I don't think I will. You asked the question, and it was open-ended. Let it stand along with its answer.

DEFENSE COUNSEL: Thank you, your Honor.

DEFENSE COUNSEL: Did the defendant or any of your co-workers in this Organized Crime Squad ever actually do anything to indicate any dislike for you?

DETECTIVE COSTELLO: They—They sure did. All of them did. They stopped talking to me. Except when they had to, like a phone call for me, then it was a "Here, you—" Real brief. And they would stop talking to one another when I came in the room, or walked up to them on the street.

DEFENSE COUNSEL: This animosity resulted from your dirty work, the role of informer, or spying on your fellow workers?

DETECTIVE COSTELLO: No, Counselor. At that time, no one knew of what you term "dirty work." All they knew was that I wouldn't do any business with the hoodlums—that I wanted to do my job just like I get paid for it.

DEFENSE COUNSEL: There is entrapment in your role, is there not?

ASSISTANT DISTRICT ATTORNEY: Your Honor, I object. The question—

JUDGE: *(Interrupting)* Sustained.

DEFENSE COUNSEL: *(Resuming questioning)* Since you place such a premium on doing what you get paid for, did you ever counsel or advise my client to do the same thing?

DETECTIVE COSTELLO: You sure you want to hear this?

DEFENSE COUNSEL: I asked the question.

DETECTIVE COSTELLO: Just before I left the Nitro bar on the day we met Big Bart Nino, I said to Bob, the defendant: "My God, you're making forty thousand dollars a year. You could never make this kind of money on the outside doing any other kind of work. You know you have a family, kids. Don't be stupid. Think about it." That was how it ended.

DEFENSE COUNSEL: Was there any response to these words of yours—any words said at all by my client?

DETECTIVE COSTELLO: No, not much. Something like, "If I really did, think about it—I'd blow my brains out."

Source: Weston, Paul B., *Criminal Justice and Law Enforcement: Cases* (Englewood Cliffs, NJ: Prentice Hall, 1972). Reprinted by permission of Prentice Hall.

Discussion Questions

1. Do the facts of this case justify a conclusion that police dishonesty is an inescapable part of the "system"?
2. Is the "thing of value" in this attempt to corrupt Detective Costello the money that would be given to him or the approval of his associates?
3. If you were a member of the jury in this case, would you consider Detective Costello to be a credible witness, and his testimony truthful?

Library Assignment

Review available material and prepare a short bibliography on police corruption and criminal behavior.

Workbook Project

Develop a list of possible influences on ethical awareness. Within your own personal experience, note the three most influential.

CHAPTER
3

The Crime-Scene Search

The preliminary investigation is the first phase of the total investigation, during which the following duties should be completed:

1. Establish whether a crime has been committed; arrest the perpetrator; determine the type of crime by category, and, if possible, by specific classification.

2. In eyewitness cases, secure a description of the perpetrator, his or her vehicle (if any), and direction of flight; transmit data to the dispatcher for radio broadcasting to other police as an alarm or "want."

3. Locate and interview the victim and witnesses; record stories and take statements, when warranted; secure and accurately record identity, addresses, and other necessary data for future contacts.

4. Protect the crime scene; search for and collect objects and traces that are obviously evidence or likely to be evidence; mark evidence for identification and protect it from change, loss, damage, or contamination; safeguard it to protect its integrity by maintaining control from the time the evidence is found to the moment it becomes an exhibit in the prosecutor's case.

5. Determine how the crime was committed, the extent of personal injuries, and the nature and value of property taken.

6. Record in field notes and sketches all data about the crime, the stories of the various participants and witnesses, the crime-scene search and evi-

dence collected and its disposition, measurements taken at the scene, and other pertinent information; arrange for a photographic summary of the crime scene and major items of evidence; make required reports.

The scene of the crime is the focus of the preliminary investigation. En route to the scene, the assigned investigator plans his or her action upon arrival and reviews the problems usually connected with any crime scene.

The first step in processing a crime scene for clues and evidence is an accurate survey of the surroundings and a careful evaluation of the situation—what is often described as "a long, hard look." Deliberate action at this time guards against false moves and mistakes. The impact of the overall picture of the scene upon an experienced investigator will provide guidelines for modifying a base plan of action. The assigned investigator must ascertain as soon as possible where the crime happened. Usually the crime scene is readily discernible.

A search for evidence starts with effective protection of the crime scene. The searcher must be certain that nothing has been removed from the scene nor added to it since the arrival of responding police—in short, that the scene is intact. Posting freeze signs *(Keep Out—Crime-Scene Search in Progress)* and stretching tape or other barriers aid in delineating the security area. Guards posted at its perimeter prevent the entry of unauthorized persons.

The main purpose of a search must always be kept foremost in the mind of the investigator. It is to look for clues and for evidence of what happened during the crime. It is not a random groping but rather a selective looking for objects and materials. The expertise of the investigator, acquired by training and experience, indicates what things are to be found at the scenes of different types of crimes. To be successful, the main purpose of looking must be aligned with some particularity in knowing what to look for. Otherwise the search lacks the necessary professional direction.

The work of the preliminary investigator concentrates on three of the basic elements of investigation: searching the crime scene, collecting and preserving evidence found at the scene, and locating and interviewing witnesses available at or about the crime scene. When crimes are not witnessed or when a reliable witness cannot be located at this stage of the investigation, the investigative leads likely to produce a solution to the crime will originate with physical evidence found at the crime scene.

The command at a crime scene is often hectic. Most law enforcement agencies specify that the "first officer" to arrive at the scene is in charge until the arrival of a patrol sergeant. This sergeant (or officer of higher rank) is in command until he or she is relieved by a detective or another sergeant or officer of higher rank. In minor crimes, the sergeant may relinquish command by calling the dispatcher and reporting that he or she is leaving the scene and reporting the name of the officer now in charge. At the scene of more serious crimes, the sergeant waits at the scene for the detective's arrival, briefs him or her about what police at the scene have learned about the circumstances of the crime, and turns over command of the investigation to this investigator. However, this sergeant will remain at the scene in command of the uniformed personnel guarding the limits of the scene, monitoring new arrivals, and like duties.

At the scene of more serious crimes, particularly homicides, larger police units field a so-called Mobile Crime Laboratory with detectives trained in forensic science or crime laboratory forensic scientists to process the crime scene.[1]

At this point, it becomes even more difficult to determine who is in charge.

Despite this identification problem, most police units have men and women who are self-starters and work together to get organized and ready for the search of a crime scene.

SYSTEMATIC SEARCH PROCEDURES

The methodology of searching depends on the case and the scene. Staffing problems in police units as well as problems associated with the proffering of evidence in court have brought about the development of the single-officer search. Associates of this officer often assist in locating evidence, but they do not disturb it or collect it. The goal is to limit the number of officers in possession of evidence found at a crime scene to the officer searching the scene. The use of double coverage in searching crime scenes is valuable as a double check for evidence, but it frequently results in conflicting testimony by searching officers.

When the search must cover a wide area, the available investigators should be assigned in teams. One member of each team serves as the single officer to collect evidence, and each team is assigned responsibility for the search of a specified segment of the crime scene. The entire searching operation is commanded by a designated investigator or a superior officer.

Prior to a search, the assigned investigator surveys the scene, noting its dimensions and whether there is an adjoining entry (approach) and exit (flight) area. A crime scene is the place of the crime including any adjoining entry or exit area. This evaluation is the basis for setting limits on the area of the search, for determining how to organize the search procedure, and for ascertaining what assistance is needed.

Traditionally, systematic searching has utilized the following methods:

1. A point-to-point movement following a chain of objects that are obviously evidence.
2. An ever-widening circle technique in which the searching officer starts at the focal point of the scene or the center of the security area and works outward by circling in a clockwise or counter-clockwise direction until the fringes of the protected area are reached. The ever-narrowing circle technique reverses this procedure: The searching officer starts at the outskirts of the crime scene and works toward its focal point.
3. A sector search in which the scene is subdivided into segments and each sector is searched as an individual unit.

4. A strip or grid search for outdoor areas. In the strip search the area to be searched is plotted like a football field. Searching starts at a sideline and moves across the field to the other sideline, searchers working back and forth across the field until the entire area is searched. The grid search begins after the strip search is completed. It covers the same area in a similar manner but at right angles to the previous search pattern. Metal or wood stakes and heavy cord are used to direct and control outdoor searches (see Figure 3–1).

Some experienced investigators dislike describing any searching method by name, as it emphasizes technique rather than purpose and has often led to criticism during cross-examination. When queried on the witness stand about searching the crime scene, investigators should state that they began the search by looking around, moved generally in a clockwise movement (if that was the technique), and made field notes as items of evidence were discovered. Their field notes then support the search as a systematic examination of the scene.

A search of deceased persons, when there is a suspicion that a criminal act is involved in the death, is often assigned to field representatives of the coroner's or medical examiner's office. In some areas the coroner or medical examiner will permit body searches by the police upon request. In any event, the search must be methodical and thorough. If the victim is a female, a policewoman or a female relative, friend, or neighbor should be asked to perform the body search. Many police units require the investigator to delay such search until it can be made in the presence of a disinterested witness and require the investigator to record the name of such a witness in his or her field notes. A complete list of all property found on the deceased victim as well as where it was found (that is, right-side pocket of trousers, hidden in bra) are made part of the officer's notes.

The ability to discover and recognize evidence at crime scenes is a prerequisite to successful searching. As the investigator surveys the crime scene preparatory to searching, he or she develops some concept of the type and nature of evidence that should be the objective of the crime-scene search. Physical evidence can be anything from massive objects to microscopic traces. The nature of the crime offers the first clue. Weapons are used in assaults; there is an entry in burglaries; a fire is set in arson cases. Possible clues in any case may be suggested by the victim, the *modus operandi* of the offender, and other circumstances that can be observed during this survey.

Where to search for physical evidence is particularized by the type of evidence the investigator is seeking. In assaults and homicides, the injuries sustained by the victim suggest a weapon and orient the search toward it. In burglaries, the means used to gain access to the premises and the place of entrance indicate the possible location of tool marks. Tabletops, glassware, and other smooth surfaces guide the search for imprints. Soft earth, mud, and dust are known sites for foot and tire impressions. Miscellaneous traces may be found anywhere at the scene.

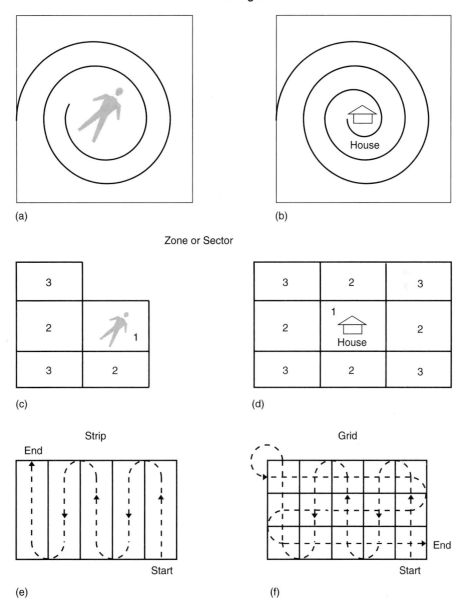

FIGURE 3–1 Searching methods: (a) indoors, (b) outdoors, (c) immediate area, (d) extended area, (e) strip search of large area, (f) grid search of large area.

Initially, then, it is a case of identifying the type of evidence one wants to find and its likely area of discovery, then making a systematic search, and finally recognizing it when it is found. The experienced investigator is always alert for evidence which may seem unimportant but is in fact material and relevant.

COLLECTING EVIDENCE

Investigators should not rush to pick up evidence, for its significance may be destroyed in the process. The investigator's field notes should record the discovery and recognition. In addition, photographs and accurate measurements are necessary to show its original position and its nature.

In searching for evidence at crime scenes, the "golden rule" of Hans Gross has been a guide for investigators in the United States since *System der Kriminalistik* was translated into English by John Adams and J. Collyer Adam in 1906: "Never alter the position of, pick up, or even touch any object before it has been minutely described in an official note and a photograph taken."

The integrity of evidence is maintained by keeping it in its original state. No alterations are made to any item that is or may be evidence. Blood, rust, grease, and dirt are not removed from objects; nor does the investigator add his or her fingerprints to the evidence or smear or wipe off any such clues. An item of physical evidence inherently important in its own substance may have another item of evidence added to it. This can range from a fingerprint on a fragment of glass to blood and fibers on weapons.

Evidence likely to be found at crime scenes and amenable to scientific analysis is divided into seven major groups: (1) weapons, (2) blood, (3) imprints or impressions (traces of a person or a vehicle), (4) marks of tools used to gain access to locked premises or containers, (5) dust and dirt traces, (6) questioned documents, and (7) miscellaneous trace or transfer evidence.

Weapons

Firearms should be handled to preserve ballistic identity. *Ballistics* is the identification of firearms, bullets, cartridges, and shotgun shells. Interior ballistics refers to the functioning of firearms through the firing cycle, and exterior ballistics is the study of projectiles in flight. Ballistics uses the inside of the barrel (the bore with its "lands" and "grooves"), the firing pin, the breech face in which the firing pin hole is located, the chamber, and the ejector and extractor as primary sources for identification.[2]

In marking firearms and cartridges/shells for identification, the investigator should avoid marking in any ballistics identity area.* When the firearm's design allows for the removal of the barrel, the frame of the weapon and the barrel should both be marked. The cylinders of revolvers should also be marked because revolver design permits the interchange, without tools, of cylinders of differing calibers. In addition, the investigator should also mark for identity the bolts of automatic rifles and shotguns, and the slides of automatic pistols, when these parts are removable without tools. The bolt and slide of such weapons contain the firing pin, the breech face, and the extractor (see Figure 3–2). When the weapon is a revolver and it is found to contain fired and/or unfired cartridges, the rear face of the cylinder should be marked to

*See Chapter 5 for the how-to of marking evidence for identification.

indicate the location of such cartridges in the chambers of the cylinder (see Figure 3–2, center right).

Investigators reject techniques for picking up firearms such as the insertion of a pencil in the barrel of a handgun and follow procedures that will not change the portions of the weapon commonly used for ballistic comparison and identification. Firearms should be picked up by their rough or checkered wooden portions, if possible, or any external metal portion except the trigger guard and trigger area and promptly placed in a container or tied to a board or strong piece of cardboard. Firearms should not be handled unnecessarily, nor should the mechanism be actuated time and time again. Safety is of paramount importance. Unloading a firearm should be held to the minimum procedure for emptying the gun. There must be no attempt to fire a gun, to dismantle it, or to interfere with the mechanism in any way.

In describing a firearm, start with the name of the manufacturer and the serial number. These data are a necessity in tracing the weapon. Record all names and numbers stamped on the firearm along with their location on the gun. Some numbers are part numbers, and one- or two-digit numbers are usually model numbers. Some marks may indicate the maker, others proof testing. (Emblems and symbols, proof marks, are used to show tests to prove the strength of the chamber of a firearm by actual firing with maximum loads.) All these marks help identify the gun. Sometimes a number has been obliterated by grinding, filing, or center-punching. The investigator should describe the damage and its location and request laboratory services to restore the number. (It is difficult to restore when center-punched, but it may be possible; and even a fragment may be helpful.)

FIGURE 3–2
Firearms should be marked for identity where indicated by arrows.

The caliber of the weapon or its gauge (if a shotgun) is also an identifying characteristic. It is often marked on the firearm in a stamping associated with the name of the manufacturer or model number. If the caliber is not marked, the investigator should qualify any estimate of the caliber by putting "unknown" in his or her field notes and noting a measurement across the bore of the weapon in fractions of an inch. This is in line with the requirement of accuracy in collecting evidence. A defense attorney can raise doubt about testimony in relation to firearms (and possibly doubt about the entire police case) by questioning police failure to make accurate notations regarding the caliber of a weapon. It is professional conduct to qualify any lack of knowledge, and it is more desirable to put down unknown than to specify an approximate caliber and later to find it is grossly wrong.

Fired (empty) and unfired cartridge cases, shotgun shells, and spent bullets should also be handled with particular attention to the portions used in ballistic identification; that is, the base and the rim or cannelure just above the base of the case, and the side of the cartridge or the shell immediately above the base (extractor marks). When possible, fired cartridges and shells should be marked for identification on the top *inside* surface or high on the side of the case; unfired cartridges and shells are marked on the side; and spent bullets are marked on the bottom (see Figure 3–3).

When empty cartridge cases or shotgun shells are picked up, the location should be pinpointed by measurements for future reference. Because some firearms throw out, or eject, the cases with some distinctiveness as to direction and force, the exact location of the cases indicates the position of the person firing the gun, sometimes at each shot fired.

Spent bullets are excellent clues to the firearm used in the crime. They must be carefully removed from their point of impact, and the location at which they are found recorded accurately in the investigator's field notes. Investigators must search for bullets embedded in walls and furniture at crime scenes. A spent bullet can be ruined by the traditional digging out with a

FIGURE 3–3 Mark fired and unfired cartridge cases, shotgun shells, and spent bullets for identification where indicated by arrows.

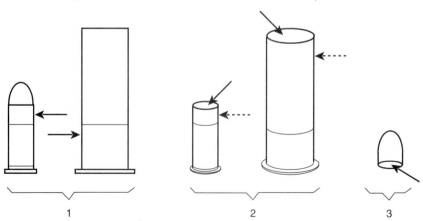

pocketknife. Care must be taken so that the drill or cutting instrument used in this operation does not ruin identifying characteristics on a bullet by coming into contact with the softer metal. Bullets also should be handled as little as possible and packaged to prevent movement and to protect the side portions used in ballistic comparison and identification. When the victim is dead and an autopsy is performed, one of the postmortem forensic science procedures is the removal of spent bullets without damage—in their original condition. In the United States, physicians and surgeons are very conscious of the evidential value of spent bullets.

Because it is sometimes necessary to establish the position of a person in crimes involving a shooting, the investigator at the crime scene should look closely for places the bullet has struck in its flight.[3] These marks or holes are items of evidence and are correlated with other positioning factors, such as the location of ejected cartridge cases found at the scene and the path of a bullet in the body of a victim.

Other weapons commonly encountered by police investigators are knives and various blunt instruments. Accuracy in describing such evidence may depend on a general description. The presence of serial numbers is not common, and clubs and similar weapons are not stamped with the name of the maker. The length of a knife blade and of the handle is easily determined without excessive handling, as are the length and other dimensions of clubs and bludgeons. Distinctive features of the object should be noted in the field notes of an investigator. The greatest possibility of error in connection with these weapons results from the tendency, when searching, to ignore as suspect weapons common items of furniture or equipment at the scene of the crime. In one case the bludgeon used in a killing was a piece of 2-inch by 4-inch lumber about $3\frac{1}{2}$ feet long—the scene of the crime was a lumberyard. In another case, an apparently innocuous empty soft drink bottle was collected; later, the autopsy report cited a depressed fracture of the skull of the victim as the cause of death, and laboratory tests discovered blood traces on the bottle.

Blood

Blood is a trace that can divulge a great deal of information about the criminal, the victim, and what happened during a crime. Police first to arrive at the scene of assaults are often smeared with blood in their efforts to help a victim. In some cases it is almost impossible to walk about the scene without stepping into some trace of blood and then transporting it around the scene. On the other hand, investigators often fail to recognize bloodstains on clothing and other objects and, therefore, fail to collect valuable evidence. To complicate the problem of blood and its stains and residues as evidence, quite frequently there is a mixture in this residue at crime scenes, when both the victim and the offender have been wounded. In addition, the evidence may have an animal as well as a human source, or a common liquid may dilute the blood.

Despite some of the problems associated with this type of human trace, blood drops and splashes help to narrow the size of the suspect group, support the identity when a suspect is located, and plot the movements of the victim and the assailant (see Figures 3–4 and 3–5). In a posttrial investigation of the famous Sam Sheppard case in Cleveland, Ohio, Dr. Paul L. Kirk, criminalist from the University of California at Berkeley, used the distribution of blood stains at the crime scene to show where the assailant stood during the assault upon the victim, Mrs. Samuel Sheppard, and the left-to-right swinging motion used in striking the fatal blows.[4]

Imprints and Impressions

Personal imprints and impressions found at crime scenes identify or tend to identify a person or vehicle as having been at the crime scene. These traces offer promising areas of inquiry, although they usually require a suspect or a suspect vehicle before their evidential value can be realized.

Imprints are markings on a surface left by protruding parts of a person or vehicle. Impressions are made by a person or object in a material softer than the item of evidence making the impression. Imprints may be lifted by dusting with a contrasting powder, applying a clean, sticky, transparent tape to the dusted area to pick up the markings, and then pressing the tape to a clean card to preserve it. The object with the imprint sometimes can be transported to the laboratory.

Fingerprints at crime scenes are usually latent prints (impressions caused by the transfer of body perspiration or oils present in finger ridges to the surface of an object) and are of great importance when sound collection techniques enhance their value in suspect identification.[5]

Chance fingerprints may be found on any smooth or nonporous surface, from the glass of windows and bottles to tabletops and doorknobs. They even have been developed by evidence technicians on semirough and porous surfaces. Plastic fingerprints, those pressed into the material, are found in soft materials at crime scenes and can be preserved by photographic means, intact recovery, or a molding process.

Tire marks of modern vehicles are highly individualistic. When suspects are identified and located, vehicles used by such persons can be processed for comparison with the tire marks found at the scene. What is more, tire marks can be clues that aid in solving a crime inasmuch as the type of vehicle used may indicate fruitful lines of investigation; it can help to know, for example, that the vehicle was a large late-model, high-priced car or a 10-year-old automobile.

Shoe, heel, and footprints in soft earth or other material that will take and hold a likeness are excellent when a suspect is located (see Figure 3–6). A trail of shoe- or footprints offers some clues to the size or weight of the person making them, his or her speed of movement, and any abnormal "walking picture."

The following procedure is suggested for casting impressions found in soil at crime scenes:

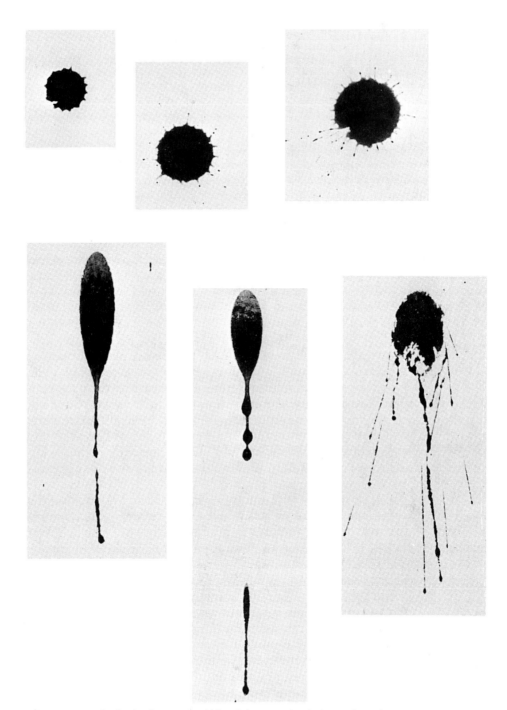

FIGURE 3–4 The hydrodynamics of blood drops and splashes—drop size
increases with the distance of the fall; the tails or pointed
ends indicate the direction of movement, the rounded edges
face the source of bleeding.

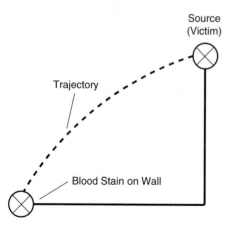

FIGURE 3–5
Blood trajectory—wall stains.

1. *Gather all the materials together.* Plaster of paris is excellent. (It is not expensive, and a great deal of it can be used to gain some skill by making practice casts.) About 3 pounds is required to cast a foot impression, slightly more for an extensive tire mark.

2. *Prepare the impression.* "Dam" the impression along its outer edges to permit an "overhang" in casting by placing a retaining frame in the ground around the impression no closer than 1 or 2 inches from the edges. Remove loose pieces of dirt and other debris from the impression.

   In fine sand, coat the impression with several (five to seven) layers of alcohol and shellac, allowing time for drying between applications. Apply indirectly with a spray gun—deflect the spray droplets with a dish-sized piece of cardboard so that the mist drifts into the impression rather than blows directly into it.

   In snow, a layer of sifted or sprayed talcum powder is applied first; next a light layer of plaster is sifted into the impression and allowed to stand for 10 to 15 minutes as it absorbs moisture from the snow. Then the cast is built up by alternate sifting with plaster and indirect spraying with a fine water mist. The center can be filled with small quantities of mixed plaster that has been allowed to stand for 5 to 10 minutes to cool and harden. When casting in snow, you should remember that, in hardening, the plaster mix gives off heat that will melt the snow and ruin the impression.

   In any substance other than firm soil, it is a worthwhile procedure to make a small impression in the same substance, not far from the impression to be cast, and to pour test casts in order to evaluate special difficulties prior to attempting to cast the evidence.

3. *Prepare the mixture.* Make a generous estimate of the amount of mixture necessary to fill the impression (the mix is 2 to 1 or 8 to 4 parts plaster to water), and select a suitable cup or pail for mixing. Then work rapidly. Place less than the estimated amount of water in the container, pour in plaster slowly until water has been absorbed, add water and plaster as

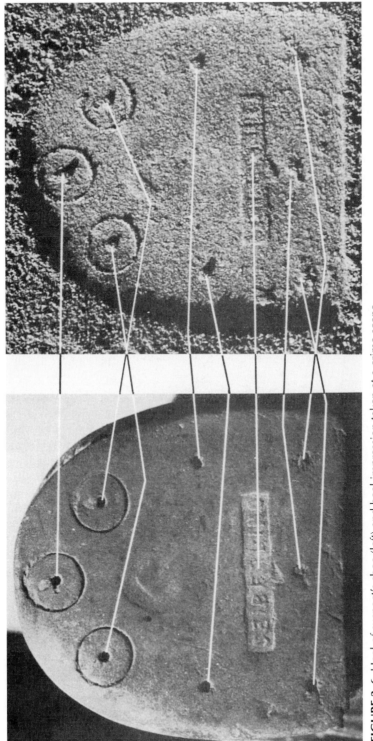

FIGURE 3–6 Heel of suspect's shoe (left) and heel impression taken at a crime scene. Lines show points of comparison—a "match."

necessary, and stir, to remove lumps and air bubbles, until the mixture is about the consistency of heavy cream.

4. *Pour the mixture into the impression.* Pour the mixture slowly, from the distance of about 2 to 6 inches, using a spatula to cushion the fall of the mixture and to direct it into all corners and angles. Pour to the halfway mark of the impression and stop.

5. *Reinforce the cast.* Reinforce the mixture with wire or gauze.

6. *Finish the cast.* Pour the mixture to the top of the impression and above it to allow for an overhang that will extend to the dam walls and support the basic impression. Casts are 1 inch thick or thicker as a general rule, and the overhang is no less than 3/8 inch.

7. *Mark for identification.* Mark the cast as it is hardening (when it is tacky), write appropriate identification (initials, case number, date, etc.) with a pencil.

8. *Remove the cast.* Be certain the plaster has hardened before you attempt removal. Remove framing, and work at one corner to loosen the cast. Tip it upward, and draw it out with a smooth motion.

9. *Clean the cast.* Allow the cast to harden completely (3 to 4 hours), then remove any adhering dirt without damaging cast.

10. *Package the cast securely.* Cushion it in a strong box to prevent movement in transit.

Other materials, such as the casting compound used by dentists and their technicians, may be equally suitable for this casting technique.[6] Investigators should experiment with compounds other than plaster of paris and determine the material they find easiest to work with and that will produce the best results for them.

Highly individual impressions of teeth are often left in partially consumed food found at the scenes of burglaries. Bite wounds in assaults, homicides, and some sex cases are impressions. Surprisingly, even the impressions left by a gloved hand or by the fabric of trousers in a knee print have uncommon characteristics, and laboratories can now develop such impressions. Fabric impressions in the paint of vehicles often are important evidence in hit-and-run cases.

Standard evidence collection procedure with these imprints and impressions is as follows:

1. Record, measure, and photograph in place.
2. Collect intact, if the article upon which the imprint or impression is made is not too large or heavy and is amenable to transport without damaging the evidence.
3. Dust and lift, if fingerprints; make a cast of impressions.
4. Mark for identification, and package carefully.
5. Transport to laboratory.

Toolmarks

Just as weapons are likely to be found at the scene of assaults and homicides, the marks of tools are likely to be found at the scene of burglaries or other crimes in which the offender forced entry into the premises or forced open locked containers at the crime scene. The criminal must gain access by force. Windows, doors, and skylights are the traditional means of ingress for such criminals. Roofs and walls have been cut and pounded in to provide entry. In some cases the criminals exit from another area of the building. The *modus operandi* of many burglars is multiple entry through rows of offices or commercial establishments, with the burglars burrowing through interior walls in a molelike progress from store to store. The places of entry or exit and all the locked desks and cabinets that were forced open along the way will bear some mark of the tools used. Safes, unless found open or opened with a combination or key, also bear traces of prying, ripping, or battering. Scientific laboratory procedures can individualize these marks and impressions. When suspect tools are discovered, laboratory technicians can make comparison analysis.

The initial procedure in collecting the marks of tools used to gain access is to locate accurately the impression at the scene and to record the general description and measurements. Accuracy, again, is the keynote. The impressions must be measured with an accurate rule and the dimensions recorded in the investigator's field notes. Photographs of the impressions should be made. If it is feasible, the substance bearing the mark should be transported to the laboratory. It is sometimes possible to make a cast impression of the mark, and this will make an effective trial exhibit. Inasmuch as the mark is small, a material more costly than plaster of paris can be used to form the impression. Various dental waxes and molding materials can be pressed into the imprint and allowed to harden. The overriding factor in reporting and collecting tool impressions at the scene of a crime is the preservation of the impression, or its reproduction, for future comparison with a suspect tool.

In the trials of offenders, many of the problems encountered in relation to toolmarks have arisen from conflicts between the size of tool impressions reported by the investigator in his or her preliminary on-the-scene investigation and the size of the impression developed later by evidence technicians on the scene or in the police laboratory. The tragedy of this conflict is that a few more minutes of the investigator's time during the preliminary search for evidence is all that would have been necessary to eliminate this problem by accurate reporting of tool mark sizes.

Quite often an investigator finds a tool that might have made an impression at the scene of the crime and attempts visually to match the tool with the impression by fitting it to the mark. This second contact of the tool to the impression ruins the evidence. Prevailing practices suggest that the best procedure is to treat any likely tool as suspect and to collect it for laboratory comparison by an expert.

Tools found on a suspect or under his or her control at the time of arrest (or traced to the suspect) become incriminating evidence when laboratory examinations show that the particularities of the suspect tool relate to the tool impressions found at the crime scene.

Dust, Dirt, and Other Traces

Traces have value as associated evidence when laboratory examination can establish identity and origin and can connect a suspect with a crime. The evidence potential of soil and mud, the debris from the underside of a vehicle and its fenders, and dust in various forms, particularly on persons and their clothing, is excellent. Minute samples of glass and paint recognized as evidence may be processed to demonstrate similarities or differences in identity and origin. Larger samples of glass may be matched physically, and chips of paint at crime scenes now can be matched layer by layer with a suspect sample. Laboratory analysis has developed an amazing range of identifications in comparing these substances and tracing origins to the crime scene, the victim, or the perpetrator.

Potential evidence in arson cases exists when the nature of the trace can be identified as a flammable fluid or its residue. Traces of volatile fluids of suspicious origin are lost if not searched for promptly and retrieved without delay. Precautions should be taken primarily to avoid loss by evaporation.

The residue of explosives should be handled similarly; the primary requirement here is to find and collect as much of the bomb as possible. Fragments of the container and timing mechanism of the bomb, if any, are loaded with residues, as are the objects close to the center of the explosion.

There is also a direction-of-force potential inherent in arson cases and crimes involving explosives. The survey of the fire scene may indicate fire trails resulting from the natural downward flow of liquid fire accelerants; laboratory tests may indicate the origin and spread of the fire from a study of the depth of charring in burnt wood collected at the scene. The expansion of gases in an explosion is discernible in a visual examination at the scene and can indicate the type of explosive and its placement. Distinctive damage at explosion sites can indicate the amount and type of explosive used in the blast.

The direction of force can be determined and some data on the force used can be gained by studying glass and its fragments found at crime scenes. Glass breaks first on the side opposite to the force applied to it. When bullets penetrate a glass window, the projectile blasts out a cone-shaped hole on the side of the glass *away* from the shooter. The shape of this exit crater gives some indication of the direction or angle at which the bullet struck the glass (see Figure 3–7).

Questioned Documents

In cases involving checks, the check itself is a questioned document and an important item of evidence. In apparent suicides the victim may leave a note. This is an evidence item, and when found, it is often processed as a questioned document.

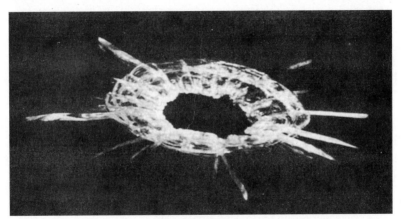

FIGURE 3–7 "Cratering" of bullet hole in glass window indicates direction of travel; bullet enters from the bottom or small side of the crater and exits from the top or large side.

Documents that have been destroyed or partially destroyed by fire can sometimes be restored by laboratory technicians. Charred paper must be sprayed with a preservative and requires special packaging and transport to the place of examination. This is a critical and time-consuming process, but the potential of charred paper as evidence is worth the work involved in its recovery.

The general style of a typewritten document, margins, separation of words at the end of the typed lines, spelling errors, paragraphing, and other indentation may all contribute to identification of the person who typed it.[7] There is an excellent opportunity of matching a suspect typewriter through a comparison of the exemplars taken from the machine and the document under suspicion.

Indented or embossed writing is sometimes found on telephone pads, blotters, and other impressionable surfaces—despite the fact that the original paper upon which the writing was made has been removed. Carbon paper sometimes contains identifiable traces of written material when the carbon process is used to prepare duplicate copies.

Other Evidence

Hair and fibers have an excellent potential for identification. The primary problem with this type of evidence is finding it. When laboratory examination indicates that hair or fibers found on the victim or on the victim's clothing are not the victim's, the possibility exists for future identification when a suspect is located. In addition, examination of the suspect for such traces may uncover hair or fibers belonging to the victim.

The stains of seminal fluid are a trace found in sex crimes. The presence of such stains is often meaningful to the investigation. They are useful and, at times vital to show the commission of a crime when the victim is too young to testify or to remember having been molested or when the sexual attack is part of a homicide.

In narcotics and dangerous drug cases (possession and sale of drugs), the evidence must be identified as a drug in violation of the law. The examination need only identify the drug as one of the illegal drugs.

Drugs and poisons may be the means of attack in homicide and assaults and the fatal substance in suicides and, as such, must be searched for and collected. When the victim becomes ill in a suspected poisoning case or is given an emetic to bring up a poisonous fluid or substance, the investigator must collect all material vomited. Urine specimens also should be collected if the victim is still alive. In poison cases precautions must be taken primarily to prevent loss, contamination, or deterioration of the substance in transit. The collected physical evidence, as well as the stories of any witnesses about the circumstances of death, should be recorded in the officer's field notes. Such data help the medicolegal experts prepare a clinical history of the death.

Cigars and cigarettes, butts, and ashes have an evidence potential. Unique brands, lipstick smears, and chewed ends may be of particular value. Wooden matchsticks and a distinguishable method of breaking them have been rewarding to searchers in some cases. Paper matches, torn from a book of matches, are evidence at the scene likely to reward a searcher if the book from which the matches were torn can be located and traced to a known suspect.

PHYSICAL CHANGES AT THE SCENE

Investigators search for and collect evidence of any observable damage to objects at the scene—things that are bent, broken, dented, or scratched, and furniture turned over, broken, or moved from its normal location at the scene. Disarrangement, damage, and theft may be useful in determining what happened and who did it. A fight or struggle of some kind is indicated by overturned and broken furniture. Damage may indicate the direction of force. Photographs of the scene preserve the "as is" quality of the change or disarrangement.

Not only may articles taken from the scene lead to a major suspect, but they also may supply incriminating evidence when recovered from the possession or the control of a suspect at the time of arrest. The responsible investigator includes a description of the stolen property in the alarm broadcast. Even articles of little value, such as snapshots or ashtrays, have a potential value as evidence when recovered.

THE AUTOPSY AS AN EXTENSION
OF THE CRIME SCENE

In homicide cases the autopsy performed on the victim is an extension of the crime scene and offers an additional opportunity to search for clues and evidence useful in the investigation. This is also true, to a lesser extent, of medical testimony about the wounds of a victim or injuries that occur in a rape or other sexual assault. The investigator searching the scene and the evidence technician lack the professional attainments of the medical examiner, the pathologist, and the toxicologist. Therefore, any examination of the victim in homicide cases by the investigator searching the scene must be a superficial one.

Many coroners and medical examiners consider an examination of the clothing of the victim to be a segment of the postmortem inquiry and desire the same laboratory personnel processing the vital organs of the deceased to examine the clothing carefully. However, in suspicious death cases it is the duty of the police investigator to make certain that an examination is conducted in a police laboratory if the local autopsy surgeon does not wish to examine articles of clothing worn by the deceased victim at the time of death or does not have adequate facilities for doing so.

The findings of these postmortem examinations usually are sufficiently clear and in adequate detail to give an accurate reconstruction of the circumstances of death.[8] The autopsy report usually provides the investigator with the following data:

1. The time of death.
2. The nature of the injuries resulting in death.
3. Any other injuries found or evidence of chronic illness or disease.
4. The weapon or substance causing death.
5. Whether the body was moved after death.
6. Amount of blood alcohol.
7. The contents of the stomach—indicative of the interval between victim's last meal and his or her death and what was eaten.
8. Any indications of virginity, sexual knowledge, rape, or pregnancy in female victims; or of sexual deviancy in male victims.
9. Any evidence of blood, hair, or other traces not the victim's.[9]

Evidence developed by medicolegal experts may include bullets removed from a homicide victim, comparison of fatal wounds with a suspect weapon, identification of the poison causing death, or data on the identification of trace material scraped from under the victim's nails or recovered from the clothing of the deceased. Because this requires a search procedure, the victim may be considered an extension of the crime scene.

Selected References

1. Evidence technicians are called scenes-of-crime officers in England. See H. J. Walls, *Forensic Science* (New York: Praeger Publishers, 1968), p. 4.
2. JURGEN THORNWALD, *Century of the Detective*, trans. Richard Winston and Clara Winston (New York: Harcourt Brace Jovanovich, 1965), p. 434.
3. J. S. HATCHER, FRANK J. JURY, AND JOE WELLER, *Firearms Identification and Evidence* (Harrisburg, Pa.: Stackpole Books, 1957), p. 286.
4. PAUL HOLMES, *The Sheppard Murder Case* (New York: David McKay Company, 1961), pp. 218–21.
5. RICHARD SAFERSTEIN, *Criminalistics: An Introduction to Forensic Science*, 5th ed. (Englewood Cliffs, N.J.: Prentice-Hall, 1995), pp. 424–35. Also J. B. Wallace, "In Defense of Tra-

ditional Technology in a High-Tech World," *Journal of Forensic Identification,* 43, no. 4 (July/August 1993), pp. 378–385.

6. CLAUDE W. COOK, *A Practical Guide to the Basics of Physical Evidence* (Springfield Ill.: Charles C Thomas, Publisher, 1984), pp. 126–28.

7. WILSON R. HARRISON, *Forgery Detection* (New York: Praeger Publishers, 1964), pp. 209–12.

8. MILTON HELPERN, "Forensic Pathology and the Law," in *Law, Medicine, Science and Justice* (Proceedings of the First Interamerican Conference on Legal Medicine) (Springfield, Ill.: Charles C Thomas, Publisher, 1966) pp. 47–74.

9. WILLIAM F. KESSLER AND PAUL B. WESTON, *The Detection of Murder* (New York: Arco Publishing, 1961), pp. 44–47.

Chapter Review

Discussion Questions

1. Is it true that a crime-scene search is a selective looking process by a person with some expertise in criminal investigation?

2. What are the major rules in collecting crime-scene evidence?

3. Explain the implications of failure to maintain the integrity of an item of evidence.

4. What suspicions about an entire police investigation are likely to develop in the minds of the triers-of-fact when standard operating procedures are not followed in collecting evidence at a crime scene?

5. Describe physical evidence likely to establish the position of a shooter in cases of attacks with firearms.

6. What marks or traces are most likely to be found at the scenes of burglaries?

7. What physical evidence may link a rapist with his victim?

8. Develop a concept of physical evidence as technical proof, rather than as circumstantial evidence to be considered only as an inference.

9. What parts of a firearm should be marked for identity? What is the most desirable place to mark fired cartridge cases for identity? Spent bullets?

Library Assignment

Trace the history of the ballistic examination of firearms.

Workbook Project

Prepare a list of physical evidence likely to be found at the scenes of (1) assaults and homicides, (2) burglaries, (3) suspicious fires, and (4) sex crimes.

CHAPTER
4

Recording the Crime Scene

Field notes made during the search of a crime scene are the basic record of the search and the evidence discovered. Photography and sketching offer opportunities to portray graphically the scene and the evidence located during the search. The investigator's report is prepared from his or her field notes. Notes and report both become permanent records in the case and have the inherent integrity of records prepared in the performance of official duties. Photographs and sketches must be made with care to represent the subjects accurately.

Sketches and photographs usually are offered in evidence as exhibits that are more realistic than words or that can assist the jurors in understanding the case or both. They must withstand the basic tests of relevancy and materiality. There is no legal presumption that graphic representations are correct. They are verified as accurate by the person who made them or by any witness having sufficient knowledge of the subject to say the sketch or photograph is a faithful representation of the thing shown.

Maps and diagrams were used to illustrate testimony long before photographs were first offered in evidence. The nonphotographic drawings of a doctor illustrating the appearance of blood as seen microscopically were admitted into evidence as exhibits to clarify the verbal description of a medical witness in a Maine case as early as 1857. When a drawing is admitted into evidence, its ability to clarify testimony and to orient evidence to the scene of the crime enhances such testimony and evidence.

Videotaping is the most recent addition to the use of graphics at the crime scene; its pictorial storytelling provides substantial benefits for investigators. Likewise, the videotape may be equally useful to defense attorneys in court.

FIELD NOTES

Field notes are memoranda made by the investigator during an investigation. They begin with assignment to the case and arrival at the scene; they are continued until the case is closed. That portion of field notes concerned with recording the search for evidence at a crime scene usually includes the time the search started, the names of assisting personnel, the weather and light conditions, a description of the area searched as the investigator proceeds, a note of any special equipment used, and an accurate note of the discovery of every significant item of evidence—when and where it was found, who found it, and what it looks like. Any measurements made to place the evidence are recorded in these notes at this time, as is the disposition of the evidence. Sketches and diagrams drawn at the crime scene are field notes that, by their graphic portrayal of the crime scene, supplement the measurements and other data recorded.

In addition, the searching officer must record in his or her field notes any damage to objects at the scene or any disturbance of furniture and other objects. Anything unusual or foreign to the scene also is noted. Moreover, the failure to locate an item of evidence commonly found at the scene of similar crimes is noted and recorded. These factual reports may be important as clues or as negative evidence to overcome defense claims regarding the theory of the crime and its reconstruction.

REPORT WRITING: THE PRELIMINARY INVESTIGATION

The place and time to get data for a preliminary investigation report are at the crime scene during the initial investigation. Anything omitted or overlooked is either lost or must be ascertained later, which is usually a difficult and time-consuming task. Information about each item of importance must be collected if an investigation is to be comprehensive; the reports required of the officer processing the crime scene are incomplete without such information. The data of this report include:

1. Victim's name, sex, age, occupation, residence and business addresses, and telephone numbers.
2. Where the event took place.
3. The time of occurrence.
4. Who reported the event, if other than the victim; personal data about this person similar to that described in item 1.

5. Date and time reported (sometimes how reported: in person or by mail or by telephone).
6. Time reporting officer arrived at crime scene.
7. Witnesses (full information along with personal data).
8. Arrestee, if any, and personal data available.
9. Suspects, named or described, with available personal data.
10. Name of reporting officer.

While at the crime scene the reporting officer must determine the method of operation of the perpetrator and collect data about this phase of the crime. These are the *modus operandi* data, and have a stylized form because data storage and retrieval are based on major segments of a criminal's technique. Attention to all these segments by the officer processing the crime scene ensures a thorough reporting of the technique used in the crime. The *modus operandi* segments include:

1. Type of crime.
2. Person attacked.
3. How attacked.
4. Means of attack.
5. Object of attack.
6. Trademark or perpetrator (peculiarities).
7. Words spoken (or the written note used).
8. Vehicle used.
9. Property stolen.
10. Name or physical description of suspect (see Figure 4–1).

Investigators must collect *pertinent* data under each segment. For this reason a checklist should be prepared as a reminder of the data to be collected in various crimes. Crimes can be grouped for this purpose as crimes against property, crimes against persons, and other crimes.

Finally, investigators must report on the details of the crime. This segment of the crime or offense report should be structured to tell the story of the circumstances of the crime to supplement the facts contained in the primary information or the *modus operandi* segments of the crime report. Many police departments suggest the following organization for this segment of the preliminary investigation:

1. *Suspect*—additional information describing the suspect or suspects, from aliases (the designation "aka"—also known as—is used to indicate aliases) and nicknames, to physical oddities and dress, including any data on employment or school attended.
2. *Property taken*—in thefts, additional descriptive data on property stolen, including the value as set by the victim, the approximate date of original

CRIME REPORT

REPORT NUMBER

| LOCATION OF OCCURRENCE | | | | | REPORT DATE | DAY | TIME | EVENT NO. | |

| OCC. DATE FROM | DAY | TIME | OCC. DATE TO | DAY | TIME | CONNECTED REPORT(S) — NUMBER AND TYPE |

CODE SECTION		F	M		CRIME TITLE
				A	
				B	
				C	
				D	

SPECIAL CRIME CATEGORIES EXIST? ☐ NO ☐ YES — CATEGORY FROM REVERSE _____

V NAME (LAST, FIRST, MIDDLE) | RES. PHONE | BUS. PHONE

RESIDENCE ADDRESS | CITY | STATE | ZIP | BUSINESS ADDRESS (SCHOOL IF JUVENILE) | CITY | STATE | ZIP

DOB | AGE | SEX | RACE | VICTIM'S VEHICLE (YR., MAKE, MODEL, LIC. NO.)

| A | B | C | D | E |
| F | G | H | I | J |

V/R NAME (LAST, FIRST, MIDDLE) | RES. PHONE | BUS. PHONE

RESIDENCE ADDRESS | CITY | STATE | ZIP | BUSINESS ADDRESS (SCHOOL IF JUVENILE) | CITY | STATE | ZIP

DOB | AGE | SEX | RACE | VICTIM'S VEHICLE (YR., MAKE, MODEL, LIC. NO.)

| A | B | C | D | E |
| F | G | H | I | J |

A. PLACE of CRIME
1 ☐ STRUCTURE   4 ☐ STREET/ALLEY   7 ☐ OTHER
2 ☐ VEHICLE   5 ☐ LOT/PARK _____
3 ☐ RES/YARD   6 ☐ BUS/STORAGE

B. DESCRIPTION OF SURROUNDINGS
1 ☐ RESIDENTIAL   4 ☐ RECREATIONAL   7 ☐ OPEN SPACE
2 ☐ BUSINESS   5 ☐ INSTITUTIONAL   8 ☐ OTHER
3 ☐ INDUSTRIAL   6 ☐ CONST. SITE

TYPE OF STRUCTURE	☐ N/A	G POINT OF ENTRY	J METHOD OF ENTRY	INVESTIGATIVE NOTATIONS

TYPE OF STRUCTURE

C NON-RESIDENTIAL
☐ 1 CONVENIENCE
☐ 2 FAST FOOD
☐ 3 RESTAURANT/BAR
☐ 4 DRUG/MEDICAL
☐ 5 GAS STATION
☐ 6 RETAIL
☐ 7 SCHOOL
☐ 8 FINANCIAL INST.
☐ 9 ENTERTAIN/REC.
☐ 10 PUBLIC BLDG.
☐ 11 OTHER _____

D TARGET(S)
☐ 1 SHOP
☐ 2 CASH REG/DRAWER
☐ 3 OFFICE
☐ 4 SAFE/BOX
☐ 5 VENDING MACHINE
☐ 6 DISPLAY ITEMS
☐ 7 CLASS ROOM
☐ 8 OTHER

E RESIDENTIAL
☐ 1 SINGLE FAMILY
☐ 2 APT/CONDO
☐ 3 DUPLEX/TOWN
☐ 4 MOTEL/HOTEL
☐ 5 MOBILE HOME
☐ 6 OTHER _____

F TARGET(S)
☐ 1 STORAGE BLDG.
☐ 2 CLOSET
☐ 3 BATHROOM
☐ 4 DEN
☐ 5 FAMILY ROOM
☐ 6 GARAGE/CARPORT
☐ 7 KITCHEN
☐ 8 LIVING ROOM
☐ 9 STORAGE ROOM
☐ 10 BEDROOM
☐ 11 DINING
☐ 12 OTHER _____

G POINT OF ENTRY
1 ☐ N/A   4 ☐ SIDE
2 ☐ FRONT   5 ☐ GR LEV.
3 ☐ REAR   6 ☐ UP LEV.

H
☐ 1 UNKNOWN
☐ 2 DOOR
☐ 3 WINDOW
☐ 4 SLIDE GLASS
☐ 5 DUCT/VENT
☐ 6 ADJ. BLDG.
☐ 7 ROOF/FLOOR
☐ 8 WALL
☐ 9 BASEMENT
☐ 10 OTHER _____

I ALARM SYSTEMS
☐ 1 YES   ☐ 2 NO
SET OFF
☐ 3 YES   ☐ 4 NO

J METHOD OF ENTRY
☐ N/A
☐ 1 ATTEMPT ONLY
☐ 2 NO FORCE
☐ 3 KEY/SLIP
☐ 4 BODY/FORCE
☐ 5 SAW/DRILL
☐ 6 HID IN BLDG.
☐ 7 CHANNEL LOCK
☐ 8 PRY TOOL
☐ 9 LIFT OUT
☐ 10 BRICK/ROCK
☐ 11 BOLT CUTTERS/PLIERS
☐ 12 WINDOW SMASH
☐ 13 TAPE/WIRE
☐ 14 DOOR PUNCH
☐ 15 DOOR KICK
☐ 16 OTHER _____

INVESTIGATIVE NOTATIONS

SUSPECT INFO PAGE
(NUMBER SUSP _____)   _____YES_____NO

PHYSICAL EVIDENCE
GATHERED BY R/O   _____YES_____NO

CSI REQUESTED   _____YES_____NO

IDENTIFIABLE PROPERTY   _____YES_____NO

ADDITIONAL VICTIMS/
WITNESSES   _____YES_____NO

NEIGHBORHOOD CANV   _____YES_____NO

PROPERTY LOSS   _____YES_____NO

PROPERTY LIST ATTACHED   _____YES_____NO

INVESTIGATIVE DIV. PERS. NOTIFIED
_____

K SUSPECT'S ACTION   ☐ N/A

☐ 1 ENTERED OCCUPIED BLDG.
☐ 2 ENTERED UNOCCUPIED BLDG.
☐ 3 VACANT RES./BLDG.
☐ 4 VANDALIZED/RANSACKED
☐ 5 USED MATCHES/SMOKED AT SCENE
☐ 6 DISABLED ALARM
☐ 7 ATE/DRANK ON PREMISES
☐ 8 VEHICLES NEEDED FOR LOOT
☐ 9 USED VICTIM'S TOOLS
☐ 10 KNEW LOCATION OF HIDDEN CASH
☐ 11 SELECTIVE IN LOOT
☐ 12 USED LOOKOUT DRIVER

☐ 13 BOUND/GAGGED VICTIM
☐ 14 RIPPED/CUT CLOTHING
☐ 15 MOLESTED VICTIM
☐ 16 FORCED VICTIM TO MOVE
☐ 17 DISABLED PHONE/ELECTRIC
☐ 18 INJURED VICTIM
☐ 19 THREATENED VICTIM
☐ 20 MASTURBATED
☐ 21 DISROBED FULLY/PARTIALLY
☐ 22 FIRED WEAPON
☐ 23 SUSPECT ARMED
☐ 24 OTHER

L PROPERTY TAKEN   ☐ N/A

☐ 1 LARGE LOSS VALUE
☐ 2 TOOK CHECKS/CREDIT CARDS
☐ 3 CONSUMABLE GOOD
☐ 4 OFFICE EQUIPMENT
☐ 5 CAMERA
☐ 6 POWER TOOLS/LAWN EQUIP.
☐ 7 FIREARMS
☐ 8 SILVERWARE
☐ 9 FINE JEWELRY
☐ 10 MONEY
☐ 21 OTHER_____

☐ 11 LARGE APPLIANCES
☐ 12 SMALL APPLIANCES
☐ 13 CLOTHING/FURS
☐ 14 DRUGS
☐ 15 CONSTRUCTION MATERIALS
☐ 16 AUTO PARTS/ACCESSORIES
☐ 17 TOOLS/CARP./MECH./ELECT.
☐ 18 GOLD/SILVER COINS
☐ 19 TV/STEREO/VIDEO
☐ 20 NO LOSS

SYNOPSIS OF CRIME

| INVESTIGATING OFFICER | | BADGE | DIVISION | SUPERVISOR | |

PAGE _____ OF _____

FIGURE 4–1 Crime report—information called for on this printed form is the primary record of the circumstances of a crime.

THIS PORTION OF THE REPORT IS REQUIRED BY LAW. REFER TO UNIFORM CRIME REPORTING STANDARDS FOUND IN THE REPORT WRITING MANUAL. IT IS **NOT** TO BE FILLED OUT ACCORDING TO CALIFORNIA PENAL CODE STANDARDS. IF YOUR CRIME CLASSIFICATION INVOLVES A BURGLARY, ROBBERY, THEFT, HOMICIDE, ASSAULT OR RAPE, BE CERTAIN TO CIRCLE WHATEVER CATEGORY BELOW IS APPROPRIATE. CODE ONLY THE TYPE AND VALUE OF PROPERTY STOLEN AS INDICATED BELOW. RECOVERED PROPERTY IS TO BE CODED DIRECTLY ON THE RECOVERED PROPERTY REPORT, UNLESS RECOVERED SIMULTANEOUSLY AT THE TIME OF THE CRIME REPORT.

PROPERTY	Stolen Value	Recovered Value	BURGLARY	ROBBERY		THEFT	
			VEHICLE AND SHOPLIFT BURGLARIES ARE TO BE CODED UNDER THEFT	TYPE		TYPE	
A CURRENCY, NOTES, ETC.	$	$		031 FIREARM		0610 PICKPOCKET	
B JEWELRY, PRECIOUS				032 KNIFE		0620 PURSE SNATCH	
METALS	$	$	ENTRY	033 OTHER WEAPON		0630 SHOPLIFT	
C CLOTHING, FURS	$	$	051 FORCIBLE	034 STRONGARM		0640 FROM VEHICLE	
E OFFICE EQUIPMENT	$	$	052 UNLAWFUL	LOCATION		0650 AUTO PARTS &	
F TV, CAMERA, STEREOS	$	$	053 ATTEMPT FORCIBLE	1 HIGHWAY		ACCESSORIES	
G FIREARMS	$	$	STRUCTURE	2 COMMERCIAL HOUSE		0670 FROM BUILDING	
H HOUSEHOLD GOODS	$	$	1 RESIDENCE	3 SERVICE STATION		0680 COIN-OPERATED	
I CONSUMABLE GOODS	$	$	2 NON-RESIDENCE	4 CONVENIENCE STORE		MACHINE	
J LIVESTOCK	$	$	(CLOSED)	5 RESIDENCE		0690 ALL OTHER	
K MISCELLANEOUS	$	$		6 BANK			
				7 OTHER		ATTEMPT VEHICLE THEFT	
TOTAL	$	$				0710 AUTO	
						0720 TRUCK/BUS	A
						0730 OTHER VEHICLE	

REPORTED DATE _____
REPORTED TIME _____
DATE OCC. _____ FROM ___ TO ___
TIME OCC. _____

SPECIAL CRIME CATEGORY		NUMBER OF VICTIMS HOMICIDE		NUMBER OF VICTIMS ASSAULTS		
A CRIMES AGAINST CHILDREN		0110 MURDER NON-NEG	0410 GUN	0440	HANDS/FEET (SERIOUS INJURY)	
01 NEGLECT/ABUSE		MANSLAUGHTER	0420 KNIFE			
02 SEXUAL		0120 MANSLAUGHTER BY NEGLIGENCE	0430 OTHER DANGEROUS WEAPON	0450	HANDS/FEET (MINOR OR NO INJURY)	
B CRIMES AGAINST ELDERLY						
C DOMESTIC VIOLENCE						
D GANG AFFILIATION						
E CRIMES MOTIVATED BY:		NUMBER OF VICTIMS		RAPE		
01 RACE						
02 RELIGION		0210 FORCIBLE	0220 ATTEMPT FORCIBLE			
03 SEXUAL PREFERENCE						

ARSON					
PROPERTY CLASSIFICATION		INHABITED	UNINHABITED	TOTAL ARSON $ DAMAGE	
091	SINGLE OCCUPANCY RESIDENTIAL (House, Townhouse, Duplexes, etc.)	1	2	$	
092	OTHER RESIDENTIAL (Apartments, Tenements, Flats, Hotels, Motels, Inns, Dormitories, Boarding Houses, etc.)	1	2	$	
093	STORAGE (Barns, Garages, Warehouses, etc.)	1	2	$	
094	INDUSTRIAL MANUFACTURING	1	2	$	
095	OTHER COMMERCIAL (Stores, Restaurants, Offices, etc.)	1	2	$	
096	COMMUNITY/PUBLIC (Church, Jails, Schools, Colleges, Hospitals, etc.)	1	2	$	
097	ALL OTHER STRUCTURE (Out Buildings, Monuments, Buildings under Construction, etc.)	1	2	$	

0981	MOTOR VEHICLES	(Automobiles, Trucks, Buses, Motorcycles, etc.)			
0982	OTHER MOBILE PROPERTY	(Trailers, Recreational Vehicles, Airplanes, Boats, etc.)			
0990	OTHER	(Crops, Timber, Fences, Signs, etc.)			

purchase or acquisition by other means ("age" of article), and the original purchase price or estimated value at the time.

3. *Physical evidence*—all items of evidence, including traces, toolmarks, and other imprints or impressions, should be described in detail, along with full information as to when and where such evidence was found and who found it, handled it, and disposed of it.

4. *Victim's statement*—the victim or victims who make statements are identified by name, address, age, and employment (or school attended) and the essential facts of the victim's story are stated.

5. *Statement of witness(es)*—each witness making a statement is identified as above, and the essential facts of the story told by the witness are stated. In addition, this segment of the report should include (a) data as to the location of the witness at the time of observation, (b) the light conditions, and (c) any relationship of the witness to the victim or suspect(s).

6. *Observations by reporting officer*—facts that are not evidence, such as weather, conditions at the scene, and sobriety of persons contacted. Opinions based on observations are permissible in this segment, with both the opinion and its objective base being reported (opinions not based on some objective fact do not belong in a crime report).

Offense or crime reports originate at the operational level. Their basic purpose is to record and transmit information. Such reports inform interested persons of the action taken at a crime scene by the reporting officer. They place the data reported in the possession of others who can take appropriate action, and ensure the continuity of an investigation with little or no need to backtrack or duplicate the work of the preliminary investigator.

Primary data, *modus operandi* information, and the "details" or narrative of the crime and its circumstances must be written legibly and in clear and simple language; they must be complete in that all available and related facts are included, but they also must be brief; and they must be accurate, with all facts reported as they are known to the reporting officer, and opinions clearly noted and differentiated from the factual content of the narrative report.

PHOTOGRAPHING THE CRIME SCENE

An investigator should not disturb the scene or any objects at the scene prior to photographing. To show the scene in its original condition it must be kept that way until photographs have been taken.

Crime-scene photography provides a permanent record of the facts at the crime scene. Photography is one means of recording facts for future use so that they can be used in reconstructing the crime scene—and sometimes the crime—but photography is not a substitute for field notes, accurate measurements, and sketches of the scene. Pictures supplement the other forms for recording the facts of a crime scene, and they are often the best way of recording and illustrating the details of a crime scene and its evidence. Sometimes, indeed, they are the only feasible means of recording and illustrating certain features of a crime and the scene.

Photographing a crime scene serves the following purposes: it provides a pictorial representation of the appearance and position of objects at the scene, and it serves as evidence to support the testimony of the investigator as to what he or she found at the scene, its location, nature, and condition.[1]

If a photo processing laboratory is not available within the limits of the chain of possession of evidence, daylight tanks for instant developing of negatives and almost automatic contact printing apparatus are available. If such developing of film is too complex or time consuming, the Polaroid camera system with its brief routine from picture taking to finished print may be useful. The finished print is ready in seconds, and if it is out of focus or did not picture the subject adequately, another photograph can be taken immediately and reviewed for quality. This 10-second trial-and-error system is excellent for instruction, and investigators soon learn to take excellent photographs with Polaroid cameras.

Color photography outperforms the black-and-white process in showing evidence as it is. When shown in court projected on a large screen, color transparencies appear to be superior to prints in fixing the attention of the triers-of-fact. The quality of life-sized reproduction and natural color in this type of photograph goes far beyond what can be achieved by any black-and-white enlarged print. The use of color slides was pioneered by experts in criminalistics, spread to medicolegal experts for autopsy photographs, and is being adopted for on-the-scene photography in many police agencies.

Investigators who do not take their own photographs should be on the crime scene ready to supervise the work of the photographer. As a general rule, police photographers working crime scenes are responsive to instructions from an assigned investigator, as they realize that the investigator is the person responsible for the adequacy of the photographs taken.

The camera positions and the range at which photographs are taken should take advantage of the natural composition at the scene. The story of the scene is to be told graphically, and coherence requires an orderly progression in picture taking. In this type of camera work, objects cannot be moved to gain better composition, but the camera is mobile and its mobility should be used to best advantage.

In general, the subject matter of crime-scene photography should move from the general to the specific. Long-range views should tell a story of what happened at the crime scene and serve as a backdrop to locate the subjects of close-up photographs of items of physical evidence. The long-range photos may show the locale, the approach route, the means of ingress to the scene or its premises, a hallway, two connected rooms, or a view of the scene from the normal entrance. Midrange photographs (10 to 20 feet) pinpoint a specific object of evidence or a significant segment of the crime scene. Close-up photographs are used for recording evidence in position and detail—the location, nature, and condition.

Aerial photographs are excellent for studying crimes in series to ascertain whether the locations of past crimes suggest a pattern of criminal behavior on which the location of the next crime in the series can be projected. They are also excellent for locating outdoor crime scenes or controlling search patterns when large areas must be searched for evidence.

To prove the *corpus delicti*,* a close-up crime-scene photograph is needed. These photographs should illustrate essential elements of the crime. This graphic exposition of the full story of the crime, insofar as it can be revealed from any mute viewing of the place of occurrence and its evidence, may be extremely important in preparing the case for presentation in court. Composition varies with the crime—a full-length picture of the victim in homicides to show the position of the body and/or the location of a wound or wounds, the place of forced entry in burglaries, and the point of origin of the fire in suspicious blazes. Close-ups include views of the weapon and wounds in homicides, tool marks at the site of forced entrance, and a fire-setting contrivance or the distinctive charring along the fire trails of the accelerant often used in arson.

Photographs also can be used to trace the *modus operandi* of the criminal and the continuity of crimes occurring in a series. Photographs of tool impressions record the characteristics of the tool used. Enlargements can be made, and the prints cut in half for comparison. Quite often a "jimmy" or pry bar can be traced from crime to crime. Linking the impressions sometimes offers a basic lead for an investigator and often provides multiple evidence when a matching tool is found in the possession of a crime suspect.

Evidence photography of crime scenes can be used to reveal blood and hair on weapons, the trajectory of flying objects from marks on floors and walls, the location and characteristics of imprints and impressions, and the full extent of injuries and wounds. Important details can be developed by close-up photography. When a close-up view does not indicate the entire item of evidence, the photographer should show a progression from one end or side of the object to the other side, in a series of sectional views. Sectional photography reassures the triers-of-fact that the entire surface of the item of evidence was examined. Thus the number of photographs taken of any single item of evidence depends on the dimensions of the evidence and the need for photographic detail.

Measurements and measurement markers always have been a problem in crime-scene photography because they intrude upon the photographer's reproduction of the scene as he or she found it. One acceptable procedure is to take a photograph without any change (as is) and then to take another picture with the measurement marker (a flat ruler, or the beginning section of a steel tape stretched out flat) placed in position.

The same principles apply to chalk marks used to isolate and identify evidence that blends into its background. It is rarely necessary to use them, but if they are used, a two-picture sequence is required—one without the markings and the other with them. In traffic accidents this is not always possible, since responding officers may remove an injured person to a hospital or push

---

Corpus delicti is a Latin term meaning literally "the body of the offence." In legal terminology it refers to the basic element of a crime—for example, the death of a victim in a murder case.

a hazardous vehicle out of position before photographs can be taken; in these cases the only record of the injured person or the vehicle may be chalk marks on the roadway.

Identification cards or markers are used in some photographs to record the date, time, location, photographer, and agency involved. However, they are not placed on the evidence nor do they conceal any part of the major subject of the photograph.

The series of photographs of a crime scene are dated and numbered consecutively (starting with 1) or identified by a series of film file numbers. Information should be linked with these numbers in the field notes of the photographer, which will supply data that can be written on each photographic print. Pertinent data consist of the case number and subject of the picture, the crime classification, the date and time taken, the name of the photographer, the camera's location, the direction in which the camera was aimed, and the distance in feet to the subject of the picture. Most photographers also enter in their field notes such vital professional information as illumination, lens setting, shutter speed, and the ASA rating (speed) of the film. Investigators using automatic or semiautomatic cameras usually dispense with such notations or restrict them to a few simple notes.

The following transcript of questioning during a trial is a good example of the line of questioning of a police witness that establishes the foundation for introducing photographs as evidence for the prosecution:

Q. Showing you exhibits that are marked 36-A, -B, -C, -D, I will ask you if these photographs fairly depict different views of the items that you have testified were found at the place of occurrence (specified).

A. Yes, sir. These are the items.

Q. And those photographs, do they depict the way these things were found?

A. Yes, sir.
[The questioning then continued by locating the area depicted in the photographs more precisely, the actual recovery of the items of evidence, the time when they were recovered, and their nature.]

Q. Were the photographs taken at that time?

A. They were taken prior to the evidence having been touched.

SKETCHING THE SCENE

The basic reason for sketching a crime scene is to provide an understanding in depth of the circumstances of the crime beyond the level of comprehension attained solely by reading a written report or studying photographs. A sketch is more than a written report and less than a photograph in depicting a crime scene. But because of its unique virtues it can supplement both reports and photographs. The advantage of a sketch is that unnecessary detail can be eliminated, whereas it cannot be eliminated from a photograph and is eliminated only with difficulty from a report. Sketching a plan or diagramming the scene in the regular course of police business records the facts available to the viewer (sketcher) so that at any time in the future the assigned investigator and the triers-of-fact both have graphic representation of the crime scene (see Figure 4–2).

There is a necessary timeliness in sketching a crime scene. The rough sketch must be made by the investigator as a part of his or her field notes; both the sketch and the notes are aligned with the search of the scene.

A field sketch is marked for identification by inserting:

1. The investigator's full name.
2. The time, date, case number, and crime classification.
3. The full name of any person assisting in taking measurements.

FIGURE 4–2 Floor-plan sketch showing walls of room and location of (1) body, (2) blood, (3) gun, and (4) empty cartridge cases.

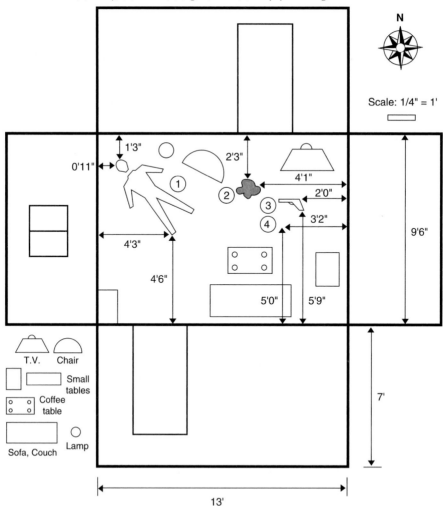

4. Orientation—address, position in building; location adjacent to building; landmarks and compass direction, if outdoors.

A common error in sketching the scene is to attempt to make an architectural reproduction of the scene or to include too many details. The crime-scene sketch is not unlike the diagram of a traffic accident. Items that do not aid in reproducing the accident should not be shown.[2] Standard symbols are used to indicate characteristics of a sketch, such as roads, walks, fences, common items of furniture, and evidence frequently encountered at crime scenes (see Figure 4–3). A sketch shows and locates important objects at the scene; unimportant ones are omitted for simplicity. No one except the sketcher should mark or correct a field sketch in any way. This is the first permanent graphic record of the investigation. It is kept for years, beyond any possible need in court, and a photocopy is attached to the investigator's report of the case.

When a graphic illustration is meant to clarify a written report, accurate measurements are needed. Steel tapes are the approved means of measuring distances in criminal investigation. The so-called measuring wheel is an accurate device, but the investigator must show that he or she knows how to use it and did use it in a manner that produced an accurate measurement. The investigator should test it against a known distance measured with a steel tape to verify its accuracy prior to use. The greatest disservice an investigator can render is to record an erroneous measurement on a drawing or in his or her field notes of a crime, for in that case no matter how many persons subsequently certify the correct measurement, there will always be a question about the initial recording and why it was erroneous.

In general, measurements are made of the area searched. They are made, first of all, with the eye. The investigator surveys the crime scene and decides what to measure and where to start. The distance lines of the sketch plan are drawn; then the actual measurements are made and recorded on the plan. Measurements should extend along and from fixed and identifiable points. Avoid any distance measurement with a floating base—that is, a reference point that may be moved or cannot be located with accuracy. Angular measurements can serve as coordinates to locate a point on the sketch only if the angle is broad and has two reference measurements from identifiable fixed points or objects.

If at all possible, nothing should be moved in the process of measuring. Remember, the movement of objects changes the scene. The sketcher can claim that the object was returned to exactly the same spot, but this is an unnecessary taint of the officer's testimony.

A crime-scene *area* diagram can supplement a crime-scene diagram. It is warranted when one or more of the basic facts in the case is beyond the crime scene itself. These sketches pinpoint the location of shoe prints, tire tracks, weapons, and similar evidence linked to the crime scene (see Figure 4–4).

Erasures may be made on such drawings. In fact, the drawings usually are completed in pencil, then inked in with a permanent ink, and the pencil marks erased after the ink has dried completely. The drawings are identified as is the crime-scene sketch, and similar symbols may be used and annotated

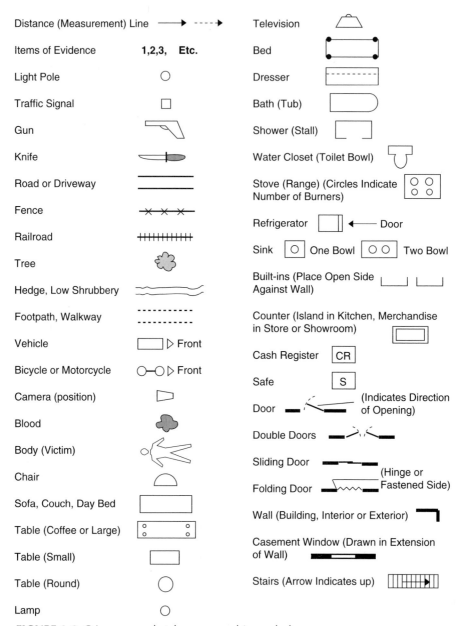

FIGURE 4–3 Crime-scene sketches use graphic symbols.

as necessary. Colors may be used for special effects, and overlays of semi-transparent paper may be used to diagram the travels of participants in the crime. Schematic diagrams are often used to show the travels (paths) of the victim, offender(s), bullets, and other moving objects.

Many graphic illustrations are drawn to scale, using the investigator's rough sketch and measurements. Recommended scales range from 1/8 inch

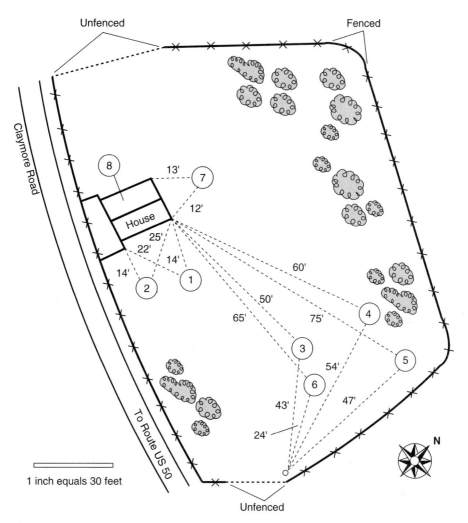

Unfenced

Fenced

Claymore Road

8

13'

7

12'

House

25'

22'

14'

14'

2

1

60'

50'

65'

75'

4

3

54'

6

43'

47'

5

24'

N

1 inch equals 30 feet

To Route US 50

Unfenced

FIGURE 4–4 Crime-scene diagram. Each numbered location represents an item of physical evidence.

equals 1 foot for indoor scenes to 1 inch equals 20 feet for larger outdoor areas. These scales usually permit the work to be presented on an $8\frac{1}{2}$-by-11-inch sheet of paper. Ideally, the investigator should select a scale that permits reproduction of the scene without completely filling the $8\frac{1}{2}$-by-11-inch paper and allows space for a key or legend and necessary identification.

The professional assistance of individuals with special training is often utilized to prepare an investigator's sketches and diagrams for use in court. These may be enlarged (blown-up), but will be to a scale noted on the drawing. They are usually endorsed or certified by the investigator as being a reproduction of his or her original crime-scene sketch.

Traditionally, the crime-scene sketch has been used as a single-purpose tool merely to indicate the position of physical evidence at the crime scene. Its major purpose has been to place various items of physical evidence at the crime scene rather than to serve as a graphic report. Basically, the objective of crime-scene sketching should be the graphic presentation of the crime scene in a manner that will permit reconstruction of the crime from the details of the sketch. Thus, an ability to draw must be placed high among the necessary skills of an investigator.

For years, sketching has been particularly effective in vehicular traffic accidents; however, it is a standard investigative technique for pictorial recording in all types of investigations.*

VIDEOTAPING

Videotaping is pictorial storytelling, and it offers compelling reasons for investigators to use it. The videotaper is not limited by the borders of a photograph or the lens of a camera, but he or she may be more careful when using the video camera to record the graphics of a crime-scene record, knowing defense counsel could use the videotape to discredit the police case during the trial.

Discovery is the term used for a request by defense counsel to the prosecutor prior to trial for disclosure of the police case against his or her client. Its objective is to aid in making certain the defendant receives a fair trial. Detectives have become accustomed to disclosing the fruits of their investigations, knowing that when a discovery request is made by defense counsel in the local courts, prosecutors must provide all crime reports, photos, sketches, and other pertinent materials.

Videotaping has been used to advantage by prosecutors at trial to show jurors meaningful views of the crime scene, but it has also been used by defense attorneys to destroy the credibility of investigators by using select segments of the video to contradict their court testimony. The segment may show only a minor oversight on the part of the officer, but it may be enough to destroy a police case by linking suspicion to police crime-scene conduct.

Today, investigators are participants in decisions on use of videotaping, along with prosecutors, local judiciary, and defense attorneys.[3]

Videotape has several advantages over photography: (1) it provides immediate results without the need for developing film; (2) tapes can be re-used by recording over the images on the previously used tape; (3) visual movement allows the viewer to perceive the scene as it is shown; and (4) sound may be utilized.[4]

The low cost of camcorders, as well as their portability, user-friendly sophistication, high-quality image, and the ease with which the tape can be moved from camcorder to table-top or large-screen monitors for viewing are

*See Department of Justice Document 2 in Appendix C.

all sound reasons for police departments to adopt this new graphic system and adapt it to their needs.

In crime investigation, videotape has been used successfully in clandestine observation of suspicious places and persons, as well as the transactions in "sting" operations. It is now being used more extensively to record interviews with witnesses, and the built-in "statement" feature has been helpful to investigators when a witness attempts to change or deny his or her initial version of the crime's circumstances. Videotaping at crime scenes has become more commonplace.

PROGRESS REPORTS (THE CONTINUING INVESTIGATION)

Progress reports are made either to inform the commanding officer of a new development in an investigation or at specified intervals—daily when there is a lot of progress, or every 5 days while the case is still "active." The purpose and scope of progress reports prepared during a continuing investigation depend on the assignment of the investigator. If the assignment is limited—to check out one of the basic leads in a case or to interview a witness—the scope of the report is limited to this assignment, and the purpose is to collect data on a possible lead or the story of a witness. But if the investigator is assigned to complete a continuing investigation, there are as many reports as necessary to report the work done, the data collected, and the status of the investigation.

Reports made during a continuing investigation have four primary objectives:

1. To inform persons reading the report of the findings resulting from an assigned investigation, including both (a) information, and (b) the precise source of the information.
2. To facilitate understanding of the entire investigation to date.
3. To foreshadow the uncompleted portion of the investigation, if any.
4. To fulfill the duties of the assignment (basic lead, witness interview, etc.).

A frequent and successful arrangement is to structure these reports according to the classic queries of news reports—when, where, who, what, how, and why. These queries and segments of the report responsive to them need not be in this order, but such queries serve as reminders to report writers to tell the entire story within the scope of their assignment.

Because a major segment of the work done in the continuing investigation is interviewing, investigators should develop a standard method of reporting interviews. This should not extend to the content of the interviews, but should list such standard items of information as the time and date of the interview, the name and other identification data on the interviewee, any relationship to others involved, and the place of the interview.

This standard method can be extended to another major segment of the continuing investigation: physical evidence. First, the item of physical evidence is identified, and then whatever facts are to be reported in connection with it are supplied.

Selected References

1. *Basic Police Photography,* 2nd ed. (Rochester, NY: Eastman Kodak, 1968), pp. 16–22.
2. PAUL B. WESTON, *The Police Traffic Control Function,* 2nd ed. (Springfield, Ill.: Charles C Thomas, Publisher, 1968), pp. 196–99.
3. KENNETH M. WELLS AND PAUL B. WESTON, *Criminal Procedure and Trial Practice* (Englewood Cliffs, N.J.: Prentice Hall, 1977), pp. 29–34.
4. LARRY L. MILLER, *Sansone's Police Photography, Third Edition.* (Cincinnati, Ohio: Anderson Publishing, 1993), pp. 111–13.

Chapter Review

CASE STUDY: THE LUCKY MARKET CASE

Police reports summarize the armed robbery of a supermarket, the subsequent investigation, and its results:

1. Details of Crime. On July 23, officers received a call at 1854 hours regarding a 211 P.C. at the Lucky Market, 56th and Broadway. Upon arrival, officers were met by the holdup victim, Edith Sheridan, who stated she was checking out at a cash register for customers. The next person in line was Suspect No. 1, and he left the groceries in the cart and didn't unload them so victim started to take them out and Suspect No. 1 said, "Leave them alone." Suspect No. 1 took a gun from his belt with his right hand and said, "Empty the till and hurry up!" Victim took the money from the till and Suspect No. 1 said, "What's underneath?" Victim said, "Nothing but checks." Suspect came around and looked for himself, taking out the drawer. Suspect then said to the victim, "Go to the next till and pull out the cash." Victim asked if he wanted the coins and Suspect No. 1 said, "No, I don't want them." Victim went to the next till and Suspect No. 1 said, "Hurry up, you're not going fast enough." Suspect said he wanted all the coins in this till. Victim told Suspect No. 1, "There's no money in the last two tills" and Suspect No. 1 said, "Open them anyway," which the victim did. Suspect told victim to "stay put" and then the two suspects went out the front door separately, the short man in front.

John Cox, off-duty Sacramento Police Officer, Badge #178, at this time was standing at the checkout counter waiting in line and knowing the holdup was in progress. When the suspects left the front door, Cox pulled his gun on the way to the front door and caught up with Suspect No. 2 and told Suspect No. 1, who was seated in the car, to "hold it right there."

Suspect No. 2 at this time was standing beside Cox. Suspect No. 2 wheeled behind Cox and pinned his arms and pushed him down. Cox then went down and Suspect No. 2 pulled his gun from his belt and shot Cox in the neck. The next thing the victim saw was Cox lying on the pavement. Victim stated she heard no shot.

Victim stated Suspect No. 2 was possibly standing behind her in the store. She did not get a good look at him.

Victim also stated she felt that if she didn't obey Suspect No. 1's commands she would be shot.

Victim also stated that the bag boy walked back to unload suspect's basket of groceries as they were at the counter and Suspect No. 1 said, "Hey, stay right there." This incident happened at No. 1 check stand.

The amount of cash taken is not known at this time. Victim will advise.

Officers: Joseph Bals, #196
George Maloney, #189

2. Casualty Report. On July 23, police officer John Cox, 38 years of age, male, white, off-duty, was shot by one of two holdup men, during robbery at Lucky Market, 56th Street and Broadway. Victim taken by Superior Ambulance to Sutter Hospital, Unit 50 following ambulance, and reporting officer was present in Sutter Hospital Emergency Room when Dr. Meehan pronounced victim DOA [dead on arrival] at 1912 hours. Victim had been shot in the neck.

Officer: Edward Leonard (Unit #50)

3. Supplementary (Progress) Investigation Reports

A. On July 23–24, 2015 to 0115 hours. I took the following photographs at the Lucky Market, 56th Street and Broadway (see Figure 4–5):

1. The front of the store: blood stains in the parking lot in front of the NW corner of the store (color).
2. The check stand area from four (4) different angles (black and white).
3. A wire basket with grocery items in it. This basket was located in front of the store office, NW corner of the store (black and white).

I checked the following items found in the wire basket for fingerprints:

1. A potato bag.
2. A paper bag of ice.
3. A carton (six pack) of Busch Bavarian beer.
4. A box of Lucky detergent (giant size; 1 lb, 15 oz). (From the face of the box of detergent I found two partial tips of fingers; latents protected with an Ace tab lift. No other latents of value found.)

I took color photographs of the deceased police officer, John Cox, at the Coroner's Morgue. These show the powder-burned area and a bullet hole in the officer's left neck, a small black and blue spot on the officer's right neck, a photograph of the officer's face, and a photograph of the officer showing his gun holster strapped to his belt on the left side of his body. (All photographs in color, and taken at f/8 and 1/50th of a second.)

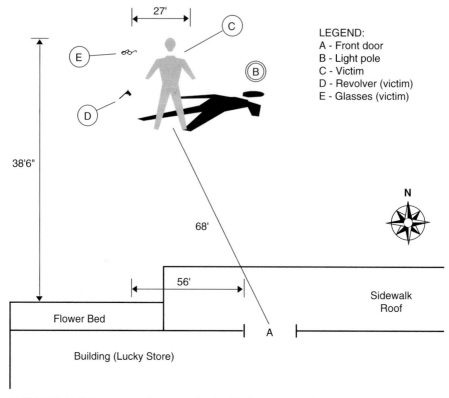

FIGURE 4–5 Crime-scene diagram—Lucky Market case study.

I checked a 1970 Red Cadillac convertible with a black top bearing Calif. license MYY 625 for fingerprints in the police yard. Numerous partial latent fingerprints were found.

Officer: Joseph Green

B. On July 23, at 1854 hours. Mr. LeRoy Kennedy, a clerk in the market, stated he was standing alongside Aisle 31 in the Lucky Store, when an unidentified man tapped him on the shoulder and said, "There's a holdup going on." Kennedy walked to the cash register at the front of the store and observed two male subjects with a female clerk, Edith Sheridan (615 Crown Road, 675-6404), as she removed money from various cash registers at the direction of a suspect wearing an orange-colored nylon shell-type jacket, who will be designated as Suspect No. 1.

His accomplice, Suspect No. 2, wearing a blue jacket of somewhat the same type, was standing by. Kennedy further stated that he could see that Suspect No. 1 had some bulky object in the waistband at the front of his trousers, and he (Kennedy) concluded that it was a gun.

When the clerk (Edith Sheridan) had emptied several registers, Suspect No. 1 took the bag and left the store. Suspect No. 1 went to a vehicle parked to the west of the front doors in the parking area and got behind the wheel as Suspect No. 2 left the store, walking toward the vehicle.

Mr. Kennedy stated that he then observed a customer (later identified as off-duty Officer John Cox), as he, Cox, pursued the suspects from inside the store and approached them at their vehicle. Cox had a gun in his hand and turned slightly away from Suspect No. 2 as he pointed the gun at Suspect No. 1 seated in the vehicle.

At this point, Suspect No. 2 wheeled around behind Cox and appeared to pin Cox's left arm behind him and then pushed down on Cox's shoulder or head with his left hand, while pulling a gun from his waistband, shoving it tight against Cox's neck, and firing once. Cox fell to the asphalt, his gun fell from his hand.

Suspect No. 2 then entered the vehicle and both suspects left, driving east on Broadway and then south on 59th Street out of sight.

Physical descriptions of suspects:

Suspect No. 1—Gunman, MWA, taller than Suspect No. 2, possibly 6', 165 lb, dark skin, medium build—wearing orange-colored nylon wind-breaker-type zipper jacket, same age-group as Suspect No. 2.

Suspect No. 2—MWA, 5'8", 165 lb, mid 20's to early 30's, wearing faded-blue nylon windbreaker and hunting-type cap with bill, dark in color.

Officer: George Maloney, #189

C. On July 23, at 1910 hours. This officer received a call via radio that a police officer had been shot and that the subjects were last seen in a late model Cad headed possibly E/B on U.S. 40 beyond the Elvis Freeway. This unit responded and rolled to the intersection of Watt Ave. and U.S. 40 and upon arrival at the Watt Ave. on-ramp E/B, observed the late model Cad E/B in the no. 1 lane with one man at the wheel. The vehicle was a late model Cad, black top over red bottom, convertible, license number MYY-625 California. The subject was ordered to the curb with the red light and the vehicle stopped. The driver alighted and stood by the rear of his vehicle. This officer was out with gun in hand and ordered the driver to lay on the ground spread-eagled and then the rear of the Cad was approached and the car was seen to move as if someone was still in it. This officer then poked his gun into the Cad's interior and the subject hiding in the rear came out from under several coats and trousers and surrendered. Subject driving was Harry W. Burrell, and the passenger was James Brainard. Brainard was the man hiding in the rear seat area.

The subjects were taken out of the car and laid on the ground on their stomachs, head to head, with their hands cuffed together. The subjects offered no resistance and were handcuffed without incident. The driver, Harry Burrell, stated as he watched this officer poke his gun into the car, "Come on out Brainard, looks like they have got us."

The subjects were transported from the scene to the County Jail.

Note: Two Colt .38 Police Positive revolvers, No. 1 loaded with four rounds and No. 2 loaded with five rounds, were found together in the front seat of the car when it was stopped.

Officer: John Gayne, #111

D. On July 23, at 1920 hour.   Upon my arrival at the scene (out/bound U.S. 40—near Watt Ave.) Officer John Gayne had two suspects on the ground on the shoulder of the freeway, handcuffed. I observed two hand guns in a red 1970 Cad convertible. The guns were on the right front seat of above Cad. Subjects transported to County Jail in my unit, number 245.

While en route to County Jail, Subject Brainard stated that he had shot the policeman. He stated he did not know that the man was a police officer until he [the police officer] pulled his gun on the two subjects. Subject Brainard stated he told the police officer to drop the gun, and when the officer moved, the subject's gun went off, and the officer fell.

Officer: Walter Morris, #622

E.   On July 23, at 2330 hours.   Following the arrest of the two subjects, Brainard and Burrell, the two weapons were brought into the Detective Bureau and examined by Harkness of the State CII (Criminal Investigation and Identification Division) and myself:

1. One .38 caliber revolver serial No. 325597 was found to contain five live rounds of .38 caliber ammunition. This gun marked and turned over to Harkness, CII.

2. One .38 caliber revolver serial No. 333563 was found to contain four live rounds of .38 caliber ammunition and one spent .38 caliber casing. This gun marked and turned over to Harkness of CII.

3. Both guns received by Harkness of CII at 2310 this date.

Officer: John Gayne, #111

F. On July 23, at 2355 hours.   Referring to attached diagram, following articles removed from 1970 Cad 2/dr convertible bearing California license MYY-625 in County Jail yard:

#1 Paper bag containing a tag from Grants dated July 23, 1972, one light socket and one jar of hand cream.

#2 Paper bag, brown containing $1,370.51 in currency and coin.

#3 Paper bag, empty.

#4 Cigarette package, opened, Marlboros.

#5 Dark glasses, bubble type.

#6 Dark glasses, flat.

#7 Hat, green with white webbing in front bearing new price tag.

#8 Bag, empty between seat and door on floor.

#9 Hat, green with white webbing in front bearing new price tag. Identical to item #7.

#10 Glove, brown cotton.

#11 Man's Naugahyde jacket, pile lining.

#12 Dark glasses, flat.

#13 Shirt, khaki tan, cotton.

#14 Shirt, orange colored with several buttons missing.

#15 Jacket, rain repellant, dark color with white lining.

#16 One glove, dark color identical to glove item #10 and found wrapped in item #13.

#17 Bag, Montgomery Ward, small size, found wrapped in shirt, Item #13.

#18 Watch, Timex.

#19 One green metal tool box containing:

   a. empty brown paper bag

   b. cloth glove similar to items #10 and #16

   c. jar, Cover Girl makeup

   d. tube lipstick, lavender color

   e. one box .38 caliber ammunition containing 33 Peters cartridges.

#20 One man's green hat, soft.

#21 One white coveralls, J.C. Penny, Big Mac brand with light-colored paint over all.

#22 Boots, brown medium high with light-colored paint on same.

#23 Two buttons, 4 hole, pearl color.

Regarding articles from the 1970 Cad (MYY-625):

   1. Items #1, and #3 to #23 inclusive turned over to Allen Harkness, State CII.

   2. Item #2 booked with Jail Sergeant.

   3. Brown paper bag, #2, containing $1,370.51 in currency and coin consisted of the following:

   a. Currency:

$ 1.00 bills	25 held together by paper clip	$ 25.00
$ 1.00 bills	loose	208.00
$ 5.00 bills	loose	535.00
$ 10.00 bills	loose	350.00
$ 20.00 bills	loose	220.00
	Currency, total:	$1,338.00

   b. Coins:

1-roll .25-cent pieces	$10.00
3-rolls .10-cent pieces	15.00
3-rolls .05-cent pieces	6.00
3-rolls .01-cent pieces	1.50
1-loose penny	.01
Coins, total:	$32.51
Officer:	John Gayne, #111

G. On July 24, at 0830 hours: The below officer was sent to the County Morgue to pick up the cartridge belt and the clothing of Officer Cox.

Officer was present when Dr. Prisinzano removed the bullet or slug from the mouth of Officer Cox. I witnessed the doctor mark same and he then handed the slug to me and I then marked same and placed in envelope. This envelope was later turned over to Allen Harkness of the CII at approximately 2230 hours.

The slug entered the neck of Officer Cox on the left side approx. 5″ below and 1″ to the rear of the ear. It then passed through the neck and then lodged itself in the lower jaw on the right side.

This slug appears to be that of a .38 cal. and it is badly damaged having smashed against the jaw bone.

Deputy Shiner of the Coroner's Office advised that he will dry the shirt and other items of clothing and will then turn same over to Allen Harkness, CII, in the A.M.

Joseph Green of our B of I took colored photos of the deceased, showing close-ups of the wounds, including the powder burns. Dr. Prisinzano removed large section of flesh from around the wound showing the powder burns and this will be preserved and turned over to the CII by the Coroner's Office.

Officer: Harry Wells, #233

Discussion Questions

1. What is the meaning of the inherent integrity of records prepared in the performance of official duties? Can this designation be applied to field notes of a crime-scene search? To photographs at a crime scene? To sketches?

2. Explain the requirement that photographs and sketches must be a faithful representation of the thing shown.

3. Relate the purposes of photographing a crime scene to the need for planned picture taking.

4. Cite the advantages of (a) photographs over sketches, or (b) sketches over photographs.

5. What are the advantages of a floor-plan sketch?

6. Who is responsible for the adequacy of crime-scene photography? Why? (Discuss.)

7. What are the primary objectives of reports made during a *continuing investigation?*

8. What is the most appropriate form or structure of investigative reports?

9. What is meant by chronological order in the preparation of reports of a continuing investigation?

10. What are the six classic queries of reporters useful in guarding against the omission of details in an investigative report?

11. Compare the real-world reports of the case study with the chapter's instructional writing.

Library Assignment

Research the area of traffic accident investigation. Prepare a bibliography of at least five references to books and articles in this field, and cite the page numbers containing material about how to prepare traffic accident diagrams.

Workbook Project

List the equipment and materials that you believe to be necessary for sketching a crime scene.

Collection and Preservation of Physical Evidence

The role of the detective or crime investigator is complex. It has a "take charge" aspect upon arrival at crime scenes and involves conferring with the first officer to arrive and his or her uniformed associates, assuming the work and responsibility of the officer-in-charge, isolating and "freezing" the crime scene, finding and holding witnesses, and similar duties. Other detectives and/or uniformed officers may arrive at the scene to assist. When all but a few available personnel at the scene are assigned to meaningful duties, the officer in charge should direct the unassigned officers to start a scene search under his or her supervision.

Many departments send photographers to a suspicious death scene; others field crime-scene units of two or more police criminalists to assist in "working" homicide scenes. With or without this skilled help, all detectives/investigators must acquire adequate skills for the collection of evidence through in-service classes at the police academy, local crime lab, and/or hands-on classes elsewhere.

During the O. J. Simpson trial in Los Angeles in 1995, defense attorneys spent weeks trying to raise reasonable doubts about the propriety of police criminalists' evidence collection and the reliability of scientific evidence. Some of the worst examples cited were one or two evidence technicians who did such an unprofessional job collecting blood samples that DNA tests seeking to link the defendant with the crime scene were considered unreliable.

The use of evidence found at crime scenes in a trial proceeding depends on trust—trust that no mistakes were made, that the evidence is untainted by partisanship or politics. *Physical evidence* is any solid, semisolid, or liquid material, however microscopic, that may aid in determining the truth during an investigation. Physical evidence has been used since 1928. In that year Locard stated his theory of transfer evidence: whenever two surfaces are in contact with each other, there is a partial transfer of material from one on to the other. Locard noted such evidence is a silent yet certain and reliable witness of a person's actions and contacts.[1] Traces from the scene may be carried away by the perpetrator, or the perpetrator may leave traces at the scene.

Physical evidence assists the investigator by supporting or confirming the facts upon which a reasonable and strong suspicion is based. It helps to establish the case for or against a suspect. In a general sense, it may be categorized within one or more of the following elements of the evidence structure of a case. Physical evidence may:

1. Supply basic investigative leads, clues, and evidence.
2. Strengthen one or more weak portions of the chain of evidence.
3. Support the accuracy of statements made by witnesses, or impeach false or improper statements.

The primary source of physical evidence is the crime scene; secondary sources are participants in the crime, places in which related acts of the crime occurred, or places visited by participants. Much physical evidence is hidden, or latent, so that scientific procedures are required to find and collect it. Some objects are obviously evidence and need little or no processing by experts to develop their basic evidential value. Other physical evidence requires scientific examination by laboratory technicians.

After being located and recognized during a search, physical evidence must be collected, marked for identification, packaged, and transported to a safe storage or the laboratory for examination. Known standards are collected at the crime scene and other areas involved in criminal operations to facilitate comparison analysis. Firearms, tools, and other suspect items also are collected for laboratory examinations, which may link these items with previously discovered physical evidence.

Physical evidence is more likely to show opportunity and identity by placing a suspect at a crime scene or in some contact with the victim; but it also may reveal motive when it connects the suspect with crimes such as rape or child molesting. It also may satisfy the necessary proof of *corpus delicti*—that is, that a crime was in fact committed where there is no percipient witness to the crime.

There is a probabilistic element to the evaluation of any item of physical evidence by investigators or by the triers-of-fact. However, the only chance of developing such evidence as effective proof is to find it, record it in place, collect it, and not ruin its value by mishandling it.

EVIDENCE KIT

Investigators require an equipment kit of miscellaneous tools, camera equipment, and items adapted to the collection of physical evidence at crime scenes and other areas searched for evidence. In addition, a variety of assorted boxes, bottles, and bags is necessary for properly wrapping and transporting physical evidence. A small attaché case can contain the major items of equipment; supplemental gear can be packed into a slightly larger piece of luggage.

A recommended kit contains the following items:

1. Flashlight and flood lamps.
2. 50-foot steel rule.
3. 18-inch straight-edge ruler.
4. Photographic equipment (cameras, filter, tripod), film, lighting equipment, and light meter.
5. Graph paper (8-by-10-inch), notebook, pen, pencils, chalk, and crayon.
6. Magnifying glass and hand mirror.
7. Fingerprint equipment, camera, powders, lifting tape, and transfer cards.
8. Casting material (plaster of paris) and dental wax, spray gun, shellac, alcohol, a large plastic cup, a pail, an adjustable casting frame, and small and large spatulas.
9. Indoor and outdoor thermometers.
10. Dissecting kit, rubber gloves, medicine dropper, forceps, tweezers, and scissors.
11. Tools—screwdrivers, hammer, wrenches, pry bar, saws, chisels, and pliers.
12. Material for packaging and transporting evidence—cardboard boxes, pillboxes, large-mouth bottles, manila envelopes, glassine envelopes, flat sheets of cardboard, sealing tape, wrapping paper, cord, twine, labels, tags, and rubber bands.
13. A compass.
14. Several small towels.
15. Plastic bags (assorted sizes).
16. Disposable gloves (latex medical examination gloves).
17. Surgical masks and protective eyewear.
18. Blood collection kit.

When a police agency employs evidence technicians to collect and preserve physical evidence at crime scenes, the evidence kit is not a great deal more elaborate or extensive; but the personnel who use it will receive a greater amount of specialized training and develop skills more rapidly because their special work requires frequent evidence collection at crime scenes. When evidence technicians are available, the investigator's kit can be less self-sufficient; but kits grow as investigators develop needs and individual preferences. Many investigators like to know the necessary equipment is at hand, so they keep up their own kits even when the police force does have evidence technicians.

HANDLING INFECTED EVIDENCE

Acquired immune deficiency syndrome (AIDS), hepatitis B, and tuberculosis are lethal and/or infectious diseases more likely to be encountered at crime scenes today than in the past. The scenes of crimes of violence involving victims with one of these diseases are likely to have blood and possibly other infectious body fluids. Therefore, it is imperative that all possible precautions be taken.

Investigators arriving at the crime scene should question other officers as to the possibility of the victim having a lethal and/or infectious disease. Because AIDS is currently affecting the heterosexual community, everyone is at high risk. The high-risk groups are homosexuals (male), IV drug users, and possibly prostitutes (male and female). A quick survey of the crime scene may indicate some warning signals: for example, condition of victim, and presence of prescription or nonprescription drugs.

The first line of defense against infectious diseases is the wearing of disposable gloves. A surgical mask and protective eyewear may also be suggested if there is any likelihood of liquid or dried blood coming into contact with the investigator's or crime-scene technician's face. The second line of defense is to avoid cutting or puncturing a finger or other portion of the body while conducting the crime-scene search and collecting evidence. A collateral line of defense is to seek medical assistance immediately if you do receive an accidental cut or other wound or believe that particles of possibly infected blood may have come in contact with your mouth or eyes.[2]

To protect others, any evidence suspected of contamination should be placed in clearly marked plastic bags and sealed. However, they should not be forwarded to the crime laboratory until it is certain that the laboratory will accept this type of evidence.

Because of the epidemic spread of AIDS, investigators are urged to meet with local health officials to discuss how to best protect all concerned. Health personnel should be able to outline possible signs at crime scenes that might indicate that a victim should be suspected of having an infectious disease; to explain the proper procedure for disposing of latex gloves after their use at a "suspect" crime scene; and to denote the best procedure to take from the time an investigator or technician believes that he or she has been in contact with blood or other body fluids likely to be infected and the time when medical assistance will be available.

COLLECTING EVIDENCE

Continuity of possession, the chain of possession, must be established when evidence is proffered in court as an exhibit. Whenever possible, if the officer locating the evidence is not the investigator assigned responsibility for the case, the evidence should not be disturbed until its location and nature can be brought to the attention of the responsible investigator, nor should it be moved until its location and description have been noted, photographs taken at the scene, and measurements made to place it.

Adherence to standard and required procedures in every case is the best guarantee that the collection and possession of physical evidence will stand court tests of what happened, or could have happened, to it from the time of its finding to its presentation in court. Any deviation from standard procedures in processing physical evidence can affect its credibility and contribute to a reasonable suspicion in the minds of the triers-of-fact about the entire police investigation.

In narcotics cases in many areas, investigators seal the evidence in manila envelopes, initial the sealing, and drop them through a slot into a locked box at local headquarters. The chemist who will make the examination has the only key to this box. He or she removes the evidence by cutting the sealed envelope open, examines it, and replaces it in the original manila envelope; reseals the envelope with gummed tape; initials the sealing; and places the envelope in a locked box. An idea of the ritual used to prove the continuity of the possession of evidence is illustrated by the questions and responses recorded during a grand jury hearing in a case of possession and sale of narcotics.

The testimony, on direct examination, of the finding investigator relative to this evidence was as follows:

Q. I believe you found a large quantity of what you believed to be drugs in the house?

A. Yes, sir.

Q. Do you recognize this plastic bag as containing the quantity you discovered?

A. Yes, sir.

Q. Where were the drugs taken?

A. They were brought to the station.

Q. Where were they put?

A. In the interrogation room and locked up.

Q. The next day did you take the drugs from the interrogation room to the Bureau of Narcotics Enforcement?

A. Yes, sir. I did.

Q. In the Bureau of Narcotics Enforcement, were they put in a locker?

A. Yes.

Q. Was this locker locked?

A. Yes.

Q. Did you have a key to open it again?

A. No, sir.

Q. Where is this locker located?

A. The chemist's office.

The chemist was then sworn and questioned.

Q. Do you recall having seen that plastic bag (indicating bag identified by previous witness) and the contents of it?

A. Yes, I have.

Q. Did you bring it with you today?

A. Yes, I did.

Q. When did you first come into contact with that particular bag?

A. On December 28 of last year.

Q. Where did you find it?

A. This was removed by me from a locked locker at the Narcotics Bureau. It is an evidence locker in my office that is used to submit evidence for analysis when I am not present to take it personally and to which I have the only key.

Q. Now, did you subsequently make an examination of those drugs in this bag?

A. Yes, I did.

Since the basic legal integrity of the evidence had been shown, the witness continued his testimony about his examination of the contents of this plastic bag.

MARKING EVIDENCE

Marking evidence serves to identify it. Marking must not impair the value of evidence or restrict the number and kind of examinations to which it might be subjected by criminalists and other experts. However, traditional marking of objects by scratching an officer's initial has been expanded to include a few details of the case. When the item of evidence does not offer opportunity for extensive marking, the officer must describe the item and the time and place and circumstances of its recovery in his or her field notes. Many officers develop a shorthand method of marking evidence, such as H-S-1/25/95-V, H being the initial of the officer's last name; S the initial of the defendant's last name, if known, or of the victim's if the defendant is unknown; 1/25/95 the date; and V the indication that the object was on or near the victim. D can be used for in the defendant's possession, or N-I to indicate the note concerning the item in the investigator's field notes.

Counterfeit money should have a dual marking. The name of the person last in possession should be signed across a corner of the bill or such person should be asked to scratch his or her initials on a coin. In addition, the investigator should place his or her own mark of identification. When currency is mutilated by marking with a tracing powder or dye, it should not be cleaned but should be placed immediately in a sealed envelope and handled with care. Later, when no longer required as evidence, this mutilated currency should not be returned to general circulation but should be redeemed at a local bank with a statement that it contains stained material added to develop it as evidence.

The item of overriding importance in identifying evidence exhibits in court is how the investigator knew that this exhibit was, in fact, the object he or she found. On direct examination, questions usually have the following format:

> **Q.** Officer, I show you this revolver, now marked as people's exhibit No. 7. Do you recognize it? (Officer takes the revolver, looks for his mark, finds it, and answers.)
>
> **A.** Yes, I do.
>
> **Q.** How do you recognize it?
>
> **A.** By my mark here on the butt. (Pointing to rear and bottom of revolver.)
>
> **Q.** Where and under what circumstances did you first see this revolver?

The witness proceeds with the testimony; the identification serves as a foundation for the remainder of the testimony.

PACKAGING PHYSICAL EVIDENCE

Evidence must be packaged so as to avoid breakage, loss, or contamination in transit. Tweezers, forceps, and similar tools are used to collect and place traces and small items in their containers. Rubber gloves are suggested for handling some physical evidence.

An evidence box or board can be utilized for transporting evidence over short distances. An evidence box with pegboard sides allows for tying or wiring small and medium-sized objects in place. A series of drilled holes and appropriately sized dowels can serve a like purpose. Items of evidence that will undergo comparison analysis for possible relationships should be packaged in separate containers to obviate any allegation of cross-contamination. No wet or soiled materials or boxes or bottles should be used. Thoroughly clean and dry containers, wrapping paper, corrugated paper, boxes, and sealing tape are the basic safeguards for physical evidence in transport.

Documentary evidence is first placed in transparent envelopes without folding or bending, then between two pieces of firm, corrugated cardboard, and then in a manila envelope or other wrapper.

Plastic pill bottles with pressure lids are unbreakable, can be easily sealed with tape, and are excellent containers for hair, fibers, and other small articles. They are ideal for spent bullets, empty cartridge cases, and cartridges because they can be packed with absorbent cotton to minimize movement of such evidence.

Plastic envelopes and bags are available in various shapes and sizes and also are easily sealed. However, when they are used for the transport of soil, debris, or clothing that may contain bloodstains, there is a strong possibility of bacterial action contaminating the blood sample. Use plastic containers with caution. To an unusual degree they can act as greenhouses for the cultivation of mold that can destroy the integrity and identity of some types of evidence.

Use only the tubes or vials with stoppers found in the blood collection kit for blood samples and swatches used to collect bloodstains, and follow directions on this kit for refrigeration and other care.

If the stain is on a solid object that can be moved, such as a firearm or other weapon, transport the object, protecting the area of the stain or completely enclosing the object in a package if it is of small size. If the stain is on clothing, the garments should be wrapped separately in paper, marked appropriately, and packaged. This is better procedure than any technique for removing a sample of the stain for analysis.

Articles of clothing, tablecloths, and similar evidence should be folded as little as possible and without pressure. If the areas of such fabric to be examined are known, the folding should protect such areas from friction with the wrapping paper or other container.

Take a soil-stained or mud-soaked object to the laboratory rather than attempting to remove and transport the soil or mud as separate items. When such traces are picked up as individual items of evidence, it is vital that every precaution be taken to keep the evidence in separate sealed containers to avoid any accidental loss or mixing in transit.

Charred wood, carpet, and drapery material from the scene of a suspicious fire may be wrapped in metal foil and sealed in an airtight container. Smaller objects, such as paper and rags, or solid samples should be sealed in the container in which they were found or placed in airtight bottles or cans. This protects the fire accelerant and its residues from evaporation.

Pills and other noncaustic substances should be left in their original containers for transport to the laboratory. Such containers often contain useful information. The investigator should count the number of pills or capsules or accurately determine the bulk quantity of fluids or powders and should place such data in the field notes.

Caustic poison should not be transported until the investigator has made certain that the container in which it was found (or placed after recovery of such evidence from sink, bathtub, or other place) is safe for a period of time equal to at least twice the likely transport time.

Food, body substances, and fluids should be placed in as many separate moisture-proof bottles or containers as necessary to avoid any contamination of evidence. Food or other substances suspected of containing or known to contain poison should be marked plainly as suspected or known samples of poison.

If a weapon is suspected of containing hair, blood, or fragments of flesh, it should be packaged as any hair, blood, or flesh sample—in a sealed container of appropriate size.

Microscopic traces, hair, and fibers should be sealed in folded paper or placed in a clean, sealed envelope or box of appropriate size.

TRANSPORTING EVIDENCE

Transporting physical evidence to a laboratory, to a place of storage, or to the prosecutor's office or courtroom is the responsibility of the investigator who found the evidence. It is usually delivered personally, but when distance is a problem, it may be shipped by registered mail, insured parcel post, or express. When food or physiological fluids or substances are collected, temperature control is a primary precaution. Refrigeration without freezing will prevent deterioration, and containers with insulating qualities are now available for the transport of such material. Evidence should be shipped by the fastest available route; local delivery should be made by the finding investigator in person or by authorized personnel of his or her employing agency.

At no time should an investigator return any part of the evidence to its rightful claimant without the authority of the prosecutor. If the prosecutor believes that the evidence is not required in the trial of the offender, he or she has the authority to dispose of it to the rightful owner or to store it until such time as it is disposed of according to law. When the case is completed, the prosecutor has the authority to release the evidence.

KNOWN STANDARDS OF EVIDENCE

Criminalistics includes the identification of physical evidence and a finding as to its origin. This individualization of evidence often requires that physical evidence collected at a crime scene be matched with a known standard of evidence or a control. Known standards may be collected at the crime scene, from the victim, from a suspect, or from other sources. Known standards of evidence must be collected in exactly the same manner as any other evidence, for they have equal evidential value. Here as elsewhere there is a need for recognition, legal possession, marking for identity, preservation of the integrity of the sample, and accuracy in reporting its acquisition.

Locating a known standard of fingerprints may require no more than a search of records for a suspect's fingerprints. Shoe prints may require the collection of a known standard of soil from the area close to a footprint or heel print for comparison with soil traces on the shoes of a suspect. Collection of a sample of hair is often required, as is the search for and the recovery of a coat or sweater or other garment that may be a known standard for fibers recovered at the crime scene.

Known samples of blood start with the victim. Samples can be secured only by a medical practitioner upon the request of the investigator. Since the Schmerber case, it is lawful to take a sample from an arrested person charged with a crime in which blood collected as evidence requires a known sample for comparison analysis.[3]

The self-incrimination clause of the Fifth Amendment to the U.S. Constitution protects against compelling a person or suspect to communicate or testify to matters that may incriminate him or her. However, the Fifth Amendment does not protect a person or suspect from being compelled to be the source of "real or physical evidence." The recovery of blood, clothing, and hair without consent is not prohibited by the Fifth Amendment, for these are all considered "real or physical evidence" and thus are subject to the controls of the right to privacy and search and seizure clauses of the Fourth Amendment, rather than to the self-incrimination clause of the Fifth.

Evidence in cases of questioned typewriting should include, first, the questioned document, intact if possible, or a complete copy of the text as it appears. Second, investigators should collect material typed at or about the known or suspected date when the questioned document was prepared, as well as known specimens typed by the investigator. This is usually a threefold process, with the investigator typing an extract from the questioned document with a light, medium, and a heavy touch. (On electric machines the touch is set with an impression control level.) In making such samples, many investigators remove the typewriter ribbon or set the machine on stencil and use carbon paper to reproduce the typed text. (If there is any chance that the ribbon on the machine may have been used to type the questioned document, it is collected as evidence.) All known specimens of typewriting conclude with the time, date, the name of the investigator, and the make, model, and serial number of the typewriter.

Handwriting analysis requires exemplars, or samples, as well as proof of authorship. These known standards are classed as either "requested" (by the investigator) or "regular-course-of-business." In death cases in which a suicide note is found, the only exemplar possible is some regular-course-of-business handwriting found on the victim or at the scene, or secured from relatives and associates and identified by a responsible person as being the victim's handwriting. In other cases such exemplars may be available at the crime scene, place of employment, or in public records. Exemplars that have been requested often are less reliable because of intentional disguising of normal writing style or distortions due to nervousness.[4]

Investigators obtaining handwriting samples from a suspect should supply him or her with paper and a pen or pencil similar to the questioned writing; dictate the material to be written or printed; and allow the suspect to spell words as he or she would usually spell them. Misspelled words can contribute to the physical match between sample and questioned writing.[5] In addition, the suspect should be asked to write out and sign a statement as to the validity and source of the sample or samples.

Requiring a suspect to give handwritten exemplars is not considered as a request for communications that fall within the protection of the Fifth Amendment. The Fifth Amendment only prohibits the compulsion of communicative or testimonial evidence from a defendant. In writing for identification in producing the exemplar, the defendant is no more than the source of identification. Handwriting exemplars have been specifically held to be such an identifying physical characteristic.[6]

As with handwriting exemplars, compelling an accused to utter words spoken by an alleged thief is not within the scope of the Fifth Amendment privilege against self-incrimination. However, voice identification is subject to the Sixth Amendment's right to representation by an attorney clause and is regarded as belonging to a critical stage of the proceedings against a suspect.[7]

The justices of the U.S. Supreme Court have expressed a minority viewpoint that handwriting exemplars and voice identification are within the scope of constitutional protection. Therefore, compelling these two types of evidence against the will of a person is at least questionable if either is the key evidence in the case. It would seem the better policy to obtain handwriting exemplars and speech for identification by consent and not by force. If the investigation is beyond the general inquiry stage and has focused on a suspect, the *Miranda,* 384 U.S. 436 (1966),* admonishment should be given to inform the person of his or her constitutional protection against self-incrimination.

Many manufacturers of paint and glass provide scientific laboratories with known standards of their products, and criminalistics laboratories maintain many reference files of known standards. However, one should not count on their being such standards on file. It is the responsibility of the investigator to seek known standards until such time as he or she is informed they are not required.

Because the legal significance of physical evidence often is based on comparison to a known standard, it is of vital importance that physical evidence and its collection be viewed as a dual process of collecting and preserving the basic physical evidence, and of collecting and preserving the known standards of such evidence.

Selected References

1. EDMOND LOCARD, "Dust and Its Analysis," *Police Journal* (London), I (1928), pp. 177–92; "The Analysis of Dust Traces," *American Journal of Police Science,* I (1930), pp. 276–98, 401–18, 496–514.
2. PAUL D. BIGBEE, "Collecting and Handling Evidence Infected with Human Disease-Causing Organisms," *FBI Law Enforcement Bulletin,* LVI, No. 7 (July 1987), pp. 1–4. Also P. R. Laska, "Biohazardous Risk at the Crime Scene," *Law Enforcement Technology,* 18, No. 9 (October 1991), pp. 66–70.
3. Schmerber v. California, 384 U.S. 757 (1966).
4. JAMES P. CONWAY, *Evidential Documents* (Springfield, Ill.: Charles C Thomas, Publisher, 1959), pp. 73–83.
5. CLAUDE W. COOK, *A Practical Guide to the Basics of Physical Evidence* (Springfield, Ill.: Charles C Thomas, Publisher, 1984), pp. 10–12.
6. Gilbert v. California, 388 U.S. 263 (1967); United States v. Blount, 315 F. Supp. 1322 (1970).
7. United States v. Wade, 388 U.S. 218 (1967). See also United States v. Ash, 413 U.S. 300 (1973), and Kirby v. Illinois, 406 U.S. 682 (1972).

Chapter Review

Discussion Questions

1. Trace the growth in the use of physical evidence in criminal proceedings.
2. Will physical evidence really establish a case for or against a suspect? Does it have real legal significance?
3. What items are basic to any evidence kit?

*See Appendix A, Case brief of *Miranda.*

4. Describe standard procedures in collecting and preserving evidence.
5. Can any one rule of evidence gathering be identified as of primary importance?
6. Explain when and why known standards of evidence should be collected.
7. Why are blood samples exempt from the scope of the Fifth Amendment's privilege against self-incrimination?
8. What other types of identification samples, in which a defendant is the source, are exempt from the protection of the Fifth Amendment?

Library Assignment

Search available literature on police rules and prepare a listing of at least five references that describe standard procedures for collecting and preserving physical evidence.

Workbook Project

Search for material as to suggested procedure for processing "suspect" crime scenes (likely to have blood and other body fluids of persons with infectious diseases), and summarize the precautions recommended and their source (library reference, local or nearby police unit, or other source).

CHAPTER
6

Laboratory and Technical Services

Reliance on the interrogation of suspects for proof of guilt in criminal cases has retarded the growth of laboratory services available to police investigators. The cost of these services and the lack of professional personnel also have been handicaps. The outlook for the future is for a steady growth in the utilization of scientific techniques to establish innocence or guilt. Years ago it may have been true that there was no other way to solve most crimes than to induce a suspect's confession, but the day of the clueless crime scene and of physical evidence not amenable to scientific analysis is gone. Today, technicians trained and equipped for the scientific collection of evidence are teamed with patrol officers to process crime scenes in a scientific search for physical evidence, no matter how microscopic, that can be examined by technical or laboratory experts. Although funds are still a problem in the growth of scientific services in criminal investigation, the number of facilities is increasing, the services are improving, and personnel of high professional qualifications are now available and being employed.

Modern processing of physical evidence owes its development to advancements in the field of forensic medicine. Public acceptance of medicolegal evidence about the causes of sudden and suspicious death was a factor in the acceptance of other scientific aids in criminal investigation. The pathologist and toxicologist based their determinations on the medicolegal autopsy and various laboratory procedures for the examination of the body tissue, bone, and fluids of the victim.[1] They were professionals, physicians, surgeons, and laboratory technicians.

In 1923 in *Fry* v. *United States,*[2] legal attention was focused on the acceptability of scientific aids in the detection of crime. The court held that the scientific principle offered for admission must first be recognized as generally accepted in the particular field of science to which it belongs. The court could then admit expert testimony deduced from the recognized principle or discovery of science.

State and federal trial courts have recently ruled that interpreting *Fry* requires some flexibility to cope with new and novel forensic scientific developments that have not yet gained adequate support in the scientific community.

There is a *de facto* hierarchy of laboratory services available to police investigators in the United States. Countywide coroners and medical examiners have laboratory facilities for the scientific analysis of physical evidence in homicides, rapes, and certain other sex crimes. Law enforcement agencies have local, regional, and statewide criminalistics laboratories. The FBI operates a nationwide facility in this field.

The following list indicates the agencies and the scientific services available to investigators:

1. County or municipal medicolegal laboratory of the coroner or medical examiner for the analysis of physical evidence in suspicious death and certain sex cases.
2. Local or regional criminalistics laboratory.
3. State criminalistics laboratory.
4. Laboratories of state and federal agencies for the service of agency personnel only.
5. The criminalistics laboratory of the FBI, Washington, D.C.

In all laboratory examinations the legal integrity of the work is maintained by tight security rules and the careful maintenance of records indicating the chain of possession. Whether an investigator forwards material to the expert or an expert returns it to the investigator, evidence is "booked" in its travels and then safeguarded. No unauthorized person is allowed in contact with the evidential materials, and a record is made of every person making tests on or handling the substance.

Standard procedures for the handling of evidence are extremely important. The proper handling of evidence submitted for examinations is the major item of routine in the laboratory. Physical evidence must pass through the laboratory in a regular manner, with no interruption in its custody, to guarantee that there will be no loss of evidence. Procedural steps in handling evidence in the laboratory are:

1. Continuous, documented chain of custody, involving receipting, indexing, storing, sealing, and unsealing.
2. Storage safe or vault meeting minimum security standards.
3. Access to evidence limited to examining criminalist when seals are broken.
4. Chain of custody and processing kept as short as possible.

CRIMINALISTICS: FORENSIC SCIENCE

The crime laboratory in which physical evidence obtained by police in the course of an investigation is examined may now be known as a forensic science laboratory, and laboratory technicians are often identified as forensic scientists. The professional group in this field, however, still identify with the term *criminalistics*.

Criminalistics is that profession and scientific discipline directed to the recognition, identification, individualization, and evaluation of physical evidence by application of the natural sciences in matters of law and science.[3]

Identification in criminalistics is aligned with the logic of set theory. All objects can be divided and subdivided into various sets on the basis of their properties. Identification in relation to physical evidence and its analysis is defined as the determination of some set to which an object or substance belongs or the determination as to whether an object or substance belongs to a given set. Fingerprints, toolmarks, blood, hair, glass, paint, and other types of evidence can be so classified. In addition, criminalistics is concerned with identity or origin. Given a bloodstain found and collected at a crime scene, the criminalist is asked to determine from whom it originated; given a spent bullet recovered from a human body, the criminalist is asked to decide if a particular firearm fired the bullet. In reaching a decision about identification, the criminalist also is asked to individualize the identification by specifying how individual or unique the item of evidence examined is within the set of its origin.

The *crime laboratory* is staffed by technicians educated and trained in the forensic science that is criminalistics. It is a subsystem in the administration of justice that studies the effect of a criminal upon a crime scene (and other sites of criminal activity), and vice versa. The informational output of a crime laboratory depends on its input: the physical evidence collected at crime scenes and forwarded to the laboratory for examination. Developing information from physical evidence, within a laboratory operation, is within the decision-making responsibility of the forensic science staff. Depending on the circumstances of the case, the general strategy is to order the analyses so that the maximum amount of information is secured.[4]

When scientific findings are interpreted, the deductions of the criminalist in reconstructing the event and the person or persons associated with it cannot be made with certainty and usually are made with prudence. Criminalists offer the most probable reconstruction on the basis of reasonable criteria and do not assign mathematical probabilities to the occurrence of two materials from different sources (two items of evidence, or one item of evidence and one known standard) having a common origin. Even the most sophisticated and specific analysis techniques do not, as a general rule, offer an opportunity for a criminalist to evaluate identification in terms of mathematical probability.

The effect on an accused person and his legal counsel of such identification and its individualization is considerable. Associative evidence placing a suspect at the crime scene ruins a not guilty pleading based on a general denial of presence at the crime scene or of contact with the victim at any time, and seriously damages a defense based on an alibi. Tracing an item of evidence found at the crime scene to the accused person or an item found on the suspect back to the scene has serious implications for any successful defense unless a reasonable explanation is forthcoming. This effect is not necessarily an inducement to confess, but it does function in this fashion by its influence on the defendant and his or her legal advisor.

FORWARDING PHYSICAL EVIDENCE TO THE LABORATORY

When physical evidence is sent to a laboratory for scientific examination, it must be accompanied by an informative report. The report must, in effect, bring the crime scene into the laboratory. This report must be on the official letterhead of the law enforcement agency with jurisdiction in the case and should contain the following:

1. Name and address of agency submitting evidence.
2. Crime classification of case by type and grade of offense.
3. Case number of agency submitting evidence.
4. Copy of the offense report or the report of the preliminary investigation or a brief history of the case.
5. List of evidence, consecutively numbered by item, with a brief description of each item and a notation as to when and where found; whether the item is a known standard for comparison; and whether any change has taken place in the evidence, either through accidental mishandling or because a sample is being submitted rather than the full amount of evidence collected.
6. List of suggested scientific examinations.
7. Brief statement of the problems in the case.
8. The name and address of the investigator to whom the exhibits should be returned upon completion of the examinations.

Packages in which physical evidence is to be shipped to a laboratory should be marked "Evidence for Examination" and should have the written request for an examination pasted securely to the outside of the package with the notation "Letter" or "Invoice" indicating its location. The criminalist receiving the package can read the request letter and have some idea of the nature of the evidence before opening the package itself.

Packages containing blood or other body fluids suspected of being contaminated by a person with acquired immune deficiency syndrome (AIDS), hepatitis, or tuberculosis, should be marked CAUTION, followed by the disease suspected. The technician in charge at the crime laboratory should be consulted prior to submitting this type of evidence.

Laboratory technicians carefully mark, tag, and otherwise identify all items of evidence while such evidence is in their custody. It is this careful handling of physical evidence by crime laboratory technicians that preserves the integrity of such evidence. Upon return of the evidence the report of the expert examiner who conducted the laboratory examination is integrated with other information collected in the investigation to date.

LABORATORY DETERMINATIONS

Laboratory personnel, after scientific examination of physical evidence, report their findings. These determinations in past cases have led to a stylized set of expectations from field investigators. It is not always possible for a finding in a specific case to achieve the optimum expectations. As a result, the field investigator may be disappointed and, perhaps, reluctant to request such technical or laboratory assistance in the future. On the other hand, an optimistic view of the determinations that are possible through scientific aid should lead field investigators to a more extensive use of technical and laboratory services.

Great expectations may be rewarded. For this reason an optimistic but realistic view of possible technical and laboratory determinations is necessary. The findings that possibly may result from a scientific examination of physical evidence have been organized in the following list for ready reference according to the types of evidence common to police cases:

1. Weapons—firearms:
   a. identification of bullets, shells, or cartridge cases with a specific gun
   b. operating condition of firearms, functioning of safety and trigger pull
   c. distance at which gun was fired
   d. position of the shooter at time of firing
   e. ownership traced
   f. obliterated serial number restored
   g. imprints (latent fingerprints) or impressions or transfer evidence developed
   h. used in other crimes
2. Weapons—knives and bludgeons:
   a. description of cutting, stabbing, or striking surfaces
   b. comparison with wounds
   c. tracing ownerships
   d. imprints, impressions, or transfer evidence developed
   e. used in other crimes
   f. direction of force
   g. position of assailant
   h. identity of assailant; sex, strength, and which hand held weapon
3. Drugs and poisons:
   a. analysis by type (name)
   b. determination of quantity of fatal dose

    c. origin (purchase, manufacturer, growth)

    d. comparison with effect—wounds, body functions

    e. used in other crimes

4. Imprints and impressions:

    a. nature of object making imprint or impression

    b. identity by manufacturer or group

    c. individual identity—comparison (imprint or impression made by or not made by submitted suspect object)

    d. individual identity—fingerprints (see Figure 6–1)

    e. individual identity—footprints[5]

    f. direction of movement

    g. transfer evidence developed

5. Toolmarks:

    a. nature of tool

    b. identity by manufacturer or group

    c. identity—for search

    d. origin (purchase)

    e. individual identity (mark made or not made by submitted suspect tool)

    f. transfer evidence developed

    g. used in other crimes

FIGURE 6–1 "Latent" print found at crime scene (left), compared with rolled fingerprint of suspect (right). Twelve points of identity indicate a match.

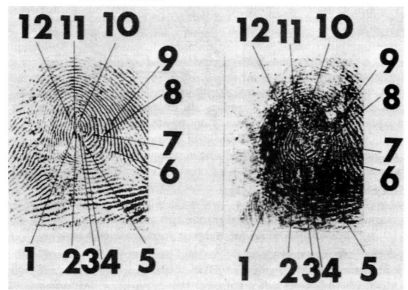

6. Traces of identity—blood:
   a. identification as blood
   b. determination (human or animal, grouping, direction, and velocity of drops and splashes)[6]
   c. direction of force
   d. position of assailant
   e. individual identity (blood of victim or of defendant)
   f. found at other crime scenes
   g. transfer evidence developed[7]
7. Blood (test):
   a. alcohol in blood (percentage)
   b. interpretation of percentage as to degree of intoxication
8. Hair and fibers:
   a. origin (human, head, body, pubic; animal; clothing)
   b. identity (sex, race—a broad grouping)
   c. individual identity—comparison of known standards of hair of victim with hair of defendant, comparison of fibers from clothing of victim (or found at scene) with material found on suspect
   d. Dog hair (victim's pet to clothing of suspect; suspect's pet to crime scene/victim)
9. Dust, dirt, debris:
   a. origin (locale, occupation)
   b. identity (group)
   c. individual identity or transfer evidence developed
10. Flammable fluids—fire and explosive residue:
   a. identity by physical properties
   b. origin (purchase, manufacturer)
   c. direction of force (flow)
   d. used in other crimes
11. Glass:
   a. identity and comparisons
   b. direction of force
   c. transfer evidence developed
   d. similar damage at other crime scenes
12. Paint:
   a. identity (group)
   b. origin (purchase, usage, manufacturer)
   c. individual identity—the same as or similar to submitted sample
   d. transfer evidence developed
13. Semen stains:
   a. identity of stain as semen

b. location and extent of stain

c. origin—individual identity—in relation to blood or other body substances or fluids of a suspect in custody[8]

14. Wood:

    a. identity (type, group, name)

    b. origin (purchase, production, growth)

    c. identity—same as or similar to submitted suspect sample

15. Suspected poisoned food:

    a. isolation and identity of noxious or poisoned substance

    b. origin (source, process)

16. Documents:

    a. authenticity of document or signature or both

    b. authorship (handwriting); authorship (typewriter); identity—"trademarks" of writer (form, spelling, vocabulary, etc.); fraudulent check "trademark"

    c. age

    d. nature of alteration or erasure

    e. copy traces, carbon paper, embossed writing, typewriter ribbons

    f. transfer evidence developed

    g. dating of ink and paper[9]

    h. used in other crimes

17. Feces—comparison with samples taken from other crime scenes, undigested food residues possible and informative

18. Vomit—comparison for identity when suspect is located with vomit at crime scene and traces on clothing of suspect; in suspected poison cases, analysis for content and identification of poison, if present

19. Urine—analysis of submitted specimens (alcohol level in blood), and analysis in suspected poisoning cases

Investigators should become acquainted with the language used by criminalists in reporting their determinations. If any doubts exist in the mind of the investigator as to the level of uniqueness achieved by the criminalist, a request for clarification should be made. A high level of exactness in identification is not always possible because of the nature of the evidence or the type of examination. Investigators should be particularly alert for the following word patterns in the reports of technicians examining physical evidence:

1. Consistent with.

2. Similar to.

3. Indistinguishable from.

4. Of the type used.

5. Matching.

6. Indicates that.

7. Has the appearance of.

MEDICOLEGAL LABORATORY SERVICES

Most local laws governing investigative jurisdiction in cases of suspicious death require that the coroner or medical examiner be notified promptly and that the body of the victim not be moved without permission of this official. The basic medicolegal service is to determine whether a death was caused by criminal agency and to identify the deceased person and the cause of death.

The report of the postmortem examination contains the autopsy surgeon's findings. The form of this report, in outline, is as follows:

1. The preamble (date, place, and identity of deceased and of witnesses to identification).

2. External appearance (site, character, and dimensions of any wounds or marks related to the cause of death).

3. Internal examination (description of brain, spinal column, organs, and contents of body).

4. A reasoned opinion of the cause of death based on the facts found.

5. Signature of examiner (title and qualifications).[10]

Autopsy technique utilizes external examination and dissection. During this work the pathologist may dictate his or her findings to a stenographer, an assistant, or a recorder. When transcribed, these notes, along with any sketches, diagrams, or photographs, are the raw notes of the examination.

The autopsy surgeon investigates all of the body cavities and makes incisions on the side of the neck to expose the neck organs for examination. A knife, saw, and chisel are used to open the head; the brain is removed and examined. The spinal cord and extremities also are examined. There is a microscopic examination of substances if there is an appearance of abnormality. The pathologist must be systematic and thorough. The recognition of the cause of death is his or her professional responsibility.

External postmortem appearances are very informative when a criminal agency is involved in the death. The areas of the body showing lividity indicate the position after death. Wounds and their appearance are particularly significant as they often assist in reconstructing the circumstances of a crime, the nature of the murder weapon, and the manner of its use. Significant data include an accurate description of where the wounds are situated, their shape, size, and direction.

Generally, pathologists classify and report the nature of wounds as follows:

1. Incised wounds—spindle-shaped in stabbing, linear in cutting.

2. Lacerated wounds—irregularly edged, some tearing.

3. Contusions—bruises, discolorations, hematoma.

4. Abrasions—scratches, trivial wounds.
5. Gunshot wounds—shotgun: "rat-hole" to dispersion; rifles and pistols: contact, entrance, exit.
6. Antemortem or postmortem.
7. The age of the wound.
8. Opinion as to wound—accidental, suicidal, or homicidal; "hesitation" wounds in suicides, and "defense" wounds in homicide.

A practitioner skilled in medicolegal procedures can reconstruct the shape of the striking area of the weapon used and the degree of force in relation to the weight and striking surface of the weapon. This can mean a possible *matching* of a murder weapon when found, and if the offender has not been identified, possibly an estimate of the sex and size of the perpetrator.

Body temperature, lividity, and *rigor mortis* indicate the time of death in on-the-scene examination, but the general appearance of the body and its stomach contents afford the pathologist a means of fixing the time of death within reasonable limits. The clinical history of the case, its revelations about persons who were the last to see the victim alive and the victim's activities, assist the pathologist in determining the time of death.

Classically, the autopsy report should provide information on the following:

1. The cause of death resulted from:
   a. natural causes
   b. accident
   c. suicide
   d. homicide
   e. undetermined origin
2. If a weapon or substance caused death, the nature of the fatal wounds or injuries.
3. Time of death in relationship to wound.
4. Whether the scene where the body was discovered was the death scene, whether marks and signs indicate the victim was mobile or that the body was moved.
5. Evidence of chronic illness or other disease.
6. Evidence of blood, hair, or skin other than the victim's.
7. Evidence of sexual knowledge or deviancy.[11]

In suspected poisoning cases the pathologist must correlate his or her clinical postmortem findings with the history of the deceased, if available, and suggest to the toxicologist the most promising area of investigation. The history in a medicolegal autopsy includes all available information about the circumstances of a case—manner of death, preceding manifestations of illness and pain, and investigation at the death scene if foul play is suspected. After the toxicologist's report has been received, the pathologist evaluates the significance of the toxicologist's findings with regard to the body conditions at autopsy and against the background of the clinical history of the deceased, and bases an opinion of the cause of death on these three types of facts.

Identification after death is determined by characteristics that distinguish the deceased from all other individuals. The usual police investigation attempts to disclose the name of the deceased in order to find responsible persons (relatives or friends) to view the body and identify it. The deceased person frequently is fingerprinted, and the inked impressions may be forwarded through the criminal justice information system for identification or verification.

Teeth provide leads to identification, and dentists can elicit valuable clues to identity. A wealth of dental information is now in the hands of the dental profession and can be useful in the identification of deceased persons.[12]

Sex, age, marks and scars, and other physical features, such as old bone fractures or deformities, are identification factors.[13] Death masks are sometimes made, photographed, and included in police bulletins when identification is a problem. These flyers are circulated in the same manner as wanted notices. Unrecognizable remains of a human body present problems. Fire, water, explosion, mutilation, and exposure to the elements and animals often make it difficult or impossible to arrive at an identification. Nevertheless, pathologists can establish some clues to identity. By correlating all available data, they may arrive at a determination of race, sex, age, and approximate height and weight.

EXPERT TESTIMONY BY LABORATORY TECHNICIANS

Technicians in crime or medicolegal laboratories can testify as expert witnesses—persons qualified to evaluate and offer an opinion based on their scientific work. An expert in technical and laboratory services is a person with a basic educational background in science, additional academic specialization, and on-the-job training or related experience. This combination of education and experience is basic to qualifying an expert in court. In addition, it must be shown that, by the nature of his or her education, work, and experience, the expert understands scientific methods and is able to explain the analytic procedures used to gain the necessary scientific acceptability. The major function of an expert is to testify in an area of expertise. He or she does not deal with the guilt or innocence of any suspect. The expert's report to the investigator and court presentation of oral evidence and any demonstration of work, such as photographic exhibits, are an analytical presentation of the physical facts of the examination and its findings and the basis of an expert opinion. At trial the meaning of this testimony can be developed only on direct examination by the prosecutor.

The trustworthiness of an expert is important to the net worth of the entire investigation. Any suspicion of subjectivity or dishonesty destroys the legal significance of evidence because the average trier-of-fact may easily view such conduct as affecting the credibility of the entire investigation. An unusual unanimous vote for reversal of an Illinois murder conviction by the judges of the U.S. Supreme Court illustrates this reaction. The case was *Miller* v. *Pate*, 386 U.S. 1 (1968):

Lloyd Eldon Miller, Jr., was convicted of murder in an Illinois state court in a prosecution for the death of a girl resulting from a sexual attack. A piece of compelling evidence against Miller was a pair of reddish-brown stained men's shorts found in an abandoned building a mile away from the scene of the crime and known as Van Buren's Flats.

The prosecution theorized that the stains on the shorts were human blood and that the petitioner had been wearing these shorts when he committed the crime. The judgment of conviction was affirmed on appeal by the Supreme Court of Illinois (13 Ill. 2d 84, 148 NE2d 455). On application for a writ of habeas corpus to the U.S. District Court for the Northern District of Illinois, the court granted the writ (226 F Supp 541), but the Court of Appeals for the Seventh Circuit reversed it (342 F2d 646). In the federal habeas corpus proceeding it was established that the reddish-brown stains on the shorts in question were not blood, but paint, and that counsel for the prosecution had known at the time of the trial that the shorts were stained with paint.

In words of unusual bluntness the unanimous Supreme Court opinion stated:

> More than 30 years ago this Court held that the Fourteenth Amendment cannot tolerate a state criminal conviction obtained by the knowing use of false evidence. There has been no deviation from that established principle. There can be no retreat from that principle here. The judgement of the Court of Appeals is reversed, and the case is remanded for further proceedings consistent with this opinion.

DNA "FINGERPRINTING"

Every human being possesses a unique genetic code. Forty-six chromosomes are used to hold the code and these are made of the chemical DNA (Deoxyribonucleic acid). Now scientists can examine evidential material (bloodstains, hair roots, semen, vaginal fluid) and read the genetic code of an individual. With the exception of identical twins, DNA "fingerprinting" (profiling) (see Figure 6–2) can be used for the elimination or association of suspects with a crime victim or a crime scene.* DNA can be utilized along with conventional blood group analysis. Private diagnostic laboratories in the United States now seek work from police agencies. However, the police crime laboratory community in the United States appears to be on the threshold of developing procedures for conducting DNA "fingerprinting." The Federal Bureau of Investigation has initiated a program to develop this technology nationwide: (1) implementation in the FBI national laboratory, serving the national police community; (2) developing a training program for the technicians of state and local crime laboratories; and (3) establishing a centralized data bank that will allow

*See Department of Justice Document 13 in Appendix C.

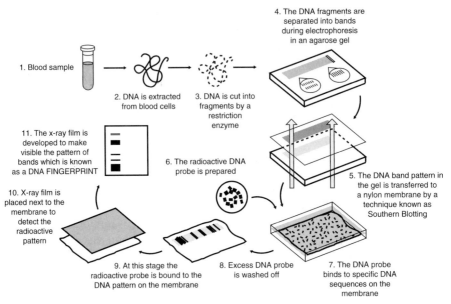

FIGURE 6–2 DNA identification process.

the DNA "fingerprints" of past violent crimes to be compared with the DNA "fingerprints" of new and similar crimes.

This is a giant step forward in the expansion of science in developing information and evidence from physical evidence recovered from the person of a victim or from a crime scene. Advances of this type are particularly important in crimes of violence: murder, aggravated assault, and forcible rape. Rape investigations will be helped by the fact that the blood, semen, or hair of the rapist is often recovered from the person or clothing of the victim, or found at the rape scene.

Another advance in the field of DNA analysis is the nationwide movement for the certification of DNA and other forensic specialists. In order for DNA evidence to stand up in court, legal counsel and judges must be confident, and a jury convinced, that a qualified (certified) forensic specialist performed the tests and analyzed the results accurately. In late 1995, the National Institute of Justice announced that it had funded the American Board of Criminalistics (ABC) to develop written tests for five specialties in forensic science, one of which is forensic biology (which subsumes DNA testing).

It is hoped that these certified experts will be able to describe in court how DNA testing works. As Judge Lance Ito, who presided over the O. J. Simpson murder trial in Los Angeles, cautioned during the testimony of a state expert on DNA testing: "If the jury does not understand it, they will not believe it!"

Almost a dozen forensic expert witnesses testified at the Simpson trial, and only one of them was able to effectively explain the intricacies of DNA analysis. This was Dr. Robin Cotton, director of Cellmark Diagnostics (Germantown, Maryland), a pioneering laboratory in DNA analysis, who has been appearing in numerous U.S. courts to further the acceptance of DNA as credible evidence. Dr. Cotton thoroughly described the tests performed and then summed up their validity by declaring that only twice in Cellmark's history (founded in 1988) have such tests resulted in "false positive" readings, adding that the last case was in 1989, and laboratory procedures were immediately altered to correct this malfunction.

Forever linked to the validity of DNA analysis and determinations is the basic requirement that evidentiary samples are collected properly. If submitted evidence is improperly collected, the validity of the DNA tests is suspect.

It is apparent that the future of DNA testing rests on gaining public confidence in its validity and trust in the people who collect the evidentiary samples.

LABORATORY EQUIPMENT

The work of criminalists concerns the physical and biological sciences, laboratories, examination of substances and things involved with crime and suspect criminals, and the use of selected equipment normally associated with scientific techniques in such disciplines. Equipment designed especially for identification of firearms and examination of questioned documents is part of the inventory of a criminalistics laboratory.

Major items of equipment, other than the basic assortment of test tubes, retorts, burners, and the like, that may be found in a modern laboratory of considerable size range from optical equipment through x-ray and spectrographic devices to machines and measuring devices utilizing the latest in space-age technology. Microscopes usually span the range of magnification, from low-power instruments of comparatively low cost to high-power instruments of high cost. The comparison microscope, designed for work in the identification of firearms, and the photographic equipment necessary for microphotography are common optical tools in these laboratories.

Equipment for spectrographic analysis has been a part of the criminalistics scene for many years. In spectrography the radiation from an incandescent gas or vapor is concentrated in certain discrete wavelengths. Such wavelengths are characteristic of the emitting elements in the gas, each element emitting a unique and characteristic pattern of wavelengths, or spectrum. A spectrograph has a narrow slit to admit the radiation, a prism or grating to distribute the radiation, and a system of lenses to focus the wavelength pattern on a photographic plate. The pattern is recorded photographically as a series of short lines, each line being an image of the slit formed by the radiation of one wavelength. In analysis the evidence sample is vaporized to incandescence by flame, arc, or spark and the radiation recorded. Evidence samples are normally composites. Therefore, spectra of all the elements comprising the evidence sample are recorded simultaneously, and the criminalist analyzes the composition of the sample by sorting the recorded lines, their widths, and their positions in the spectrum. Spectra of known standards and charts of the standard wavelength of various elements are used for identification. A medium-sized, quartz prism instrument with a range into the ultraviolet region disperses incident light on a 10-inch photograph plate. The spectrograph is an all-purpose instrument for criminalistics,* which will produce a complete elementary analysis of evidence samples containing mineral and other inorganic compounds.[14]

Chromatography is a method of separating compounds in order to identify the components. Modern equipment in this area is capable of identifying compounds. Gas or vapor chromatography employs a columnar device in which the evidence sample is injected into the system at the beginning of the column and carried along by a stream of carrier gas. Each constituent of the sample being tested is separated, emerges at a definite time from the time of injecting the sample (retention time), and is fed into a recorder. The recorder provides a trace in which the peaks and their position on a time axis (the retention time) identify each of the components of a sample. Gas chromatographs are valuable analytical tools, because with them microsamples of complex composition, such as gasoline, fuel oil, perfumes, hair dressings, and paint thinners, can be separated and identified from their constituents—a difficult problem with other scientific techniques when only minute quantities of evidence are available.[15]

X-ray crystallography is useful for the identification of any crystalline solid or compound from which a crystalline solid derivative can be made. X-ray diffraction is also of use in processing very small samples, in examining samples with noncrystalline impurities, and in identifying inorganic and mineral substances. X-ray spectra are used for analysis and identification. Equipment is based on standard x-ray devices adapted to testing and recording x-ray spectra and diffraction patterns.

The newest laboratory equipment is the type of research nuclear reactor used for neutron activation analysis, a technique that can analyze samples one hundred times too small for ordinary spectrographic techniques. It is not equipment easily purchased by a local laboratory, but a centrally located radiochemistry laboratory can make this new technique available to any local criminalistics laboratory.

Neutron activation analysis is a very sensitive method of analyzing samples for the elements in their composition. It involves bombarding the samples with neutrons in a nuclear reactor, which causes the different elements in the sample to become radioactive, thus making it possible to identify the different radioactive elements present and to determine the quantity of each. The great sensitivity of this method allows the detection of mini-micro elements. The research reactor is much smaller and simpler than a nuclear power reactor. In operation it produces vast numbers of neutrons by the uranium fission chain reaction, but under precise control. When an evidence sample is inserted into this intense field of neutrons, the various elements in the sample undergo a nuclear reaction that causes some of these elements to become appreciably radioactive. After the irradiation the activated sample is removed for counting. The different radioactive elements present emit radiations of different energy

*See Department of Justice Document 4 in Appendix C.

and decay at different rates. Some die out within seconds, some within minutes or hours, some require days, weeks, or even longer. A very sophisticated apparatus, the gamma-ray spectrometer, is used to measure the very distinctive radioactive gamma-ray emissions and thereby to identify the elements from which the rays come. The data are printed on paper tape and also displayed on the face of an oscilloscope. As the number of elements found at the same concentrations in two samples increases, the matching of the two samples becomes increasingly positive.[16]

The neutron activation analysis (NAA) technique and its application in the study of gunshot residues has returned a potential item of evidence to investigators. Testing for gunshot traces had fallen into disuse when the old "paraffin test" was found to react to urine and a few similar substances as well as to gunshot residues. Now paraffin-lifting kits are used on a suspect's hands, and NAA measurements for the presence of antimony and barium, common gunshot residues, have indicated a new and useful discrimination and particularity.

Distinctive "signatures" of handguns, tools, and other metal objects are now available to investigators through an innovative trace metal detection technique (TMDT) which makes the patterns of these objects visible on the skin or clothing of suspects when the suspect area is treated with a test solution and examined under ultraviolet light.[17]

Ultrasonic cavitation is an etching method that may replace chemical, electrolytic, and magnetic particle methods of restoring obliterated serial numbers on firearms and other metal objects. Cavitation is similar to boiling liquids; there is a formation of vapor bubbles in a liquid agitated by a vibrator. An ultrasonic generating system is used for inducing cavitation. Since the bubbles produced are of high energy, they have the effect of etching a metal surface. It is a rapid and very effective method for serial number recovery.[18]

Lasers (argon ion; copper vapor) are widely used in the detection of latent fingerprints. Recently, laser examination of questioned documents has been found to be useful in some alteration or obliteration cases. Laser examination can reveal information unattainable by any conventional, nondestructive means.[19]

The equipment found in crime laboratories is extensive. Basic cameras, microscopes, spectrographs, and fluoroscopes are being supplemented by computers and space-age devices. As new equipment is obtained and utilized by laboratory technicians, the director of the laboratory will inform local police managers of the additional services available. It is important that investigators be alert to these changes in the availability of such services and utilize them whenever it is in the best interests of an investigation.

VOICEPRINT IDENTIFICATION

Voiceprinting is the graphical identification of voices. Voiceprints are an innovative concept in personal identification, and they are fast becoming useful tools in criminal investigation, their use limited only by the adaptation of this new technique to the many areas of verbal communication encountered in an investigation.

Voiceprint identification is based on the physical characteristics of each individual's vocal cavities (the throat, mouth, nose, and sinuses) and the manner of manipulating the lips, teeth, tongue, soft palate, and jaw muscles. It is a technique of personal identification that may challenge fingerprints as the most positive means of personal identification. The chance that any two individuals have precisely the same size vocal cavities and have learned to use their articulators in the same manner is remote. This premise has survived some thousands of attempts to disprove it to date. Attempts to disguise the voice or to imitate the voice of another have been easily discerned. Whispering, muffling, noseholding—even filling the mouth with marbles—can be detected.

Suspect voices are recorded on a good tape recorder. Known standards for comparison also are tape recorded. Tape recordings are fed into a specially designed spectrograph, which reacts to the sound of the recorded voice and produces a voiceprint in much the same way as the polygraph produces a chart. The voice spectrograph reacts to voice frequency, volume, and the timing of a person's speech. Voiceprint techniques of identification are particularly applicable to the identification of voices involved in kidnappings, obscene language telephone calls, and telephoned threats.

Automatic methods of voice identification are in the process of development. This is a machine-aided speaker recognition: naming, identifying, or distinguishing the speaker, who has produced a given voice sample, from other speakers. This is a mechanized, computerized extension of the ability of people to recognize voices. Speech samples will be processed for their unique features and categorized by these extracted features, from which recognition will be automatic, and based on digital computer technology rather than on any skill of a technician, "user," or operator.[20]

CRYPTOGRAPHY

The use of simple ciphers and codes to protect the security of messages is increasing in the world of crime. It is common in unlawful gambling cases where records of wagers made by customers must be kept; it also is utilized by organized crime personnel because written communications have been found to be less susceptible to investigative examination than telephone conversations. And it is likely to be used for communications among extremist groups planning crimes, as well as by various types of offenders who want to protect the security of personal telephone and memo books.

The most common cipher in use by criminals is a simple substitution cipher in which a symbol, letter, or digit stands for another symbol, letter, or digit. The simplistic thinking of many criminals confines the substitution to some simple order such as 1 represents A, 2 represents B, 3 represents C, etc.

Transposition ciphers are characterized by a change in the order of the enciphered material. Investigators find it fairly common in recording telephone numbers. This may be a reversal transposition, in which the telephone number 445-1769 becomes 967-1544, or any split combination, for example, 176-4459, 769-4451, 544-1769, etc. Of help to investigators is the fact that most criminals are amateurs in cipher work, and the solution of their ciphers is a simple matter. A criminal does not have access to the few sources of information available about ciphers, and when he or she sits down to evolve a cipher there is no one to tell the person that his or her invention is, in truth, hundreds of years old.[21]

A stolen bonds fraud case involving members of the Mafia in a typical national crime syndicate operation with international overtones was successfully solved by federal agents when a key to a code was found hidden in the wallet of one of the gang members. The code had been used in cable communications between members in New York and London to communicate secretly the name and denomination of stolen bonds available for sale and the asking price. Court action by the Federal District Attorney brought the records of these communications into court, and the knowledge of the code key made their content intelligible to the trial jury and showed the joint action of the conspiracy.

Investigators can learn to solve simple substitution or transposition ciphers by running down the alphabet with the first eight or ten letters of the message and then testing for substitution. This requires substituting letters one further on in the alphabet in the first runthrough, then two further on in the second testing, and so on. This means try b for a, then c for a, and so on. Julius Caesar is said to have used a cipher based on the simple substitution of a letter three letters further on in the alphabet. Simple transposition ciphers can be solved by trial and error when the enciphered word or numerical prefix in telephone numbers is known or suspected. Telephone and memo book codes usually are solved by using the local telephone exchange prefix of three numbers to break the method of transposition by trial and error. A frequency distribution study will solve more complex ciphers, but this requires the work of experts with tables of letter and word frequencies. However, an investigator may break a complex cipher or code if he or she has some knowledge or can guess that a certain word is likely to appear in the message and then looks for this word.[22]

When the use of a cipher or code is suspected, the investigator should attempt to collect as much of the suspect writing as possible and to ascertain the languages and skills with which the defendant is familiar. Knowing the language fluency of the suspect and whether he or she has any particular skill such as stenography, printing, piano playing, or the like may be helpful in deciphering the communications, because these areas of skill or experience often form the base of the cipher or code scheme. When expert assistance is required, the enciphered material should be forwarded to the police laboratory in the same manner as other questioned documents, with the data above noted under the details of the case along with some of the possible words likely to be frequently used in the enciphered communications.

CLASSIFICATION OF CRIME LABORATORIES

The classification of crime labs is ongoing and nonpartisan, is made by local detectives and their supervisors, and is based on the past performances of the lab and its staff—initially in the lab itself but later in the courtroom at trial time. If a municipal or county lab fails to meet local needs, detectives will begin to use a regional or state lab, and if still dissatisfied, will go to the FBI's national crime lab in Washington, D.C. For DNA testing, detectives may look to a privately owned lab such as Cellmark Diagnostics.

In a 1990 homicide case in Virginia, the physical evidence was processed in a local (county) lab, a state lab, and a lab in an adjoining state.

To some extent, in preparation for trial, the assigned district attorney develops a proprietary interest in a case and will fund a search for an honest evaluation by a forensic scientist who can survive a hostile cross-examination and be viewed as a credible witness by most of the trial jurors. Experienced investigators have long been aware that their best expert witness is a qualified person who is telling the truth.

Ideally, there should be a national classification of crime labs, listing the full-service labs first, followed by those that who provide fewer services. At present there is no need to grade these labs, since those who need their services in court already have this information.

Selected References

1. THOMAS A. GONZALEZ et al., *Legal Medicine—Pathology and Toxicology* (New York: Appleton-Century-Crofts, 1954).
2. Fry v. United States, 293 Fed. 1013 (1923).
3. JAMES W. OSTERBERG, "What Problems Must Criminalistics Solve?" in *Law Enforcement Science and Technology* (Chicago: Thompson Book Co., 1967), pp. 297–303. The term "forensic science" is commonly used to describe criminalistics. See Richard Saferstein, *Criminalistics: An Introduction to Forensic Science,* 5th ed. (Englewood Cliffs, N.J.: Prentice Hall, 1994).
4. BRIAN PARKER AND JOSEPH PETERSON, "Physical Evidence Utilization in the Administration of Criminal Justice," in Carroll R. Hormachea, *Sourcebook in Criminalistics* (Reston, Va.: Reston Publishing Co., 1974), pp. 50–58.
5. LOUISE M. ROBBINS, *Footprints—Collection, Analysis, and Interpretation* (Springfield, Ill.: Charles C Thomas, Publisher, 1985), pp. 183–207.
6. HERBERT L. MACDONELL, *Flight Characteristics of Stain Patterns of Human Blood* (Washington, D.C.: U.S. Department of Justice, National Institute of Law Enforcement Assistance Administration, Superintendent of Documents, Stock No. 2700–0079, 1971), pp. 1–29.
7. "Examination of Biological Fluids," *FBI Law Enforcement Bulletin,* XLI, No. 6 (June 1972), pp. 12–15, 30.
8. *Ibid.,* pp. 15 and 30.
9. RICHARD L. BRUNELLE AND ROBERT W. REED, *Forensic Examination of Ink and Paper* (Springfield, Ill.: Charles C Thomas, Publisher, 1984), pp. 6–8.
10. GONZALEZ et al., *Legal Medicine—Pathology and Toxicology,* pp. 29–47, 698.

11. WILLIAM F. KESSLER AND PAUL B. WESTON, *The Detection of Murder* (New York: Arco Publishing, 1961), pp. 44–47.

12. LOWELL J. LEVINE, "Forensic Odontology Today: A New Forensic Science," *FBI Law Enforcement Bulletin,* XLI, No. 8 (August 1972), pp. 6–9, 26–28.

13. T. D. STEWART, "What the Bones Tell Today," *FBI Law Enforcement Bulletin,* XLI, No. 2 (February 1972), pp. 16–20, 30–31.

14. H. J. WALLS, *Forensic Science* (New York: Praeger Publishers, 1968), pp. 60–61.

15. *Ibid.,* pp. 49–55.

16. DONALD E. BRYAN et al., "High-Flux Neutron Activation Analysis as an Investigative Tool in the Field of Criminalistics," in *Law Enforcement Science and Technology* (Chicago: Thompson Book Co., 1967), pp. 371–77.

17. *Trace Metal Detection Technique in Law Enforcement* (Washington, D.C.: U.S. Department of Justice, National Institute of Law Enforcement and Criminal Justice, Law Enforcement Assistance Administration, 1970), pp. 1–16.

18. RICHARD S. TREPTOW, *Handbook of Methods for the Restoration of Obliterated Serial Numbers* (Cleveland, Ohio Lewis Research Center, prepared for the National Aeronautics and Space Administration, 1978), pp. 73–82.

19. RONALD E. BLACKLOCK, "The Laser: A Tool for Questioned Document Examination," *The Journal of Police Science and Administration,* XV, No. 2 (July 1987), pp. 125–26.

20. R. W. BECKER, F. R. CLARKE, F. POZA, AND J. R. YOUNG, *A Semiautomatic Speaker Recognition System* (Washington, D.C.: U.S. Department of Justice, Law Enforcement Assistance Administration, 1973), pp. 1–26.

21. PARKER HITT, *Manual for the Solution of Military Ciphers* (Fort Leavenworth, Kans.: Press of the Army Service Schools, 1916), p. vii; David Kahn, *The Code-Breakers* (New York: Macmillan Publishing, 1966), *passim.*

22. DAN TYLER MOORE AND MARTHA WALLER, *Cloak and Cipher* (Indianapolis, Ind.: The Bobbs-Merrill Company, 1962), pp. 17–19, 98–112.

Chapter Review

Discussion Questions

1. Are laboratory personnel handicapped by the legal precept that the admissibility of any scientific process in relation to evidence must be tested against acceptance of the scientific principle involved?

2. Is there any difference between the terms *forensic science* and *criminalistics?* How does *medicolegal* differ from *criminalistics?*

3. Cite similarities and differences in the determinations of a criminalist and the findings of an autopsy surgeon.

4. Project the likely growth and development of the present nonsystem of laboratory services.

5. Who are the decision makers as to the best strategy (or strategies) for the forensic science examination(s) of physical evidence?

6. Describe spectrographic analysis; trace metal detection technique; ultrasonic cavitation.

7. Is there a true scientific objectivity to the determination of criminalists?

8. Discuss the perspectives of voiceprinting in criminal investigation.

9. Explain the meaning of one word or phrase used by criminalists in describing comparison analysis determinations.

10. In relation to the laboratory examination of physical evidence, define a *physical match*.

Library Assignment

Compile a selected bibliography of at least three references to cryptology and its use in crime or among criminals.

Workbook Project

Prepare a 500-word theme on trace evidence and discuss the value of this type of evidence in criminal investigations.

CHAPTER
7

Basic Investigative Leads

The problem of who did it is a simple one when the offender is caught in the act or apprehended in flight from the scene shortly after the crime. When the perpetrator is not promptly arrested, the direction of the investigation varies according to whether the case falls into one of two categories—known identity or unknown identity. The case is one of known identity when the perpetrator is known and has been named by the victim or witnesses. All other cases are of unknown identity. Cases involving named suspects are a high percentage of the cases cleared by arrest in any police agency. In these cases the principal lead to the perpetrator's identity has been furnished by the victim or witnesses. The challenge to the skill of any investigator is the case without a named suspect. In such cases the basic investigative leads must be developed by the investigator to reveal the identity of the perpetrator.

Motive and opportunity (or presence) are broad areas of investigation basic to any crime. The people and things involved in a crime offer leads to the identity, motive, and opportunity of any perpetrator, known or unknown.

The victim offers the initial basic lead. The background of the victim furnishes data, as do his or her activities just prior to the crime. A group of suspects can be developed from inquiries about who would benefit from the crime and who had the requisite knowledge about the target—the object of the crime. Field contact reports of interviews by patrol police officers at and about the time and place of the crime offer data about suspects and sometimes about vehicles. When motor vehicles or weapons are involved in a crime, inquiries often link these material things with their owners or users. Latent fingerprints and other trace evidence found at crime scenes confirm that a suspect has been at the scene and indicate opportunity. Another trace of a presence at the crime scene is the manner in which the crime was committed—the *modus operandi*. Sometimes recovered stolen property can be traced to the thief; and police records contain photographs of persons previously arrested, which can be viewed by witnesses when investigators develop suspicions about the identity of suspects. When photographs are not available, composite drawings may be used. Finally, injuries characteristic of certain crimes furnish leads that often help to link a suspect to a crime. (See Figure 7–1.)

Experienced investigators dislike associating the development of investigation leads with any intuitive process; they believe that a hunch is out of place when dealing with people. Developing leads is probably a combination of know-how, the cognitive process, and an ability to work rapidly. Time is of the essence in criminal investigation. Time has an effect upon witnesses and the investigator; it gives the criminal an opportunity to dispose of evidence, to develop defenses against the shock of being arrested, or to get farther away, if he or she is in flight. No time can be lost making inquiries indicated by the basic leads of a case.

In cases of *known identity* the objective is to corroborate the story of the eyewitness. The investigator follows the basic investigative leads, but particular effort is also made to corroborate the eyewitness's stories. In addition, parallel inquiries are pursued to avoid error in identity and to make the case compelling rather than subject to doubt.

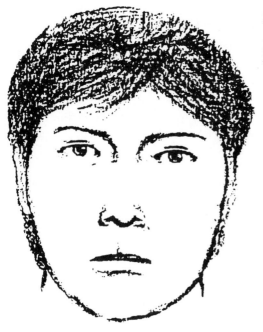

FIGURE 7–1
This composite sketch resulted in prompt identification of the "shooter" in a double homicide outside the CIA's headquarters in Virginia. (See the case study in Chapter 20.)

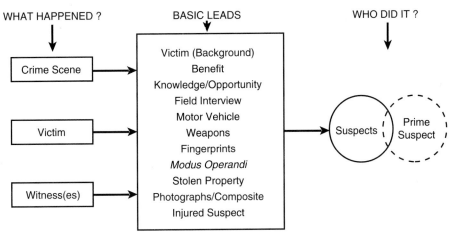

FIGURE 7–2 Basic leads are the linkage between what happened and who did it.

In cases of *unknown identity* the objective is to develop suspects—to follow the basic investigative leads with a goal of identifying the perpetrator. The action is oriented to expanding the universe of suspects, to identifying prime suspects, and to finding the guilty person or persons among the prime suspects.

It is well to keep in mind that determining who committed the crime should *not* terminate the investigation. All elements of the crime must be proved beyond a reasonable doubt. Some crimes have unique elements or possible defenses; thus the investigation should continue until all evidence, positive or negative, is gathered to prove the crime, to identify the perpetrator, and to disprove, when possible, defenses such as justification, excuse, lack of specific intent, lack of malice, diminished capacity, intoxication, ignorance, error, insanity, and the like.

Basic leads suggest lines of inquiry likely to provide an investigator with information. (See Figure 7–2.) *Active* information leads to the establishment of a group of suspects. The strength of the information accumulated against each member of this set depends on the nature of the evidence, but it may indicate prime suspects. *Passive* information is associative evidence that can be of use only if a group of suspects has been developed. Passive information often confirms suspicions against a person as a prime suspect who can be associated with the crime scene or the victim. These basic types of information lead by two routes to sufficient evidence to reveal the person or persons who are guilty of the crime being investigated.[1]

VICTIM'S BACKGROUND

Police investigators have been criticized by uninformed people for cross-examining a victim and for probing his or her background and relationship to the crime. To the uninitiated, prying information from the unfortunate victim of a crime instead of promptly taking up the hue and cry for the perpetrator seems unjustifiable. However, a chase without a clearly defined objective is just aimless activity. Very promising leads can be developed from a review of the background of the victim, which can give the pursuit defined goals.

There are many classic avenues to probe in regard to the victim. Some of these classic queries are:

1. Did the victim know the perpetrator? If so, what is the relationship?
2. Does the victim suspect any person? Why?
3. Has the victim a history of crime? A history of reporting crimes?
4. Did the victim have a weapon?
5. Has the victim an aggressive personality?
6. Has the victim been the subject of any field contact reports?
7. What is the license number and description of the victim's car?
8. Was the victim mistaken for someone else?

This does *not* mean that an investigation of crime boomerangs into an investigation of the victim. However, any fact of significance about the victim should be unearthed at this stage of an investigation inasmuch as it may contribute a vital basic lead, and it may aid in the future evaluation of the case by the prosecuting attorney.

BENEFIT

The question of who might benefit from a crime provides an excellent focus for making inquiry. The factor of benefit often can provide investigative leads. In homicide cases the motive of jealousy or elimination is a standard avenue of inquiry. Whenever a wife or husband dies and the death is unexplained, the survivor is suspect. Necessary action is taken to discover the classic love triangle. If a third party is involved, the triangle is considered a promising lead.

In arson cases the benefit may be complex—a rational motivation for financial gain in fraudulent fires of insured premises; an irrational motivation in psychopathic fire-setting.

These are particularized motives, in that the identity of the perpetrator can be deduced from the exposure of a relationship to the victim or the crime. Generally, the relationships between the victim in homicides and persons who might benefit from the fact of death are most productive in providing significant leads. The more universal motives of profit and sexual release common to burglaries, robberies, rapes, and other sex crimes usually do not offer investigators specific leads about the identity of the person who will benefit from the crime.[2]

OPPORTUNITY

Searching for and identifying persons with the opportunity to commit a crime is a valid basic lead. Admitted or suspected presence at the scene of a crime at or about the time of its occurrence may be no more than an immediate investigative aid, but it is a lead.

When offenders know they are suspected of being at the crime scene, and thus vulnerable to this "opportunity" line of inquiry, they often fabricate an alibi—a claim of being elsewhere. Investigation into an alibi will often disclose any fabrication, justifying other inquiries directed at this suspect. However, an effective alibi does not summarily exclude a suspect from further screening.

KNOWLEDGE

In theft cases the victim is questioned about the identity of persons who might know their way about the premises and about the presence and location of articles of value. This is done in order to establish who may have had the knowledge necessary for committing the crime. In armed robberies the victim is questioned about the identity of persons who knew of the routine of the victim or the business firm victimized. This tracing of knowledge provides a natural group of suspects, including:

1. Persons who have access to the premises at which the crime occurred or who are familiar with them.
2. Persons who knew of the value and place of storage of property or the routine of the victim or the business victimized:
   a. any present employee and spouse
   b. any former employee and spouse
   c. service and maintenance personnel (employed in area, building, or making frequent service deliveries)
   d. neighbors
   e. professional "finger-men" with contacts among the persons listed above
   f. criminals with contacts among the persons above
3. Persons noticed in the area or on the premises recently:
   a. acting strangely (sex cases, fires, homicides)
   b. applying for work, soliciting sales, conducting surveys, etc.

Possession of the knowledge needed to commit a crime suggests possession also of the skill and capacity to have done it. What kind of criminal could accomplish the crime under investigation? Did it require a special (and identifying) skill in using a torch to open a safe or knowledge of the fast cutting action of demolition-type burning bars? Did it require a special knowledge in a trade or occupation? The use of the hydraulic jimmy suggests a person who has worked in body and fender shops where this device is used to pry apart bent fenders, and employees know about its fast and powerful push-and-heave action. Did the crime require a person who was not afraid to kill, such as the cat burglar, who enters occupied homes, even occupied bedrooms?

The multiple murders of the Clutter family in Kansas would have been solved months earlier if the basic lead of former employees had been pursued. Floyd Wells, a prisoner in Kansas State Prison, had worked on the Clutter ranch and had mentioned the extent of the ranch to a cellmate. The murders took place shortly after the release of the cellmate. Wells, weeks after the crime, identified himself as a former employee of the victims and supplied the authorities with this basic lead; it identified one of the two killers. A check of this man's associates led to a rapid identification of his crime partner.[3]

FIELD CONTACT REPORTS

Field contacts are an aggressive police patrol tactic. A field contact report records the "stop-and-frisk" interview with persons stopped in their cars or on foot about the city or country because of their suspicious appearance or actions. These reports place in police records the names and descriptions of the persons coming to police attention, and the time, date, and place they were seen and interviewed. These reports are confidential, in that they are not disclosed to the public, but they are filed in police records systems for the use of investigators. The data on who was "about," and where and when, are valuable aids to investigators seeking basic leads. Field contacts represent a broad surveillance involving observations of an entire patrol sector by alert, assigned officers. Often an investigator confronted with a burglary without apparent clues to the identity of the offender will find a field contact report of a known thief being stopped in the early morning hours not more than a few blocks from the crime scene. An apparently innocent suspect in a sex case who pleads that he hardly ever leaves his home at night may be revealed by field contacts to be a nocturnal roamer in the city's parks.

Some police units have an automated filing system for field contact cards of youngsters under 17 or 18 years of age for the purpose of revealing group identification. Because most juvenile crimes are committed by groups, this cross-reference offers information about the associates of an offender. When the field contact cards of a juvenile are requested, these group associations should be probed for basic leads along the lines of race, sex, age, and associates of previous arrests.

MOTOR VEHICLES

There is no better clue to the identity of a criminal than the identification of a vehicle. True, time is important when a stolen vehicle is used. Professional bank robbers and other criminals who plan their crimes with care abandon the getaway car before an alarm can be broadcast. However, two killers of a police officer were once observed as they changed cars, and thus a crucial basic lead that led to their arrest was gained.

Even a fragmentary description of a vehicle is often helpful. In a series of bank robberies in northern California, the robber walked away from his crimes. The first basic lead offering any promise followed the third robbery, in which a witness noticed a man acting suspiciously going from a bank to the parking lot. All he could offer was a fragment of a license number, EPC. Federal Bureau of Investigation agents sought help from the California Department of Motor Vehicles, but without results. Then the "EPC" fragment was checked against reports of cars stopped at barricades set up after each robbery. The agents found one promising lead. A car had been stopped and passed through a road block with registration letters CPC! Again motor vehicle records were scanned. The vehicle was registered to William Liebscher, Jr., a used-car dealer. Motor vehicle files provided an in-the-course-of-business exemplar of Liebscher's signature on a registration application. Agents compared it with another basic lead—previously useless for lack of a suspect—the handwriting on a fictitious money order dropped by the robber at one of the crime scenes. The handwriting was similar. Other evidence corroborated these leads, and Liebscher was arrested and convicted.

Enterprising detectives scan stolen car reports for similarities with the descriptions of cars used in crime. The anxious criminal who used his or her own car may become worried that the vehicle has been seen by witnesses, and abandons it. Then, after an appropriate interval, he or she reports it stolen. The criminal hopes to throw off suspicion by such action if the car had been identified with the crime. Usually, the fragments of description are not enough to locate a vehicle, but they are sufficient for alert detectives when a criminal directs attention to an automobile by reporting its loss.

Motor vehicle records are statewide records filed under name and license (registration) number. Often a name not known to be used by the suspect under investigation is detected in searching for the owner of a vehicle used in a crime or known to be operated by the suspect. Motor vehicle records may contain a thumbprint or a photograph or both, and they usually will have some physical description of a licensed operator. Both owner and operator records usually contain a person's date of birth, previous residences, and dates of residence at such locations. Accident and violation reports cross-indexed to these basic motor vehicle records may reveal something of the activities of the suspect, such as dates and locations of accidents and driving record.

Of importance to investigators is the finality of identification possible in using motor vehicles as a basic lead. Time and time again the suspect's shock upon learning that he or she has been identified has led to full cooperation with police and a plea of guilty.

WEAPONS

It is not often that clubs and other blunt instruments are engraved with an owner's name, but firearms are marked with a maker's name and a serial number, and their ownership often can be traced through sales and firearm registration records. The lead developed from such tracing may reveal that the weapon was stolen, but this fact links the crime under investigation with another crime—and that is a basic lead.

The ownership of knives often can be identified even though they do not have serial numbers. Clubs and other striking weapons often provide promising leads to identity. Poisons and drugs used in crime sometimes can be traced, and the purchase of dynamite is often traced in bomb cases.

Bullets and fired cartridge cases, pattern wounds, and the distinctive effects of several poisons provide passive information useful to associate a suspect, when identified, with a crime.

FINGERPRINTS

Fingerprints found at crime scenes have a very high potential for identifying perpetrators of crime once the imprints of the victim and other nonsuspects are screened out. There is an increasing emphasis on searching for these chance imprints at crime scenes. Latent imprints, normally invisible, are developed by dusting various surfaces at the crime scene with contrasting fingerprint powders or by iodine fuming. The growth in the use of evidence technicians at crime scenes has resulted in more effective searches for these hidden fingerprints.

Computerized fingerprint searching systems in some large police agencies permit a rapid scanning of thousands of ten-finger records against chance imprints found at crime scenes. Police expertise at other police agencies is developing slower but equally effective procedures for the rapid comparison of fingerprints found at crime scenes with the fingerprints of known offenders on file:

1. Crime-scene fingerprints are evaluated as being of value or of no value. Imprints of value have an adequate number of identifying characteristics.
2. Crime-scene fingerprints are compared with the imprints of persons legally at the scene: victim, witnesses, police, and other known visitors.
3. Fingerprints on file are searched to identify the suspect making the crime-scene fingerprint(s):
   a. *Request search.* Investigator assigned to case names one or more suspects and asks for search.
   b. *Single-digit search.* Identification technicians search files such as those containing other crime-scene fingerprints, or containing the ten-digit fingerprints of repeat or career criminals.
   c. *Cold search.* Identification technicians search through an entire ten-digit fingerprint file. Unless the police agency is small, or has a computerized search capability, the scope of this cold search should be reduced to: (1) known criminals operating in the same geographical area and/or with the same *modus operandi,* and (2) recent arrestees.[4]

Of importance is the finality of identification in this area. Fingerprints found at crime scenes reveal the opportunity or presence factor, an important lead. When fingerprints pinpoint a person with a history of like crimes or link the suspect with other latents from another crime, the lead is significant.

STOLEN PROPERTY

A search for stolen property is a search for identifiable things. Police have been using this technique skillfully for so many years that it is sometimes overlooked as a routine, albeit successful, technique. Novice investigators are not aware of its potential value until they have worked on cases in which stolen property has been recovered and, in tracing its possession, they have noted the ease with which the identity of the burglar or thief has been developed.

Tracing the proceeds of a theft is facilitated by the establishment of special investigative squads whose duties are to visit pawnshops, secondhand dealers, junk shops, and other places where stolen property is likely to be offered for sale and to coordinate the local search for locally stolen property. It is supported, also, by laws in many states and municipalities that require the pawnbroker to report to the police the pawning or purchase of specific secondhand merchandise (guns, watches, televisions, radios, and like articles that are commonly stolen). These laws often require places of business handling such merchandise to maintain a log, or register, of their business describing each item purchased, and this record is open to police inspection at any time. The level of cooperation extended to police by many such business managers, often far above the legal demands, results in the recovery of vast amounts of stolen property. In some cities pawnshop proprietors have personally defrayed the cost of hot lines to, and silent alarms in, nearby police stations for prompt notification of offerings by suspicious persons.

A computerized stolen property record system within a police department will:

1. Shorten the time required to search these reports for items of stolen property.
2. Allow for searches leading to the identity of persons who frequently sell or pawn used property.
3. Offer opportunities long after a crime has been committed to locate stolen office equipment by periodic examination of the records of the repair services of manufacturers (authorized agents).[5]

Serial numbers and other positive identifying data necessary for the recovery of property are not always available from the victim of a theft. It may be necessary for the victim (or the investigator) to visit the store in which the property was purchased. Most merchants keep a record of sales in detail. When jewelry and furs are stolen, merchants can provide information regarding scratch marks on items of jewelry or hidden identification stamped on the inside lining of fur garments or on the skins themselves. These merchants, along with pawnbrokers, sometimes mark this type of property when it passes through their establishments for repair or cleaning or as collateral for a cash loan. Often markings are hidden and require information about where to look for them or ultraviolet light for viewing. Happily, when skilled thieves believe they have removed all labels and identifying marks from stolen property, these markings remain for the investigator's use.

No assumptions should be made in regard to describing identifying characteristics of stolen property. Recovery depends on identification. For instance, when jewelry is described, it is better to state the appearance of the metal and stones than to assume a basic classification. What is described by a victim as a yellow gold ring is best detailed in a wanted notice as a yellow metal ring, and the diamonds and rubies said to be part of the setting of such rings are best described as white and red stones of a particular size and cut. Stolen property notices or wants sometimes contain lengthy listings of stolen property, and for this reason these notices are indexed by number to each item of property listed, starting with number one. Investigators also group property in general classifications, such as jewelry, clothing, furs, within this numbered sequence. In communicating with agencies locating the property, this numbering system aids in identification and shortens the necessary communications between agencies. Know-how based on experience and some intuition can lead an investigator to the prompt recovery of stolen property and offer a valuable investigative lead.

Akin to tracing stolen goods is verifying the use of stolen credit cards. It is a trail that offers many opportunities for basic leads. Large commercial organizations issuing credit cards are generally nonlocal because a central accounting office provides nationwide coverage. However, their billing procedures give effective assistance in tracing fugitives, which more than justifies the labor of communications. Because gasoline is a prime credit card item, local service station dealers offer good chances for inquiries about a suspect and the use of a credit card. Recent receipts, not yet forwarded to the central accounting office, may still be available at gas stations and will reveal the name of the purchaser, credit card number, and the name of the gasoline company handling his or her account. These credit card accounts reveal recent billings and show the activity of a suspect on the days when purchases were charged to the credit card. Problems resulting from loss, theft, and misuse of credit cards have led to a security consciousness among the accounting personnel of these firms, and their cooperation with police is excellent.

MODUS OPERANDI

The choice of a particular crime to commit and the selection of a method of committing it is the *modus operandi* of a criminal. All criminals do not have a particular *modus operandi,* but enough of them have distinctive methods of operation to justify classifying crimes by like characteristics. The *modus operandi* of a criminal is his or her "signature."

For this reason, investigators compare the manner in which a crime was committed with relevant records stored in the *modus operandi* section of the police record systems. If any of these comparisons are successful, the detective secures data on possible suspects. The use of *modus operandi* by police agencies is both current and extensive. Its successful use in robbery, burglary, grand theft, fraud, sex offenses, and fraudulent checks amounts to a mandate to search the *modus operandi* files for basic leads in these crimes.

A *modus operandi* file contains information about the methods of operation of known criminals and the methods used in unsolved crimes. This file has three major capabilities:

1. Identifying a perpetrator by naming suspects whose *modus operandi* in past crimes fits the facts of the crime being investigated.
2. Linking an unknown perpetrator with the *modus operandi* of past crimes committed by unknown perpetrators for the purpose of structuring the identity of a suspect from the *modus operandi* and leads from several connected crimes.
3. Storing data on unsolved crimes according to *modus operandi* to allow comparison with the crime technique of an apprehended criminal and to connect unsolved crimes with an arrestee.

Of course, past offenses and their operations must be sufficiently similar to be meaningful. They must possess a number of common features with a crime under investigation to warrant the inference that if the suspect committed the other acts, he or she must have committed the act being investigated. Similarities in methods of operation (in combination with other basic leads) also are an important tool in the realm of identity, for they decrease the likelihood of a claim of a mistake, or a real mistake, in suspecting a person of crime.

PHOTOGRAPHS OF KNOWN CRIMINALS

A search through *modus operandi* records often provides photographs of suspects made at the time of a previous arrest. These photographs, called "mug shots," are available, and if the crime being investigated has been witnessed, the investigator has an opportunity to ask an eyewitness to view them. Usually, it is a casting-out process. The witness is not asked to identify any photo but is requested to scan no less than a half-dozen photographs and to cast out those that offer no resemblance to the perpetrator. When one or more photographs appear to resemble the perpetrator, further inquiry is conducted. The investigator concentrates on the whereabouts of the persons selected as possibles. It may be that the suspect was in prison, out of town, or living in a distant city at the time of the crime. Every reasonable circumstance that eliminates persons from a group of suspects reduces the group and allows concentration upon the remainder. There is also a humanitarian casting out of any suspects known by the investigator or associates to be working and living within their means and to have a reputation for no longer being involved with crime.

Mug books are often prepared. The FBI provides photos of known bank robbers to agents investigating bank robberies. These photographs were collected before the crime being investigated happened and thus permit a rapid viewing by an eyewitness of persons who have committed crimes similar to the crime under investigation.

This practice does not destroy the validity of future testimony of these witnesses as long as the photographs show five or ten suspects of various types and origins. When a photograph of only one person is exhibited to an eyewitness, or when the other photos in the group are of a nature that a single suspect is isolated by some physical or racial characteristic, the future testimony of the witness is compromised. This viewing of photographs is likely to be criticized in present-day trial procedures and likened to a conditioning process. The witness may be compromised and his or her potential credibility toward establishing identity may be ruined. When two or more eyewitnesses are available, it is possible to use one of them to view photographs for basic leads to the identity of the offender and to reserve the remaining witness or witnesses for later identification. There is little justification for ruining the potential of a major witness by having him or her confirm identification at this initial stage.

COMPOSITE SKETCHES FOR IDENTIFICATION

When photographs are not available, the victim and any witnesses may be asked to collaborate with a police artist in developing a composite sketch of the suspect. Artists have the necessary skill to develop a portrait of a suspect from the description of a victim or witness, or the descriptions given by several witnesses. The usual procedure is for the artist to make a tentative sketch and then show it to the victim or witness and ask how closely it resembles the suspect. After some trial and error, this collaboration of the artist and the victim and/or witness frequently results in a drawing that is likely to be of value in identifying the suspect.

Identi-kit is another visual means for identification through the cooperation of victims/witnesses. An Identi-kit is a system of several hundred plastic slides containing photoreproductions of one small portion of a human face: hair styles, foreheads, eyes, nose, mouth, chin, ear, glasses, and so on. Police personnel trained in the use of an Identi-kit can work with a victim or witness in developing a composite sketch in accordance with the description and trial-and-error viewing.

Computer software for computer art recently became available. It is called "Suspect I.D." and is produced by Imageware of San Diego, California. The composites created with this program are in color and "drawn" by a witness in response to queries in the computer program.

INJURED SUSPECTS

In homicides, assaults, and arson cases the criminal is sometimes bloodied or burned. An injured person may be a basic lead. In most states physicians are required to report gunshot and knife wounds when patients seek treatment. In some cases local hospitals are asked to be alert for persons seeking treatment for various injuries. In one case the investigator believed that blood and a broken glass window suggested a wound with glass in it. The emergency room of the local hospital was requested to report any such wound, and 48 hours later a call was received describing "a wound with a great deal of powdered glass." In a rape case the attacker was surprised in the act and ran off in the dark through a wooded area. Two days later the police received a call about "a patient . . . who did not seek treatment for his broken ankle for two days." An anxious suspect may wash off blood and postpone treatment for a severe injury; but if medical treatment is sought, there is an excellent chance for a basic lead.

Searching for injured persons to develop a group of suspects is similar to an exhaustive search for witnesses. The search may develop information and it may not, but this work of the investigator reveals a determination to follow every reasonable line of inquiry in seeking leads to the identity of the perpetrator.

Similar determination to follow every suggested line of inquiry as basic leads are developed not only reassures the people of a community that criminals are being sought systematically but also favors exoneration of an innocent person originally suspected of the crime. Diligent inquiry in following up basic leads gathers the active and passive information that will identify "who did it," sometimes will reveal the perpetrator's presence at the crime scene, and often will contribute to an understanding of why the crime was committed.

LINKAGE BETWEEN SUSPECT AND CRIME PARTNER(S)

When more than one person is responsible for a crime, the assigned investigator must develop the identity of all the individuals involved. An arrested suspect may or may not identify his or her crime partners. An identified but unapprehended suspect may be located by identifying and locating one or more crime partners.

While crime partnerships may be based on the underworld skills of an individual (ability to neutralize burglar alarms; getaway car driving skills; "torch" capability for opening safes and locked boxes), they also depend on mutual trust and compatibility. When crime is a person's business, there is no doubt that partnerships are only formed with someone who is known, liked, and trusted.

The types of relationships that form strong personal links between persons engaged in criminal activity are:

1. *Neighborhood friendships.* These friendships may date from early childhood, such as from membership in a youth gang, or the social interactions between neighboring families and co-ethnics.
2. *Juvenile hall and prison contacts.* Incarceration in a correctional facility brings persons who are convicted of a crime, or who are adjudicated as

delinquent and made wards of a children's court, into close contact. Many of these contacts ripen into friendships that can be traced through juvenile institutions to prisons for adult offenders. Inmates band together with others they trust.

3. *Family relationships.* Many persons have a strong sense of family trust and loyalty, which may be extended to persons without kinship linkage who have exercised some form of unofficial parental control, guidance, or support.

4. *Co-ethnic contacts.* In ghetto neighborhoods, juvenile halls, and prisons, each ethnic group tends to band together. This is emotionally similar to family relationships.

5. *Buyer–seller interactions.* This is a business relationship between the person wanting the crime committed for profit and the criminal actor. The common type of buyer–seller relationships are the business owner and the "torch," the planner of a murder and the "hit man," and the receiver of stolen property and the thief.

6. *Lovers.* An identifiable and often easily traced friendship is one between husband and wife (legal or common law); a "triangle" relationship in which a lover of either sex is added to the husband–wife duo; and heterosexuals or homosexuals living together, or otherwise identified as lovers.

When basic investigative leads do not disclose the identity of a crime partner, investigators must probe among the common kinds of relationships for "possibles."

The investigator who probes a criminal or personal relationship may gain information that is meaningful to the success of the investigation. There are few relationships that can survive the temptation of "better him than me." Ethnic gangs have their informants or potential informants; prison friendships may succumb to self-preservation; families often have hidden internal hostilities; and the instances of lovers-grown-cold are legion.

INFORMANTS

Informants have long been a source of information to investigators seeking basic leads to a crime under investigation. In fact, one class of informants has been termed the "basic-lead informant" (see Chapter 10). However, informants are not basic leads, but a means through which basic leads can be developed.

One of the criticisms of criminal investigation in its early years was that police investigators (more commonly termed detectives in those days) were prone to rely on informants in solving crimes and paid little or no attention to processing the crime scene or to following up on available basic leads.

Today, the starting point in investigating any crime is a thorough examination of the crime scene, if known, and a scrutiny of the basic leads discovered in the course of this examination. The follow-up investigation picks up on these data, and expands and develops them.

Investigators no longer depend on informants, but they do seek help from the general public in locating anyone with information about the crime under investigation.

Selected References

1. M. A. P. WILLMER, "Criminal Investigation from the Small Town to the Large Urban Conurbation," *British Journal of Criminology,* VIII, No. 3 (July 1968), pp. 259–74.
2. JAMES W. OSTERBERG, "The Investigative Process," in *Law Enforcement Science and Technology* (Chicago: Thompson Book Co., 1967), p. 591.
3. TRUMAN CAPOTE, *In Cold Blood* (New York: Random House, 1965), pp. 159–64.
4. JOAN PETERSILIA, *Processing Latent Fingerprints—What Are the Payoffs?* (Santa Monica, Calif.: The Rand Corporation, 1977), pp. 13–14.
5. JOHN E. ECK, *Solving Crimes: The Investigation of Burglary and Robbery* (Washington, D.C.: Police Executive Research Forum and the National Institute of Justice, U.S. Department of Justice, 1983), pp. 269–70.

Chapter Review

CASE STUDY: THE SHUGARS AND SMITH CASE

At 3:40 P.M. on November 5 officers on patrol were instructed to investigate a call from a Greyhound Cab Company driver saying that the door of a pawnshop at 424 J Street was open and the owner not there. On arrival the officers discovered the body of the proprietor apparently dead of knife wounds in the chest. There was evidence of a struggle, and blood was found in several areas of the crime scene. A display case, which was a container for handguns, was open; the tags (identification of guns) were there, but six guns were missing (see Figure 7–3). No wallet was found on the victim. The victim was pronounced dead by the coroner at 1624 hours (4:24 P.M.). The location of the pawnshop is in an area frequented by laborers and transients; occupancies are low-cost hotels and small stores.

The Investigation

Immediate action was instituted to develop all possible basic leads.

Eyewitnesses

1. Interviewed all employees of hotel and adjoining Greyhound Taxi Terminal and cab drivers. Checked all neighborhood hotels and shops. Results negative.
2. Questioned bus driver C. Gardner, who stopped at 4th and J Streets from 2:30 to 3:00 P.M. He noted two people in pawnshop. No definite description. States he saw a green station wagon in front of pawnshop with woman in front seat and possibly two children in rear (not positive about children).
3. Questioned all cab drivers who worked at that time. Negative.
4. Open book in pawnshop with last entry Richard Moriarity.
5. Contacted Richard Moriarity at his home. He had redeemed a rifle belonging to his brother at 1500 hours. Negative. Moriarity states there was a Mexican

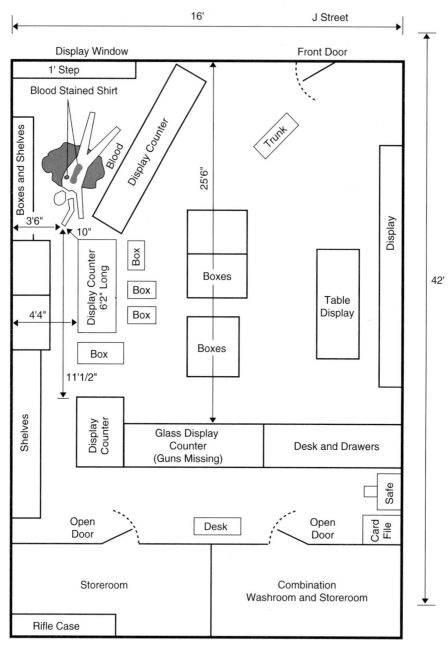

FIGURE 7–3 Crime-scene diagram—Shugars and Smith case study.

customer in pawnshop. He gave a complete description of this person but said he left before he (Moriarity) left the shop. Also interviewed his wife, Mrs. Moriarity. Negative.

6. Interviewed George Samuel, who told cab driver Petovitch he saw door of shop open but could see nobody inside; he was worried.

7. Petovitch interviewed, said he went to door, saw the mess, and asked his dispatcher to call police. He said he had not seen any suspicious people around at the time.

8. Questioned B. Knursem, cab driver, who picked up a man at 4th and J. Street at 4:00 P.M. Man said, "Let's get out of here. Dead man in there." States he took him to 8th and E, where he had a soda with him. Six other cab drivers interviewed. Negative.

Victim's Background

1. E. Martin, desk clerk at Olympic Hotel, had received phone call from some elderly person (victim's father) earlier but was too busy at the time to call victim to phone. (Victim used this phone, no telephone in pawnshop.)

2. Interviewed parents of victim. They said he carried a brown wallet, no credit cards, and had a car (which was found in nearby parking lot). They said he (father) had worked with son but had no idea of inventory.

3. Outer door of the safe open, but inner door still closed. Money in safe intact, but pocket of victim turned inside out; wallet is missing. Inventory made of money in safe: total was $4,693.70.

4. Questioned cab driver Caleb Leyhe. Saw victim at approximately 3:00 P.M. talking with two men and one woman. Negative.

5. Interviewed Robert Head, cab driver. Negative.

6. Questioned Harry Isuki, jeweler, who was a friend of victim and did work for the pawnshop. He said victim had been beaten up three months ago by two men who had given no reason. No report had been made of the assault to police.

Informants

1. James Chambers came to the police station. He said he had information regarding the murder in the pawnshop. Said he had been standing on the corner of J and 2nd Streets on November 5, and a white man asked for "Jerry King." Wanted to know if he was still living on 10th Street. This man said he had heard that King was in trouble because of a "shooting" in a pawnshop someplace. Chambers stated that King runs with a man named Mason and that both are good with knives. Chambers has not seen them since the murder. King is called the "Cowboy," wears a big white cowboy hat and boots. Chambers also states that Mason bought a green station wagon, a Ford. Officer sent Chambers back to street for more information.

2. Questioned informant Chambers, who gave a complete description of one Jerry King. He is afraid to tell where he got the information that King was going to borrow a car and "knock over" a pawnshop the night of the homi-

cide. Promises more information. Said he thinks he bought a car at Del Mar Market.

3. Questioned Joe Note at Del Mar Market. Note said that on November 3 he sold a 1990 green station wagon to Eugene Mason. He said Mason had a guy with long hair with him and that Chambers (our informant) lived with Mason.

4. Again questioned Chambers, and he admitted he had lived with Mason *and* King. King, Chambers states, had later lived with a Mexican woman on 10th Street. He said some man had told him that Mason and Sanchez had showed up at his house at 1815 6th Street with a 1989 or 1990 green station wagon a couple of nights ago, loaded it up and left, and that there was a third man in the car. He also said that Mason had a reputation with a knife and had knifed someone on 6th Street some time ago. He promised more information.

5. Re: Jerry King. Information from Willie Park (1815 6th St.). Knows of suspect, refers to him as "Big Foot." Big Foot wanted Park in on a deal. Park did not want anything to do with it, so Big Foot talked about getting "Walkie Talkie" to go in on the deal with them. Park states that Walkie Talkie is a MAA [male, African American, American] about 50 years, 5′8″, 175 lb, sort of heavy build; wearing a cap made of corduroy material; grayish type suit coat and blue pants. Park states that Walkie Talkie sometimes sleeps in the shack behind 1815 6th St. Park stated that Big Foot, in talking about the job he had lined up, said they were going to use three men on the job. One was to be on the outside, one on the roof, and one was to be let down by the fellow up on top through the skylight into the shop. Big Foot talked about a lot of guns, watches, and cameras that were in the place. When they were done they would take the stuff to a room they had. Big Foot is supposed to see Park tonight (1815 6th St., November 12) and bring over some pants and a bottle of wine. This was supposed to be around 1800 to 1900 hours.

6. Re: Elroy Robin (Walkie Talkie) DOB [date of birth] 7/19/49 (Texas), MWA, gray/black [hair color], brown eyes. Elroy Robin was spoken to in the Detective Division regarding the above offense. Robin stated he did not know anyone by the name of Jerry King and that the nickname Big Foot meant nothing to him. Stated he only knew what he had heard on the street about the killing at the pawnshop. Robin was asked if he had ever been approached by anyone who attempted to get him to go along on a burglary of a pawnshop. He stated he had not, that he had been in prison once and didn't want to go back.

7. Re: George Brendon Williams ("Tex"), MWA, bald/gray, DOB 2/6/56 (Texas). Williams stated he was approached by a subject he knows as Jerry King on Saturday at 0900 hours at 2nd and K Street in front of the Bank Exchange Bar the day the pawnshop man was killed. King asked him to loan him his car. Williams asked King why he wanted his car. King stated he had to go pick up some money. Williams told King that his car was not running. King was with a small man with gray hair at this time. Williams later saw the two walking east on J Street near the Olympic Hotel about 0930 hours.

Williams states he did not see King again until November 10 around 1200 hours. This was at 6th and S Street near the park. After a short conversation of small talk, King told Williams he had a hot gun he had bought down on 2nd Street. Williams asked what kind of gun, and King replied it was a .22 caliber pistol. Williams stated he advised King that he had heard the cops were looking for him. King stated he knew they were. Williams told King if he knew the cops were looking for him why didn't he go in and get straightened out. King stated he was going to do that but he was going to throw the gun in the river first. The same man who was with King when they had met on 2nd Street was with him at this time. He had walked away, going to a nearby gas station. On his return King stated he was fixing up to leave town. He was going to steal a car and make it. Williams stated the last time he saw King, he and the other man were walking in the direction of town. Williams described the man with King as short, thin, gray hair, about 45 or 50 years.

8. Received phone call at police department from J. Drum of 1909 P Street. Drum states that on the previous night he was drinking at the Village Club and a man said he had killed the pawnbroker. This man was about 37 years, 5'10". He stated that the bartender seemed to know him because he changed a lot of dimes to bills for him, no questions asked.

9. Contacted bartender at Village Bar re: customer changing dimes. He states the man works for the Purple Heart Thrift Shop, that his name is Bill Donal, and that he was drunk at the bar with Drum and probably did talk about the murder because the victim of the homicide had refused Donal a loan at an earlier date. This story was checked out with Donal. Negative. Donal was in Los Angeles and en route on bus (checked out) at time of murder.

10. Willie Park (informant) called and said King would visit the 6th Street address in the evening (November 12) for sure.

Benefit and motive

No reports.

Knowledge

No reports.

Field interview reports

1. Jerry King is a supposed associate of a Eugene Mason. Field interview cards checked: On July 20, 1966, Eugene Mason, PD S-7836 was stopped at 2nd and I Streets. DOB given, May 3, 1938, MWA, 5'9", 155 lb. Add[ress] of California Apartments in Broderick. Car being used was a 85 Mercury, 4 dr. Lt. Blue, ANZ-009. At the time he was with an Agapito Casteneda.

2. FI card on Agapito Casteneda shows DOB 11/20/38, 5'7", 138 lb. Add. 100 Lucas Street, Laredo, Texas.

Motor Vehicle

1. Witness states he observed a blue Renault in alley in back of pawnshop with four occupants who seemed to go into shop. Secured license number, to dispatcher for check.
2. Legal owner of Renault is RZ Auto Sales; no contact on Sunday. Followup on Monday.
3. Checked out witness's story, and showed photo of undercover police officer working in alley area on another investigation. Witness identified photo as one of men seen. Negative.

Weapon

1. No weapon found at crime scene.
2. Interviewed Mr. John Daven, a resident of Olympic Hotel who said he observed a man displaying a knife with an 8-inch blade in the lobby around the time of the homicide. Daven identified Albert Richards, who surrendered the knife to officers and said he was intoxicated that day and lives in neighboring hotel. Identified himself. Negative.

Latents at crime scene

1. Six latent prints were lifted and photographed at crime scene.
2. Compared latent prints found at scene. Found they were of victim, of the last customer in shop (Richard Moriarity), and remainder not identified at this time.
3. The latent prints obtained were checked against all persons on the list of police and coroner's personnel present at crime scene with negative results.

Stolen property

1. Thorough check of inventory of shop. Six tags for handguns found in showcase, but no guns. Description and serial numbers of guns on tags. This case had been broken into. Missing were one .25 caliber automatic, three .22 caliber revolvers, one Smith & Wesson .38 caliber revolver, and one .32 caliber revolver. It also appeared that some rifles were missing. Further checks with accountant.
2. With assistance of brother-in-law of victim, checked records in pawnshop and made list of all guns on hand, guns taken in pawn and not redeemed, and guns sold. Checked all guns bought by victim for past year and a half. Bookkeeper contacted. He had invoices for all new guns. Impossible to find out what weapons should be in shop—poor records.
3. After further check with accountant: 7 guns (handguns) missing.
4. Inspector Serro of the pawnshop detail called and said he had picked up a 17-year-old MWA by the name of Steven Russell while he was attempting to pawn some "junky" jewelry; a search of his car revealed a .38 caliber Smith

& Wesson revolver, serial #190452. Inspector Serro stated that he had seen the TT [Teletype alarm, wanted notice] on the pawnbroker stabbing and noticed that some as yet unidentified guns had been stolen, and he offered this information for what it was worth.

5. Phone call received from Wayne Cooper. Has in his possession three guns obtained from a Henry Smith as security on a loan. Checked serial numbers—all three missing from pawnshop. Cooper called after he had been told by his sister that Smith was wanted. These guns were taken as evidence.

Modus operandi comparison

1. Checked all local pawnshop owners for any unusual occurrences. Negative.
2. Attempted holdup at Southside Junk Yard. Gun displayed but victim could not identify make. There is a good description of the robber, who was scared off by a customer.

Photographs of known criminals

None available. Identi-kit likeness prepared from descriptions given by informants. (The Identi-kit is a trademarked device utilizing plastic inserts of facial characteristics to reproduce a likeness of a suspect from verbal descriptions and visual supervision; it is a substitution for a police artist drawing a portrait sketch.)

Injured suspects

1. Checked adjacent hotel. Interviewed witness who saw a man with blood on face and hands in washroom of hotel at the time of the homicide. This was traced to a resident who had a fight with another resident. Negative.
2. I went to the Olympic Hotel and took two photographs of the blood droplets in the lobby and in the bathroom in front of the toilet bowl. I obtained a sample of this blood at the same location and booked it as evidence. Receipt #30551.
3. Patrol Division Captains: Re: Homicide at 424 J Street, Pacific Jewelry & Loan Co. It appears that the victim fought with the suspect, and perhaps the suspect has injuries. Please be on the alert for subjects being arrested with injuries that may have been caused during a struggle, and bring it to the attention of the detective division.
4. Contacted the clerk at the desk in the Travelers Hotel and obtained a list of checkouts this morning. There were six, and R/O [reporting officer] in company with the housekeeper (Clacey Brown) checked each room; three had been made up and the floor maids indicated that no signs of blood or other evidence noticed. Three rooms not yet made up were checked, particularly bathrooms and towels, but no signs of blood or anything of evidential value seen. The floorman responsible for cleaning the common washrooms on each floor was also contacted, and he reports that there were no bloodstains or anything suspicious noticed in any of them.

The Arrest

On November 12 about 1800 hours a team of investigators went to 6th Street in separate vehicles, positioning their cars to keep the vicinity of 1815 6th Street under observation. After a short interval a man wearing a white cowboy hat and having the general appearance of the suspect Jerry King was observed on the sidewalk walking toward the house at 1815. The suspect was stopped and questioned. Also stopped with the suspect was another man who identified himself as Henry Smith and who said they both lived at 912 S Street. Smith had identification. King had none. Both men were searched; King had a .22 caliber revolver, loaded, in his belt, and Smith had a .22 caliber revolver, loaded, in his right pants pocket. Both King and Smith were handcuffed and taken to the police station.

Post-arrest investigation revealed Jerry King to be Lyle E. Shugars. His companion was identified as Henry E. R. Smith, the person named as Eugene Mason during the investigation by informants. Both men were warned of their rights to silence and legal counsel (the Miranda warning) but waived these rights and made statements to police.

The Trial

Both Shugars and Smith were represented by legal counsel. However, guilty pleas were entered for both men. The proceeding was brief; both men admitted their guilt in open court. They were sentenced to state prison for life.

Critique

1. The lack of eyewitnesses, despite diligent search, indicated this case was likely to be one in which the police would not have a named suspect.
2. Investigator's reports of their day-to-day activity document a series of parallel inquiries along avenues suggested by basic investigative leads.
3. There was an excellent gathering of information from reliable informants.
4. Investigators followed the doctrine of warning suspects of their constitutional rights to silence and to legal counsel. Grand jury testimony indicates rights of both accused persons were fully protected while in custody during questioning. Wording of statements and content indicates voluntariness.
5. Continuing and diligent search for witnesses and evidence indicated impartial attitude of investigators, which allowed the case to focus within its own evidence structure and without any preconceived theory of who did it.

Source: Sacramento, California, Police Department and Public Defenders Office.

Discussion Questions

1. Compare the objectives of investigations in which the offender is known with those in investigations in which the identity of the offender is

unknown. Compare these objectives with the basic objectives of any investigation.

2. Discuss in some depth one of the classic queries to be probed in victim–offender relationships.

3. Explain the concept of benefit in relation to motive for a crime.

4. Is the basic lead of knowledge more likely to be concerned with motive or opportunity for a crime?

5. Are field interviews justified? Why?

6. Why does the shock of being connected with a crime often lead to a prompt acknowledgment of guilt? What basic lead or leads are likely to have this "finality of identification"?

7. Can the imprint of a single finger found at a crime scene lead to identification of a suspect? Explain.

8. Discuss the role of tracing stolen property in the day-to-day investigation of crime and criminals.

9. Discuss the three major capabilities of a *modus operandi* file.

10. What is the common theme between the use of photographs for identification and the hue and cry for injured suspects?

11. What is the role of composite drawings in identifying a suspect?

Library Assignment

Search available literature on homicides and list at least five bibliographic references to motivation for murder. If possible, itemize page references of motives for murder related to the concept of benefit. Prepare an abstract or digest (100 to 200 words) of the most meaningful reference.

Workbook Project

Review the case study in this chapter. Describe the items of information that served to identify the perpetrators and name the basic investigative lead concerned with each.

CHAPTER
8

Locating Witnesses

The solution to most crimes is obtained through locating witnesses. Investigators must seek information from people. They must learn how to win the trust of strangers. Police investigators have a duty to locate witnesses and to ask for information about an event suspected of being a crime: there is also a nebulous public duty for witnesses to identify themselves and to assist the police by providing information.[1] The U.S. Supreme Court has noted that police officers have a right to expect a high level of responsiveness among citizens interviewed in a general inquiry into the facts surrounding a crime. The court's words in *Miranda* v. *United States,* 384 U.S. 436 (1966), regarding this responsibility of citizenship were: "It is an act of responsible citizenship for individuals to give whatever information they may have to aid in law enforcement."

The first objective of seeking out witnesses is to find enough people who will give their impressions of the circumstances of the crime so that the investigator can feel as if he or she has personally witnessed the entire crime. The ultimate objective is to use the testimony of witnesses to present the case against the accused person in order to convince the triers-of-fact that the accusatory pleading against a defendant in a criminal action is true.

A single witness may be quite accurate, but two mutually independent witnesses decrease the possibility of human error. The stories of several persons may allow puzzling aspects of an investigation to be resolved, and the testimony of one witness may strengthen or destroy the evidence given by others. There is no such thing as a perfect witness. Many individuals are notoriously poor observers; some for one reason or another are liars. The story of a casual passerby cannot be naively trusted to be the truth about what happened.

Persons sought as witnesses fall into three general classes: (1) victims and complainants; (2) witnesses who may give testimony before a grand jury, at a preliminary hearing, or at the trial of the offender; and (3) persons concerned with the events but removed from the actual circumstances of the crime, or those serving only as sources of information.

The new creed among police investigators is that the methodology of locating witnesses must be exhausted in all of its major forms in every investigation. It is time consuming to ring doorbells in search of witnesses, to follow up the standard chain of inquiries into the identity of witnesses, and to devise ways of locating missing witnesses; but there is no other way for investigators safely to conclude that they have discharged their preliminary responsibility in any attempt to solve a crime—locating all the witnesses and gathering all available information.

There are eyes in the street belonging to the nearby residents, the users of the thoroughfare, the stores, bars, and restaurants. Businesspeople and their employees are street watchers, and the lady in the window of ghetto neighborhoods is an example of a resident who observes everything that goes on.[2] In suburban areas the shopping centers are the locale of activity generated by people on errands, at business, or engaged in some activity related to food, drink, or recreation.

Moreover, there is no way other than thoroughness to guard against witnesses being overlooked by police inquiry and used by the defense in the trial of the case. Defense counsels have long used the end of the police investigation as the beginning of the defense investigation. This is especially true now that pretrial discovery increasingly gives defense counsel access to the reports of the police investigation. Failure to locate witnesses is now readily discoverable. A thorough search for witnesses during an investigation forestalls an attack by the defense that the investigator has failed to seek diligently for all the witnesses to the crime, and it also guards against defense investigators finding previously undisclosed witnesses and using them on behalf of the defendant.

Contacting persons who are, or may be, witnesses requires skill and patience. The barriers to an investigator searching for a witness are silence, the withholding of information, and the deliberate avoidance of the role of witness. In some areas there may be a barrier of general unwillingness to speak honestly to any police employee.

WITNESSES AT THE CRIME SCENE

It is the duty of the first officer at the scene of a suspected crime to "contain" it. Standard regulations require responding officers to detain witnesses and other persons at the scene. These officers secure adequate information as to the identity of all persons found at a crime scene, their names, addresses, telephone numbers, and their employers' names and business addresses. Of course, the perpetrator is arrested if he or she is at the scene and so identified; but at this time the major concern with regard to witnesses is to locate them, secure a description of the perpetrator and the facts of the crime, and record their identity and where they can be located.

A witness is often reluctant to identify himself or herself at a crime scene. Police no longer cry out "Let's get the witnesses over here." In fact, police officers avoid prefacing their remarks at a crime scene with the word *witness*. Officers responding to crime scenes learn to pick out a key individual as a person likely to provide information. It may be the proprietor of the premises, a person comforting an injured victim, an unusually alert individual, or a person known to the responding officers. It is not necessary to appeal to persons found at a crime scene; individuals who remain on the scene until police arrive usually want to give information about what they saw or heard. The fact of the crime now has some relationship to them. The police officer, in these contacts, acts out the role of a reporter working with members of the community who are as eager as the officer to bring together a true story of the event.

Revisiting the crime scene area has been effective in locating witnesses. Motorists and pedestrians who do not live or work in the area but who travel the area at about the same time daily or weekly are often witnesses; but they leave the scene prior to the arrival of responding police, sometimes not even knowing that the event they witnessed was a police case.

The technique of revisiting a crime scene area in a search for witnesses has been adapted from the investigation of hit-and-run crimes. The solution of these cases of motorists who are involved in an accident and flee the scene usually requires locating the vehicle involved. Investigators can utilize only the identification potential of the physical evidence found at the scene and, when the suspect vehicle is located, the damage to the suspect car. For this reason, witnesses who can give some clue to the identity of the vehicle and its operator must be discovered. When the initial inquiry at the scene does not produce witnesses, investigators revisit the scene for an hour or more each day, spanning the time of the accident, for a week or two, then revisit on the same day of the week for three or four weeks. Traffic accident investigation units have used this technique for years to find witnesses and collect information about the identity of a hit-and-run vehicle. Key witnesses have been located as much as a month after an accident. The procedure is now formalized as follows:

1. Revisit the accident scene daily for no less than a week and weekly on the day of the week of the accident for no less than a month at the same time of day that the accident occurred.
2. Question motorists and pedestrians, with particular attention to school children and service personnel, such as operators of delivery vehicles.[3]

VIEW-AREA CANVASS FOR WITNESSES

An inquiry in the view area of the crime scene is also standard practice. When a crime is committed within a building, as in an office or apartment, the universe of possible witnesses may be small; but when the crime is committed in a store or in the street, there is a large group of persons who might have witnessed it. This requires a search for persons who may have been witnesses but who have not been so identified. Officers visit places of business, apartments, and residences near the scene. Customers and employees of markets, taverns, and service stations, and residents at home and their visitors are all questioned. This is a solicitation for information about the crime and about anyone who might have seen the event, witnessed suspicious persons in the area before the crime, viewed the perpetrator's flight from the scene, or heard anything unusual—or who knows of someone who has or might have information.

THE NEIGHBORHOOD CANVASS

Superior officers supervising the criminal investigation often assign additional personnel to an extensive neighborhood *canvass* in order to find a witness. The plan used in such a canvass may be based on the approach and flight route of the perpetrator, the travels of witnesses, or the path of a bullet in sniper cases. There is a pattern for a canvass for witnesses in the neighborhood of the crime. It starts with revisits to persons residing or employed in the view area of the crime scene and extends to establishing contacts with employees of service firms such as laundries, dairies, and public utilities. This canvass expands to nearby areas and bus stops and public transit stations beyond the crime scene but within a convenient distance of it. Such a canvass involves the traditional task of ringing doorbells. Often it appears to be a hopeless assignment, yet time and again an investigator canvassing an area finds a witness or, equally important, a person who knows the identity of a witness.

This knocking on doors and asking questions is a very productive source of evidence in homicide cases. The seriousness of the crime impresses most people, and they respond meaningfully when questioned. In these cases investigators are seeking information about the victim as well as the killer or killers.[4]

The attempt to locate witnesses in a canvass of a neighborhood includes the following steps:

1. Friends and immediate relatives of the victim living in the neighborhood are located and interviewed.
2. A house-to-house, apartment-to-apartment, door-to-door canvass is made of:
   a. residents and shopkeepers and their employees
   b. delivery boys, utility, and other service personnel
   c. bus and taxi drivers

Supermarkets, which are isolated within the moats of their immense parking lots, have created problems in locating witnesses. It is not that the view area is curtailed; people are still in and about this area. However, they are tran-

sients in the view area. They do not reside in it, nor is it a place of employment. They walk or drive to a view area, then leave it and return to their
homes or places of business. The tremendous population of people and vehicles in and about shopping centers complicates the problem of locating witnesses to crimes and has led to the concept of the shopping-area canvass for
witnesses (see Figure 8–1). Unlike the neighborhood canvass, developed by
detectives in large urban central cities, this shopping-area canvass can be very
extensive geographically. The canvass in urban centers encompasses the area
in which the *perpetrator* may have traveled to and from the crime scene; the
shopping-area canvass encompasses the area in which *witnesses* travel to and
from the crime scene.

It may seem that the distinction is highly technical or abstract, but many
individuals who are otherwise very cooperative with the police reject any
semblance of the informer role. But these persons often feel that to reveal the
name or whereabouts of a witness is not in the same category as revealing the
identity of a person who might have committed the crime.

Investigators successful in locating witnesses in this way are skilled in
establishing liaisons with persons likely to have information and in maintaining contacts with such individuals until there is need for their cooperation.
This is not normally a procedure that can be developed for a specific investigation. The contacts must be established first. Then when a crime occurs and
there is a need for this type of cooperation, the investigator has sources of
information available.

FIGURE 8–1 Shopping-area canvass for witnesses—Brown case study.

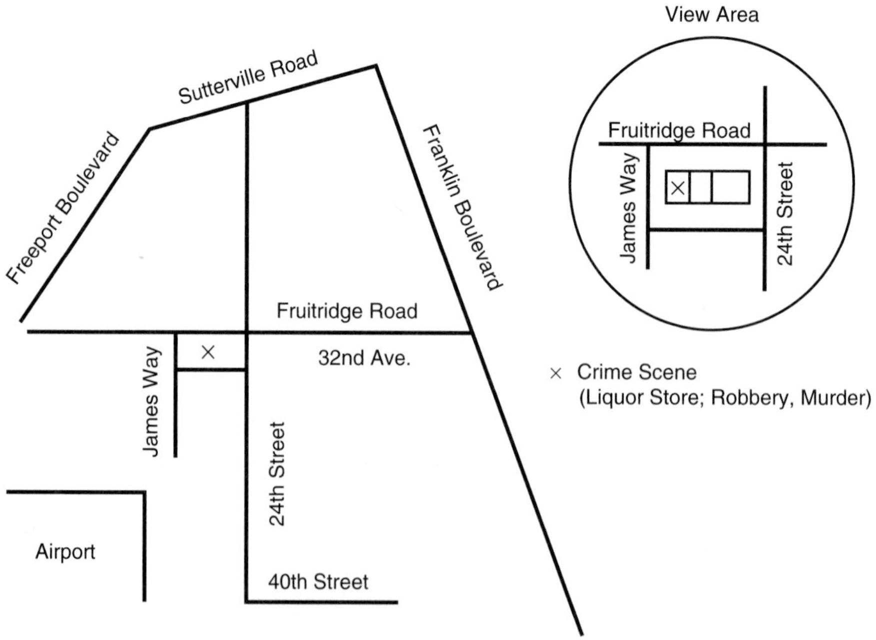

PLEA FOR PUBLIC COOPERATION

In serious felony cases receiving unusual publicity, the police receive a great many investigative leads from members of the community. These offers of help reach unusual heights when the crime is child molesting, a series of murders or rapes of housewives, and robberies or thefts of very large sums of money or immensely valuable jewelry. Unfortunately, the great majority of these calls are from persons justly classified as cranks. Most of the leads are useless, and the time spent making inquiries is lost entirely. An investigator cannot afford to verify every offer of information from such sources. There is need for selectivity; techniques for auditing these unsought messages should be developed. In the audit all messages containing the name and address or other identifying data of a potential witness are separated from letters and calls presenting theories of the crime or suspicious persons. A prompt follow-up inquiry is made on the witness leads, and the remainder are set aside for later analysis.

Police officials, in attempting to locate witnesses to crimes of importance, use all the modern communications media: newspapers, AM and FM radio, and local television outlets. In New York, Chicago, San Francisco, Miami, and other large cities the standard plea to the public is to contribute any information about the case to police, and it is now made easier for them to do so by publication of a special telephone number. In some cases the posting of a reward hastens the response to these pleas for public cooperation. However, this mercenary inducement for help should be avoided unless it is deemed absolutely necessary. For gain, some persons may supply false or meaningless information solely in the hope of making a future claim. Silent Witness programs seek the same help but offer rewards and confidentiality.

A technique has been developed with local television stations. This is a telecast of clues about an unsolved and recent crime. This "clue-in" offers the viewers a minimum of facts about the case, and the core of the program is a request for listeners to call the local station if they believe they may have witnessed any of the travels of the suspected offender or offenders. Several radio stations across the country have cooperated with police in a similar fashion. Listeners in either instance are conditioned to respond by calling the station because of the growth of contests and opinion polls requiring a prompt telephone response.

In both the information wire and the multimedia programming of clue-ins, the emphasis is not on finding people with theories of the crime or ideas of techniques the police should utilize in searching for the offender, but rather upon locating witnesses. Listeners and viewers are asked to call a specific, easily remembered telephone number under either of the following conditions: If you witnessed any segment of this crime, any act concerned with its preparation, any of the postcrime travels or other activities of the criminal or his or her associates, or if you know the identity of the criminal or his or her associates from other sources of information; or if you know the identity of any other person who might have been a witness or who might know the identity of the offender and his or her associates.

One of the problems that police have in the United States has been in securing the cooperation of the public in solving crimes. However, when the crime is widely recognized as vicious and hurtful there is an excellent potential for community support. Persons who would not normally cooperate will do so when the atrocity of a crime inspires their sympathy for the victim and the public appeal for information orients them to the police. It is a technique in searching for witnesses that has optimum potential because everyone in the community is exposed to multimedia. Notices in the media do communicate to people and can be used successfully in discovering witnesses.

Selected References

1. Giske V. Sanders, 9 Cal. App. 13 (1908).
2. Jane Jacobs, "Violence in the City Streets," in *Violence in the Streets,* ed. Shalom Endleman (Chicago: Quadrangle Books, 1968), pp. 214–26.
3. J. Stannard Baker, *Traffic Accident Investigator's Manual for Police,* 4th ed. (Evanston, Ill.: The Traffic Institute, Northwestern University, 1963).
4. Barbara Gelb, *On the Track of Murder: Behind the Scenes with a Homicide Commando Squad* (New York: William Morrow & Company, 1975), p. 26.

Chapter Review

CASE STUDY: THE BROWN CASE

The Brown case is one in which the identity of the perpetrator was not known at the time the investigation was started, and only extensive work by assigned investigators disclosed the identity of the suspect and led to prompt apprehension. A known identity case is likely to be under-investigated, but the work commonly necessary in a serious felony investigation in which the perpetrator is unknown develops the type of evidence structure necessary in *any* prosecution of an accused person.

Although the killing of this liquor store proprietor might be considered accidental, it was legally classified as murder because it was a homicide committed in the course of committing a felony (robbery).

Synopsis

At approximately 3:20 P.M., March 12, officers on patrol received a call to proceed to the Bank Bottle Shop, a liquor store. The first patrol officer arrived at 3:25 P.M. and walked into the scene of a murder. The scene survey showed the appearance of a struggle and robbery, and the victim apparently dead from massive wounds and extensive bleeding. The officer checked the body for signs of life, looked for other occupants, then called for detectives and the coroner. A neighborhood inquiry by the responding police officers located two witnesses. One witness, an adult, observed what was believed to be the killer's automobile in the parking area immediately in front of the liquor store. Another witness, a child, observed what was believed to be the killer and his automobile leave the parking area immediately in front of the liquor store. This witness also saw the automobile scrape the curb in front of the liquor store. Two nights later, evidence was found in a ditch near a golf course along a nearby street. Among the items in the ditch was a hammer later proved to be the murder weapon. A witness who observed the automobile from which the items were thrown obtained its license number, and this led police to the defendant. This witness also identified the defendant as the driver of the car at a later lineup. In a jury trial the defendant was found guilty and sentenced to death.

The Investigation

Sketches and diagrams were prepared by the police to detail pictorially the crime scene. Photographs of the crime scene and the extension of the scene were taken. In conjunction with the sketches there were (1) a written report describing the items depicted on the sketches, and (2) measurements to show the exact location of the evidence illustrated (see Figures 8–2 and 8–3).

Recovery of physical evidence at the crime scene included a hat, hair samples, paint scrapings from the area of the parking lot curb in front of the store, the glass particles from the floor. Physical evidence recovered at the extension of the crime scene (the ditch) included clothing in a bundle and, separated from the bundle, a wheel weight tool (hammer) and hair samples from the clothing.

FIGURE 8–2 Brown case crime-scene area—position of witnesses.

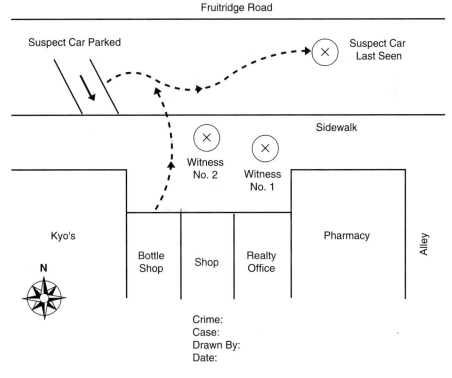

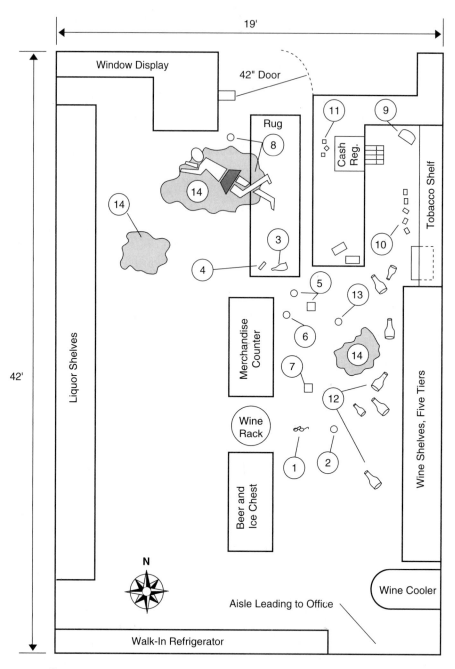

19'

Window Display

42" Door

Rug

⑪ 11   ⑨ 9

Cash Reg.

⑧ 8

⑭ 14

Tobacco Shelf

⑭ 14

③ 3

⑩ 10

④ 4

⑤ 5   ⑬ 13

Liquor Shelves

42'

Merchandise Counter

⑥ 6

⑭ 14

⑦ 7

Wine Shelves, Five Tiers

⑫ 12

Wine Rack

① 1   ② 2

Beer and Ice Chest

N

Wine Cooler

Aisle Leading to Office

Walk-In Refrigerator

Case:
Crime:
Drawn By:
Date:

FIGURE 8–3 Brown case crime-scene sketch. Numbered locations indicate items of evidence (listed on crime report).

At the time the suspect was arrested, the shoes of the suspect and a hair sample of the suspect were secured. At the suspect's home after the arrest, a sample of the suspect's dog's hair and a sample of paint from the tire of the suspect's automobile were taken for comparison tests.

Interviews of two witnesses at the scene developed the following evidence at the trial:

Witness No. 1. (Previous questioning elicited testimony that established the age and identity of the witness.) The questioning included a number of leading questions, which are sometimes necessary and permissible when the witness is quite young. This witness was 11 years old. The prosecutor phrased the questions.

Q. Do you know the shopping center that is located on the corner of Fruitridge Road and 24th Street?

A. Yes.

Q. On March 12th, a Sunday afternoon of this year, were you in the area of that shopping center?

A. Yes.

Q. What was your purpose for going there?

A. Had to get something at the grocery store.

Q. What were you going to get?

A. Some milk.

Q. And that was at which store?

A. Raley's.

Q. Raley's market located in that shopping center?

A. Yes.

Q. Which way did you come from when you approached Raley's?

A. By Fruitridge Road.

Q. Do you know where the Bank Bottle Shop is?

A. Yes.

Q. Did you walk past that?

A. Yes.

Q. Do you know where Kyo's is?

A. Yes.

Q. Did you walk past that?

A. Yes.

Q. You passed Kyo's before you approached the Bank Bottle Shop?

A. Yes.

Q. Did you look in the Bank Bottle Shop as you passed?

A. Yeah.

Q. Did you see anything?

A. Saw a pair of legs lying down on the floor.

Q. Did you see anything else?

A. Blood.

Q. Where did you go then?

A. I went to the store.

Q. And what did you do?

A. I just got the milk, and I left after I paid for it.

Q. Did you go back past the Bottle Shop again?

A. Yes.

Q. How long did it take you between the time you passed the Bottle Shop on the way to the store and the time that you passed it on your return?

A. About 5 minutes.

Q. Would you tell these ladies and gentlemen what you saw?

A. Well, I saw a man coming out from the store. I didn't see him run out from it, but he was coming from that direction. Then he got in his car and drove away.

Q. What did you notice about the man, if anything?

A. He had blood on him, a lot of blood, and he was carrying something in his hand.

Q. What was he carrying in his hand?

A. A small hammer.

The witness continued to relate that the man appeared as if his leg was injured and that when he started to drive away his car scraped the curb in front of the liquor store. (When arrested, the defendant had a broken leg.)

Witness No. 2. This was an adult witness who saw the car used by the robber and killer while it was parked in front of the liquor store, the Bank Bottle Shop. After giving testimony concerning his identity, he was questioned by the prosecutor as follows:

Q. Are you familiar with the shopping center at the southeast corner of Fruitridge Road and 24th Street?

A. I live in that area.

Q. Did you have occasion to be in front of that area, the shopping center, on Sunday, March 12th, in the afternoon?

A. Yes, I walked down the sidewalk past the Bottle Shop.

Q. Are you referring to the Bank Bottle Shop at 2346 Fruitridge?

A. Yes.

Q. Where were you going at that time?

A. I was going to Kyo's right next door.

Q. What time was it?

A. Approximately 3 or a few minutes after.

Q. Did you see any automobiles in that area?

A. There was one car parked out in front.

Q. Would you describe that automobile please.

A. It was a light, cream-colored, two-door Thunderbird with chrome down the side, and curved fenders, and it had "Thunderbird" written across the side on the front fender. (This described the defendant's automobile.)

Medicolegal (autopsy) evidence developed the following data from the autopsy report: Countless wounds were found about the scalp, ears, forehead, and eyes (see Figure 8–4). These lacerations are generally sharp in character and are

FIGURE 8–4 Coroner's report—wounds of victim in Brown case.

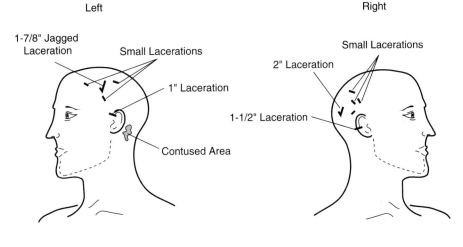

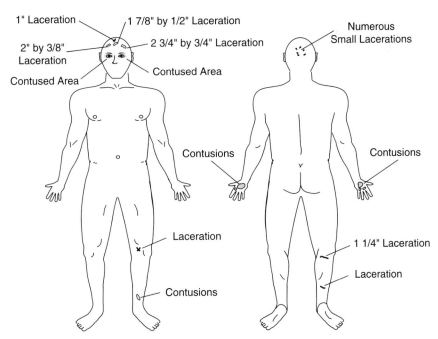

made by a relatively sharp instrument. They show a bruising along the edge and vary in size from 3 to 4 inches in length to virtual puncture wounds. There is one virtually continuous laceration across the entire frontal area from right temporal bone to left temporal bone. Both ears have been partially divided, again by a sharp instrument. There are innumerable other smaller marks, approximately six around the left eye, approximately six to eight around and under the right eye. There is extensive bruising in these areas. These wounds are basically small and appear to be virtual gross puncture wounds. Through one of the lacerations over the left frontal area, there is palpable fracture.

Extremities: There are several small bruise lacerations about the left upper arm, left forearm, and left hand. There are similar lacerations over the right hand. There are two or three superficial abrasions and lacerations over the left lower extremity and a laceration over the right heel. All of these wounds, head, arms, and lower extremities, appear to be made by basically the same type of instrument.

Head: There are three areas of fracture involving the skull. The first is in the left frontal area, the second is in the right posterior temporal area, and the third is in the right occipital area. All of these are relatively undisplaced fractures, the intracranial depression being approximately 5 to 10 millimeters in each case. The most severe of these is the right temporal bone fracture, and even in this area there is little or no underlying hematoma. No trace of glass fragments found in head area.

I had occasion to reexamine the subject for the purpose of comparing the wounds inflicted with a weapon supplied by the coroner's office. This weapon was a hammer with a green composition handle and a peculiar type of head. There was a flat surface at the front, a side extension resembling a screwdriver, and in the rear a two-pronged structure, one prong being relatively straight and the other being curved, somewhat on the order of a bottle opener. The sutured lacerations over the left frontal area were removed, and the area of peculiar dual penetration of the skull was exposed and, upon examination, was found to fit perfectly with the end of the hammer described above as two-pronged. In addition, multiple lacerations over the hands and face demonstrated virtually perfect conformity to the small screwdriver-like side arm on this hammer. It was my impression, after examining the wounds again, and the hammer supplied by the coroner's officer, that this instrument or one very similar inflicted said wounds. The skull fracture in the left frontal area appeared to be made by the pronged end of the hammer; the two other skull fractures appear to have been made by the flat end of the hammer. The hammer was then returned to the custody of the coroner's officer (see Figure 8–5).

Cause of death: Cerebral concussion due to multiple skull fractures with multiple lacerations of the head.

Laboratory technicians in criminalistics tested the physical evidence and reported their findings as follows:

1. The hair samples from the hat recovered at the scene were similar in appearance and physical characteristics to the hair samples taken from the suspect.
2. Hair samples found on clothing recovered at the scene extension (ditch) were traceable and similar to the hair samples of the suspect's dog.

FIGURE 8–5
Murder weapon in Brown case.

3. Glass fragments from the crime scene and glass fragments in the soles of the suspect's shoes could not be differentiated one from the other.

4. Paint scrapings from the curb in front of the crime-scene store appeared similar in color and type to the paint transfer found on the tire of the suspect's car.

5. Blood on the hammer and clothing found at the scene extension (ditch) was human and the same type as that of the deceased.

Critique

The success of the prosecution was ensured by:

1. The careful documentation and recovery of physical evidence at the crime scene.

2. Location and interview of the two witnesses at the scene.

3. Careful documentation and recovery of physical evidence at the scene extension (ditch).

4. Initiative of the witness at the scene extension (ditch) in recording the automobile license number and his ability to identify the driver.

5. Postarrest documentation and recovery of physical evidence from the suspect and his home and car.

6. Successful comparison of physical evidence connecting the suspect to the crime scene.

Source: Sacramento, California, Police Department and Public Defender's Office.

Discussion Questions

1. Describe a canvass for witnesses.

2. What is the rationale for the concept that investigators must exhaust every investigative technique in a search to locate and identify witnesses to a crime?

3. Why are many persons in the United States reluctant to identify themselves as witnesses? Do you believe that this is true in England and other countries?

4. In what areas are residents unwilling to accept the role of informer?

5. Does the public response to requests for information differ when the objective is locating witnesses rather than finding the perpetrator?
6. Cranks usually volunteer meaningless information to police when a crime receives wide publicity. Is there any way such data can be screened or audited for useful information without following up every proffered lead?
7. Review the means by which an investigator can expand the universe of witnesses.
8. What is the rationale for revisiting the crime scene and the view area?
9. Name the witnesses in the case study and describe their contribution to the solution of this crime.
10. Describe the items of evidence that served to identify the perpetrator, the item(s) establishing the *corpus delicti*.

Library Assignment

Research the area of police-community relations. Prepare a bibliography of at least ten sources in this area, and extract comments from each source about public attitudes likely to void attempts to locate witnesses.

Workbook Project

Select a local supermarket and delineate on an outline of a street map the most appropriate limits of its shopping area. Assume that a robbery-murder had been committed in this market. Prepare a series of statements and questions for an investigator ringing doorbells on such a neighborhood canvass, that will (1) identify the "caller," (2) offer a door-opening reason for the visit, (3) seek information, (4) make the subject of the visit feel at ease, and (5) leave a request for cooperation and a means of future contact.

CHAPTER
9

Interviewing Witnesses and Interrogating Suspects

You are going to have to talk to people . . . talk to people and make them feel like people . . . you get a lot of results that way . . . very smooth, very quiet.*

Interviewing in criminal investigation is a face-to-face conversation with a purpose—to get information. The persons interviewed are individuals who have been located and identified as individuals with a knowledge of the crime or its circumstances. A successful interview develops a story of what the witness saw and heard. In total, all the information gathered from witnesses should allow the investigator to understand it as if he or she had been present at the time. Second, the reliability, competency, and credibility of the witness is reviewed. It is a case of knowing what the witness knows and does not know, and of knowing the witness.

Persons suspected of a crime are interrogated. The purpose of interrogation is to secure a confession of guilt. It is an offensive–defensive situation in which the investigator probes, pries, and pushes an investigation to its climax with a confession. The suspect, guilty or innocent, explains, lies, or stands mute.

*E. W. Count, *Cop Talk—True Detective Stories from the NYPD.* (New York: Simon & Schuster, Pocket Books, 1994), p. 4.

THE TIME AND PLACE OF INTERVIEW

Witnesses should be interviewed without delay. When witnesses are interviewed early in a case, there is a notable willingness to talk and to tell the truth. Moreover, a witness cannot take refuge in an evasive "I don't remember" when an interview is conducted early.

Time is not a factor, however, when there is a problem about the condition of the witness. Serious doubts have been raised about the wisdom of interviewing persons who are intoxicated, under sedation, or otherwise under the influence of drugs. For this reason, a witness under the care of a physician or in a hospital for emergency treatment who may have been given sedation should not be interviewed until the physician has been contacted and has stated that the witness is fully conscious and that any forthcoming story will not be affected by any medication. A witness who admits to a recent dosage of drugs or narcotics of any kind, or who acts in a manner that indicates recent drug use, should not be interviewed at this time. Any person so under the influence of alcohol that he or she is legally unfit to drive a motor vehicle also should be rejected. Finally, the investigator should be satisfied prior to a full-scale interview that the witness is not psychotic. A witness is suspected of being emotionally disturbed when there are indications that he or she is confused or disorganized and out of contact with reality.

Not interviewing persons in this condition only postpones this task in the majority of the cases. Individuals recover from the effects of drugs and alcohol, and even psychotics have periods of lucidity. Postponement makes certain that the story of the witness is uninfluenced by any deteriorated mental condition, and such a story can be carried beyond the interview and into court for trial.

Interviews on the scene cannot be staged formally, but so long as group interviews are avoided and the witnesses are separated after the police arrive and before and after interviewing, the physical conditions will not meaningfully interfere with the interview. Nor are interviews resulting from a canvass of neighborhood residents postponed or formalized in any way. They are an extension of the initial contact, and the location of the interview is the home or place of business of the witness.

In the *Miranda* decision, 384 U.S. 436 (1966), the U.S. Supreme Court specifically approved the crime scene as a place for interviewing witnesses and expressed the opinion that the home was a likely site for such questioning. The words of the decision noted that a person's home and other familiar surroundings are free of any implied compulsion. When an interview is not conducted at the crime scene or as an extension of an information-seeking contact, a primary factor influencing both the time and the place of the interview is the convenience of the witness.

THE TIME AND PLACE OF INTERROGATION

The interrogation session offers the suspect an opportunity to clear himself or herself or to spill everything and to hope for the best. The element of compulsion that continues to exist in post-*Miranda* interrogation is not the coercion of past police interrogation practices but rather an inner stimulus prompting a prisoner to talk to the police.

Unlike an interview situation, the investigator conducting an interrogation must be prepared; must be up to date on the reconstruction of the crime; must be cognizant of the facts secured in parallel inquiries into motive and opportunity; and must know as much as possible about the suspect and the facts connecting him or her with the crime. If any physical evidence has been collected, the investigator should know the findings of the criminalists examining the evidence.

A custodial interrogation takes place in a police building, in an interrogation room or other secure, private room. Prior to any questioning the investigator must make certain the suspect is not in an emotional state that might impair his or her capacity for rational judgment. As in interviewing witnesses, the investigator must ascertain if the suspect is intoxicated or under the influence of any drug. Sedation after injuries or because of illness is a problem that should be discussed with an attending physician. The questioning should take place only when the investigator is advised by the doctor that the suspect is not so much under the influence of drugs or alcohol that he or she would not be able to answer questions intelligently and rationally. Obviously intoxicated persons are easy to detect, but drugged persons sometimes appear to be acting normally. This is also true of the obviously abnormal person, but a person in a deep psychotic episode may appear normal in actions. In either case the responsibility of the questioner is to probe the suspect's contact with reality, his or her memory, and his or her rationality.

CUSTODIAL INTERROGATION: THE *MIRANDA* WARNING

After the decision of the U.S. Supreme Court in *Escobedo* v. *Illinois,* 378 U.S. 478 (1964), in which the court ruled an accused person should be warned of his or her right to silence and should not be denied the advice of an attorney during police interrogation, a confusing series of state appellate decisions followed about the timing of this right to a warning and to counsel—the "when" factor—in the pretrial period. The court's action in *Miranda* v. *Arizona,* 384 U.S. 436 (1966), clarified this point. In the absence of an intelligent waiver of the constitutional rights involved, confessions and any other statements obtained by custodial police interrogation are held inadmissible in evidence.

A suspect being questioned is in custody when under arrest or deprived of freedom of action in any significant way. The crux of the definition is that it identifies a legal point in time, the time at which the Anglo-American adversary system of criminal proceedings commences and the safeguards established for the protection of individuals against self-incrimination become operable.

The *Miranda* doctrine requires a warning be given to the suspect relative to his or her privileges under the Fifth and Sixth Amendments—the right to avoid self-incrimination and the right to legal counsel. Prior to any questioning, the police must make known to the suspect that:

1. He or she has the right to remain silent.
2. Anything stated can be used against him or her in a court of law.
3. He or she has the right to consult with an attorney and to have an attorney present during questioning.
4. If the suspect cannot afford an attorney, one will be appointed prior to any questioning, if desired (see Figure 9–1).

Procedural safeguards supplement this warning and lay a foundation for a waiver of constitutional rights. Suspects may waive such rights after such warning has been given and such opportunity afforded them, but the waiver must be made knowingly and intelligently. After such waiver, opportunity to exercise these rights must be afforded to the suspect throughout any subsequent interrogation. Unless and until such warning and waiver are demonstrated by the prosecution at trial, no evidence obtained as a result of interrogation can be used against the person questioned. The burden of demonstrating that the defendant knowingly and intelligently waived the privilege against self-incrimination and right to a retained or appointed counsel rests on the prosecution.

Standard procedure to demonstrate this decision of the suspect is the person's signature on a copy of the *Miranda* warning or a signed statement equally extensive. The investigator must offer affirmative evidence that the suspect was willing to waive these privileges and participate in the interrogation and that at no time before or during the resultant interrogation did the suspect indicate in any manner that he or she wished to remain silent or state that he or she wanted an attorney.

Since *Miranda,* the courts seek more than silence when a suspect is interrogated and the introduction of a confession is sought. They expect testimony that will explore the waiver of rights by the suspect, and they will look for testimony about the time span of the interrogation. When was the suspect first taken into custody? At what time was the *Miranda* warning given? What is the time of the statement? At what time did the interrogation begin? When did it end?

A study of the interrogation practices and the techniques rejected by the court in *Miranda* indicates how the integrity of an interrogation can be jeopardized. Also, by exclusion, acceptable techniques are revealed. The *rejected* areas of questioning are:

1. Suggesting the invincibility of the forces of law enforcement by conducting the interrogation only in police buildings, where privacy was certain, and in surroundings unfamiliar to the suspect.
2. Viewing the guilt of the suspect as a fact; displaying an air of confidence in suspect's guilt.
3. Minimizing the moral seriousness of the offense.
4. Offering legal excuses for the criminal action.

Miranda Warning

Report #_____

1. You have the right to remain silent.

2. Anything you say can and will be used against you in a court of law.

    a. Do you understand that you have the right to remain silent?

        ❑ YES_____   ❑ NO_____

    b. Understanding that right, do you wish to talk to me now?

        ❑ YES_____   ❑ NO_____

3. You have the right to talk to an attorney and have an attorney present before and during questioning.

4. If you cannot afford an attorney, one will be appointed free of charge to represent you before and during questioning, if you desire.

    c. Do you understand you have the right to talk to an attorney?

        ❑ YES_____   ❑ NO_____

    d. Understanding that right, do you wish to talk to me now?

        ❑ YES_____   ❑ NO_____

SIGNED_____

OFFICER:_____   BADGE: _____

OFFICER:_____   BADGE: _____

TIME: _____   DATE: _____

The suspect should initial the appropriate answer to each question (yes, no) and sign the waiver. The officer should then sign and date the form. Juveniles must be informed of their rights whether or not the officer intends to question them

FIGURE 9–1 Miranda warning—action indicating a suspect about to be questioned by police while in their custody has thoughtfully waived his or her *Miranda* rights. (See Appendix A, Case Briefs, for a digest of the *Miranda* case.)

5. Using the scheme of dogged persistence, over a period of time, to dominate the suspect and overwhelm him or her with the interrogator's inexorable will to obtain the truth.

6. Using "Mutt and Jeff" questioning (the friendly–unfriendly team interrogation).

7. Utilizing the trickery of a false lineup, with identification by witnesses coached to identify suspect.

8. Pointing out the incriminating significance of a suspect's refusal to talk.

9. Patiently maneuvering the suspect into a position from which the desired object, a confession, may be obtained.

10. Rejecting requests for legal counsel or contact with relatives or friends by suggesting that an innocent person does not need an attorney or other contacts or that telling the truth must be a prelude to access to counsel or contacts with relatives and friends.

Use of these techniques by interrogators is unacceptable. If any of them are used to obtain a confession, the confession will be rejected.

Strangely, instead of citing real-life instances of the use of the foregoing techniques, the main references of the court in this decision were to textbooks written to instruct police in interrogation. This may be the key to the extensive instructional writing contained in this decision. In previous confession cases the court has been satisfied to reject the circumstances of a particular questioning; but in the substance of this opinion, the court rejected the discipline of interrogation, the body of knowledge collected in the authoritative literature on this investigative technique. Simply, the likely rationale of the court was that little would be gained by rejecting *Miranda's* questioning session and declaring his confession inadmissible without rejecting the body of knowledge that had been built up and was being taught to every police recruit in the United States.

One of the problem areas for years has been the trustworthiness of confessions. The *Miranda* decision makes it abundantly clear that even a true confession will be ruled inadmissible unless adherence to the *Miranda* warning and its procedural safeguards can be shown affirmatively to overcome what may now be termed a standing suspicion of coercion in police interrogations. (See Appendix A, case brief on *Miranda*.)

THE INTERVIEW STRUCTURE

An interview, like any work of art or science, has a beginning, a main portion, and an end. During the introductory segment the witness is scanned and appraised by the investigator and put at ease. It is a leisurely opening of a meeting between two people. The investigator meets the witness, introduces himself or herself, puts the witness as much at ease as possible, and begins by asking the witness for identity data. As these data are secured, the investigator makes a brief appraisal of the witness. Investigators do not make this appraisal as a prelude to an interrogation but rather for a better understanding of the manner in which the witness will perceive and report what was witnessed. For this reason, the appraisal is mainly of the broad personal characteristics of the witness and of his or her motivation to tell the truth. If the witness does not appear to be willing to cooperate, it is wise to repeat the introductory phase and seek ways of motivating the witness.

The closing of the introductory segment of an interview is of vital importance. In this termination the investigator quite plainly informs the witness by his or her actions that "this is it." This action by an investigator is usually wordless, but it does convey to the witness that no future additions or corrections of the story he or she is about to tell will be possible. Investigators reject any suggestion at any time that a witness will be reinterviewed or given any other opportunity to add to or change a story. Follow-up queries may be necessary at a later date, but any overt communication by the investigator to this effect may result in the witness withholding vital information until a later interview. The willingness of a witness to speak the truth is not as readily apparent as are his or her personal characteristics, skills, and interests. An investigator can shape a tentative image of the attitude of a witness during the introductory segment of an interview. Behavior that is illustrative of the apparent position of the witness in relation to the crime, signs of any overt or covert interest in the crime or in the perpetrator, or an emotional problem in relating the story of the crime, all offer clues to the witness's attitude. Investigators should have some understanding of the basic motivations of people being interviewed as witnesses.

When the witness relates to the victim of the crime and wishes to aid in the apprehension of the criminal, he or she is motivated to communicate—but will do so only when believing that the investigator will be able to apprehend the criminal. Thus the interviewer is seen by the subject of the interview as an agent who can bring about a desired change. This provides the normal extrinsic motivation, unless the interviewer disturbs the relationship by some thoughtless act implying a rejection of the witness.[1]

Intrinsic motivation depends on developing a personal relationship between the interviewer and the witness in which the witness receives satisfaction from the personal level of communication with the interviewer. The basic condition for such motivation to talk is that the person being interviewed believes the interviewer is a person who is likely to understand and accept him or her and what he or she has to say.[2]

Many willing witnesses become reluctant to cooperate with an interviewer when they can identify attitudes or viewpoints with which they are not in sympathy. Intolerance and impatience are handicaps, but indications of the interviewer's bias or prejudice are major faults. On the other hand, sincerity and compassion are important factors in gaining cooperation. One of these attributes at an observable level is most helpful. An investigator who apparently possesses both of them is a person to whom most witnesses will relate and talk with as much confidence as with an old friend.

Many experienced investigators suspect some long-forgotten instinctual alarm mechanism or unconditioned reflex warns witnesses of an investigator with adverse attitudes or unconscious hostility and antagonism. There is belief verging on superstition among such experienced personnel that trustworthiness, sincerity, and compassion must be a way of life for an investigator. It is almost a folklore among individuals who have made investigation a career that these attributes will not surface and be identified by witnesses unless they are genuine characteristics of the investigator.

The main portion of an information-gathering interview is structured as follows:

1. The investigator requests the witness to tell in his or her own words, as briefly as possible but omitting nothing of importance, what the person has seen and heard in relation to a certain time, place, and event.

2. The investigator listens and may make brief notes as the witness tells his or her story.

3. The investigator asks questions that explore various aspects of the story of the witness, but does not cross-examine. Open-end questions assist the witness in continuing a story: "Then what?" "What gives you that impression?" "What was the distance?"

4. The investigator establishes the foundation for the story told by the witness:

   a. "How did you happen to be in this place where you made the observation?"

   b. "Where is this place exactly in relation to the movement of the crime—its happening?"

5. The witness is asked to state any relationship that may exist with others concerned with the crime or its circumstances. If it becomes clear the witness is not a chance bystander or passerby, a few questions probing beyond the apparent facts of the crime and collecting information on the stated relationship are justified.

Just prior to concluding this main segment of the interview, the interviewer may attempt to resolve any minor conflict between the story of the witness being interviewed and the circumstances of the crime known to the interviewer from information collected previously. This inquiry must be made without departing from the nondirective interview technique. The interviewer must develop the theme that accuracy is important in gathering information, and then he or she must ask the witness to "look back" within the general area of conflict. The specific nature of the conflict should not be stated because it raises the suggestibility factor in the interview; nor should the tactic of asking the witness to "look back" be repeated or used unnecessarily because it is open to criticism when so used. Some conflict between the stories of witnesses may be healthy. However, major conflicts between the story of a witness and the circumstances of the crime as developed during an investigation are reviewed when testing the credibility of each witness in the postinterview period and eventually in court.

In many ways the main body of an interview is similar to the major portion of a one-to-one teaching interview in which the witness is the instructor and the investigator learns what he or she knows. (See Figure 9–2.)

The closing segment of the interview is fairly abrupt and is indicated by the classic question: "Is there anything else you would like to add?"

Normally, it is not recommended that witnesses be reinterviewed repeatedly. However, in testing the credibility of a witness the need may arise for a reinterview to inquire into problems that have developed. It may be a simple matter of confirming information that indicates a witness is not reliable and not likely to be telling the truth; it may be complicated by the investigator's need

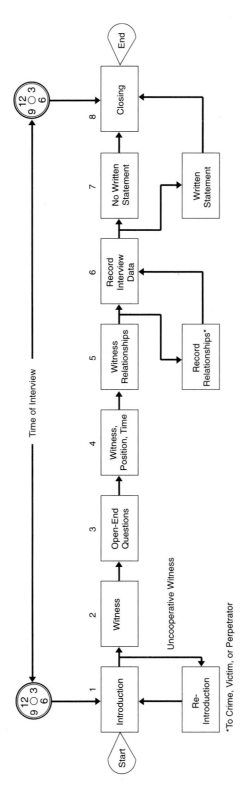

FIGURE 9–2 Interviewing witnesses—nonsuggestive structure.

to discover why the witness has failed to measure up to reasonable standards. It may be that the story of another witness has opened up vistas indicating gaps in the story of a witness interviewed earlier, and reinterviewing is necessary in an attempt to fill voids in his or her memory. Major conflicts may develop, and earlier witnesses must be reinterviewed to determine how and why such conflict came about. Whatever the reason for reinterviewing, the basic concept is to hold these sessions to a minimum and to record in the report of the later interview(s) the basic justification for it. Follow-up interviews are structured in the same manner as the basic interview, but the scope of the inquiry should be limited to the problem that has developed since the basic interview.

THE INTERROGATION STRUCTURE

Interrogations are similar to interviews in structure in that they have a beginning, a main body, and a conclusion (see Figure 9–3). After the introductory material necessary to establish the integrity of the interrogation, the interrogator completes the beginning of the interview by clearly stating the reason for the suspect's presence, the crime about which he or she is to be questioned, the name of the victim, and the time and place of the crime. The day of the pretext interview is past. Today the practice is to level with the suspect as an indication the interrogation is not an attempt to deceive but an inquiry being conducted because evidence has indicated the suspect's knowledge of, or participation in, the crime under investigation.

The main body of the interrogation concerns the activity and whereabouts of the suspect at and about the time of the crime—who he or she was with, who observed or might have observed him or her in this period of time, what was done, and where. Any discussion about damaging evidence is avoided because it may be misinterpreted as a threat to the suspect.

If the story of the suspect is that he or she was not at the scene of the crime or was not in contact with the victim, the second half of the main body of the interrogation concerns whether the suspect had ever been at the scene or in contact with the victim and under what circumstances. This is a safeguard against any later attempt to compromise physical evidence putting the suspect at the crime scene or in contact with the victim by admitting being there or in contact at another time.

The closing of the interrogation is similar to that of an interview. The possibility that a formal statement (confession) may be taken exists. There is also the classic concluding question: "Is there anything else you wish to talk about or any correction you wish to make in your story at this time?" A suspect who has made a full disclosure may be asked for permission to search certain premises, to ride about with the investigator to identify other locations or criminal activity and persons involved, and to participate in an identification lineup.

The basic voluntariness of a statement during an interrogation can be tainted by a promise or a belief that some leniency has been offered in return for a confession. To ensure against this possibility, the investigator must be

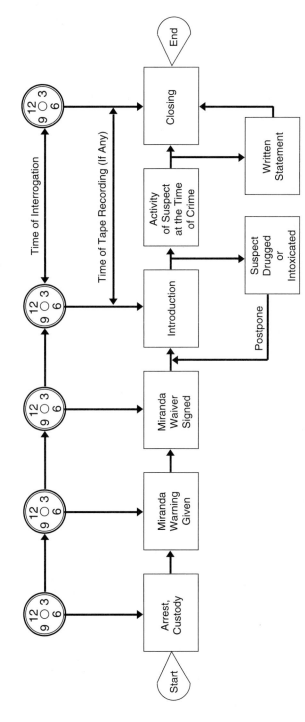

FIGURE 9–3 Custodial interrogation.

certain that no promises are made or implied prior to or during the questioning. Affirmative responses from the suspect should be elicited to the following questions:

Q: You realize I haven't made you any promises?

Q: Has anyone else in authority or associated with me in any way made you any promises? These promises I refer to are in relation to an exchange of some favor or benefit in return for a statement of guilt or a confession from you in relation to this offense [here the specific crime is stated]. Do you understand this?

Q: Is it true that no such promises have been made to you?

Adherence to the foregoing procedure places the investigator in a position to respond appropriately on direct examination to questions that are necessary in laying a foundation for the introduction of a confession.

THE WRITTEN STATEMENT OF A WITNESS

Statements are an excellent means of indicating the story told to the investigator by the witness, which is important in the trial of an offender. They usually are little more than ruled paper forms on which the witness writes a brief summary in his or her own words of what he or she has seen and heard and of how he or she happened to be in a position to make this observation. If the statement is not in the handwriting of the witness, it should be signed by him or her as a guard against repudiation. Investigators are expected to exercise judgment as to the number of statements taken if there are a great number of witnesses.

When a statement is taken, it should have a dual accuracy; it should reflect what the witness has said and what, in fact, happened. The statement should contain the essential facts of what the witness is prepared to testify to, under oath, about his or her observations. If there is any contradiction, defense counsel may seize it as an opportunity to destroy the credibility of the witness.

The purpose of taking a statement from a witness is generally to:

1. Provide a written record that will allow a prosecutor to evaluate the case and plan its presentation at trial.
2. Enable the prosecutor to monitor the testimony of the witness in court.
3. "Hold" a witness—that is, discourage surprise testimony by providing a possible base for impeaching the witness.

If statements are taken, or if the interview develops as a situation in which a statement should be taken in accordance with standard local operating procedures, a note of the taking of a statement, or the failure to do so when a statement is warranted, should be made part of the investigator's field notes and report of the investigation.

THE WRITTEN STATEMENT (CONFESSION) OF A SUSPECT

Confessions of suspects, when taken, are similar to the statements of witnesses. The modern method of taking a statement is to be nondirective, to allow the suspect to write the story in his or her own words or to dictate it into a tape recorder. A verbatim transcript of the recording should be signed, as the handwritten story would be, and witnessed by the interrogator. However, an added dimension in interrogation is very important in connection with taking a statement; no action of the investigator should indicate belief in the story of the suspect. Today, a confession or admission is accepted for what it is worth. Often an exculpatory statement accusing someone else may serve as an admission; or the suspect may phrase a confession so that it will contain justification or excuse for the criminal act.

In either event, and in line with the present methodology of interrogation, the investigator is in a position to testify honestly that this is what the suspect said (possibly wrote) and signed after the conversation reported. It was not a joint effort of the interrogator and suspect but is an entirely voluntary statement of an accused person fully aware that the adversary system of U.S. justice had commenced and fully aware of the constitutional rights to silence and legal counsel.

At one time it was considered good procedure for interrogators to review the written confession and to correct it, but this is now thought of as coaching a witness and creates the beginning of a credibility gap between the investigator and the triers-of-fact. If errors occur in the confession, they should be allowed to stand; they can be pointed out in support of the credibility of the entire process.

Question-and-answer confessions, in which the questioner phrases questions in the manner of a cross-examiner, also have been criticized because of the strong element of suggestion and the potential for leading the suspect into a story. A second confession is undesirable because it appears to be coercive and implies continual pressure for change in the story of the suspect. It is likely to bring the entire confession into doubt.

AUDIOTAPING SUSPECT/WITNESS

Tape recordings have been suggested as appropriate to record accurately a statement made during an interrogation and also to record accurately the characteristics of the interrogation. A New Jersey Supreme Court decision[3] established a half-dozen guidelines for the admissibility of sound recordings.

1. The tape recorder must be capable of recording conversation.
2. The operator must be competent.
3. The recording must be authentic and correct.
4. No changes, additions, or deletions may be made.

5. The operator should read into the tape the time the tape began and ended, and the recorder should be left on at all times during the interrogation. If the tape breaks during the recording, it should not be spliced, but a new segment should be started, with a new time of beginning.

6. When the person being interrogated makes a statement amounting to a confession, it must be elicited voluntarily and without inducement.

These reasonable rules for recording the interrogation of the suspect illustrate the theme of interrogation in the post-*Miranda* period, which is that the entire procedure is replete with a basic integrity that not only confirms the existence of procedural safeguards but also suggests strongly the basic trustworthiness of any confession or statements given during an interrogation.

Witnesses are audiotaped as a routine and integral part of interviewing. It is a casual process to which witnesses usually do not object.

VIDEOTAPING OF SUSPECTS

The videotaping of suspects is a natural outcome of the availability of video cameras and television sets. Originally used primarily to reveal the conduct of persons arrested for driving while intoxicated, the videotaping of suspects in homicides and other serious crimes is becoming more and more popular— thousands of law enforcement agencies videotape interrogations and confessions of major-crime suspects. Usually the video camera is out in the open and the suspect is informed of the planned taping. Covert videotaping, to date, is restricted to various "sting" operations or general surveillance.

It is likely that videotaping will foster many pleas of guilty, and be more compelling than written statements or verbal testimony. In New York's Central Park "wilding" case (a gang of youths running wild in the park who were accused of assault, rape, and attempted murder), the videotapes of the defendants and their questioning were compelling evidence in court. In addition, it is likely that suspects will not be questioned as vigorously as in the past; after all, the videotape is a graphic portrayal of the interrogation.

To gain the maximum integrity for this technique, the camera should be turned on when the suspect is read his or her Miranda rights and not turned off until the session is completed. This start-to-finish rule is better than any partial taping, which is wide open to challenge by defense attorneys.

Interrogators must also remember that their conduct and questions are all part of the videotape. In a recent California case of the prosecution of a caregiver for physical child abuse resulting in the death of the child, the videotape of the defendant's questioning may have had a negative impact on the jury, as the interrogator did not inform the suspect that he was a homicide detective, that the child was not injured but dead, that the suspect was about to be arrested for murder-one homicide. All of this left open the possibility that the suspect was tricked into responding to questions.

This is an emerging area of expertise in criminal investigation. It should reveal guilt if present, and it will reveal misconduct by the interrogator if also present on the tape. It is certainly an area worthy of *Miranda* in all of its protections.

Videotaping of witnesses is not yet common, but the cost/benefit as compared to audiotape favors its use, and it is likely to soon become common practice.

THE OFFENSIVE–DEFENSIVE SITUATION— INTERROGATION

Investigators do not focus investigations on persons who have reasonable explanations for incriminating evidence. These individuals usually are cleared in the early stages of an investigation. The persons interrogated are individuals upon whom the investigation has focused. The basis of the offensive–defensive roles in an interrogation is that the interrogator has one or more items of evidence *against* the suspect before an interrogation. He or she attempts to exploit this evidence. The innocent as well as the guilty suspect is defensive, aware he or she is in the presence of an unfriendly questioner.

The investigative situation itself accounts for the growth of this offensive–defensive technique. A person would be a poor investigator if he or she did not become personally involved in unraveling the event under investigation. Two opponents are moving toward one another on a collision course— one the accuser, the other the accused. The interrogation is a face-to-face confrontation. If a confession is secured, all the tensions and concern about the reconstruction of the crime and the stresses of personal involvement are relieved. The interrogator and the suspect are no longer opponents. Taking the statement in the postinterrogation period is often a friendly and informal interview. A confession is a pseudo-approval of the work of the investigator. Diligence, hard work, and expertise will focus an investigation against a suspect, but an investigator is always very happy to receive a suspect's approval of a job well done.

THE SUSPECT'S DILEMMA: THE CRIME PARTNER

The suspect has a problem when he or she committed the crime with a partner, an accomplice. The suspect must decide whether to sacrifice a crime partner for some mitigation of the suspect's involvement in the crime—and must make the decision before the crime partner does. This dilemma is often referred to as simply *Better him than me.*

Advising a person being interrogated that a crime partner has talked is a practice that may taint an interrogation, if done to persuade a suspect to waive his or her right to remain silent. If done honestly, it can—at times— be an effective technique. The offensive–defensive situation of an interrogation session is replete with covert communication. The threatening aspect of the experience may be perceived with little outward awareness, but subliminally there is a strong anxiety response on the part of the person being interrogated. There is no need for comment by the interrogator; the worry and concern about whether a crime partner has talked is a natural form of anxiety. Many offenders assume that their partner has talked or is about to talk, and the only smart thing to do is to talk first, or better—to spill everything.

Interrogators should be alert to situations in which the person about to be interrogated is a professional criminal with an amateur crime partner. It may be the "torch" of an arson ring, it may be the hired killer of a heavily insured partner in commerce or industry, or it may be the burglar and thief with a businessperson receiver, who buys all the thief can steal. In any event these pros apparently look upon this relationship in crime as future insurance in the event of arrest, rather than a dilemma.

NONVERBAL COMMUNICATIONS

The ability to "read" the body movements of a suspect has been a long-sought-after goal of police interrogators. Some interrogators place great faith in noting whether a suspect under interrogation is perspiring, or makes sudden body movements when asked critical questions However, the unreliability of such visual assessment of conduct has relegated nonverbal communications to no more than a clue or "signal" status.

In the social interchange between individuals there is no doubt that anger, hate, love, and other milder emotions can be assessed visually, but these interchanges lack the threatening atmosphere of police interrogation. Therefore, the body language that is "spoken" during an interrogation may not be a signal of guilt or guilty knowledge, but a reaction to the police environment and a threatening situation.

Micromomentaries is a term for micromomentary facial expressions that happen when a person lies or otherwise avoids the truth. Researchers in human behavior have developed some evidence that rapid eye movements and split-second facial twinges indicate deception. Again, a shifty-eyed person may only be responding to the police questioning and not to any feelings of guilt, and a tendency of a facial "tic" under any emotional pressure will ruin micromomentaries as an indication of deception. On the other hand, individuals with a hearing problem often become rudimentary lip-readers in order to gain clues to words and phrases of a conversation they do not fully hear; and experience in interrogation no doubt will enable police interrogators to develop rudimentary skills in understanding the meaning of rapid facial movements of a suspect during an interrogation.

Nonverbal communication can become a valuable investigative aid because it reveals what is otherwise hidden. Body and facial language has been used by trial attorneys, together with other techniques, in jury selection. However, the likelihood of any technique of "reading" nonverbal communications becoming more than an investigative aid is slight. Courts that reject polygraph examination results will be even more reluctant to accept any testimony about body language as an indication of a person's credibility.

Selected References

1. ROBERT L. KAHN AND CHARLES F. CONNELL, *The Dynamics of Interviewing* (New York: John Wiley & Sons, 1957), pp. 45–46.
2. *Ibid.,* pp. 46–47.
3. State v. Driver, 38 N.J. 255 (1962).

Chapter Review

Discussion Questions

1. What has been the impact of the U.S. Supreme Court's *Miranda* decision upon criminal investigation? What are its future implications?
2. Is the offensive–defensive situation common to all interrogations?
3. Explain the similarities and differences between interviewing witnesses and interrogating suspects.
4. Is it likely a case would cease being a general inquiry into the circumstances of a crime when a person is taken into custody and questioned by police as a suspect?
5. Describe the *Miranda* warning. What are its related procedural safeguards?
6. What is meant by affirmative evidence?
7. Explain the legal significance of the nonsuggestive structure of interviewing witnesses to crime.
8. When a witness is not interviewed at a crime scene or during a canvass of a neighborhood, what are the primary factors to be considered in selecting the place of the interview?
9. Discuss an investigator's problem when two witnesses tell conflicting stories of the same event.
10. Why is it necessary to record the fact that a statement was not taken when it normally would have been taken?
11. Discuss the problem of motivation in regard to witnesses. What is extrinsic motivation? Intrinsic? What personal characteristics of an investigator lead to trust and confidence?

Library Assignment

Review the available literature on constitutional law in the area of police interrogation and confessions. Prepare a list of U.S. Supreme Court cases, with appropriate citations, that traces the body of case law known as the confession cases.

Workbook Project

Prepare an outline of the introductory segment of an interrogation that could serve as a guideline for your opening of an interrogation session with any suspect or accused person.

CHAPTER
10

Snitches and Other Informants

Revealing other people's secrets is snitching. In the world of crime and criminals, snitching is a social felony. It is treachery in the underworld when a crime partner reveals his or her associates to police investigators and becomes a prosecution witness at subsequent court proceedings.

Words long used to describe individuals who "inform" to police are denigrating. They tend to disparage the character and/or reputation of the informer: snitch, tipster, stool, stool pigeon, rat, canary. More recently, police investigators employ "informant" as a generalized—and euphemistic—term.

Anyone can be used as an informant. Most informants can testify in a criminal trial as long as they are acceptable as witnesses and their testimony meets the rules of admissibility.

Informants generally wish to remain anonymous. They particularly want to avoid the public identification inherent in becoming a witness for the prosecution. There is a lifesaving need to conceal the identity of informers or to protect them from attack once their identity is disclosed, for professional criminals are not unwilling to kill or maim informants. Concealment of cooperation is difficult because criminals use every available source to learn the identity of informants.

The use of informants is a questionable option in criminal investigation, as the investigator relinquishes his or her basic role and seeks the help of criminals and/or persons associating with criminals. Even noncriminal informants are often less objective than claimed. Some of the more common motivations for snitching are less than benevolent: hatred, revenge, jealousy, greed.

Informing is a dirty business because informants may lie to implicate innocent persons or to exculpate a favored crime partner. Inherent in some forms of snitching is that the snitch trades his or her version of what happened during a crime for immunity to prosecution, a reduced charge, or leniency at the time of sentencing.

It is also a dirty business because it brings investigators into close contact with individuals who are street-smart and have low thresholds to ethical, moral, and criminal misconduct. The attempt to corrupt an investigator may begin with pleas for a "license" to operate so-called minor illegal scams (illegal gambling, after-hours or unlicensed beer and whiskey establishments, pimping, receiving stolen property, low-weight drug sales). Later, or even initially, the pressure is to recruit the investigator as a crime partner. In New York, two general-assignment detectives were corrupted by an informant who used the detectives' unwise social contacts with him to corrupt them and turn the wife of one into a prostitute, and both detectives into willing accomplices in selling seized drugs back to drug dealers. In Alabama, a state narcotics agent was charged with murder, along with his snitch of several years, for the killing of the informant's wife in an insurance fraud case. In Miami, a drug rip-off and murder ring of rogue police officers is likely to have had its beginnings in the corrupt influence of an informant.

It is a dirty business because retaliation for snitching is often violent and fatal. Abe Reles, one of a murder-for-hire gang in New York City, talked about his associates and their killings because a politically ambitious prosecutor promised him immunity for his own role as a killer. For six months Abe appeared in court and testified against several of his crime partners indicted for murder. Then, late one night, a mob hit team entered his sixth-floor hotel room, avoided his police bodyguards, and threw Abe out of the window. He died from injuries sustained in the fall. Mobsters throughout the city gleefully described the dead man as "the canary who could sing but couldn't fly!"

Noncriminal informant Arnold Schuster identified a new neighbor as Willie Sutton, a notorious bank robber and most-wanted fugitive. Police promptly arrested Sutton and paraded Schuster on television as an example of a good and dutiful citizen who informed police of Sutton's identity and whereabouts. Several days later, Schuster was shot to death by a local hoodlum who denied knowing either the victim or Willie Sutton; he claimed his only motivation was a generalized dislike of snitches.

To counteract the foregoing problems in using informants, investigators must verify any information received, maintain a nonsocial relationship with them, and keep secret the informant's identity unless it is vital to the prosecution's case that the informant become a witness or a trial court orders disclosure of his or her identity. Ideally, the function of an informant is investigative only, and, hopefully, compelling evidence of a defendant's guilt can be obtained from other sources.[1]

Despite the genuine concern of many investigators about the use of informants, there is no doubt that they are in common use by investigators throughout the United States at federal, state, and local levels. The aid of informants is generally sought in four major areas:

1. To uncover primary or secondary basic leads.
2. To initiate the ritual of "making buys" to justify the arrest of drug dealers.
3. To gain up-to-date information on the operations of a terrorist or other criminal group.
4. To provide meaningful evidence in a pending trial (see Figure 10–1).

BASIC-LEAD INFORMANTS

Informants are a traditional starting point in seeking basic leads. In fact, informants sometimes offer data about an unreported or undiscovered crime or one in its planning stages.

The successful use of basic-lead informants is a complex combination of an alert and knowledgeable investigator knowing where to seek information, finding the contacts having it, and probing and prying to gather as much meaningful information as possible.

This type of informant is motivated to divulge information to a police investigator for a multitude of reasons. He or she may have encountered it by chance or wants to do a citizen's duty by divulging it. Or criminals may provide information to get rid of a competitor—a common practice in the fields of gambling and prostitution and not uncommon among thieves and receivers of stolen property. Jealousy and revenge sometimes motivate such informants. The "woman scorned" has done great harm to the victims of her fury by informing about their criminal activities.

Former girlfriends and wives often serve as unpaid informants. In the world of crime, the women friends of criminals often fear them with some jus-

FIGURE 10–1 The informant network in criminal investigation.

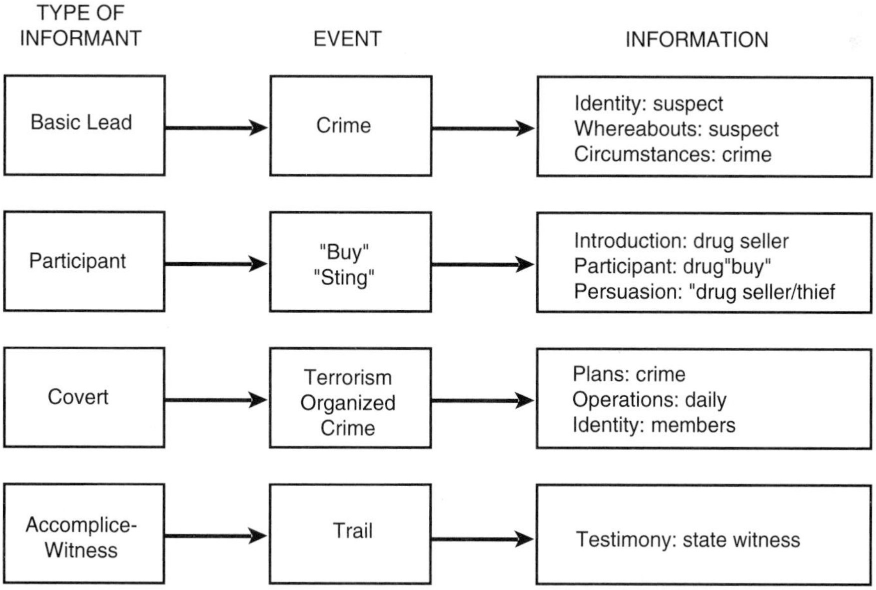

TYPE OF INFORMANT	EVENT	INFORMATION
Basic Lead	Crime	Identity: suspect Whereabouts: suspect Circumstances: crime
Participant	"Buy" "Sting"	Introduction: drug seller Participant: drug"buy" Persuasion: "drug seller/thief
Covert	Terrorism Organized Crime	Plans: crime Operations: daily Identity: members
Accomplice-Witness	Trail	Testimony: state witness

tification. A frightened and knowledgeable ex-girlfriend or ex-wife, in self-defense, has often allied herself with police efforts and delivered vital information about the criminal activities of the ex-boyfriend or ex-husband.

Other informants seek pay for information leading to arrests. Investigators with unsolved jewelry thefts, suspicious fires, and homicide cases often are contacted by such informants proposing to supply information. Recently released prison inmates may be confronted with the choice of going back into crime or "earning" money, and they know of this resource. They often sell information as a stopgap livelihood until they find employment or return to crime.

"Secret Witness" programs of local news media in many areas are an innovative way of paying informants for basic leads. Cooperating business firms contribute to an "informant" fund; local police request publicity about most-serious crimes or those without substantial leads. The news medium involved publishes the details of the crime and specifies the amount of the reward (varies by nature of crime). Inherent in these programs is a means by which informants can contact local police investigators without revealing their identity, by providing a code word or number that will substantiate their claim to the reward. Rewards are paid when police have verified the information and found it meaningful and useful in the identification of a suspect, in learning the whereabouts of a known suspect, or in discovering what happened at the time of the crime.

PARTICIPANT INFORMANTS

The role of the participant informant in enforcing the law against illegal drug sales is that of go-between: to identify the drug seller and to introduce the undercover investigator as a potential buyer, or to "instigate" the transaction in some fashion.[2]

Participant informants are workers who participate directly in gathering sufficient evidence to warrant an arrest. One type of participant informant is the *special employee.* He or she is paid a fee set in advance for this work. A special employee may be hired because of his or her knowledge of the local drug scene, friendships among local drug sellers and users, or the ability to deceive suspects as to his or her role.

Another type of participant informant on the drug scene is the arrestee who has been "turned" or "flipped" by the arresting officer. The anatomy of this procedure is that the arrest is on a minor charge of possessing and/or selling illegal drugs, and the arresting officer can persuade the arrestee to cooperate in identifying his or her source of supply of drugs: in effect, a more important arrest in return for some consideration by police, prosecutor, or court because of the informant's cooperation.

At one time, this was an informal procedure, but current procedure usually requires discussion with the prosecutor and approval of the "deal" by this official. Often, a formal plea bargain is entered into between the prosecution and the defendant and his or her legal counsel.

Participant informants may be used by an investigator in solving crimes other than those involving the sale of illegal drugs. A few of these informants have been used as shills in police "sting" operations aimed at discovering burglars and thieves and recovering stolen property. This role requires the informant to sell property to the police "buyers" in order to lure real burglars and thieves to do likewise.

The Federal Bureau of Investigation (FBI) used a participant informant to uncover political corruption in Chicago. The informant's role was to lure politicians to meetings where payoffs could be videotaped by FBI agents.[3]

The FBI's ABSCAM investigation pioneered this videotaping of public officials accepting bribes. The name derives from the original cover story about the informant's relationship to a group of wealthy Arabs owning "Abdul Enterprises Unlimited." In the ABSCAM prosecutions a U.S. senator, six U.S. Congress members, several local public officials in Pennsylvania and New Jersey, and numerous associates were found guilty. These verdicts were decided despite defense claims of unfairness and entrapment in this cash-for-political-favors "scam." The videotapes presented to the juries in these trials apparently convinced them that the government's action was not unfair, unscrupulous, or unethical.[4]

COVERT INFORMANTS

Covert informants are not classified as persons who assist in developing basic leads in a criminal investigation, nor do they serve the "instigator" role of participant informants. They are men and women who report to a police investigator information about a terrorist or other criminal organization from a position of trust and confidence within the group. These agents-in-place are known as "moles" in the area of international espionage, as they are often "buried" for years prior to being activated.

This person may or may not be remunerated for this work. He or she is not used for spot intelligence. The use of such persons is akin to the practice of having spies in the enemy's camp. These agents-in-place are a spin-off from military and international intelligence.[5] They can provide information over a lengthy period as long as their identity is protected. Such individuals must be developed fully, cultivated over a long period, and used only when absolutely necessary. These sources of information are not developed solely to provide information for current investigations, but can be set up to provide information at a future time.

The ever-widening organized crime syndicate and hate extremist groups are sites for agents-in-place. Homicides are frequent among hate groups, and organized crime is constantly expanding its operations. The hoodlums and extremists are an ever-present threat. When there is a need for information, after-the-fact intelligence operations are useless with either of these groups.

A man or woman may be established within the terrorists or crime group when they begin cooperating with an investigator. On the other hand, the investigator may recruit a person who he or she believes trustworthy and capable, and suggest a means by which the new covert informant can infiltrate the target organization.

A Canadian woman, a member of the *Front de Libération du Québec (FLQ)*, went to the Montreal police to avoid involvement in an armed robbery planned by members of this terrorist group. She was promptly recruited as a covert informant. She was an excellent source of information for several months as she was never suspected of being an informant by any of her terrorist associates. Her police "contacts" avoided disclosing her identity until the day she appeared in open court as a witness.[6]

Most terrorist groups have established high thresholds to any penetration by informants; new members are always greeted with suspicion and distrust. Therefore, in seeking a productive informant, investigators should make every effort to cultivate and recruit as an informant a person who has been an active member of the group for some time.[7]

The "family" aspect of organized crime groups, regardless of its ethnic nature, is a real handicap to infiltrating an informant as a new member. However, the need for covert informants in these groups has diminished in recent years because of the success of prosecutors in "turning" or "flipping" accomplice–witnesses.

THE ACCOMPLICE–WITNESS

An accomplice–witness is a person who is liable to prosecution for the identical offense charged against the defendant or defendants in a pending trial. He or she has been arrested along with one or more crime partners, and the police–prosecutor team offers leniency in return for his or her cooperation. Accomplice–witnesses testify for the prosecution, identifying the defendant or defendants and testifying to acts done by them in furtherance of the crime.

Some prosecutors develop compelling evidence of guilt on the part of one person in a criminal operation, bring them to the prosecutor's office for a briefing on this evidence, and offer the alternative of (1) arrest, conviction, and prison; or (2) cooperation, a bargained plea to a lesser charge, and a "walk."

A special state prosecutor in New York broke a complex case involving many police officers by confronting two of the police suspects with compelling evidence of guilt. Facing prison for their own crimes, these two officers *flipped* and agreed to inform on their co-workers in exchange for their own freedom. While "wired for sound," they continued their criminal activities (ripping off drug dealers primarily) while secretly recording and incriminating their colleagues in crime.[8]

Recruiting a defendant in an organized crime case begins with a reiteration of the theme "every man for himself." Once the witness seeks more information, the standard "package" deal is detailed.

1. In return for full cooperation, the witness will be given partial or full immunity.

2. After testimony is completed, the witness will be accepted in a witness-protection plan (federal/state) which will furnish the witness with a new identity, funds, and assistance in relocating the witness and his or her family, and security measures sufficient to conceal his or her where-abouts.

When a pending case does not involve organized crime members, the accomplice–witness does not usually need the protection afforded by a witness protection plan, and the prosecutor offers the potential informant only immunity or partial immunity. In a widespread diamond fraud case involving no less than $5,500,000, the mastermind (Irwin Margolies) ordered two of his crime partners killed (his accountant and her assistant). After the contract killer in this case was sentenced to over 100 years in prison for these two homicides plus the wanton killing of three accidental witnesses to the murder of the accountant, the prosecutor was determined to indict Margolies for murder. All the evidence secured by hard-working police investigators, however, was circumstantial. Rather than allow the mastermind to avoid trial and conviction, the prosecutor offered a co-conspirator in both the fraud and the murders a "deal": He would be named in future indictments in the conspiracy to murder unless he freely told all he knew and agreed to testify against Margolies in any future trial. If he did cooperate, he would be granted immunity from prosecution. He did talk; Margolies was convicted of murder, primarily on the testimony of the accomplice–witness that he brought Margolies and the "shooter" together and was a party to the murder "contract."[9]

CONTROLLING THE INVESTIGATOR/INFORMANT RELATIONSHIP

Official controls of the investigator/informant relationship are now common in most police departments. Early on, these rules did no more than forbid social contacts between an investigator (and his or her family) and an informant, and warn investigators to be alert for criminal misconduct by the informant and to take measures to prevent it.

Extensions of these control measures have been established primarily to protect the integrity of the investigator and the ongoing investigation, and the reputation of the police unit. These controls now call for bringing informants "out of the closet" through a registration procedure in which the real and code names of the informant, and other meaningful data, are placed in the confidential records of the police department. In addition, investigators cannot utilize informants until they are registered and approved by the investigator's superior or higher authority; and disciplinary action is threatened against any investigator who uses an unregistered and unapproved informant.

Acceptance or rejection of a proposed informant may be because he or she is in a "wanted" status, on parole, under the age of 18 (usual minimum), or has a past "unsatisfactory" record as a registered informant.

Disapproval need not have an objective basis. It may be based on the decision maker's own experience and professional insight.

The superior officer of an investigation unit responsible for these yes/no decisions should reject a proposed informant if he or she has a criminal record and there is reason to believe that the proposed informant will (1) commit crimes while working with assigned investigators, and/or (2) attempt to corrupt police associates.

If an investigator's request to register an informant is approved, he or she is usually designated as the "contact" person to manage and supervise the informant. An alternate contact person from the same investigative unit as the requesting investigator is also designated at this time to serve as necessary. When a uniformed officer recruits an informant, this officer may be designated as contact person or alternate.

Investigators designated as contact persons or alternates will make whatever arrangements are necessary to keep in touch with the informant. The practice of giving an informant the residence telephone number of the investigator is not recommended. All communications should be through an on-duty investigator or directly to the contact investigator or alternate. Codes can be arranged to guard the identity of the informant on these calls. Any mail contact should also be conducted in a prearranged code. Similarly, meetings should be carefully discussed with the informant as to places and times, so that no one knowing the investigator and/or informant might chance on them. A good safeguard is to have a backup cover story in case persons observe the meeting who are likely to disclose it. This is a story the informant can use to justify meeting the investigator.

Registration of an informant begins with a written request of an investigator to his or her commanding officer. This request is expected to contain the name of the informant, aliases, criminal history, and an overview of how the informant can be utilized in an ongoing or future investigation.

Upon approval of an informant, his or her registration file should contain the foregoing request for services and other data, such as:

1. Copies of criminal record, if any.
2. A current photograph.
3. A summary of any prior use of informant, locally or elsewhere.
4. Records (and receipts) of payments to informant.
5. Records of all meetings with informant.
6. Records of all work by informant (introductions, caused arrests, useful information).
7. Arrests of informant while registered.
8. Code name assigned.
9. Signature of informant (both real and code names).
10. Name and assignment of contact person and alternate.
11. Prior disapprovals and comment, if any.

Necessary precautions to protect the integrity and confidentiality of these informant-registry files must have the highest priority of police managers. Access should be on a need-to-know basis only, and approval or disapproval of access requests should be the responsibility of the superior officer in charge of such files. In addition, all department reports concerning registered informants should refer to them by code name only.

An interesting aspect of a central registry of informants is that snitches no longer are the exclusive property of any one investigator. Any investigator should be able to obtain the services of a registered informant by filing a written request citing the general thrust of an ongoing investigation and the type of informant sought. In the event a scanning of the registered-informant files by the officer responsible for them reveals a possible match-up, the investigator will be informed and arrangements made for a discussion between him or her and the informant's contact person.

Older investigators, habituated to concealing an informant's identity from their closest co-workers and never inclined to share an informant and his or her information with anyone, may resent these new rules—as well as the basic concept that higher authority in the investigative unit has a vested interest in examining the character and reputation of a proposed informant and deciding whether or not it is in the best interest of all concerned to utilize this individual as an informant.

It is a new discipline for investigators, but a procedure that protects all parties involved. The opening up of this relationship to any kind of official scrutiny is certainly preferable to the former hush-hush arrangements.

DISCLOSURE

Unfortunately, the disclosure of the identity of informants is sometimes necessary to ensure a fair trial for the defendant. The requirement of a fair trial is balanced against the viewpoint that anonymity of the informant is the only effective method of preserving the informant system and of protecting informants. The disclosure of the identity of an informant at trial or in pretrial proceedings depends on the relationship of the informant to the guilt or innocence of the accused. Disclosure may be sought by defense counsel for a number of reasons:

1. To gain a tactical advantage by seeking dismissal of the charge rather than disclosure.
2. To test the actual existence of the informant.
3. To ascertain differences between the informant's information and the story of the police witness.
4. To determine the reliability of the informant.
5. To obtain the testimony of an informant–participant who is a principal witness to the offense charged against the defendant.

There are jurisdictions requiring the police or prosecutor to make reasonable arrangements for the production of informants who are material witnesses to the guilt or innocence of the defendant. This duty falls on an investigator at the time that he or she can reasonably be expected to know of the informant's materiality to the issue of guilt or innocence.

The identity of an informant need not be disclosed when the question is whether there was probable cause for an arrest or a search, rather than the fundamental issue of guilt or innocence. When it appears that law enforcement officers making the search or arrest relied on facts supplied by an informant they had reason to trust, there is no constitutional requirement that the informant's identity be disclosed at any preliminary hearing.

This is the doctrine of *McCray* v. *Illinois*, 386 U.S. 300 (1967). In this case, the two officers making a warrantless arrest on information supplied by an informant testified, in open court, fully and in detail as to what the informant had told them about the defendant and as to why they had reason to believe that the informant was reliable and his information was trustworthy. Both officers were under oath, each withstood a searching cross-examination, and the presiding judge was obviously satisfied that truthful statements were made by each officer.

The best safeguard against being forced to disclose fully the source of information received from an informant is to base the justification for action on the investigator's own independent inquiries after hearing from the informant.

JAILHOUSE INFORMANTS

A jailhouse informant is an inmate of a local jail who offers to testify for the prosecution against a fellow inmate either currently on trial or whose trial is pending. The claim by the informant is that the inmate–defendant confessed the crime or made guilty-knowledge admissions to him or her while both were in the jail. The expected reward for this public-service cooperation is one or more favors, generally some form of meaningful leniency in the informant's pending trial or sentence.

There is no doubt that many innocent defendants have been convicted by the false testimony of jailhouse informants intent on the reward to be granted by the prosecutor. Of course, many of these prosecutors acted in good faith; some accepted the offer because their case needed this compelling testimony, and some may have actively sought this help.

One informant publicly admitted several such perjured-testimony events, saying he used the jail telephone to gather information about a fellow inmate awaiting trial (posing as a law enforcement agent), and then composed a fairly credible confession: "as told to me." Investigators found that this informant testified in more than one trial and received rewards from each court upon the in-court request of a prosecutor.

Investigators in law enforcement agencies may encounter a jailhouse informant from contacts during a prior case, referral by another inmate, or pure chance. Infrequently, a prosecutor may ask for a check on the informant's reliability and credibility.

The role of an investigator is to gauge an informant's credibility as a witness and reliability as a person. The credibility factor should be scanned as it would be for any witness: (1) possibility of jail contacts with defendant–inmate, (2) privacy of contacts, (3) level of friendship developed, (4) the "how come" factor—why were the confession and admissions made to the informant, and (5) how the facts in the alleged confession jibe with the known facts of the crime concerned. It is difficult to determine the reliability of a jail inmate awaiting his or her own trial or sentence, possibly a career criminal. However, an index of past performances can reveal how often the informant has sought this role, been accepted or rejected, and what favor(s) were attained because of past testimony.

The core area of this report should alert prosecutors to informants who may have fabricated the alleged confession or admissions and who have served in this role—or sought it—on previous occasions.

Selected References

1. LARRY C. RISSLER, "The Informer-Witness," *FBI Law Enforcement Bulletin,* XLVI, No. 5 (May 1977), pp. 29–31.
2. JAMES Q. WILSON, *The Investigators—Managing FBI and Narcotics Agents* (New York: Basic Books, Publishers, 1978), p. 62.
3. IRA ROSEN, Wheeler, Dealer, Squealer, "60 Minutes" transcript, March 6, 1988, pp. 5–9.
4. IRVIN B. NATHAN, "ABSCAM: A Fair and Effective Method of Fighting Public Corruption" in *ABSCAM Ethics: Moral Issues and Deception in Law Enforcement* (Washington, D.C.: The Police Foundation, 1983), pp. 1–16.
5. THOMAS WHITESIDE, *An Agent in Place: The Wennestrom Affair* (New York: The Viking Press, 1966), p. 150.
6. CAROLE DE VAULT (with William Johnson), *The Informer—Confessions of an Ex-terrorist* (Toronto: Fleet Books, 1982), pp. 115–44.
7. JAMES M. POLAND, *Understanding Terrorism—Groups, Strategies, and Responses* (Englewood Cliffs, N.J.: Prentice Hall, 1988), p. 196.
8. MIKE McALARY, *Buddy Boys—When Good Cops Turn Bad* (New York: The Putnam Publishing Group, 1987), pp. 25–37.
9. RICHARD HAMMER, *The CBS Murders* (New York: William Morrow & Company, 1987), pp. 215–20.

Chapter Review

Discussion Questions

1. Define a basic-lead informant.
2. What are the major roles of participant–informants?
3. What basic factors should be considered in whether or not to approve a proposed informant?
4. How does the role of accomplice–witness differ from that of covert informant?
5. What precautions should be taken by investigators designated as "contact" persons in order to protect an assigned informant?
6. Discuss the basic reasons for court-ordered disclosure of an informant's identity.

Library Assignment

Update bibliographic references to informants and their use in criminal investigation.

Workshop Project

Interview and poll from five to ten of your friends or fellow students as to their attitudes concerning the use of informants in criminal investigation.

Discovering the Hidden and Unknown

Identifying a suspect with compelling evidence of guilt often goes beyond hours of making inquiries and miles of footwork and driving. The combination of an eyewitness, a suspect, and a police lineup may achieve this goal.

Monitoring the activities of a subject by ordinary observation can be supplemented by videotaping, court-ordered wiretaps, and fluorescent chemicals and can reveal contacts and actions of great importance to an ongoing investigation—even when the suspect is aware of (or fears) a police interest. Patience is essential in this area, but on occasion a suspect is not as cautious as he or she should be and the investigator is able to unearth a valuable piece of information as a result.

The "lie box" capability to defeat a suspect's own nervous system has been known for years, but now that its use is supplemented by a computer that can monitor responses and software that aids the decision making of the polygraph examiner, it has great promise in disclosing guilt or guilty knowledge.

Investigators assigned to covertly scan the activities of the known criminals of organized crime often are not the arresting officers; but when homicides occur, the information these investigators can provide their associates will lead to arrests.

Undercover police agents assume a similar role. Seeking information in this manner can be life-threatening to agents; nevertheless, facts gathered in this way become solid evidence when the agent testifies in court.

The method of last resort used by investigators who cannot acquire the facts they need is investigative hypnosis. This has long been a temptation of detectives who are hopelessly roadblocked by a witness who cannot recall some aspect vital to a case. However, its use became questionable over time. Hypnosis is likely to reemerge, in a better-structured framework that follows professional procedures.

LINEUPS

The solution of a crime may rest on the identification of a suspect in custody. The lineup has been the traditional identification procedure used to focus a case against a suspect when eyewitnesses were available, but this process has an inherent evil of suggestibility that has now been legally recognized. The post-indictment lineup has been cited as a *critical stage* of the pretrial period in which the suspect is entitled to legal counsel. (*U.S.* v. *Wade,* 388 U.S. 218 (1967).

The major objective of placing a suspect in a lineup with other persons for viewing and possible identification by an eyewitness, or several such witnesses, is to make certain the suspect is the perpetrator of the crime. The witnesses are asked: "Is any of them the man (or woman) who committed the crime?"

A lineup format is common throughout the country. From four to six persons are utilized. They are allowed to select their position; then they are placed in line under a numeral against a wall marked to indicate clearly their height in feet and inches. A record is made of their descriptions and physical characteristics. They should be photographed for the record, in color, if possible. Viewing may be under lights, with the witnesses out of view of the persons lined up for identification. Many police units have installed complex dimmer switches to permit a simulation of the light conditions at the time of the crime. The individuals lined up may be asked to speak for identification; and in some cases they are asked to put on various items of clothing. The witness or witnesses viewing the lineup may be requested to prepare and sign a statement, noting whether they could make an identification.

There is a grave potential for prejudice, intentional or not, in the pretrial lineup. Investigators in the United States are now aware of this fact and are beginning to understand why this identification technique has required the presence of friends or legal counsel in many foreign countries. In England the suspect must be allowed the presence of a solicitor or friend. In Germany a retained counsel must be present. In France there can be no confrontation of the suspect with any witness in the absence of counsel.

Eyewitnesses have been destroyed on cross-examination in the trial of an offender because of substandard investigative procedures in arranging an identity lineup. Contentions of the abuse of the integrity of a lineup can be overborne by the testimony of the eyewitness, the investigator, and police officers present at the time.

It is difficult to defend a lineup when an eyewitness is asked to view an injured person in a hospital bed. When a witness is told that the culprit has been apprehended and the hospital bed is guarded by a uniformed police officer, it is a difficult situation to justify; but when police use professional care in the arrangements, a hospital-bed identification may be justified.

It has been suggested that the presence of legal counsel at such lineups would avert prejudice of any kind and assure a meaningful confrontation at trial. This concept has persuaded the U.S. Supreme Court to determine that the lineup is a *critical stage* of the proceedings against the defendant and that he or she has a right to counsel at such lineups. In 1972, the Court modified its position regarding lineups by specifying that the provisions of the *Wade* decision applied only to indicted defendants.

Many investigators believe the presence of legal counsel at a lineup impedes legitimate inquiry. However, if the presence of counsel prevents the taint of an improper lineup from affecting the eyewitness testimony upon trial, then his or her presence actually is an aid to the investigator. The attorney cannot interfere with the witnesses; they view the lineup and make or do not make their identification without help or hindrance from such legal counsel. The attorney's presence can bring the identity evidence into court without taint and strengthen the testimony of the prosecution's eyewitness.

Defense counsel are divided on what their duty is in the lineup procedure. Some feel this role should be passive. However, most of them see their role as a new and active one. If they do not actively seek a fair lineup they will be in a poor position to complain about it at the trial or upon appeal. A look at the type of action a defense counsel might take during the course of a lineup will alert investigators to possible problem areas.

Basically, a defense counsel proceeds under the following theory: Miscarriages of justice are related to the degree of suggestion inherent in the manner in which the prosecution presents the suspect to the witness for pretrial identification.

Defense counsel will request an interview with the accused prior to the lineup. At such interview he or she obtains an overview of the defendant's involvement by asking the circumstances of the arrest, whether any witnesses have seen him or her since arrest and prior to the lineup, and what statement has been made to the police. Counsel advises the accused of basic rights and answers questions the accused may ask regarding the future proceedings.

After talking to the accused, defense counsel should interview the investigating officer and request the names and addresses of the witnesses who are to view the lineup, information regarding the nature of the offense and the time and place of its commission, and whether the witness or witnesses have previously described the suspect (and if such description has been reported on an official police report), have been shown photographs of the accused, or have viewed the suspect since arrest but prior to the lineup.

Defense counsel will request that others in the lineup be of the same general age, build, and appearance as the accused. Counsel will note the physical procedure of the lineup, should request that a photograph be taken of the lineup viewed by each identification witness, and may suggest that the accused person be allowed to change positions after each witness has viewed the lineup. He or she will request a separate lineup for any other accused persons.

Counsel may object to any voice identification, but if overruled will insist that all persons in the lineup say the same words.

Counsel will insist upon being present when each witness views the lineup and says whether he or she does or does not identify any person there. Counsel also will note any comments made by the officer or investigator in front of the witnesses.

This new constructive role of defense counsel depends on the fairness of the procedure used in the particular police department. The presence of an attorney representing a suspect is not akin to the interrogation of suspects where an attorney representing a suspect is likely to advise a client not to talk at all or not to answer certain questions. An attorney in this bystander role should be welcomed and used by police to strengthen their identification procedures and thus strengthen their eyewitness case at trial by foreclosing the charge of unfairness or of suggestion heretofore often raised by defense counsel.

Case law has established five factors likely to establish the net worth of a witness identification of a suspect in a pretrial police lineup:

1. The opportunity of the witness to view the criminal at the time of the crime.
2. The witness's degree of attention.
3. The accuracy of the prior description of the criminal given to police by the witness.
4. The level of certainty demonstrated at the confrontation (lineup).
5. The time between the crime and the confrontation.*

SURVEILLANCE

Surveillance is observation of people and places by investigators to develop investigative leads. Often hidden, not just unobtrusive, it is a seeking for specific activity and significant information rather than a mere passive onlooking. Its basic objective is to bring an investigation into sharp focus by supplying detailed information about the activities of a person or place and about the associates of a person or the individuals who visit a place.

Visual Surveillance

Visual surveillance is nothing more than keeping a watch on a particular suspect, vehicle, or place. It may be aided by binoculars or a telescope or replaced by a photographic surveillance. The use of binoculars permits observation from a distance of two or three city blocks. A twenty-power telescope is effective at ten to fifteen city blocks. A robot camera can replace personnel manning a fixed surveillance. Infrared viewing devices permit observation in the dark.

*See Appendix A, Case Briefs, for digest of *Wade*.

A fixed surveillance, a *stakeout* or *plant,* is located within a building, if possible, the observations being made through available windows or doors. Panel trucks and campers have been converted to fixed observation posts using peepholes or curtained windows for viewing. Rooftops are excellent for a long-range surveillance; stores and hallways are suitable sites for short-range viewing. Sometimes long-term positions are possible; in some instances it is necessary to move frequently to avoid notice. The static quality of a fixed surveillance requires skilled judgment in selecting a rewarding area of observation. To be effective in scrutinizing a suspect's activities, the presence of the observing investigator must not be detected. For this reason a fixed observation post in a building is preferable because the investigator is not only concealed but through a rental arrangement has the rights of a resident or tenant.

Some investigators, because of their height, size, race, or national origin, may have difficulty blending into certain environments as residents or tenants. In fact, several well-hidden fixed surveillances in apartments have been compromised by the appearance of the investigator entering the premises. In the *de facto* segregated ghetto areas of urban centers across the country, an investigator not conforming to the appearance of the residents or tenants is certain to be suspect.

A moving surveillance, a tail or shadow, may be on foot, in a vehicle, or may use a combination of walking and riding. The suspect being followed is often alert and may take evasive action. Suspects "double door" the trailing investigator by entering a street-level shop and leaving by a rear, side, or basement entrance. They utilize the modern traffic system with its "platoons" of traffic and one-way streets to break contact or force the investigator too close to a point at which his or her presence can be noted by an alert suspect. It is difficult to supplement a moving surveillance optically, although camera equipment can be utilized. A moving surveillance is a dynamic technique in that it does not depend on the appearance of the suspect at a certain place; rather, it keeps the subject in view from place to place.

To avoid detection, a mobile surveillance often uses a two- or three-person surveillance team, with members rotating in the "close contact" position. This leapfrogging technique of following persons under surveillance is useful on foot or in vehicles. Its particular value is that the chance of detection by the suspect is diminished because the same person is not following the suspect continuously. The close contact position is behind the suspect, and an alert and anxious suspect will identify a person who is in this position for an extended period. With the leapfrogging technique the suspect just about makes an identification when a new member of the surveillance team or a new vehicle moves up into contact and the other team member drops back into a position well to the rear or across the street. All that is required of the personnel who drop back is to keep the contact position investigator in sight. When vehicles are used, such contact can be maintained by radio.

A device that electronically signals the location of automobiles, or other objects to which it is affixed, is known as a *bumper beeper.* Sophisticated receivers in the vehicle(s) of a mobile surveillance continually trace the otherwise silent signals emanating from the bumper beeper and locate the vehicle (or other object) under surveillance. These devices are particularly helpful during investigations of ongoing, conspiratorial criminal activities involving a high degree of organization (gambling, fraud, drug selling) and in which the person or persons under surveillance are likely to "make" (identify) one or more of the vehicles in a mobile surveillance if they follow the target car too closely.

Monitoring beeper signals from a radio transmitter that was placed in a container of chloroform has been held not to invade any legitimate expectation of privacy and not to constitute search or seizure under the Fourth Amendment. The U.S. Supreme Court's decision in *U.S.* v. *Knotts,* 75 L. Ed. 55 (1983), noted that the scientific enhancement of the beeper raised no constitutional issues that would not be raised by visual surveillance.

Investigators develop their own methods for blending with the surroundings on mobile surveillances. A device or technique suitable to one individual may draw attention to another. Appearances can be corrected to some extent. A change of clothing may suffice for one individual; another may use clothing to suggest a trade or service. Conduct and behavior can be coordinated with appearance to communicate some cover or excuse for being in a neighborhood. Carrying something is a common practice with some investigators adept at hiding their occupation, and it is true that most persons are not suspicious of a person carrying a bag of groceries or some similar load.

Vehicles used in mobile surveillances do not blend with surrounding traffic units if they are too distinctive in design or color. The number of occupants and the seating arrangement may also identify a vehicle to a suspect under surveillance, as will the design and position of headlights at night. Apparent changes in the number of occupants and their in-car positions are a defense against identification, as is driving without lights when safe, or using a vehicle with the capability to change the appearance of headlights.

Fortunately for investigators, most suspects are alert but anxious; they are on the lookout for a surveillance, but they really do not want to discover it. They want to know if the police are watching them, and yet they do not want to know it. This is the only possible explanation of heavy-footed mobile surveillances going undiscovered and fixed pickup posts operating for weeks unnoticed adjacent to the meeting places of known hoodlums and crime syndicate gangsters. At the Los Angeles International Airport, police intelligence unit personnel, federal agents, and state narcotics officers are frequently standing shoulder to shoulder among the throngs greeting incoming planes from Las Vegas, but the subjects of their observations never seem to notice the tail they pick up. One notorious hoodlum was so oblivious to this surveillance that he was apprehended in a minor shoplifting episode at the airport newsstand.

A combination of fixed and mobile surveillances (both on foot and by vehicle) has been found to be effective in on-the-scene apprehensions of criminals who have committed a series of crimes. The irrational fire-setter who sets several fires a night and who cannot be traced by normal investigative leads can be apprehended by isolating the area of suspicious and known incendiary fires and establishing extensive surveillances. Burglars and series rapists who enter residences and continue their operations until arrested also may be surprised in their operations by the technique of staking out an area.

The object of a surveillance is to collect information on the activities of a suspect, the persons in contact with him or her, and the places frequented. Therefore, the assigned investigator and associates must keep a running commentary, or log, of their observations. Notes are made in the field as the surveillance discloses associates of the suspects, cars used by the suspect and associates, and the ownership or reputation of places frequented. When surveillance is aligned with use of the investigator as a witness to what he or she observed, the surveillance investigator must personally verify vehicle registrations, identities of unknown persons in contact with the suspect, or data on premises or locations frequented by the suspect or others. With such a foundation the witness can show personal knowledge of the surveillance and the investigation that disclosed pertinent and related facts.

It should be noted that there is some limit on visual surveillance. In a federal court decision in 1968 the court said that without a valid warrant or reasonable cause, a person should be free from the eyes of the law while within the privacy of his or her own home. The action complained of was the peering into the defendant's window by stealth.

Audio Surveillance

Wiretapping and electronic eavesdropping are the primary forms of surveillance by listening. It is the observation technique that has been termed a "dirty business" by the U.S. Supreme Court and that is viewed with mixed emotions by law-abiding citizens, who apparently see it as the epitome of an unjustified and nondirective invasion of privacy.

The interception of telephone communication is a difficult surveillance to detect. Telephone wires lead from the instrument cable to a house cable, to an area cable, to a main cable, and to the "bays" of a central office. At each point a junction box containing an array of wires and binding posts facilitates the work of the telephone company's service personnel in providing service to subscribers. The wires of an individual telephone appear in terminal boxes and are identified by pair and cable numbers located at various points from the telephone instrument to the distant central office. A telephone tap easily can be hooked up at any of these locations. Equipment varies from the basic headset for monitoring intercepted conversations to an elaborate voice-activated automatic recorder and a device for recording the numbers dialed on outgoing calls (pen register).

Testimony is sometimes required on the mechanics of the interception—for example, how the wires used were selected as the wires of the telephone that was meant to be tapped. A common practice in dial-phone areas is to use a regular portable telephone instrument equipped with wire clips. The investigator hooks up to the selected wires, makes certain no one is using the line, and dials the subscriber's number. There is a distinctive sound of the busy signal without conversation on the line. In other areas an associate may have to call the subscriber and hold a "survey" conversation while the listener clips in and verifies the line by recognizing the associate's voice.

Years ago a record was kept at these listening posts by stenographers, and it was later transcribed in the same manner as court testimony is recorded and transcribed. Tape recording devices now permit direct recording of overheard conversations and offer a verbatim record for review.

Places or people may be wired for sound. This has been termed "bugging." When properly installed, the electronic equipment necessary for eavesdropping is almost as difficult to detect as wiretap connections and equipment. The pickup microphone may be wired directly to a tape recorder or it may broadcast the conversation by radio a short distance to a receiver located on the person of an investigator or in a nearby car or building.

Surreptitious or covert entry of private premises to install a microphone (bug) is in conflict with expectations of individual privacy. However, in a 1979 case, *Dalia* v. *United States,* 99 S. Ct. 1682, the U.S. Supreme Court stated: "We find no basis for a constitutional rule proscribing all covert entries. It is well established that law officers constitutionally may break and enter to execute a search warrant where such entry is the only means by which the warrant effectively may be executed."

The facts of *Dalia* are that the U.S. District Court authorized the interception of specified oral communications at a particular location in compliance with Title III of the Omnibus Crime Control and Safe Streets Acts of 1958. Dalia was convicted of receiving stolen goods and conspiring to transport, receive, and possess stolen goods. At a hearing on petitioner Dalia's motion to suppress evidence obtained under the "bugging" order, it was shown that the order did not explicitly authorize entry of petitioner's business office, but the District Court ruled that a covert entry to install electronic eavesdropping equipment is not unlawful merely because the court approving the surveillance did not explicitly authorize such an entry. (FBI agents assigned the task of implementing the court's order had entered petitioner's office secretly and installed an electronic bug in the ceiling.)

The court considered two questions in *Dalia:* (1) May courts authorize electronic surveillance that requires covert entry into private premises for installation of the necessary equipment? (2) Must authorization for such surveillance include a specific statement by the court that it approves of the covert entry? The court held that: (1) the Fourth Amendment does not prohibit *per se* a covert entry performed for the purpose of installing otherwise legal bugging equipment; (2) Congress has given the courts statutory authority to approve covert entries for the purpose of installing electronic surveillance equipment; and (3) the Fourth Amendment does not require that a Title III electronic surveillance order include a specific authorization to enter covertly the premises described in the order.

Audio surveillance is an investigative technique about which appellate courts have rendered many decisions. Fortunately, the U.S. Supreme Court, in *Katz* v. *U.S.,* 389 U.S. 347 (1967), consolidated judicial thinking in this area and established the doctrine that such eavesdropping may properly be conducted under court supervision similar to procedures now available to police in securing search warrants and warrants of arrest.

The U.S. Supreme Court reversed the conviction of Katz, saying: "Wherever a man may be, he is entitled to know that he will remain free from unreasonable searches and seizures." In this decision the court slashed away at a confusing collection of previous decisions in this area, involving, among other things, whether or not there was a physical penetration or a technical trespass, by pointing out that the trespass doctrine is no longer controlling: "For the Fourth Amendment protects people, not places." The final words for the decision suggest that antecedent court review of the probable cause for eavesdropping and a court order similar to a search warrant would have resulted in the court's sustaining Katz's conviction. (See Appendix A, Case Briefs, for *Dalia* and *Katz*.)

An application for a court authorization to intercept oral communications by a wiretap or the installation of a concealed microphone (bug) must establish probable cause that the person to be "searched" has been or is involved in a crime. For the issuance of such a court order, the probable cause must be based on recently acquired information as to the criminal offense that has been, is being, or is about to be committed.

Other information generally required in the audio surveillance application consists of:

1. A statement of the necessity for the electronic surveillance, based on the inadequacy of alternative investigative techniques.
2. Target identity and location.
3. Objectives (type of communications) sought.

Consensual electronic surveillance (as opposed to nonconsensual) is also known as "participant monitoring." Its primary use is to secure a record of a conversation to which the person wired for sound is a participant. Undercover police agents and cooperative informants such as accomplice–witnesses can provide police with a record of conversations in which they participated. This record proves exactly what was said and is important when the substance of the conversation is later disputed by one of the other participants. Since electronic surveillance that is carried out with the consent of one of the parties to a conversation is not a "search" within the meaning of the Fourth Amendment, this type of surveillance does not require prior judicial authorization. Telephone conversations that are recorded with the consent of one participant are in this class of consensual electronic surveillances.

Since a collateral purpose of consensual electronic surveillance is to expose wrongdoing, particularly in relation to an ongoing investigation, it is important that police investigators know that the Fourth Amendment does not shield a suspect/defendant from a misplaced belief that a person to whom he or she voluntarily confides wrongdoing will not reveal it.

Investigators contemplating the use of audio surveillance should avoid it unless the means–end factor justifies its use. Because of its overtone of being dirty business, any results obtained by this technique are often mitigated or negated by the means used.

Any electronic eavesdropping technique may be subject to countermeasures. Technicians skilled in surveillance countermeasures make extravagant claims about "debugging." An electronic device *(bug)* that is wired to its receiver is difficult to detect, as is a properly connected wiretap, or the installation of a pen register to record the numbers to which outgoing calls are directed. If an electronic transmitting device is used, however, its radio transmissions can be detected by other electronic devices that are commercially available.

Countersurveillance activities may also include deliberate conversations intended to be heard and recorded: (1) incriminating statements involving innocent persons; (2) exculpatory conversations transferring or excusing guilt or guilty knowledge; and (3) scenarios intended to "blow" the surveillance by confirming the target suspect's belief in police eavesdropping. Fortunately, police investigators carefully screen incriminating or exculpatory conversations for their basic worth, and avoid acting on any conversation calling for police response (search, arrest) unless confirmed by other independent information.[1]

Contact Surveillance

Contact surveillance techniques are based on the capability of certain fluorescent preparations to stain a person's hands or clothing upon contact and thus to offer observable proof of a connection between the stained person and the object under surveillance. It is difficult to deny the connection and to offer a reasonable explanation for extensive and vivid fluorescent stains in blue, orange, or green. Contact surveillance techniques may be used alone or in supplementing a visual surveillance. They are very useful when visual surveillance is not feasible, as in cases of dishonest employees and of transactions involving the payment of money.

These tracer preparations usually are in the ultraviolet spectrum and become visible only under ultraviolet light. Persons who make contact with the object under surveillance are not aware of the treated surface nor of the transfer to their clothing or hands until questioned about the contact and examined under ultraviolet light. Tracer paste is available for objects exposed to the weather, such as fire alarm boxes, automobiles, and the drops used in underworld or espionage activity. A marking powder is available in plastic bottles for puffing tracer powder on money or any object not exposed to weather. Felt pens are available for tracer marking of objects such as money or merchandise.

Ultraviolet light is not required for contact surveillance. A dye powder is available that is also invisible when dry but becomes visible when wet, although it is difficult to wash off. This is convenient in cases of petty thefts investigated in schools and business offices because a school or office supervisor can monitor the surveillance without ultraviolet-light equipment.

These tracers are available from police equipment suppliers, and most police agencies have an assortment in stock from which an investigator can select the appropriate dye, powder, paste, crayon, or pen. The selected preparation should be applied liberally to the object likely to be contacted by the suspect or suspects. It should be tested prior to field use for its invisibility—its ability to blend in normal light—for its adhesiveness, for the life of each application, and for the difficulty of removing the stain by ordinary washing with soap and water.

A variation of this contact surveillance is the technique of adding a tracer substance to objects or liquids commonly subject to theft. The U.S. government has added various dyes to gasoline at federal garages to enable the ready identification of government gasoline in privately owned vehicles; state agencies have marked containers of foodstuffs for state institutions (when unauthorized possession is suspected); and department stores attach tracer tags to merchandise to alert personnel at store exits unless removed by a salesclerk upon purchase.

POLICE INTELLIGENCE: CRIMINAL INVESTIGATION INFORMATION

Intelligence is the secret or clandestine collecting and evaluating of information about crime and criminals not normally available to investigators through overt sources. The detection and investigation of crime and the pursuit and apprehension of criminals require reliable intelligence; otherwise, the investigator is limited to overt acts and volunteered information and thus severely handicapped in many cases.

The collection and analysis of information discovered by undercover police agents or confidential informants usually is channeled to a special unit within a police department. There the data are analyzed and evaluated so that they may be used on current or future investigations. To a certain extent, intelligence is warehoused until it is needed.

The police intelligence process is cyclical: a series of linked activities beginning with the needs of users (consumers), and ending with intelligence reports to specific users (see Figure 11–1).

The six stages of the police intelligence process are:

1. *Needs.* Clear needs for information develop as police investigate unsolved crimes and attempt to block the commission of planned crimes. Police personnel demonstrating such needs are the users of police intelligence.
2. *Collection.* The gathering of information on matters of interest, in response to user needs, is investigatory reporting: Raw intelligence (information) is reported, along with a field evaluation of the information and its source, and how access to the information reported is gained. The *overt* collection of information is from public sources or from nonintelligence police personnel; *covert* collection of information is from sources such as undercover police agents and confidential informants, or from various types of surveillance of unaware targets.
3. *Evaluation and collation.* The evaluation of information screens out useless, incorrect, nonrelevant, and unreliable information. Collating evaluated information is its orderly arrangement, cross-indexing, and filing so

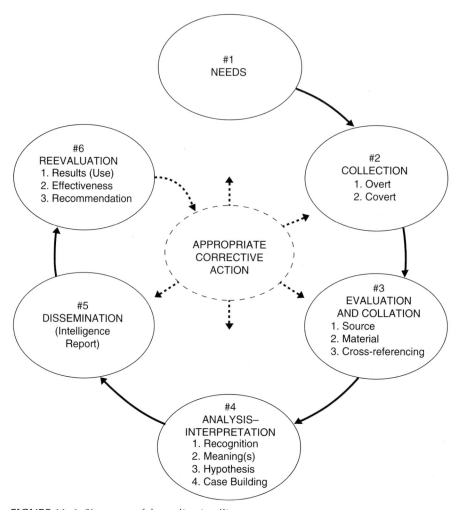

FIGURE 11–1 Six stages of the police intelligence process.

that meaningful relationships can be developed between apparently unconnected bits and pieces of information.

4. *Analysis—interpretation.* This is the core area of the police intelligence process. This activity converts information into intelligence. Unanalyzed raw information gives little data about a developing pattern of criminal activity or a target suspect. As a result of analysis, a new recognition of the significance, meaning, and interrelationships of incoming information can be developed. Interpretation is an inseparable part of analysis, as it is the dovetailing of collated information with the problems of users. Interpretation is the developing of a hypothesis and a tentative statement as to the meaning of the information involved.

5. *Dissemination.* Police intelligence reports are only released to users with a legitimate need for such intelligence. This need-to-know factor must be

credibly established and strictly enforced. Unused or misused police intelligence reports sabotage a criminal investigation technique that is unique and often the only means of disclosing to police information as to ongoing and planned crimes.

6. *Reevaluation.* This final element of the police intelligence process is a postmortem review of the effectiveness of police intelligence reports, and subsequent action likely to improve the process and its effectiveness.[2]

Criminal investigation information is police intelligence oriented to the solution of ongoing investigations. A Criminal Investigation Information Center (CIIC) within a police agency can assist investigators in clearing assigned cases by:

1. Reviewing and collating items of information common to police reports.
2. Providing information in response to requests by investigators.
3. Organizing information on criminal activities in other jurisdictions for connect-ups to local crime activities.
4. Arranging for information "sharing" between investigators and investigative units.[3]

POLYGRAPH TESTING

A technique useful in investigation is the instrumental detection of deception. With a cooperating subject, it is a valid investigative tool.

Modern polygraphs have three components, or channels—that is, three separate capabilities for recording anatomical responses to the questioning situation. These devices and their action are:

1. The pneumograph—records respiration (breathing rate and depth).
2. The galvanograph—records electrodermal response (skin electrical resistance changes).
3. The cardiograph—records changes in pulse rate and blood pressure.

Generally, the cardiogram is considered to be the most reliable indicator of deception. The galvanic skin response (GSR), which is measured by the resistance of the skin to the passage of a small electric current, is the least dependable.

Instrumental detection of deception is based on human anatomy. The sympathetic division of the autonomic nervous system, when stimulated by reactions such as anger and fear, mobilizes the body and its resources for emergencies. The effects are similar to those produced by adrenalin. Sugar is released from the liver for use by the muscles, the heart rate increases, and the coagulability of the blood is heightened.

Because the autonomic nervous system reacts automatically to threat in this fight-or-flight reaction, a subject cannot hide his or her involuntary responses to a situation. If there is a threat to the subject, there will be fear;

and when a person is fearful, there is an involuntary, animalistic preparation within the body for fight or flight—a prehistoric form of survival insurance.

A guilty subject fears relevant questions during an examination. He or she is in a stress situation: fears telling the truth, which would expose him or her as the guilty person, and fears lying, which may be revealed by the "box," exposing him or her as a liar and, therefore, a suspect in the case.

If these tests of deception are to succeed, cooperation between investigator and examiner is necessary. Just as the investigator must do an effective job of collecting evidence and delivering it to the criminalist at the police laboratory if he or she is to secure an adequate examination from the criminalist, so too must the investigator guard against contaminating the subject of a lie detection test by any action prior to the testing session that will make it difficult or impossible for the examiner to make an effective test. The investigator should not discuss the lie detector or the possibility of such tests with a suspect until a decision has been made to request tests. It is not so much that silence is a safeguard against the subject's use of tranquilizers, for a drugged response level will be apparent when the subject is initially tested on the instrument; rather, it is a safeguard against any future allegations that the subject had been threatened with the use of this scientific device. When talking with possible subjects of tests, investigators also should avoid any mention of key facts of the crime and its circumstances. Examiners use these facts for questions at the peak of tension. For example, in larcenies the exact amount of money taken and sometimes the denominations of the larger bills in cash thefts, or in assaults and homicides the type of weapon used or some detail about it, are facts useful for questions at the peak of tension.

The procedure in lie detection sessions may vary slightly with the examiner, but it is similar to interviews and interrogations in that these sessions have an introductory period, the actual testing phase, and a closing.

During the introductory period, the examiner explains the operation of the instrument and its capability for detecting bodily responses. The use of questions calling for a simple yes or no response is also explained, and the subject is instructed to remain silent if he or she does not understand the question and to reserve explanations for the period after the questioning. The subject is put at ease and allowed to ask questions to which the examiner replies in an easily understood conversational style. The transition to the testing session for suspects in criminal cases usually is accompanied by an assurance that questions will be asked only in relation to the event under investigation. The questions may even be shown to the subject prior to the test. Some operators believe this to be a more effective procedure. This reassures the subject that the testing period will not be a "fishing expedition" into a lifetime, and it validates responses as emanating from the present situation and not from any past feelings of guilt or fear about other crimes.

The testing begins after the subject is comfortably seated, and the various tubes and wires are attached securely and without discomfort. The first questioning contains irrelevant questions to establish a normal level of response for the individual being questioned. After these questions have established a response level, the examiner may ask the subject to select a card from a deck of cards, to demonstrate the capability of the machine. The examiner directs the subject to answer no to questions about the value of the card. Then, by examining the graph, the examiner determines the identity of the card and tells it to the subject. The examiner is cued to its identity by the subject's reaction, which is shown on the graph made by the instrument when the subject lied by giving the required "no" response.

The core area of the testing session follows this display of the device, and the relevant questions are interspersed with irrelevant questions. The so-called peak-of-tension questions relate to the actual circumstances of the crime; the remaining relevant questions may relate to events shortly before or after the crime.

No suspect can be forced to take a lie detection test. The privilege against self-incrimination, guaranteed to individuals by the Fifth Amendment to the Constitution, protects against such coercion. However, there is an area of psychological coercion merely in requesting a suspect to take a lie detection test and this is likely to negate any claim of voluntariness. That is, there are "damned if you do" and "damned if you don't" overtones to this testing.

The process of lie detection by use of instruments and a skilled examiner has not gained the general acceptance in its field to warrant court acceptance of the process as scientifically valid. In 1923, in *Frye* v. *United States,* 293 Fed. 1013 (1923), this doctrine of general acceptance was established: "While courts will go a long way in admitting expert testimony deduced from a well-organized principle or discovery, the thing from which the deduction is made must be sufficiently established to have gained general acceptance in the particular field to which it belongs."

One of the major criticisms of lie detection is that the examiner's role and the mechanics of testing jeopardize the scientific aspects of the instrument. The relationship of the examiner to the instrument in the detection of deception has been compared to that of a pilot to an airplane. The emphasis on operating skill brings the entire process into question as a way to detect truth or lies.

UNDERCOVER POLICE AGENTS

Use of police personnel as undercover agents is an ethical approach to the problem of securing information about criminal operations from the inside. It is a surveillance from a position of advantage. It is dangerous work but often preferable to using an underworld informant, probably the only other source of such information. Undercover agents make excellent witnesses. Unlike underworld informants whose credibility can be attacked because of criminal histories, the police agent is a person of good reputation and character. Jurors recognize the hazards of this work and tend to accept police undercover agents as very credible witnesses.

Investigators often go underground in searching out the operations of criminals. In one case a covert investigator arranged with an underworld informant for an introduction to a gambling operator. The agent had a good cover story of being interested in gambling, and he posed as a man who had been arrested and sentenced to prison. A few weeks later this agent was able to identify thirteen members of a gambling syndicate operating illegally and extensively and to offer legally significant evidence against them at their trial.

Many police units on the West Coast use young recruits fresh from police academy classes for this work. They are not known to local members of the underworld, and they do uncover meaningful information of help to the investigator. Statewide narcotic and alcoholic beverage control units use their young trainees during their first year or two of employment in undercover work. Federal agencies transfer suitable personnel to areas in which they are not known to facilitate the clandestine collection of information.

INVESTIGATIVE HYPNOSIS

Hypnosis is a state resembling normal sleep. A person may be placed under hypnosis by the suggestions and operations of a hypnotist, a person who has studied the science or art of inducing hypnosis. Hypnosis in one form or another has been practiced for centuries, but its use in criminal investigation is a relatively recent phenomenon.

The use of hypnotically aided recall to enhance the memories of persons who have witnessed a crime but are unable to recall critical facts about the event is based on the belief that human memory is like a videotape machine that (1) faithfully records, as if on film, every perception experienced by the witness; (2) permanently stores such recorded perceptions in the brain at a subconscious level; and (3) accurately "replays" them in their original form when the witness is placed under hypnosis and asked to remember them.

This "videotape recorder" theory of law enforcement hypnotists, however, is not supported by a survey of professional literature in this area. Highlights of these writings are the following: (1) hypnosis is by its nature a process of suggestion, and one of its primary effects is that the person hypnotized becomes extremely receptive to suggestions that he or she perceives as emanating from the hypnotist; (2) the person under hypnosis experiences a compelling desire to please the hypnotist by reacting positively to these suggestions, and hence to produce the particular responses that he or she believes are expected; (3) during the hypnotic session, neither the subject nor the hypnotist can distinguish between true memories and pseudomemories; and (4) neither the detail, coherence, nor plausibility of the resulting recall is any guarantee of its veracity.

The California legislature, as a response to California's Supreme Court banning the testimony of witnesses who have been hypnotized to aid in recollection, enacted legislation that allows such a witness to testify under very limited circumstances. For instance: The substance of the prehypnotic memory of the witness must be preserved in written, audiotape, or videotape form prior to the hypnosis session; the session must be extensively recorded; and the hypnosis can be performed only by a licensed medical doctor or psychologist experienced in the use of hypnosis and independent of and not in the presence of law enforcement, the prosecution, or the defense. Finally, the testimony of a witness who has undergone a memory-jogging hypnosis session is limited to "those matters which the witness recalled and related prior to the hypnosis" (California Evidence Code, Section 795, 1984).

It is, therefore, risk-taking behavior for a criminal investigator to use investigative hypnosis. In some cases, the importance of discovering the identity of the person or persons responsible for a crime are so overriding that an investigator is justified in suggesting a hypnosis session for a witness whose recall of events appears to be blocked. Kidnappings in which the victim is still under the control of the kidnapper(s), terrorist acts, and series crimes such as rape and murder are examples of instances in which hypnosis may be justified. In effect, the investigator sacrifices any future value of the witness in court to gain information about the identity of the criminal and associates, if any.

Selected References

1. National Commission for the Review of Federal and State Laws Relating to Wire-Tapping and Electronic Surveillance (NWC), *Electronic Surveillance* (Washington, D.C.: U.S. Government Printing Office, 1976), pp. 151–52.
2. E. Drexel Godfrey, Jr., and Don R. Harris, *Basic Elements of Intelligence: A Manual of Theory, Structure and Procedures for Use by Law Enforcement Agencies against Organized Crime* (Washington, D.C.: U.S. Department of Justice, Law Enforcement Assistance Administration, 1971), pp. 11–35.
3. Don R. Harris, *Criminal Investigation Information Center: A Manual Describing the Organization and Analysis of Criminal Information* (Washington, D.C.: U.S. Department of Justice, 1979), pp. 1–8.

Chapter Review

Discussion Questions

1. Explain the public's approval of visual surveillance, and its rejection of electronic eavesdropping.
2. Why is collected police intelligence vital to the success of investigation into the operations of organized crime?
3. What restrictions exist as to the surreptitious entry of homes or places of business by police to install hidden microphones (bugs)?
4. Under what circumstances is it likely that a court would authorize police to enter a home or office surreptitiously for the purpose of installing hidden microphones?
5. How does consensual electronic surveillance differ from nonconsensual electronic surveillance?
6. What is the common scope of countermeasures used by "targets" of police electronic surveillance?
7. Justify the sequential arrangement of the six stages of the police intelligence process.
8. What anatomical responses are recorded by the polygraph?
9. Are undercover police agents useful? Is their work ethical?

Library Assignment

Prepare a selected bibliography on wiretapping; list at least ten references. Abstract or digest no less than three of the references that appear to have unusual or timely significance in this area of audio surveillance.

Workbook Project

List five methods of becoming the "invisible investigator" during a visual surveillance.

CHAPTER
12

Arresting the Accused Person

The accused person may be known and easily located. On the other hand, the suspect's name may not be known, he or she may have no known address, and he or she may be in hiding or in flight. Early in the investigation an alarm or pickup order containing only fragmentary identification is broadcast locally. Its purpose is to apprehend the perpetrator in flight. The investigative search for a perpetrator, when the initial hue and cry alarm has failed, must collect and publish more detailed information about the perpetrator. This is the means by which other officers, distant in time and space from the crime, locate and identify a person in flight from justice.

The tracing of fugitives depends a great deal on the expertise with which sources of information are exploited for adequate and meaningful information about the wanted person. Although the crime and its circumstances provide the basic information, data about the suspect as a person also are available to a diligent investigator in the records of criminal justice agencies, credit reports, telephone records, employment histories, and public records. Basic research often rewards the investigator with meaningful information.

An arrest brings the investigation into close focus. The prisoner can be searched and booked, and in the process of recording facts, fingerprinted for positive identification. Evidence that can be collected at this time will be collected, recorded, and preserved. The prisoner may be anxious to talk to the police, to deny or to admit being the criminal. It is time to warn arrested persons of their constitutional rights to silence and legal counsel, and it is time to ascertain if the accused person will waive such rights and participate in an interrogation session and otherwise cooperate with the investigator.

THE BROADCAST ALARM OR PICKUP ORDER

The initial hue and cry in pursuit of the perpetrator of a crime emphasizes the distinctive identifying characteristics of the person, vehicle, or property wanted. Transmission of these alarms, or orders to pick up a suspect, which alert other police units to the recent crime, usually are done first by radio and then by Teletype. The police officer first on the scene of a crime or the investigator receiving the report of a crime has the responsibility of obtaining the best possible physical description of the criminal and his or her car, if any. A broadcast detailing a want is most effective when it is sent promptly.

Despite the need for getting the alarm or pickup order on the air to alert other officers, there must be an emphasis on accuracy. Law enforcement agents no longer ask leading questions in obtaining descriptions, and they emphasize in their reports that the description is a *composite* inasmuch as it usually is secured from both victim and witnesses. Officers do not change the composite description once it is entered in their field notes or other records, nor is the composite description changed when the wanted person is arrested or when a wanted vehicle is recovered and found to differ from the composite description.

Identifying characteristics that make a person or a vehicle different from other persons or vehicles are the basis for success in the apprehension of suspects. Partial descriptions, if distinctive, such as a damaged fender on a vehicle coupled with a fragment of the registration number, have resulted in apprehensions. In cases involving juveniles, a painted identification or other marking on the car may be very distinctive. Several weak, general descriptions of persons individually insufficient for identification often total up to significant identifying characteristics when they are broadcast as the occupants of a vehicle.

The content of wanted notices at this time in the investigation is oriented toward characteristics that are observable and that will guide searching police. Although a brief description of the crime (including the proceeds of a theft) is included, the major content usually is limited to describing persons, vehicles, and weapons.

The brief description of the crime is no more than the offense the offender is suspected of and the date, time, and location of occurrence. Stolen property is not described, but a few details of the amount of currency taken or the kind of item stolen are included. Whether a weapon was used and its type and description are included in the broadcast to alert police that the fleeing suspect is likely to be dangerous.

When more than one perpetrator is described, a listing by number (Suspect No. 1, Suspect No. 2) is recommended. The following characteristics, in the order listed, are standard for these notices: sex, age, height, weight, color, complexion, build.

A suspect's height and weight are usually reported in blocks or ranges: upward from 5 feet in 3-inch intervals, and from 100 pounds in 20-pound intervals.

Clothing is an observable characteristic that affords excellent opportunities for recognizing a wanted person. In the "How Dressed" section of this notice, the clothing of each suspect is described and the color, cloth, and design of the outer garments noted. The absence of such garments, when normally worn by others in the area, is also noted. The following items, in the order listed, are standard in such alarms or pickup orders across the nation: bareheaded; hat (color and design: black, gray, porkpie, skimpy brim); cap (color); overcoat (color, cloth, design); jacket (color, cloth, windbreaker, fingertip); suit (color, cloth, design); shirt (color, dress, or sport); trousers or shorts (color); dress; slacks; or shorts (color, cloth, design).

Vehicle descriptions in these alarms or pickup orders generally are limited to the following: year, make, model, color, state license number, damage or suspected damage, number and sex of occupants.

The usual categories of sedan, station wagon, convertible, and sport car have been supplemented by pickup, "crew" pickup, jeep, and pickup with camper.

The direction of flight, if it is known, is also included. Roadblocks may be set up, buses and other transportation may be searched, and a surveillance of the area may be conducted for criminals who seek refuge temporarily by hiding in the yards, basements, hallways, and roofs along the escape route.

The initial notices usually are concluded with a statement of the authority for the alarm or pickup order—at the local level, the name of the investigator and assignment; at other levels, the name of the issuing police department.

All broadcast alarms are distributed locally, but their coverage is expanded as the interval from the time of the crime indicates the possible enlargement of areas of flight. An all points bulletin (APB) is justified when adequate descriptive information is available. The geographical coverage of an APB depends on the locale, but may extend to neighboring states.

As facts become available to the investigator and associates during the search, there is an urgency to add information to what was originally broadcast. This added information may be simply a notice that the vehicle, when located, should be protected but not processed until evidence technicians can visit the scene and search the vehicle for fingerprints and other evidence. Additional facts on the identity of a vehicle may relate to information secured from the Department of Motor Vehicles, such as the full license number and the name and description of the registered owner. Additional knowledge about the suspect may relate to no more than a fragment of information about appearance, but it may be a full name and description of the perpetrator when a prompt and specific identification has been made. The objective of broadcasting facts as soon as they are available is to provide searching police with enough identification to pick out a fleeing person or vehicle with some certainty that the person or vehicle being stopped is the subject of the alarm.

RECORDS AS SOURCES OF INFORMATION

Agencies that may provide an investigator with information useful in locating a fugitive range from criminal justice agencies that might have processed the suspect at some previous time to the vast data banks of agencies providing credit or telephone service.

Investigators develop a knowledge of where to look for useful information. It may be found among records systems common to all localities, but it also may be in records native to a specific locality. For instance, in Reno, Nevada, the records of the County Clerk contain records of every divorce granted in this mecca of unhappy spouses, and these records are dated and cross-referenced with the names of wives, children, parents, and witnesses. Public records in the Miami to Hollywood section of Florida have been a source of information about holidaying husbands and their girlfriends when they were arrested on some minor charge. In every section of the country there is a local record system unusual in its information and generally known only to investigators who have stumbled upon it or have been advised of its existence by friends or associates.

Investigators should develop their own ready reference file as to sources of information. In working on an investigation, the assigned investigator has a general idea as to what he or she is looking for, and a ready reference information sources file will provide information as to (1) where such information may be found, (2) the form in which it may be found, and (3) how to gain access to it.

A suggested form for a file of this type includes type of information, source, and name and other identification data of a "contact" (for example, telephone number).*

Among the sources of information are:

1. *City/county*—Vital statistics, tax, welfare, courts, schools, jurors, voting records, prosecutor, public defender, etc.
2. *State*—Tax, corporate records, courts, alcohol beverage records, consumer affairs data, motor vehicle license and registration files, etc.
3. *Federal*—Federal Bureau of Investigation and other federal law enforcement agencies (Secret Service, Treasury, Postal Service, courts, U.S. Attorney, Naturalization and Immigration, Securities, Social Security, Military, etc.)
4. *Private*—Moving companies, telephone company (public directory and directories on file at company office), other public utilities, credit reporting agency, banks and finance companies, Better Business Bureau, Chamber of Commerce, business (trade) directories, industry and trade associations, professional associations, etc.[1]

---

*These contacts are invaluable when a speedy response to queries is necessary, despite the reciprocity inherent in these calls. Some networks include graduates of the FBI Academy, former members of the FBI and the New York Police Department, and alumni of college/university criminal justice degree programs.

Computer software may soon supplement—or even replace—most of these sources of information. Computer Information Systems of Skokie, Illinois, is a pioneer in this field and offers software designed to track suspects and fugitives.

WANTED NOTICES

A wanted notice should provide full information about the fugitive and about areas in which he or she is likely to be found. Copies are sent to police in neighboring areas and mailed to police in areas that the fugitive is likely to visit. These usually are large cities in adjacent states and resort centers. The basic content of a wanted notice is a photograph or sketch of the fugitive, fingerprints, and an extensive personal description.

The standard mug shot taken at the time of a previous arrest, if available, is made part of the wanted notice. When this is not available, any close-up photograph may be substituted. These are often available from public records or from associates of the suspect. Full-length shots of the suspect alone or with a group of associates often are available and can be used to supplement the standard front and profile photographs. Ideally, color photography and printing should be utilized in wanted notices because it offers a lifelike image of the wanted person.

The fingerprint classification of a fugitive in the wanted notice is a major point of identification. Often these notices contain a facsimile of the fingerprints of a suspect, and a comparison can be made by the local agency making the arrest. In recent years the fingerprinting of persons not charged with a crime has increased, and these records are available to police agencies preparing wanted notices. It is the classification and comparison of fingerprints that guarantee against the apprehension of the wrong person. Any other identification always includes the possibility of error. For this reason investigators should search diligently for a fingerprint record for the wanted notice.

Observable and distinctive characteristics are used in describing a person. Identifying physical characteristics are necessary to locate the fugitive and to offer some positive identification for an arrest.

The standard base of details for describing wanted persons is sex, age, height, weight, color of eyes, and color of hair. Racial appearance or national origin is also an identifying characteristic. Many police units use a standard listing and suggest the most descriptive designation applicable to the fugitive to be used. The usual list is as follows: White, African American, Mexican, Indian, Chinese, Japanese, other.

Observable physical characteristics found useful by police in tracing fugitives have been codified in a "relevant matter" listing of key items in a personal description. These are the items of identity believed to be important:

1. Face—shape.
2. Hair—color, type, and cut.
3. Eyes—color, type, and defects.

4. Nose—shape and size.
5. Mouth—shape, size, and unusual characteristics.
6. Chin—shape, size, and if dimpled.
7. Ears—type, size, and defects.
8. Eyebrows and beard—appearance.
9. Scars and marks—location and type.
10. Amputations and deformities.
11. Speech.
12. Peculiarities.

In using these relevant characteristics, a person may be described as being round-faced with long, red, wavy hair; blue, bulging, cross eyes with hooded lids; a broken nose; a wide mouth with full lips; a receding chin; flaring ears; bushy eyebrows meeting in the center; long sideburns, mustache and light beard; a forehead scar about 1 inch long over his right eye and needle marks on his left arm. He also may be described as walking with a pronounced limp.

A fugitive's occupation, associates, friends, relatives, habits, and hobbies are often significant factors in a police manhunt. A person's occupation or profession is often a form of habituation. Known criminal associates are likely to offer promising leads, and data on relatives and friends may suggest promising areas of inquiry. Habits and hobbies are related to places frequented or areas in which the fugitive is likely to be found. Amusement and resort areas may offer promise in one instance; theatrical and cabaret districts may be indicated in the habits of another person. This field is wide open to innovative practices by both the investigator preparing the wanted notice and police seeking the fugitive.

A final segment of the description of a fugitive concerns whether he or she may resist arrest. All investigators seeking the apprehension of a fugitive have a duty to specify in every wanted notice whether the fugitive is armed, whether known to use weapons, whether a weapon has been used in crime, and whether the fugitive has used weapons on previous occasions to avoid capture or to escape from custody. The cliché "armed and dangerous" may appear to be routine, but the unnecessary injury and death of arresting officers is not routine and can be avoided by adequate notice. Officers manning roadblocks and stopping suspicious cars on the highway late at night usually are prepared for any aggressive action by the occupants of a vehicle. However, officers on many other occasions likely to be met in the pursuit of a fugitive are not always as alert to possible aggression—unless they are warned in advance.

Armed with the knowledge that a person is wanted, all police seek fugitives. It is part of the general police role. Traffic officers making so-called routine stops have apprehended fugitives. Police on patrol, in responding to a call for help or in handling a minor crime investigation, encounter fugitives and take them into custody. Investigators allow some time out of their daily routine for inquiries about wanted persons.

Investigators, however, must exercise care in questioning people about a fugitive. They may encounter a person who knows the whereabouts of the suspect but who is more friendly with the fugitive than with the police. A warning to the suspect of the inquiries being made may result in flight, and an excellent chance for capture will be lost forever.

Traditionally, a wanted notice has always been aimed solely at locating and apprehending the fugitive. It now has an additional purpose: to discover, to collect, and to preserve evidence at the time of the arrest. The four purposes of a modern wanted notice for a fugitive from criminal justice are:

1. To provide sufficient identifying characteristics (constituting reasonable grounds for belief) to allow other law enforcement agents to identify provisionally the fugitive upon initial contact and to make positive identification when the suspect is taken into custody.
2. To alert other law enforcement officers to the nature and character of the fugitive, his or her criminal history, and whether armed and dangerous.
3. To suggest activities and areas in which a search or surveillance may locate the fugitive.
4. To delineate the crime in sufficient detail to alert arresting officers to potential legally significant evidence available *at the time of arrest.*

THE ARREST

Today it is no longer generally believed that legally significant evidence can be developed *after* an arrest has been made. Investigators are now assembling evidence beyond the strong suspicion or probable cause level, basic to any lawful arrest, before they attempt to arrest the major suspect in a case. Of course, a great deal of meaningful evidence may be collected at the time of the arrest. The arrest is an excellent opportunity to find evidence that will connect the prisoner with the crime, the crime scene, or the victim, or with other crimes and other criminals. It is also an excellent moment in the investigation to guard against faulty identification of the arrestee.

All arresting officers should be alert to the nature and type of evidence that might normally be encountered at the time of arrest. In collecting evidence at this time, the finding officer must exercise the same care he or she would use if the evidence had been discovered in a crime-scene search. The officer finding it should make an appropriate entry in his or her field notes and in the records of the arrest, mark it for identification, and protect its integrity.

The search incidental to an arrest may not only recover the proceeds of a theft, but may also produce transfer evidence that will link the suspect with the crime, the scene, or the victim. The search should be confined to the person of the arrested individual and to the vicinity of the arrest.[2] A complete body search is made at the time of booking. In serious crimes it is not uncommon to seize the clothes of a suspect for processing by vacuum cleaner to collect dust and debris for analysis and to search them for blood and other stains that may connect the defendant with the crime scene or victim.

The search of a person should not verge on conduct that shocks the conscience, as in the case of *Rochin* v. *California,* 342 U.S. 165 (1952), in which an offender's stomach was pumped out in a hospital in order to recover two capsules of heroin. The search should fulfill the obligation of an arresting officer by protecting the arresting officer from harm and removing any material that might aid in the escape of the arrested person, and by avoiding the destruction of evidence or failure to collect evidence.

The doctrine of immediate control indicates the area in which a search is justified. If the arrest is made on the street when the suspect is walking, his or her person and the immediate public area may be searched; if arrested in a parked or moving vehicle, the vehicle may be searched; and if the arresting officer witnessed the jettisoning of some article just prior to the arrest, he or she should search for such article. If the arrest is made inside a premises, the search usually is restricted to the area over which the arrested person has control. (See Appendix A, Case Briefs, for *Chimel.*)

The police department issuing the wanted notice is notified of an arrest, cancels the want by issuing a Teletype notice of the arrest, and makes the necessary arrangements to pick up the prisoner. If the locale of the arrest is outside the state in which the crime was committed, extradition proceedings are required unless formally waived by the fugitive.

When a perpetrator is arrested locally, the search incidental to the arrest may involve the home of the prisoner, if it is the place of arrest. Burglars and thieves in possession of recently stolen property often conceal it in their homes. Experienced detectives know there is a great deal of promise in "hitting" the residence of a suspect in burglary and theft cases. The present doctrine is to seek search warrants when looking for evidence in any building during the post-arrest period unless the search is incidental to the arrest. The investigator can cite the fact that an arrest has been made and should be able to establish probable cause for a search of a specific location for particular items of evidence. The search warrant avoids tainting evidence, and it is a simple matter to conduct a search pursuant to a warrant and to report in full to the court upon the results. The investigator can arrange for a surveillance of the premises or place to be searched, which will secure it from disturbance while the warrant is being obtained.

An investigator may ask the arrested person to consent to a search of an office or residence. If another person has dual or joint control of such premises, consent also should be requested of such individual. Landlords and managers of multiple housing or office structures can consent to a search only of the so-called public portions of such buildings and cannot consent to the search of a room or apartment or office under the sole control of a tenant. Since the *Miranda* decision, the compelling atmosphere of police custody has been delineated as inherently in conflict with the intelligent waiver of any constitutional right. Therefore, the waiver should be formal, should state it is a voluntary act, and should be signed by the prisoner and witnessed. Ideally, the police should discuss the nature of the evidence and where in the premises it will be found with the prisoner. A post-arrest consent to search is not illogical conduct if the arrestee is "cooperating" with police, and it should be requested.

PEDIGREE

At the time of arrest the booking process either begins the prisoner's criminal history file or adds to it. The police apprehension process has concentrated on identifying a logical suspect as the perpetrator and, after ascertaining sufficient information about the appearance of the suspect for a pursuit, locating and arresting him or her. In these pursuits the searching police are advised of the suspect's name and whereabouts when these are available. Sometimes, however, pursuits for wanted persons are based on little more than an eyewitness description and a sketch. Therefore, when an arrest has been made, positive identification of the arrestee is required.

The arrest record should reflect as much information about an arrestee as possible. Such basic information should include:

1. Name (including alias—aka—and nickname).
2. Sex, race, age.
3. Residence, employment.
4. Social condition, next of kin.
5. Physical description:
   a. height and weight
   b. hair color and style
   c. eye color, and any defects
   d. ears, nose, lips, chin, teeth
   e. complexion and general build
   f. facial hair
   g. tattoo marks; amputations/deformities; visible scars, moles, birthmarks, needle tracks.
6. Speech.
7. Peculiarities.
8. Habits (known to . . . , frequents . . . , hobby is . . .).
9. Type of crime, and area of geographic operations.
10. Associates (neighborhood, crime partners, other).

Unless forbidden by local laws stating that they may not be taken in minor cases, the fingerprints and photograph of every person arrested should be taken. Sufficient copies of fingerprints should be taken for circulation to other records systems; and both front and profile pictures should be made. The basic records systems for a fingerprint search are the files of the arresting agency, the state criminal justice files, and the huge records system of the FBI. The search determines whether the fingerprints of the prisoner are on file. The fingerprints taken at the time of this arrest are matched against the base files of these agencies, a report of the search is made to the police agency forwarding the prisoner's fingerprints, and the fact of this arrest is filed in all these records.

The report of the records search may be a simple "No record." However, it bears a date, and a person's name, and it is evidence that a records search in that agency, based on a set of fingerprints of an arrestee, was made and failed to disclose any record. On the other hand, the report may be several pages long and list arrests and imprisonments in various sections of the country. (This is the "rap sheet" of a person with a criminal record. The prior arrests, and other contacts with police and criminal justice agencies, were once referred to as raps. The name is synonymous with criminal record or criminal history. The term "bum rap," signifying a false charge of crime, is quite common in the argot of criminals.)

At the same time the current criminal justice status of the arrested person is reviewed by the agencies searching their fingerprint files. When warranted, the arresting agency is notified if the arrestee is wanted by police in other jurisdictions as a suspect in a crime, as a fugitive from justice, as an escapee from a correctional institution or mental health facility, as under the supervision of a probation or parole officer, or as being at liberty on bail pending trial upon a previous arrest and charge of crime.

The criminal histories of persons are serially numbered in the local agency, the state records system, and in the FBI. In effect, the arrestee is given a lifetime identification (ID) number. In some areas a letter prefix reveals the grade of the crime: serious—usually a felony, but sometimes a "high" misdemeanor; and minor—usually misdemeanors, sometimes not including minor offenses, such as traffic violations. In New York City, the prefix B is for serious crimes and E for lesser crimes. In the state records systems, the number usually has a simple prefix of letters representing the name of the agency. In California it is CII, for the California Bureau of Identification and Investigation. At the federal level, it is FBI.

If an arrestee has never been arrested within the jurisdiction of the local police agency in which he or she is being booked, a local number will be assigned. If previously arrested locally, the arrestee is booked under a previously assigned ID number.

The collection of data about the prisoner at the time of the arrest does not relate primarily to the offense but rather to the pedigree of the offender. Pedigree is an odd word; yet the questions asked and the information sought at the time of booking an arrestee provide just that—complete information about a person. When an arrested person is in contact with law enforcement agencies as an arrestee for the first time, the facts of the pedigree may be minimal. As a criminal prosecution moves from arrest to trial to sentencing, a great deal of information is collected and filed under the arrestee's ID number. Now it is more than a personal description; it is a person delineated against the background of the crime charged and sometimes a record of behavior when in prison and on parole. When another arrest occurs, similar data are collected and integrated with the base file. This is probably the reason the word has persisted as a reference. The criminal history of a person is a pedigree.

For an investigator the compilation of an offender's data sheet upon a first arrest is a routine that should be serviced in full recognition of the future use of such data as an investigative aid by other investigators.

Selected References

1. HERBERT EDELHERTZ, EZRA STOTLAND, and MARILYN WALSH, MILTON WEINBERG, *The Investigation of White-Collar Crime: A Manual for Law Enforcement Agencies* (Washington, D.C.: U.S. Department of Justice, Law Enforcement Assistance Administration, 1977), pp. 267–75 (Appendix B, Sample Guide to Sources of Information). For an in-depth coverage of the sources of information, see HARRY J. MURPHY, *Where's What: Sources of Information for Federal Investigators* (Washington, D.C.: The Brookings Institution, 1975).
2. Agnello v. United States, 296 U.S. 20 (1925).

Chapter Review

Discussion Questions

1. Explain the relationship, if any, between sources of information and tracing fugitives.
2. What are the common faults of broadcast alarms and wanted notices?
3. What are the obligations of an arresting officer in searching a prisoner at the time of arrest?
4. Discuss the making and keeping of records about persons arrested.
5. What is the primary role of fingerprinting at the time of arrest?
6. What special features of an arrestee's personal appearance are likely to be recorded as to facial hair? As to nose? Ears? Speech?
7. Why is data as to an arrestee's associates and area of criminal operations recorded at the time of arrest?
8. Are arrestees a potential source of information? (Explain.)
9. How do you obtain an arrest warrant?

Library Assignment

Prepare a selected bibliography of at least twenty references about public and private record systems serving as sources of information for investigators.

Workbook Project

Prepare a checklist of action to be taken (things to do) when serving as an arresting officer in a fugitive felon case.

CHAPTER
13

Case Preparation

Case preparation is organization. It is the orderly array of information collected during an investigation—all the reports, documents, and exhibits in a case. It is also the preparation of a synopsis of the individual material in the case, an abstract written without personal conclusions, opinions, or "facts." A so-called final report is undesirable. The collected reports and other data are the final report, the package forwarded to the prosecutor. There is no intrusion by the investigator. The synopsis is no more than a summary of the package contents. In the evaluation of a case in this pretrial period, investigators must discriminate between evidential material and personal conclusions and opinions, between potential evidence and "facts." In a criminal action fact leads to truth, and courts admit relevant evidence at trial to determine fact.

This is the round-up time of an investigation. The investigator collates the work of the entire investigation, confers with associates, prepares the case folder and its synopsis, forwards the case to the prosecutor for the preparation of the formal accusatory pleading and the legal development of the case prior to trial, and marks the case closed by arrest.

THE IDENTITY OF THE DEFENDANT

The identification of an individual as the person accused of the crime leads to an array of witnesses and evidence. Identification usually results from some combination of testimony and other evidence. This evidence structure is sometimes supported by a pretrial statement of the accused person and is oriented to proving the identity of the individual as the person responsible for the crime alleged in the indictment or information, the accusatory pleading.

Guidelines to evidence likely to have legal significance in establishing the identity of the person or persons responsible for a crime can be summed up as follows:

1. A witness (or witnesses) who has seen the offender commit the crime or some part of it.
2. A witness (or witnesses) who has seen the offender at the crime scene at or about the time of the crime.
3. A witness (or witnesses) who observed the offender in the neighborhood of the crime at or about the time of occurrence.
4. Physical evidence discovered in the crime-scene search that indicates the offender was at the crime scene or in contact with the victim.
5. Physical evidence found on the offender or among his or her effects at the time of arrest, or secured by other lawful means, that indicates that the offender had been at the crime scene or in contact with the victim.
6. Connect-ups:
   a. the offender possessing the vehicle that witnesses will testify was used in this crime
   b. the offender having the proceeds of the crime (in theft and burglary cases)
   c. the offender having an unexplained injury (in assaults and homicides)
   d. the offender having the weapon used in the crime
   e. the offender having been interviewed by an officer at or near the crime scene at or about the time of the crime (the officer having reported it in the regular course of business and being available to so testify).

This appears to be a formidable array of witnesses and evidence, but it must be evaluated against the background of the problem areas in proving the identity of a person accused of crime. These are:

1. Variances in the original descriptions and the actual description of the accused person.
2. Other errors in evidence or variances in statements of witnesses.
3. A well-supported claim of "alibi"—being elsewhere at the time of the crime.
4. A widespread distrust of eyewitness identification because of the many publicized mistakes in such identifications.

THE DEFENDANT AND THE *CORPUS DELICTI*

The accusatory pleading must show that at a specified time and date in a specific place, the person named therein has committed an act or omission in violation of a particular law specified by both name and section number and in force at the time of the act or omission.

Therefore, the first major area of case evaluation is the affirmative evidence of a real-life *corpus delicti*—the classic "body of the crime" plus the identity of the person charged with it:

1. The time and date of the crime and the territorial jurisdiction in which it happened (the venue).
2. The name by which the accused person has been identified.
3. The essential elements of the crime charged.
4. A specification of the criminal agency utilized to accomplish the crime and of the name of the victim.

This is a combining of "what happened" and "who did it" with the knowledge that the happening as reported violates a specific law, for which violation the offender has a legal responsibility to answer.

NEGATIVE EVIDENCE

The second major area of case preparation concerns negative evidence and is oriented to countering defenses to the crime charged. Standard defenses are:

1. The defendant did not commit the crime. The defense allegation is that the accused person is the victim of mistaken identification, faulty police work, or pure coincidence and was somewhere else at the time.
2. The defendant did commit the crime, but:
   a. it was excusable (usually a claim of self-defense or provocation)
   b. it was an accident
   c. it was the result of legal insanity
   d. there were mental factors that diminished the defendant's responsibility for the act.
3. No crime was committed:
   a. attack on the sufficiency of the *corpus delicti*
   b. attack on the sufficiency of the evidence
   c. attack on one or more of the essential elements of the crime charged (intent, proximate cause, etc.).

If any essential element of the crime charged is not proved beyond a reasonable doubt, the defendant is entitled to acquittal.

LAWFUL PROCEDURES

The third major area of case preparation concerns procedural foundations in the securing of evidence. This requires affirmative proof to dispel any allegations of unlawful activity by police that may be presented to a court. The investigator must point out the procedural lawfulness. In most cases, such evidence will show one or more of the following:

1. Nothing suggestive or otherwise improper in locating and interviewing witnesses.
2. The reasonableness of the search and the integrity of collecting and preserving evidence.
3. A reasonable surveillance, which meets the requirements of due process.
4. The voluntariness of a confession or admission, together with the other due process requirements.

ARRAYING EVIDENCE

Evidence must be tabulated in some orderly array. A suggested outline includes the name and a summary of the background of each witness, a synopsis of the story told, and a reference to the name of one or more witnesses who can give corroborating or supporting testimony. The array is usually, in order of importance, the identity of the defendant, relationship to the *corpus delicti* of the crime, essential elements of the crime charged, and negative evidence likely to block common defenses.

Another means of tabulating testimonial evidence is a timetable of the crime. This is a chronological exposition of the movements of all persons involved in the crime and a brief description of the evidence that pinpoints the time and the relationships. It can be broken into any convenient subdivisions.

This tabulation of evidence in some relevant arrangement helps an investigator avoid disorder in an investigation, facilitates review by others, and permits an overview of the case not possible in any other fashion. This "taking in of the case at a glance" was a principal objective of Hans Gross's "table" of a crime, suggested over half a century ago, to allow the investigator to determine if work on the case was complete or where additional work was necessary.[1]

THE "PACKAGE" OR CASE FOLDER

File folders, with metal or fiber devices to bind the enclosed papers, are used by major police departments to forward the case to the prosecutor. Police reports and other documents usually are placed in chronological order. The offense or crime report is on top, and the various supplementary or progress reports follow in sequence. Photographic exhibits in the form of color or black-and-white prints or transparencies are integrated with the folder. Physical evidence, if any, may be delivered to the prosecutor or held until requested by him or her. The content of the various reports should be sufficient to indicate the physical evidence and its nature.

A synopsis (brief) should accompany each case folder. In preparing a synopsis an investigator must keep in mind that this is an abstract or digest of the material in the case folder, nothing more and nothing less. It must be brief. It can deal only with the pertinent facts in the complete case folder being forwarded to the prosecutor. Every point covered in the synopsis must be supported by a police report or other document in the case folder being forwarded, and the elements of the synopsis should be organized in the same order as the police reports and documents in the case folder. A quick reading of the synopsis and a scanning of the case folder should inform the prosecutor of the crime committed, the time, date, and place of its happening, and the evidence collected.

A recent innovation is a "face sheet" on the police reports, documents, and exhibits forwarded to the prosecutor. It is an outline synopsis of the case, which requires only a few notations in appropriate spaces under printed captions. It can be utilized to serve the same purpose for the transfer of the facts of a case from the prosecutor to the defense attorney under the rules of pretrial discovery.

THE DECISION TO CHARGE

In the office of the prosecutor the case is reviewed and assigned to a staff member for further investigation and preparation for trial, if warranted. This review of the case by a public official trained in law is a learned review of the work of the investigator. Conferences with the investigator and witnesses usually are scheduled by this legal expert, and physical evidence and the reports of its analysis are examined. If the case is a homicide, the staff of the coroner or medical examiner and their reports may be involved in these sessions. The assigned prosecutor makes his or her decision and moves through the necessary stages for trial or recommends that no action be taken at this time and details reasons for not taking action. The decision to charge is not a function or responsibility of the investigator.[2]

Cases are not moved for trial or rejected as possible trial material solely on the basis of the work done by the investigator and the legal significance of the collected evidence. Tactical factors and the needs of law enforcement may indicate that a trial is not advisable. Prosecutors may waive prosecution in exchange for information or testimony against a more hardened criminal; the conservation of resources may suggest a negotiated plea of guilty to a lesser charge; or the application of the sanctions of the criminal justice process does not appear justified by the circumstances of the case—for example, in processing first offenders and emotionally disturbed persons.[3]

Review of case preparation by the staff of the prosecutor prior to arrest is not uncommon. Of course, an investigator habituated to the traditional separation of the roles of investigator and prosecutor is reluctant to ask the prosecutor to step into an ongoing investigation. However, legal advice on the measure of proof appears to be an area in which the prosecutor's expertise is valued by investigators. When the measure of proof is less than the amount necessary to move the case to the prosecutor, there is a natural tendency to seek help. It is within the concept of the role of the prosecutor to accept difficult investigation as just that—incomplete and insufficient. In such instances, and in a case with promise, the prosecutor has an ideal investigative device in the local grand jury, with its powers of subpoena and the right to administer oaths and take sworn testimony. It is a route for promising cases previously marked by police with the notation "no further results possible."

CLOSING AN INVESTIGATION

An investigation is successful when the crime under investigation is promptly solved and the case closed. Measurable results occur when the case is closed by the arrest of the perpetrator. Cases cleared by arrest are a statistical measure of the efficiency of the criminal investigation function of any police unit. However, case clearance also may be a statistical measure of efficiency in cases where an investigation is terminated without an arrest. A review of reasons given by police executives for closing investigations in this manner shows the following authorized case clearances in lieu of an arrest:

1. The investigation discloses the case is unfounded; no crime occurred or was attempted. However, the return of stolen property, restitution, or refusal by the victim to prosecute does not justify this classification.
2. The offender dies.
3. The case is found to be a murder and suicide; one person kills another person and then commits suicide.
4. The perpetrator confesses on his or her deathbed.
5. Arrest and charge of an identified offender is blocked by an uncooperative victim.
6. A confession is made by an offender already in custody for another crime.
7. The person identified as the perpetrator is located in another jurisdiction, and an unsuccessful attempt is made to gain custody; or the prosecutor does not believe the expense of an attempt to gain custody is justified.
8. The person identified as the perpetrator is prosecuted for a less serious charge than that cited at the time of arrest—upon the decision of the assigned prosecutor.[4]

If the investigator's case preparation reveals that the identity of the perpetrator has been definitely established, has been located, and there exists sufficient information and evidence to support an arrest and a charge of crime, there is no valid reason not to close the case by arrest if it is not covered by any of the foregoing exceptional clearances. The identification of the perpetrator solves the case and justifies such action.

An investigator should recommend on a supplementary report the termination of a case when no further results can be secured. In addition, a follow-up officer should have the authority to file cases in an inactive or "hold file" when no further results can be obtained despite due diligence.

Therefore, the criminal investigation function can be terminated in the following instances:

1. Results have been obtained in full; cleared by arrest or exceptional clearance.

2. Results have been obtained in part, and no further results can be obtained.

3. No results can be obtained.

Recognition that a bona fide conclusion to a case can be achieved without an arrest is important to the new frontiers of investigation. Such action strips the deadwood from the work load of an investigator, leads to new definitions of responsibility and accountability in the criminal investigation function, and strengthens the concept that arrests are not the primary objective of criminal investigation.

In pursuing the main objective of an investigation—truth—investigators must view all aspects of a case, particularly information pointing to the innocence of the accused person. It is no longer sufficient to present a *prima facie* case and to hope and trust it will withstand the contradiction of a defense attack. The case must be so prepared that legally significant evidence presented in court will withstand attack by the defense and establish guilt beyond a reasonable doubt.

An investigation is a search for truth in which all possible information in a post-factum inquiry is searched for, collected, and analyzed. The investigative process examines all the data, both for and against the person accused of crime. Therefore, it is always appropriate to view a case throughout an investigation from the viewpoint of the defense, and particularly appropriate to do so in preparing the case for presentation to the prosecutor. Along with scrupulous accuracy in reporting information, viewing the defense side of a case is the ultimate technique for conducting investigations that exonerate the innocent and discover and identify the guilty.

Selected References

1. Hans G. A. Gross, *Criminal Investigation,* trans. John Adam and J. Collyer Adam (Madras, India: Higginbotham, 1906), pp. 34–35.

2. Wayne R. LaFave, *Arrest: The Decision to Take a Suspect into Custody* (Boston: Little, Brown and Company, 1965), pp. 5–6, 320–24.

3. Institute of Defense Analyses, *Task Force Report: The Courts* (A Report to the President's Commission on Law Enforcement and Administration of Justice) (Washington, D.C.: U.S. Government Printing Office, 1967), pp. 5–7.

4. International Association of Chiefs of Police, *Case No. 5: Criminal Investigation* (Washington, D.C.: International Association of Chiefs of Police, Inc., 1966), p. 18.

Chapter Review

CASE STUDY: DOUBLE MURDER—MS. WYLIE AND HOFFERT _____

This case involves a double murder and a lengthy investigation in which George Whitmore, Jr., is arrested and charged with the crime. For clarity, the case is presented in the form of a chronology, beginning with the day of the crime.

Wednesday, August 28
The Day Of The Crime

Janice Wylie, twenty-one, and Emily Hoffert, twenty-three, were found bound and stabbed to death in Apartment 3-C at 57 East 88th Street, New York City. Their bodies were found by Max Wylie, father of Miss Wylie, and by Patricia Tolles, a roommate who shared the murder-scene apartment with the two victims.

Miss Tolles, who had last seen the victims when she left for work at 9:30 that morning, returned from work at 6:40 P.M., and found the apartment in disarray. Shocked and upset, she did not go through the apartment, although she did glance into the bathroom. She called Max Wiley from the telephone in the foyer of the apartment, and he came directly over from his home a few blocks away. They examined the apartment and found the bodies of the two victims in a bedroom, between a wall and a bed. Miss Wylie was nude, Miss Hoffert was fully clothed. Two knives were found near the bodies, and there was another knife on the basin in the bathroom of the apartment which was opposite the crime-scene bedroom. The wrists and ankles of both victims were tied, and their bodies were bound together at the wrists and waists. Cloth strips, torn or cut from a bedsheet and a bedspread, were used for this restraint. (See Figure 13–1.) There was no blood in any room other than the bedroom in which the victims were found. The drawers of dressers and cabinets were open, and their contents were dumped on the floor, on beds, and on dresser tops. Miss Tolles said that nothing was missing, and that neither the victims, nor she herself, possessed any valuable jewelry or large sums of cash. Preliminary police investigation revealed no sign of forced entry, and no witness who had seen or heard anything suspicious was found. Chief Medical Examiner, Dr. Michael Halpern, said the bodies of the victims had been mutilated viciously, but there was no apparent evidence of sexual assault.

Thursday, August 29
1 Day After The Crime

A search of the apartment by police identification technicians revealed numerous fingerprints. All such traces were collected and then processed by the police. The two knives found in the crime-scene bedroom had broken blades, but the broken-off portions of the blades were recovered from the floor nearby. The knife found in the bathroom was intact, and identified as a standard pointed steak knife. The origin of knives was apparently the kitchen of the apartment.

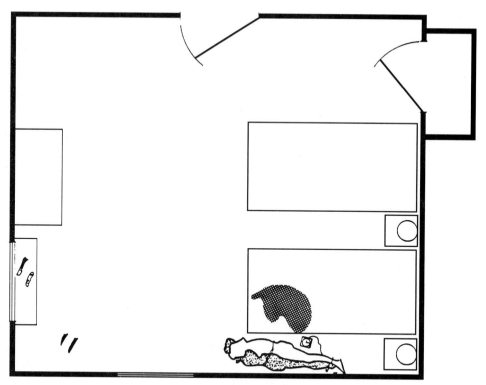

FIGURE 13–1 Janice Wylie and Emily Hoffert were found dead, tied together, in one of the bedrooms of their two-bedroom apartment. (*Source:* Paul B. Weston, *Criminal Justice and Law Enforcement—Cases, 1972.* Reprinted by permission of Prentice Hall.)

Continued questioning of neighbors and building employees failed to locate anyone who had seen or heard anything suspicious or directly related to the crime apartment. One neighbor reported meeting a stranger in the elevator, who he described as of medium build and "baby-faced."

Chief Medical Examiner Halpern said, in a preliminary autopsy report, that the cause of death for both victims was multiple stab wounds in the neck, chest, and abdomen, and that Miss Hoffert had head wounds in which glass was found, indicating blows by a weapon such as a soft-drink bottle. An electric night-table clock was found near the bodies. Its plug was out of the wall and on the floor a few feet from a wall outlet, and a good portion of its electric cord was partially under the torso of victim Wylie. The time on the stopped clock was 10:35.

Max Wylie stated that his daughter Janice had received a threatening phone call on or about August 18, and that she was terrified by it. The caller left a name, Joe Hunter, and a telephone number, Wylie added, but when his daughter called the number a woman who identified herself as the subscriber for that telephone number said she knew of no man named Hunter or any similar name.

Friday, August 30
2 Days After The Crime

Newsweek, where Miss Wylie had worked, offered a $10,000 reward for informa-tion leading to the arrest and conviction of the murderer or murderers. Continuing investigation revealed that Miss Hoffert had left the apartment shortly after her roommate, Patricia Tolles, left for work at 9:30 A.M. The victim then drove north to Riverdale to return a borrowed car and pick up her own automobile. She was placed in the Riverdale area up until 11 A.M., through contacts with friends and the garage proprietor. The time span of the crime could now be set between 9:30 A.M. and 6:40 P.M. for victim Wylie; and 11:30 A.M. to 6:40 P.M. for victim Hoffert. Police established a public information telephone number, and asked for public cooper-ation in their search for both witnesses and the person or persons responsible for the killings.

Friday, September 6
9 Days After The Crime

No substantial clues were revealed by the continuing investigation, despite a far-reaching search for witnesses, and numerous inquiries among relatives, friends, and associates of victims. No motive for the crime was discovered either. Burglary was not believed to be the actual motive, although an attempt was apparently made to create the illusion of a burglary. However, no cash was stolen, and sev-eral pieces of jewelry and a watch were left untouched. Over 100 detectives were assigned to the case by this time. The canvass for witnesses had been concluded without success. All known sex offenders and all known daytime burglars had been questioned by the police, and their activities on August 28 had been investi-gated—all to no avail.

Friday, September 13
16 Days After The Crime

The report of the fingerprint search and processing revealed that no fingerprints were present on the suspect murder weapons (3 knives), and that a total of nine partial sets of fingerprints were found in the apartment. Seven of these sets corre-sponded with those of the victims, relatives, friends, or occupants of the apart-ment. The two remaining sets of partial fingerprints did not have sufficient char-acteristics for overt identification by any search of criminal justice files; but they were marked for possible use as suspects were developed through other informa-tion and evidence in the case.

September 27
33 Days After The Crime

In the continuing investigation of the Wylie-Hoffert murders, detectives had inter-viewed over 500 persons, but to date no identity of the murderer or murderers had been revealed, nor had any witness been found who observed anyone leaving the apartment or any suspicious person in the building during the time span of the crime. Investigators had been seeking someone who observed a blood-spattered person, or one carrying a bundle or bag. The police believed that the killer's clothing was splashed with blood during the crime, and he then would have had blood-stained clothing when he fled from the scene—unless he had changed clothes at the crime scene. In that case, he would have carried out his bloody garments in a bag or bundle.

Thursday, October 31
64 Days After The Crime

Continuing investigation exhausted all leads contained in telephone and memorandum books of the victims, and all other memoranda such as cards and letters with names, telephone numbers or other identification that were found in the apartment. Police had also investigated all names and other leads supplied by friends and relatives of the victims, including the "Joe Hunter" lead supplied by Max Wylie. They also followed leads gathered through the over 1,000 telephone calls received by the special public information number. To date, no description or other identification of the murderer or murderers, or of any suspicious person seen leaving the death-scene apartment or its vicinity on the day of the crime, had been secured. The detail of detectives, now reduced to twenty-four, had reoriented the continuing investigation to investigate (1) all previous crimes in which knives were used; (2) all persons moving out of the neighborhood; and (3) persons who left state mental-health institutions or prisons just prior to the crime, or who had been admitted or committed since the crime.

Thursday, February 27
183 Days After The Crime

Detectives assigned to the continuing investigation had now interviewed, questioned, and investigated over 1,000 suspects. Most suspects had been fully exonerated. About ten of these individuals required some verification of their activities on the day of the crime. To date, no one of these persons was classed as a major suspect, and no substantial clue to the identity of the murderer or murderers had been discovered.

Saturday, April 24
240 Days After The Crime

George Whitmore, Jr., nineteen, was arrested for the Wylie-Hoffert killings. At about 6:00 A.M., Friday, April 23, a Brooklyn police officer who was searching an area in which an assault, robbery, and attempted rape had been committed a few hours earlier, spotted a suspect and took him to the police station. The victim of the robbery and attempted rape, Mrs. Ella Borrero, was brought to the police station and identified the suspect—George Whitmore. He confessed to the crime. He was booked for the robbery and attempted rape of Mrs. Borrero. A search revealed no weapon and no drugs, but two photographs were found in his wallet. The suspect said they were "girlfriends." Further questioning led to Whitmore confessing to the murder of Mrs. Minnie Edmonds, age forty-six. Mrs. Edmonds' body had been found in a backyard at 444 Blake Avenue, Brooklyn, on April 14—ten days earlier. Death had resulted from multiple stab and slash wounds from a knife or similar weapon.

Detective Edward Bulger, who was present at the questioning of Whitmore in the Edmonds case, had been assigned to the investigation of the Wylie-Hoffert murders in its early stages. He thought the two photographs found in Whitmore's wallet resembled the blonde, blue-eyed Wylie girl and her roommate-victim. Further questioning resulted in Whitmore admitting to the murders of Misses Wylie and Hoffert. Whitmore's formal statement of guilt in the double murder was taken under the direction of Peter Koste, an assistant district attorney in the Manhattan district attorney's office.

Whitmore seemed to know details of the double homicide that had never been made public. In his statement, Whitmore gave the brand name of the broken soft-drink bottle that had been found, and he stated that he broke the blades of two of the knives used in the attack by using his heel and the floor, as in breaking a stick of wood. Lastly, he admitted that he took the photograph of Miss Wylie from the dresser of the crime-scene bedroom.

Whitmore was arraigned before Judge James J. Comerford in a Brooklyn court. An attorney, Jerome Leftow, was appointed to represent Whitmore when he stated that he was without legal counsel. After a brief out-of-court conference between Whitmore and his new attorney, both returned to court and Mr. Leftow told Judge Comerford that his client had made certain statements to the police but that they were made under duress and stress, and that his client now recants and repudiates all the confessions he had made. Whitmore was remanded to jail without bail by Judge Comerford for a hearing on the next Thursday.

Tuesday, April 27
243 Days After The Crime

Jerome Leftow now claimed that his client, George Whitmore, Jr., had asked police to give him a lie detector test when he was arrested. Additional data released by police connecting Whitmore to the Wylie-Hoffert murders was the substance of an unofficial statement published in the New York *Journal-American*. This press story stated that Whitmore knew the location of a razor blade found on the floor of the crime-scene bedroom, knew where its wrapper had been found in the bathroom, and was able to describe a Noxzema jar left on the bloody floor, and told of blood spots that were found on the bedroom window shade.

Wednesday, May 6
253 Days After The Crime

Whitmore was indicted by a Manhattan grand jury in the knife slaying of Janice Wylie and Emily Hoffert. The jury presented a two-count murder indictment to Justice Charles Marks, who ordered Whitmore taken into custody and arraigned for pleading. Whitmore pleaded "not guilty" to the murder charge.

Friday, October 17
317 Days After The Crime

Psychiatrists at Bellevue Hospital found George Whitmore, Jr., sane and able to stand trial for the Wylie-Hoffert murders. The finding concluded the longest study of any one patient in the long history of Bellevue's Psychiatric Center. Whitmore had been committed to Bellevue last May by Justice Charles Marks, following his arraignment and not-guilty plea in the Wylie-Hoffert case.

Saturday, January 2
393 Days After The Crime

Manhattan's district attorney, Frank S. Hogan, refused comment on the eight-month delay in the trial of Whitmore for the Wylie-Hoffert killings. Police reporters pointed to three factors that might account for the delay: (1) identity of the young blonde girl in the photograph found on Whitmore was in dispute; (2) whether the photograph was really taken from the death-scene apartment in 88th Street was also in dispute.

    Note: A few weeks after detectives arrested a new suspect in this case, D. A. Frank Hogan quietly asked the Manhattan court to release Whitmore in "the interest of justice." Whitmore was released to the Brooklyn District Attorney for trial in homicide cases in that jurisdiction.

Source: Paul B. Weston, *Criminal Justice and Law Enforcement—Cases* (Englewood Cliffs, N.J.: Prentice Hall, 1972). Reprinted by permission of Prentice Hall.

Discussion Questions

1. Is extensive case preparation necessary when an agency requires its investigators to submit progress reports throughout an investigation?
2. What is the rationale for organizing a final review of an investigation around a theme of witnesses and exhibits of evidence?
3. What is the emerging concept inherent in an *exhaustive* search for witnesses? An *intensive and scientific* crime-scene search for evidence? The *objective and scientific* laboratory services for processing physical evidence? Setting *limits on suggestibility* during interviews with witnesses and lineups for identification?
4. On the basis of available legally significant evidence likely to be admissible in court upon trial, is further action by the prosecutor against George Whitmore, Jr., for the Wylie-Hoffert killings justified?
5. Does the role of prosecutor in making the decision to prosecute an accused involve a preliminary evaluation of evidence on the issue of guilt or innocence?
6. What evidence collected by police, other than Whitmore's confession to the double murder, supports the police theory about this crime, and the conclusion about Whitmore's guilt?

7. Present an argument in support of the validity and reliability of reviewing a case from the defense frame of reference—that is, from the point of view of the case for the accused person.

Library Assignment

Prepare a list of at least five cases (court decisions) about the rights of defendants in custody awaiting trial.

Workbook Project

Summarize any one of the case studies in preceding chapters.

CHAPTER
14

The Investigator as a Witness

At the conclusion of an investigation, an investigator does know the victim, the circumstances of the crime, the identity of the offender, and sometimes possesses data on the motive for the crime. He or she has collected facts, linked them together, and mentally shaped a pattern of the crime and a narrative of the event with form and order. However, the events and incidents of a crime are known to the investigator only indirectly, through the interviewing of witnesses and other techniques of investigation. No matter how much intelligence and honesty went into the many decisions common to any investigation, the sum total is a subjective impression in the mind of the investigator.

The investigator as a witness is confined to the same narrow band of personal knowledge as any other witness, and he or she is under the same requirement to establish a proper foundation to show personal knowledge prior to giving any oral evidence.

Criminal investigators have a basic obligation to court and community when testifying as a witness in a criminal case, and this is to tell the truth as they have found it. They also have a basic obligation to themselves and their employing agency not to allow any item of their appearance or any act done within the courtroom to affect adversely their testimony on the witness stand. The legal significance of an investigator's testimony can be damaged by behavior on the witness stand not in harmony with his or her role as impartial fact-finder and reporter.

Men and women serving as trial jurors evaluate witnesses on what they say, how they say it, and their overt behavior while saying it.

ACTION PRIOR TO COURT APPEARANCE AS A WITNESS

Investigators should review the substance of their testimony before the trial of the defendant. Investigators can easily review areas of likely inquiry in direct examination in a friendly questioning by an associate, the prosecutor. Unfortunately, investigators can never prepare fully for cross-examination. This is usually hostile questioning by an unfriendly attorney, the defense counsel.

Major areas for this self-analysis are the following:

1. Is the possible testimony arrayed in a manner that allows the investigator to relate it simply and convincingly so that the triers-of-fact will both understand it and believe it?
2. Is the investigator willing to state that he or she does not know or cannot recall certain facts?
3. Is the investigator ready to acknowledge mistakes made in the investigation when questioned, and is he or she prepared to answer questions truthfully and directly, without hedging?
4. Is the investigator prepared to refute and rebut any allegation of "improving" the case against the defendant?
5. Will the investigator prepare for being a witness by refreshing his or her memory immediately prior to trial?

The legal significance of evidence demands a pretesting for credibility. Self-analysis is often difficult, but it is vital to the integrity of an investigator's testimony. The facts told by the investigator as a witness will be tested in court against standard bases of credibility.

Investigators should confer with the assigned prosecutor a short time prior to the date of court appearance for a last-minute check. No doubt the prosecutor is well informed as to the expected testimony and possible areas of difficult cross-examination. A brief review just before a court appearance can be helpful to the investigator–witness. Ethical prosecutors will make certain that any conference with witnesses does not degenerate into a "coaching" session, and an investigator–witness should promptly admit to any such meetings under questioning, as they are normal case-preparation procedure.

On the date an investigator is scheduled for a court appearance, he or she should allow a generous amount of time for the trip to the courthouse. This is a safeguard against unexpected traffic delays or other events that make the trip longer than anticipated. In court appearances, it is better to be very early than to rush in at the last minute.

On arrival at the courthouse, and prior to opening of court, the investigator should sign in or check in as required by local regulations, and make contact with the assigned prosecutor. If witnesses are excluded from the courtroom until they have testified and been excused, the investigator must wait outside the courtroom until a bailiff calls his or her name. If witnesses have not been excluded, the investigator should take a seat within the courtroom and await his or her call.

This is an excellent time to get rid of the "stage fright" not uncommon among witnesses about to testify. This is a nebulous fear, often based on no more than a reluctance to get up and talk in front of a group of people. With investigator–witnesses it may be complicated by knowledge that the presiding judge is known to have a short-fuse temper, or by their last experience with an aggressive cross-examiner.[1]

Stage fright is often cumulative. Initially, there is an increase in the blood pressure and respiration rate of the witness: a feeling of being "charged up." This is accompanied by a noticeable dryness of the mouth, and sometimes, a shaking of the hands. This is unusual and uncomfortable, and the common reaction is greater anxiety.

Stage fright can be controlled. Planning ahead is the first step. Therefore, quickly review the substance of the case and possible questions. Second, mentally scan past experiences that can be termed "satisfactory" or better, and relax in the thought that such past experience will be helpful in successfully concluding the forthcoming session as a witness. Finally, remember that anxiety at this time is nothing more than the witness's body preparing the person to do his or her best.[2]

GENERAL BEHAVIOR AS A WITNESS

Upon being called as a witness the investigator walks promptly to the front of the courtroom. He or she stops in the "well" of the court, usually in front of the witness stand, to take the oath to tell the truth. This is an important stop on the way to the witness stand. A court officer proffers a Bible. The witness-to-be places his or her hand on it. The court officer then administers the oath (usually slowly and clearly) and the witness-to-be replies in the affirmative. The investigator's behavior during this portal ceremony should reflect a deep and sincere belief in the oath.

The first questioning of a witness that is not within the scope of any previous examination of the witness is the direct examination conducted by the party calling the witness (subpoena). In the case of investigator–witnesses, this is most often the prosecutor. This questioner guides the witness to prevent deviation from relevant facts. This stage of the examination is followed by cross-examination by defense counsel. Cross-examiners are likely to be aggressive. In either stage of this examination a witness is expected to be responsive to questions.

Cross-examiners often prefer to limit the responsiveness of a witness by phrasing questions calling for a yes-or-no answer. A "yes" means that the witness accepts the idea expressed in the question; a "no" indicates that the witness rejects the idea. If a cross-examiner does not use simple language in his or her query, then "yes" or "no" is not a simple response. Therefore, if a witness does not fully agree with the idea expressed in the question, he or she should give a negative response: "no." A "qualified yes" is often a responsive answer, but it is not usually allowed as the scope of the question may be extended when the witness explains the need to qualify the answer.

As a general rule, the investigator–witness is not alone at this time. The prosecutor will usually speak out and ask the court to have the question withdrawn, reworded, or thrown out.

Any witness who does not understand a question has the right to ask that the question be repeated, usually read by the court reporter. Sometimes, when this request is made, the questioner will withdraw the question and rephrase it.

How best to answer questions? Speak up! Speak clearly and loudly enough for everyone in the courtroom to hear all the testimony, and use simple language in making responses.

Simple language is plain talk. It helps people to understand what the meaning of each answer is. Beyond the limits of a yes-or-no answer, an investigator–witness should speak in complete sentences rather than sentence fragments. Normally, each sentence should express no more than one idea. Short sentences space out ideas. Jurors, as well as others in the courtroom, get a breathing spell between them.[3]

Open-end questions are often asked of investigator–witnesses during direct examination. These queries detail one segment of the investigation and ask the witness to respond "in your own words." The key to a responsive answer, and one that will usually be understood by all listeners, is to use short sentences arranged in chronological order.

The time element in responding to questions is also important in any evaluation of a witness by in-court listeners. A short pause before responding is good behavior. It allows the prosecutor to interpose an objection to the question if he or she wishes. It also indicates a thoughtful reflection upon the substance of the question and the response.

Investigator–witnesses should avoid using underworld slang and police lingo. Jurors are unfamiliar with such language and will not understand it—and possibly a good portion of the witnesses's response in which this language is used. To many jurors a "hit" does not mean to kill, a "piece" does not indicate a pistol or revolver, and a "scam" does not describe a criminal conspiracy. Similarly, jurors have little understanding of words common among police personnel; for instance: "pinch" (arrest), "frisk" (search), "DOA" (dead on arrival), and "FOA" (for other authority).

An investigator–witness must be courteous to questioners. This may be difficult with some defense attorneys, but it is an imperative rule. Questioners should be carefully addressed. Avoid the prefix "Mister," as it may be viewed as sarcasm. Be cautious of "Madam," as it not only means a lady, but also a woman in charge of a brothel. "Counselor" seems to be fairly safe as a general term for either the prosecutor or defense counsel, man or woman.

The apogee of discourtesy is to interrupt a questioner when he or she is phrasing a question. An interruption usually damages the ability of jurors to understand the question and any response made by the witness when the question is finally completed. Jurors, as well as others in the courtroom, view this conduct as argumentative. This evaluation can be harmful to the goals of the prosecution.

Another caution for any investigator–witness is: do not argue with defense counsel. Arguing destroys the image of the witness as an impartial fact-finder and reporter. Jurors do not expect investigators to be friendly with the defendant or his or her counsel, but any argument during cross-examination can antagonize many jurors, as it projects a hostility toward the defense beyond the expectations of these men and women (remember: defendants are innocent until proven guilty).

A final caution is not to lie or misrecollect on the witness stand. Unfortunately, many investigator–witnesses are sensitive about one or more areas of the investigation in which they failed to perform up to standard, or were overzealous in their performance. Rest assured that no circumstance of this area of the investigation will be left unexplored when a cross-examiner detects this sensitivity. It is also reasonably certain that any attempt to "stonewall" or "cover-up" can be disastrous to the credibility of the witness.

If any sensitive areas do exist, the best procedure is to discuss them with the assigned prosecutor prior to trial and obtain his or her guidance. These guidelines will probably be to admit to any substandard practice, inefficiency, or incompetency if questioning begins to exploit one or more of these areas. It is better to have the jurors think of a witness as a bungler (a common human condition) rather than a perjurer (an unacceptable human condition).

One survival technique for withstanding the most aggressive and belligerent cross-examination is to think and rethink constantly the fact that cross-examination of a witness is a constitutional right of all defendants—an absolute right.

NONVERBAL COMMUNICATION

Nonverbal communication is anything someone does that another person finds meaningful. It is a process of a person transmitting nonverbal cues that have potential meaning to one or more observers.[4] Nonverbal communication is "body language." Body movement and eye behavior send signals to observers.

In the drama of witness and questioner as it is staged in U.S. courtrooms during criminal trials, the observers and listeners are jurors. These men and women are alert to what the witness is saying, and they are also alert for any body language signs that will help them to better understand the testimony of the witness and evaluate his or her credibility. There is little doubt that many jurors mentally note what they do not hear to evaluate fully the net worth of what they do hear from a witness.

Communication without speech is transmitted through body movements and eye behavior. Facial expressions (smiles to frowns), head nods and shoulder shrugs, gestures (clenched fists to folded arms), leg crossing, and toe-tapping are all body movements. The direction of eye movement, and the frequency and duration of eye contact, sum up common eye behavior.

A good portion of "body language" is involuntary and difficult or impossible to control. On the other hand, anyone can learn to mask some basic emotions.

Investigator–witnesses can easily learn the rudiments of masking nonverbal communication that indicates to observers that the witness is bored, impatient, anxious, surprised, angry, or fearful. Then a conscious effort to avoid these indicators while testifying should not interfere with the testimony of an investigator–witness.

As far as any body movement is concerned, most basic police academy lectures on being a witness have long emphasized "Don't fidget." Sit down. That's what witnesses are supposed to do on witness stands. Better yet, sit still.

Eye behavior is a nebulous area. "Do what comes naturally" is generally good advice. In making eye contact initially, the eyes should move casually to the presiding judge, the jury, prosecutor, defense counsel, defendant, and to the spectators. When asked a question, the eye contact is with the questioner. In answering, the eye contact moves from the questioner toward the jury, where the witness scans the jury box as he or she responds. If reading from notes or exhibits, the investigator–witness should look upward toward the jury box now and then and briefly make eye contact with one or two jurors. When extensive answers are called for by questions, the witness may pick out jurors who he or she believes to be more attentive than others and make a less-than-staring eye contact.

Clothing is also nonverbal communication, but investigator–witnesses are usually police officers, and most police departments have established rules for the appearance of their members in court. If a man or woman is working in uniform, these rules usually require court appearance in uniform. For members working as investigators in an out-of-uniform assignment, there is usually a "dress code" specified—or stylized by custom—for appearance in so-called plainclothes. To identify the latter group as police officers, most departments require that badges or identification cards be pinned to the outer garment of the witness. Many badge cases are designed so that one-half of the case slips into the breast pocket of a coat and the other half hangs out and over the pocket—displaying the badge or ID card as if pinned to the coat.

To be identified as a police investigator by uniform or badge is not out of order. After being sworn in, police witnesses must give their name, assignment, and the name of their employing agency. What may be a negative nonverbal communication is to stress this class membership by displaying a holstered revolver or pistol through an open jacket. (See Chapter 9, Interviewing Witnesses and Interrogating Suspects, for a discussion of nonverbal communications during interrogation sessions.)

CONDUCT AFTER TESTIFYING

After testifying, the investigator–witness should make a graceful exit from the courtroom. Stopping to shake hands or chat with the prosecutor on the way out is definitely taboo. If the witness has not been excused by the court, he or she should wait in the hallway until the next recess prior to speaking to the prosecutor in a low-key conversation. Also, this is the time for the witness to speak to the prosecutor about segments of his or her testimony about which the witness may be concerned.

Many prosecutors want the investigator–witness to be available for recall to the witness stand, and they will make whatever arrangements are necessary. While in or about the courtroom during this period, the investigator should not discuss his or her testimony with anyone except the prosecutor assigned to the case or a person designated by this official.

At this time, or shortly thereafter, the investigator should review in his or her own mind as much of the testimony given as possible. These are self-teaching sessions in which the investigator impartially (as possible) examines his or her performance on the witness stand. In this fashion, every minute spent on the witness stand can be educational and serve as a means of improving future performance in court.

Selected References

1. John J. Burke, "Testifying in Court," *FBI Law Enforcement Bulletin,* XLIV, No. 9 (September 1975), pp. 8–13.
2. John F. Wilson and Carroll C. Arnold, *Dimensions of Public Communication* (Boston: Allyn and Bacon, 1976), pp. 34–36.
3. Rudolf Flesch, *The Art of Plain Talk* (New York: Harper & Brothers, 1946), pp. 31–56.
4. Loretta A. Malandro and Larry Barker, *Nonverbal Communication* (Reading, Mass.: Addison-Wesley Publishing Company, 1983), pp. 4–28.

Chapter Review

Discussion Questions

1. Can "stage fright" be controlled? How?
2. Why are investigator–witnesses advised not to argue with a cross-examiner?
3. Define nonverbal communication.
4. What body movements indicate boredom, impatience, anxiety?
5. Do you believe eye contact between an investigator–witness and jurors in a criminal trial is important? Why?
6. Sum up the recommended behavior for investigator–witnesses following their appearance on the witness stand.

Library Assignment

Review library materials available on nonverbal communication. Prepare a summary of findings.

Workbook Project

Prepare an outline of major body movements. List what you believe is the likely message transmitted to jurors when a witness makes each of these movements during his or her testimony.

CHAPTER
15

Homicides and Assaults

Criminal homicides, from murder to manslaughter, and common and aggravated assault are major crimes against the person. The crime scene and the circumstances of the attack are the focus of these investigations.

Criminal homicide is usually divided by statute into murder in the first degree, murder in the second degree, and manslaughter. Murder in the first degree is well defined by statute, but second-degree murder is frequently defined as any murder that is not first-degree murder, and manslaughter may be defined as any criminal homicide that cannot be legally classified as murder.*

The *corpus delicti* of *all* criminal homicide is:

1. An evidentiary showing of the death of a human being.
2. An evidentiary showing of a criminal agency.
3. An evidentiary showing that the criminal agency was the proximate cause of the death.

The death must be of a human being and occur within a certain period of time after the act causing the injury. The time may vary in different jurisdictions from one to three years.

*Most of the criminal law material in this and the following chapters was excerpted from Kenneth M. Wells and Paul B. Weston, *Criminal Law* (Santa Monica, Calif.: Goodyear Publishing Co., 1978), pp. 177–264.

The *criminal agency* means that the death was caused by another person's unlawful act or omission. The form, manner, means, or instrument are not material. A failure to act where a duty exists may provide the unlawfulness. A physical touching is not necessary. The only requirement is that the act (or omission), manner, or means be unlawful.

The proximate cause is that cause which produces a result without the aid of any intervening cause: the direct cause.

The *corpus delicti* of homicide is an essential element of homicide and must be proved beyond a reasonable doubt before any conviction may stand.

MURDER AND MALICE AFORETHOUGHT

State statutes uniformly describe murder as the willful and intentional killing of a human being with malice aforethought.

Except where the felony-murder doctrine applies, an essential element of murder is malice in addition to proof of the *corpus delicti*.

Malice aforethought (malice, maliciously) denotes a particular state of mind on the part of the criminal agent. It is an inexcusable, unjustified, and unmitigated person-endangering state of mind. At common law, *malice aforethought* meant the intentional killing of one human being by another without legal excuse or without circumstances that would reduce the offense to manslaughter.

The essential element of malice aforethought may be proved in several different ways:

1. The specific intent to cause death or grievous bodily harm.
2. Knowledge that the act will cause death or grievous bodily harm (use of a deadly weapon).
3. The specific intent to commit any felony.
4. Resisting arrest or escape from arrest or custody.

Malice does not necessarily import an ill will toward the victim but at the least it must include a general malignant recklessness toward the lives and safety of others. Usually it is an intention to commit the act and a concurrent appreciation of the likely result. The malice must preexist the act and can be implied from the character of the act.

Malice aforethought is shown "where the defendant for a base, anti-social purpose, does an act which involves a high degree of probability that it will result in death." The specific determinations to satisfy this definition are:

1. Was the act (or acts) done for a base anti-social purpose?
2. Was the accused aware of the duty imposed upon him not to commit acts that involve the risk of grave injury or death (or was there diminished capacity)?
3. If so, did he or she act despite that awareness?

Modern statutes define malice aforethought. For example:

Such malice may be express or implied. It is expressed when there is manifested a deliberate intention unlawfully to take away the life of a fellow human being. It is implied when no considerable provocation appears, or when the circumstances attending the killing show an abandoned and malignant heart.

Malice aforethought should not be confused or equated with deliberation and premeditation, which are additional elements necessary to find a murder to be in the first degree.[1]

FIRST-DEGREE MURDER

Most jurisdictions specify that the circumstances of a first-degree murder should additionally include deliberation and premeditation.

A significant number of states list one or more of the following circumstances, which will also prove a first-degree murder:

1. Poison used.
2. Lying in wait (ambush).
3. Torture involved.
4. Act greatly dangerous to life.
5. Use of a destructive device (bomb, grenade, etc.).
6. Killing of a law enforcement officer.
7. Killer(s) hired.
8. Killer(s) previously convicted of murder.
9. Killer(s) serving life sentence.
10. Killing of a witness.
11. Killing in the commission of specified felonies (robbery, burglary, arson, etc.).

Premeditation and *deliberation* denote a willful and specific purpose and design to kill. *Deliberate* means a full and conscious knowledge of the purpose to kill. *Premeditated* means a design that must precede the killing, no matter how short the time between the design and the killing.[2]

The law does not undertake to measure the length of the period during which a thought must be pondered before it can ripen into an intent to kill which is deliberate and premeditated, and the true test is not the duration of time but the extent of the reflection.

The words *willful, deliberate,* and *premeditated* indicate that the legislature meant, by reiteration, to emphasize its intent to ensure considerably more reflection than the mere amount of thought necessary to form intention. If not, every intention to kill would be first-degree murder. There must be more than malice for a finding of first-degree murder.

THE FELONY-MURDER RULE

The felony-murder rule imposes a particular criminal liability upon the perpetrator of a felony for a death that occurred during the commission of that felony. The attack resulting in the killing must be done while the crime is in progress, and not after it is over.

A limitation on felony murder is the merger doctrine, that the felony must be independent of the killing. Robbery would be an independent felony. Aggravated assault would not be independent since the attack (assault and battery) merges with and is an essential step toward the killing. The purpose of the rule is to deter felons from killing in the course of their crime. The killing during the commission of the felony needs no further proof of malice, but is itself sufficient proof of malice.

The felon must be the agent of the killing. Thus, the felony-murder rule may not extend to a case in which the police officer shoots the defendant's crime partner while they are fleeing the robbery scene.

Most states class felony murder as first-degree murder; a major percentage of states specify rape, robbery, burglary, and arson as the felonies essential to the first-degree felony-murder rule; a few states expand the specified felonies to such offenses as mayhem (maiming), kidnapping, sexual offenses, larceny, sodomy, illegal drug sales, aircraft piracy, and escape; and some jurisdictions simply state "during the commission of a felony."

SECOND-DEGREE MURDER

Murder in the second degree is best described as a criminal homicide committed with malice aforethought but without the elements of deliberation and premeditation. Second-degree murder may be committed without intent to kill, and in the course of any felony inherently dangerous to human life.

MANSLAUGHTER

Manslaughter may be divided into degrees by number or by name. A common division is the following: voluntary manslaughter, involuntary manslaughter, and vehicle manslaughter.

Voluntary manslaughter is an unlawful killing *(corpus delicti)* without malice, during a sudden quarrel or heat of passion, upon adequate provocation. There is also a hidden but most important element: an intent to kill. This intent to kill is an essential element of voluntary manslaughter, and must be formed during a sudden quarrel or heat of passion. If the intent was so formed the law will presume the absence of malice. Malice is, of course, actually present but the law will presume it is absent where, because of human infirmity and with sufficient provocation, the defendant acts rashly and with his or her reason obscured. Anger, sudden resentment, jealousy, or terror may render the mind incapable of cool reflection and may reduce the degree of crime to manslaughter.

And the authorities are all agreed that the question is not alone whether the defendant's passion in fact cooled, but also was there sufficient time in which the passion of a reasonable person would cool? If in fact the defendant's passion did cool, which may be shown by circumstances, such as the transaction of other business in the meantime, rational conversations upon other subjects, evidence of preparation for the killing, etc., then the length of time intervening is immaterial. But if in fact it did not cool, yet if such time intervened between the provocation and the killing that the passion of an average person would have cooled, and his or her reason has resumed its sway, then still there is no reduction of the homicide to manslaughter.

If the fatal wound be inflicted immediately following a sufficient provocation given, then the question as to whether the defendant's passion thereby aroused had in fact cooled, or as to whether or not such time had elapsed that the passion of a reasonable person would have cooled, is a question of fact to be determined upon a consideration of all the facts and circumstances in evidence; but, when an unreasonable period of time has elapsed between the provocation and the killing, then the court is authorized to say as a matter of law that the cooling time was sufficient.

Ordinarily one day, or even half a day, is in law much more than a sufficient time for one's passion to cool; and *a killing committed upon provocation given some 9 or 10 months before is not, on account of that provocation or any passion, engendered thereby, reduced to manslaughter. A deliberate killing committed in revenge for an injury inflicted in the past, however near or remote, is murder.*

In order for a killing to be voluntary manslaughter, there must be both heat of passion (or sudden quarrel) and adequate provocation.

Involuntary manslaughter is an unlawful or negligent killing without malice and without the intent to kill necessary for voluntary manslaughter. The requisite must be gross negligence—negligence amounting to a reckless disregard of the consequences and of the rights of others. It is not mere negligence or carelessness; it is an extreme or gross negligence, tantamount to a wanton disregard for the safety of life and limb.

There is an additional definition of involuntary manslaughter that is similar to the felony-murder rule: If a death is the result of an unlawful act not amounting to a felony (misdemeanor), it is involuntary manslaughter. Knowledge of potential danger is not necessary in this definition. Gross negligence is imputed by the doing of the unlawful act.

It is well to keep in mind that the *corpus delicti* of a criminal homicide is an essential element of the crime of manslaughter as well as murder.

Vehicle manslaughter is similar to involuntary manslaughter: a vehicle-caused death resulting from an unlawful act not amounting to a felony which is the proximate cause of death. If there is gross negligence (entire failure to exercise care or such a slight degree of care as to show indifference) the manslaughter may be tried as a felony. If there is mere negligence it may be deemed a misdemeanor.

The rise in the number of deaths caused by the operators of vehicles has caused the lawmakers of many states to enact specific vehicle-homicide laws.

The Uniform Vehicle Code proposed by the National Committee on Uniform Traffic Laws and Ordinances suggests the following:

(a) Whoever shall unlawfully and unintentionally cause the death of another person while engaged in the violation of any state law or municipal ordinance applying to the operation or use of a vehicle or to the regulation of traffic shall be guilty of homicide when such violation is the proximate cause of said death.

(b) Any person convicted of homicide by vehicle shall be fined not less than $500 nor more than $2,000, or shall be imprisoned in the county jail not less than three months nor more than one year, or may be so fined and so imprisoned, or shall be imprisoned in the penitentiary for a term not less than one year nor more than five years.

The laws of most states and of the District of Columbia specifically mention homicide caused by the operation of a vehicle which is comparable to the offense and penalties set forth above.

"SUSPICIOUS DEATH" INVESTIGATION

Police investigators conduct a "suspicious death" investigation in all cases in which the circumstances of the death indicate violence or "foul play"—that is, some criminal agency; when death occurs in a place other than the residence of the deceased; or when the deceased is not under the care of a physician at the time of death. From the preliminary investigation of a suspicious death, the facts may result in a decision to close the case because death resulted from natural or accidental causes or was a suicide; or a decision may be made to continue the investigation because the facts disclosed indicate a criminal—that is, unjustified or unexcused—homicide.

The "suspicious death" concept is more than the traditional "foul play is suspected" in which the circumstances of a death strongly suggest murder. It is a classification of certain unexplained deaths so that they will be investigated until either the circumstances indicate that death was due to natural, accidental, or self-inflicted causes, or the criminal agency is determined and the criminal "agent" identified.

The autopsy is a major method of detecting murder. This postmortem examination of the victim in a suspicious death case is performed by a competent physician, generally a surgeon specializing in this field. These surgeons are the professionals who determine the cause of death. If the autopsy surgeon reports that the nature of death is natural, accidental, or suicidal, then the death is not classed as a criminal homicide. When the autopsy surgeon's report states that a death resulted from a criminal agency, a criminal homicide has been detected.

Although police investigators can make no contribution to the professional conclusions of an autopsy surgeon as to the cause of death, they can assist such surgeons by supplying information related to the means used to cause death. Current prevailing practices in the detection of criminal homicide have led autopsy surgeons throughout the United States to expect a report from a police investigator prior to the time of the autopsy which will inform the autopsy surgeon of all the facts in the case known to police at that time. These include the details as to the scene of the crime, possible weapons, and other matters that relate to the death. The autopsy surgeon does not participate in the linking of the perpetrator to the criminal agency that caused death. This is the role of the investigator.

Thus, the detection of criminal homicide is based on finding the answers to four classic questions:

1. What was the cause of death?
2. What were the means (agency) that caused death?
3. Was the homicide excusable or justifiable?
4. Who was responsible for causing death (the agent)?

The autopsy surgeon shoulders the major responsibility in response to the initial question as to the cause of death. He or she and the police investigators work together in seeking to find the agency of death and whether the agency is criminal, excusable, or justifiable. The police accept the sole responsibility for identifying the person responsible for the killing.

SUICIDE, ACCIDENT, OR CRIMINAL HOMICIDE

Persons who kill themselves adopt methods similar to techniques used in criminal homicides. Many suicides do not leave classic notes explaining their reasons for self-destruction and do not foreshadow their intent to commit suicide in any observable fashion. Even when the circumstances of a suspicious death reek of murder, a comprehensive investigation may indicate that the death was suicidal.

Circumstances of a suspicious death often invite an investigator's conclusion of self-destruction. However, a great number of murderers attempt to hide their crime by cloaking it in a dressing of clues and traces that will indicate suicide. The greatest problem exists when the circumstances of the death show that someone has a motive, or could have a motive, for murder. An investigation into the background of a victim may strongly indicate an apparent suicide is out of character with the victim's lifestyle, a fact that must be weighed heavily before closing a suspicious death case as a suicide.

The techniques of criminal homicide are similar to accidental causes of death. Death can result from being pushed out of a high window, or from accidentally falling out of the window; it can result from being shot by another person, and a fatal gunshot wound can be the result of an accident while cleaning a firearm; it can be caused by another's plunging a knife into a vital area, and an accidental fall on a bottle can drive shards of glass into the same vital area and cause similar fatal injuries; a fatal dose of poison can be administered by another, or taken by mistake; and a skull can be crushed with a blunt instrument, or the same injuries may result from falling down a flight of stairs.[3]

IDENTIFICATION OF VICTIM

In most homicides there is no problem in identifying the victim. He or she is known and can be identified by relatives and friends. Identifying a victim becomes a problem when death occurs in a public place, a hotel, or a place not the domicile of the victim. This is particularly true when the victim is one of the large transient population in the United States. Although the transient population is made up primarily of homeless men, the drug scene has contributed a great number of runaway girls and boys to the ranks of those who move about from place to place in the United States.

A major problem of victim identity occurs when the killer attempts to avoid detection by doing away with the remains of his or her victim through burning, sinking the victim in a substantial body of water, cutting the victim up, or destroying the victim's remains by chemical means.

Sometimes the killer does not seek complete destruction of the body, but may attempt to destroy only portions of the remains to prevent or delay identification. There are scientific means for the identification of the partial remains of victims in suspicious deaths. Among the possibilities are:

1. *Fingerprints.* If the victim had been fingerprinted in his or her lifetime, this is a positive means of identification.
2. *Dental work.* This is a comparison identification, with the dental work of a victim being matched with the dental work of a person who has been missing from home or is otherwise unaccounted for.
3. *Bones.* Bones serve as a broad index of identification when other means are not available because of the condition of the victim's remains. They may indicate sex, height, and age; and sometimes time of death, cause of death, and other features of identification.
4. *Surgical procedures.* Surgery that took place during the lifetime of the victim may also aid in identification.

Estimates of the size, age, sex, and race of a homicide victim are possible from the study of the victim's remains, but identification of the unknown victim must depend on finding a sufficient number of unique physical characteristics for comparison with records that were made during the victim's lifetime. Insofar as skeletal remains are concerned (no fingerprints), dental records and body x-rays are the most likely means of identification. Dentists can be queried and identification made from dental records, and bone injuries severe enough to suggest hospitalization during the victim's life can lead to existing x-rays in hospital records and result in a positive identification.[4]

TIME OF DEATH

Criminal homicide investigations have a built-in time clock keyed to the time of death. Methods for establishing this vital time, or period of time, range from the testimony of witnesses (the person who saw the killing, or who last saw the victim alive, or the person who discovered and reported the crime), to the testimony of autopsy surgeons as to the condition of the body of the victim when found or examined, which generally can indicate the time of death.

The time of death connects the events that happen prior to the crime with the actual killing in homicide cases. The important questions related to this time-clock sequence are:

1. What activity was the victim engaged in at the time of the fatal assault?
2. What activity did the victim engage in immediately prior to death (24 to 48 hours, and longer if warranted)?[5]

Inasmuch as the only certain time element in the beginning phases of a homicide investigation is the time the crime was discovered, the witness or witnesses who can testify to this aspect of the case are carefully questioned as to the circumstances that first aroused their interest or suspicions, and *the time* of that event; how they found the victim and if he or she was found dead; *the time* of the discovery of the victim; and the circumstances *and time* of reporting this discovery to police.

As a homicide investigation continues, witnesses are located who talked to the deceased victim prior to the fatal assault, either in person or over a telephone. Such witnesses can give information as to the content of the conversation and its *time*. Sometimes, the activity in which the victim was engaged prior to or at death can be *timed* within reasonable limits. This is particularly true of habitual activities such as travel to and from employment and organized recreation.

In the reconstruction of the last hours of the victim, there is a tracing from one individual to another in chronological sequence from the time of death to the discovery of the crime. Who was the last person to have contact with the victim? Where was the last place the victim visited or was physically present prior to appearance at the death scene? Can this person who last saw the victim provide information as to where the victim had come from and who he or she had seen just prior to this time? Can the person or persons at the place where the victim was last seen, prior to being at the death scene, provide any information as to where he or she was prior to this time? Reconstructing the last hours of a homicide victim's life is a leapfrog procedure from one individual and one place to another person and place as far back in time as is necessary to gather some understanding of the dispute or of the onset of the circumstances that led to the homicide.

To "bracket" the time of death as closely as possible by the testimony of witnesses who can provide information, homicide investigators have adopted a tactic developed in hit-and-run cases, where the offending motorist flees the scene of an accident without helping the victim or reporting the event to police. Investigators assigned to hit-and-run cases regularly return to the accident scene looking for witnesses. They return at the same time of day, and day of the week, as the accident. They question passers-by and residents or store personnel in the neighborhood of the crime scene who were not located and interviewed previously.[6]

Witnesses located in this manner may be able to provide important items of direct evidence in the event they witnessed the fatal attack or a related circumstance. Officers who persevere at these revisits to the death scene and its neighborhood discover witnesses to corroborate other evidence as to *when* the victim was last seen alive, the *time* of the crime's discovery and report, or even a new time of death.

EXHUMATION

A court order must be secured for exhumation—the removal of the body of a deceased person from its place of burial for a medicolegal examination to disclose the presence of previously unknown or improperly identified injuries, or the presence of poison or other noxious substance which would indicate a criminal agency caused death.

Examination after burial is rarely as satisfactory as an autopsy prior to burial. However, full autopsy procedures should be carried out, and the body should be fully x-rayed before and after the autopsy, and photographs of the body in both color and black-and-white film should be made prior to the autopsy and after the autopsy.

CHECKLIST FOR THE INVESTIGATION OF CRIMINAL HOMICIDE

A checklist for a criminal homicide investigation should be divided into stages to allow for the orderly progression of the investigation from its beginning, to its focusing, and then to the arrest of the perpetrator and crime partners, if any (see Figure 15–1).

Stage I: The Crime Scene

1. Be alert at the approach to and the entrance of the crime area for the perpetrator and others leaving the crime scene. All persons at or leaving the crime scene should be stopped and identified before they leave. Interviewing of such persons may be done at the scene or later.

2. The "good hard look" when entering the crime scene is important for an overview:

    a. *The Victim.* Give first aid or summon medical help, if necessary; note if victim is apparently dead or pronounced dead by physician; take dying declaration, if possible.

    b. *The Scene.* Check entrances, exits, extent; protect weapons and other evidence; prevent entrance of unauthorized persons; call for techni-

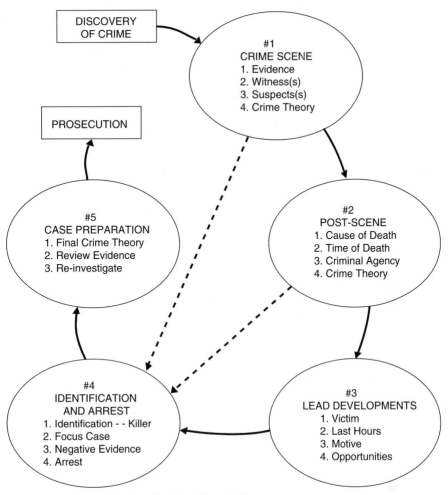

FIGURE 15–1 Investigation of criminal homicide.

cians (if available) to take photographs and process scene for finger-prints and other physical evidence.

3. Protect the integrity of the scene by warning all present not to smoke, use any plumbing (sinks, tubs, showers, toilet bowls), or towels, touch any objects or surfaces at the scene, or walk in or otherwise contaminate blood traces at the scene.

4. Identify witnesses, interview, get a statement of their knowledge of the crime, and begin the search for additional witnesses.

5. If an apparent suspect is at scene (case is focusing), warn him or her of rights, note appearance, clothing, physical and mental condition, and record any spontaneous utterances. All present at scene are possible suspects until the case has focused. Begin a search for suspicious persons and vehicles that were at the scene prior to or at the time of the crime.

Checklist for the Investigation of Criminal Homicide **221**

6. Record the scene:
   a. Photograph.
   b. Measure and sketch the scene.
   c. Make notes.
   d. Collect evidence and record where it was found and who found it; mark the evidence, transport it, and secure it with the property officer.
7. Seal the scene: Do not open the scene without prior agreement of associates, technicians, and the prosecutor.
8. Identify victim.
9. Develop a tentative crime theory.

Stage 2: Post-Scene

1. Determine time of death; "bracket" the time period:
   a. Witness(es) who saw victim alive or talked to victim by telephone before his or her death.
   b. Witness(es) who discovered victim (the crime).
   c. Medicolegal testimony setting a maximum and minimum time of death (report of autopsy surgeon).
   d. Other evidence.
2. Determine the place of fatal assault (when different from the place of discovery of the crime).
3. Determine cause of death:
   a. Apparent cause at the scene.
   b. Medicolegal autopsy report.
4. Determine means of death:
   a. Criminal agency.
   b. Specific weapon.
   c. Weapon recovered.
5. Develop tentative crime theory.

Stage 3: Lead Development

1. The background and activities of the victim.
2. Last hours of the victim:
   a. Contacts.
   b. Activity at time of death and prior to death.
3. Vehicle(s) used.
4. Injured suspects.
5. Informants.
6. Weapon.
7. Tie-ups with other crimes.
8. Knowledge of victim's activity; access to premises.
9. Motive: "pattern" of the criminal homicide.

10. Opportunity:
    a. Known persons at the scene.
    b. Possible persons at the scene.
11. Develop tentative crime theory to include the identification of one or more "prime" suspects.

Stage 4: Identification and Arrest

1. Develop evidence that will identify killer. Review evidence for *corpus delicti,* identification, and consistency with the crime theory.
2. Focus the case.
3. Exonerate innocent suspects.
4. Arrest killer and crime partner(s), if any.
5. Gather negative evidence as needed:
    a. Alibi.
    b. Self-defense.
    c. Intent:
        i. Mental state of suspect.
        ii. Sobriety.
        iii. Crime record of suspect.
    d. Crime or treatment (medical, psychiatric) records of witness(es) and victim.

Stage 5: Case Preparation

1. Reconstruct crime.
2. Summarize physical evidence.
3. Summarize testimony of witness(es).
4. Review motive (reason), intent.
5. Confer with associates and prosecutor.
6. Reinvestigate as warranted or directed by the prosecutor.
7. Prepare "cover sheet" (synopsis) to forward case records to prosecutor.

PATTERNS OF CRIMINAL HOMICIDE

The basic pattern of a criminal homicide ordinarily is disclosed in the initial investigation of a suspicious death. Even though a killer may attempt to falsify the facts of a dispute or cast the suspicion of guilt upon another person, a routine investigation should disclose the facts.

Among the basic patterns of criminal homicide are the following:

1. *The anger killing.* This pattern is an extension of the crime of assault. There is a dispute, anger develops; there is an attack on the victim with or without weapons, and the victim is fatally injured.

2. *The triangle killing.* The possibility that there is an errant husband, lover, or mistress should rarely be ignored. If there is a wife dead and a woman in a triangle situation, there are grounds for suspecting a husband who wished to rid himself of an unwanted wife. The reverse situation is frequently encountered; the wife is anxious to rid herself of an unwanted husband because of a developing romance. When the person who may have the motive in this triangle was also the last one to see the victim alive, the investigation starts to gather momentum in its development as a triangle killing.

3. *The revenge or jealousy killing.* The initial investigation of who the victim was, and the history of the involvement between the victim and suspects usually will disclose the motive of revenge or jealousy—and thus a suspect.

4. *Killing for profit.* The elimination of another person because the murderer would gain some benefit has long been a standard motive for murder. *Who would profit?* This is a splendid avenue of investigation for developing suspects. When the circumstances of a suspicious death show that persons who would profit from the death are among those who last saw the victim alive, there is support for developing a theory of criminal homicide along these lines. Murder for profit is closely aligned with the triangle-killing situation; the victim is eliminated to gain some benefit.

5. *The random killing.* Every killing has a motive, if "motive" is defined as a reason for the slaying. Even the random killing, where there is no prior connection or tie with the victim, has a motive. This type of killing is often termed unmotivated because the reason for the killing is clouded and unknown until the suspect is discovered. The killing of a complete stranger is perhaps the most difficult to solve. This pattern of murder may be disclosed by first excluding the usual or common patterns of criminal homicide.

6. *Murder-suicide.* This self-explanatory pattern of criminal homicide is one in which the killer self-destructs shortly after the fatal assault on the victim. These are often "compact" killings in which a husband and wife, boyfriend or girlfriend, or parent and child agree that both should die and one takes the responsibility for killing the other and then committing suicide.

7. *Sex and sadism.* This pattern of criminal homicide is marked by unusual violence. It may follow child molesting, rape, acts of perversion, or sadistic acts. It often has bizarre overtones. In one New York case the two girl victims were stabbed repeatedly, undressed, tied together face to face, and the killer rubbed Noxema on and about the rectums of his victims. In a Nevada case the victim's vagina and breasts were slashed deeply with a sharp instrument.

8. *Felony murder.* In these cases, the victim's death does not result from an angered attack, a triangle, revenge, jealousy, profit motivation, random chance, a murder-suicide compact, or sex-and-sadism; rather, death resulted from injuries inflicted by someone in the act of committing a felony. The criminal intent of the original crime carries over to the killing.

The investigator must not close his or her mind or the investigation too quickly. A homicide investigation may appear to fit one of the criminal homicide patterns, and evidence developed in a continuing investigation may reveal sufficient data to change its classification to another pattern, or to a combination of patterns.

A criminal homicide case in St. Paul, Minnesota, first appeared to be a burglary gone wrong. Mrs. Carol Thompson was found semiconscious and bloody in her home. She was rushed to a hospital where she died as a result of bleeding from multiple fractures of her skull. The death weapon was a blunt instrument, and when fragments of pistol grips were found in a pool of blood in the Thompson living room, it was assumed to be a pistol-whipping. Evidence of a burglary was apparent at the crime scene in the ransacking of bureau and desk drawers.

Continued inquiries developed the fact that the husband of the victim had been intimate with another woman and a new potential pattern developed: elimination of an unwanted wife. A few days later, when local insurance executives responded to police inquiries with the news that the housewife victim was insured for over $1 million with the husband as sole beneficiary, the "killing for profit" pattern was added as a possible motive for the crime.[7]

MOTIVE FOR MURDER

In a trial for murder, proof of motive is always relevant but never necessary. In a criminal homicide investigation, a motive is necessary and useful. It may surface while following the basic leads of benefit and opportunity or upon reviewing the relationships of the victim. Spouses, lovers, and former spouses and lovers of the victim promptly become suspects, as friends and relatives, not strangers, are often the killers.

Terms useful in describing these relationships are:

1. Spouse (or ex-)
2. Common-law spouse (or ex-).
3. Boyfriend; girlfriend (or ex-).
4. Live-in boyfriend; girlfriend (or ex-).
5. Sister; brother.
6. Mother; father.
7. Daughter; son.
8. Other relative (includes in-laws).
9. Friend of family; relative (specify).
10. Neighbor.
11. Business associate (specify partner, co-worker, other).
12. Acquaintance.
13. Seen before (as "known from neighborhood").

Terms useful in describing the frequency of the contacts common to a relationship are: live together, see daily, see weekly, see monthly, or hardly see at all.

SERIAL MURDERERS

Serial murderers repeat their crimes. Each murder is similar; each killing is an event complete in itself, but part of a series. Commonly, these killers act alone, but several of them have operated with a single crime partner.

This random selection of victim has a terrorism aspect. Murder in a series is frightening. Newspaper, radio, and television news reports not only give the gruesome details of the latest murder, but also imply "where it will happen next—who the next victim will be." As a result, these are investigations in which pressure from the general public is a constant factor.

Because of the random selection of victims, investigators find few leads to the killer's identity in working back from the victim, and very few witnesses are ever located who can give information about the appearance of the killer or the killer's vehicle.[8]

The victims in these crimes have been children, both boys and girls, and men and women of all ages. They are strangers to their killers. However, among the victims there is a high percentage of "street people": runaway children and adolescents, female and male prostitutes, and hitchhikers.

In a minority of cases no overt sexual component is present. One killer shot and killed his victims with a super-caliber revolver. He never had any physical contact with them. England's Jack-the-Ripper may have had sexual contact with his prostitute victims, but it appears that his only physical contact with them was incidental to his fatal stabbing attack.

Series murder is a crossover between the random-killing pattern (number 5 above) and the sex-and-sadism pattern (number 7 above). Unfortunately, searching for suspects among known sex offenders has not been rewarding; most of the serial murderers arrested have not been found to have an extensive criminal record of sex offenses.

A man-in-a-car is a major characteristic of most serial murders. The killer (with or without a crime partner) needs the vehicle to cruise for a victim; once successful in luring the victim into the car, he uses its confined space to partially control his captive, and its mobility to transport him or her to a place for the sexual attack and murder (sometimes two different places). Finally, he needs the car to dispose of the victim's body (see Figure 15–2).

An exception to this *modus operandi* is the serial rapist–burglar turned serial killer. This criminal selects homes at random, breaks and enters them, rapes and brutalizes female residents, and murders them and (possibly) their spouses and children. However, he uses a vehicle only for transport to the general area of his crimes.

As in any other homicide investigation, the emphasis is on a crime-scene search. In serial murders, this is the body recovery site (the disposal site to the killer). Second, a major effort should be made to locate witnesses who

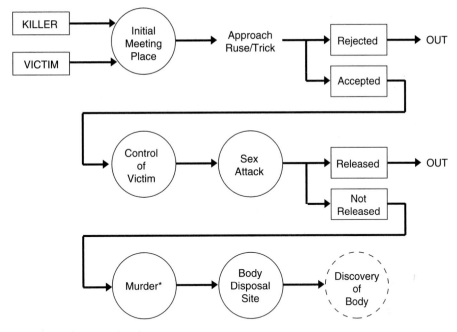

KILLER → Initial Meeting Place → Approach Ruse/Trick → Rejected → OUT

Accepted

Control of Victim → Sex Attack → Released → OUT

Not Released

Murder* → Body Disposal Site → Discovery of Body

*At sex-attack site or elsewhere

FIGURE 15–2 Man-in-a-car serial murderer.

observed the killer's vehicle at or near where the body was discovered. Most of these killers use great care in disposing of bodies so as to avoid any observation by others. Therefore, physical evidence has become of great importance in these cases.

Fibers from carpets (killer's home, vehicle) or the killer's clothing have been found at these scenes, as have human head hairs, pubic hairs, and other microscopic transfer evidence linking victim and killer. This physical evidence may not identify the killer, but it has great legal significance once the killer has been identified and arrested. Whenever the assigned investigator can manage it, he or she should request the services of a crime-scene-evidence technician, if available, and this person should work each body recovery site as the cases progress in the series. This continuity of assignment should be extended to the crime laboratory; the investigator should request that the same criminalist be assigned to process the evidence found at each body recovery site. Newly assigned scene and "lab" technicians may not perform at full efficiency because they are not aware of the evidence found and processed in previous murders in the series.[9]

The mobility of serial killers is extensive. Now investigators can find out if similar murders have occurred elsewhere in the United States. The Violent Criminal Apprehension Program (VICAP) of the Federal Bureau of Investigation is the clearinghouse for this information. Investigators send in data on their local murders (VICAP Crime Analysis Report), and when cases are linked, the reporting investigators in the local agencies are given each other's names so that they can coordinate their work. All reports are confidential, and the only intrusion on the local scene is the help provided by linkage reports.[10]

Linkage is also possible at local levels through an examination of crime reports concerning a "failed" approach or the release of a victim after the sexual assault. One girl's story of the "approach" linked up with past murders in the series, and her description of the vehicle led to its identification and the arrest of its owner; and in another case, the released victim immediately reported to police and gave them an excellent description of her rapist and his vehicle. When arrested, this suspect soon confessed to a series of murders being investigated locally.

The apogee of linking local with "foreign" jurisdictions to improve the investigation of violent crime is the recently formed Homicide Investigation and Tracking System (HITS) based in the state of Washington and serving a regional area of surrounding states (California and Oregon) and across-the-border areas of western Canada. HITS is a computerized program that collects and analyzes information about murders, attempted murders, missing persons (with suspected foul play), unidentified persons believed to be murder victims, and predatory sex offenses.* HITS relies on law enforcement agencies in Washington State and out-of-state cooperating jurisdictions to voluntarily submit information on these crimes as they occur, and this information is stored in the files that compose the system. The major benefit to local detectives assigned to investigate a murder and/or rape case is early and ongoing access to relevant information not available in any one police agency.[11]

STALKERS

About half of states in the United States now have penal code provisions to combat stalking. For instance, in Kentucky, stalking is defined as an intentional course of conduct that:

1. is directed at a specific person or persons;
2. seriously alarms, annoys, intimidates, or harasses the person or persons; and
3. serves no legitimate purpose.

Stalking ranges from phone calls and letters, through personal confrontations, to attempted murder, murder, and/or rape. A recently developed typology of stalkers may be helpful to investigators who are suddenly confronted with the activity of a stalker. This classification of stalkers is:

1. Celebrity (victim is known on an impersonal level—actor, sports star).
2. Lust (predatory sex, escalates to murder).
3. Hit (professional killer).

*Predatory sex offenses are those in which the victim is a stranger to the assailant.

4. Love-scorned (intends violence against known victim).
5. Domestic (ex-lover or spouse, "get even" violence).
6. Political (selected victim is personal stranger; political aspect).[12]

INVESTIGATING ASSAULTS

An *assault* is an unlawful attempt, coupled with the present ability, to commit an injury on the person of another. In other words, it is an attempt to commit a battery: an unlawful beating or other wrongful physical harm inflicted on a human being without his or her consent.

In assaults the victim is usually alive and willing to cooperate with investigators. In many cases the assailant is known to the victim, and the investigation becomes one in which establishing the identity of the perpetrator is not a problem. When the assailant is not known to the victim, the investigation of assault is closer to homicide investigation than it is to any other investigation.

Assault without a weapon, and in which serious injury is not inflicted on the victim, is a relatively minor crime. Assault with a deadly weapon or an assault in which serious injury is inflicted with or without a weapon is aggravated assault—a serious crime.

Aggravated assaults are often murder attempts that have failed as a result of the intervention of witnesses, prompt medical treatment, or pure luck. For this reason, the characteristics of assailants in either crime are likely to be similar.

The term *violent injury* is synonymous with *force* in assault cases. It includes any application of physical force even though it entails no pain or bodily harm and leaves no marks.

The assault scene must be protected and its integrity preserved. Of course, the victim must be given first aid and prompt medical attention, if required, and furniture may have to be moved to care for the victim. The investigating officer at the scene should make note of these changes in the crime scene, and if the victim is moved from the position he or she was in at the time of the officer's arrival, the victim's original position should be noted (possibly by a chalk outline on the floor, street, or other surface).

The crime scene is processed for evidence that will assist in reconstructing the crime and identifying the participants as to the roles of the attacker and the victim; witnesses at the scene are interviewed for the same purpose. The work of investigators at this time is concentrated on securing the details of the attack and of the dispute that led to the attack.

When the victim is seriously injured and requires medical care, the investigating officer should accompany the assault victim to the hospital. The situation is flexible, but the objective is to gain as much information as possible from the victim as to the circumstances leading to the attack, the nature of the attack, and the identity of the attacker. The information provided by a victim in periods of consciousness after being seriously injured may be compelling evidence in a future trial. If a victim is *in extremis* and is aware of impending death, the officer may secure a dying declaration indicating the victim's mental condition and the circumstances of the attack.

If the circumstances warrant, the officer accompanying an assault victim to the hospital should collect, mark, and retain the victim's clothing as evidence. Future processing by criminalists may indicate the direction of force in bullet holes and the damage caused by knives or other sharp instruments, bloodstains and their origin, and similar evidence.

It is particularly important that the weapon or weapons involved in an assault be promptly identified, recovered, and related to a participant in the assault event. The police search of the crime scene should disclose the presence of all weapons at the scene at the time of arrival of police; police interviewing of eyewitnesses should seek disclosure of any weapons used in the attack and not found at the crime scene.

Prior to an actual assault, the offender and the victim usually have had some interaction. Generally, this was an "altercation"—a verbal dispute. The dispute's origin may be domestic difficulties or a pushing-and-shoving situation to prove masculinity among drinking partners. Although intoxication (drugs or alcohol) may not be a factor, the high incidence of assaults during late evening and early morning hours suggests that many disputes arise in some leisure-time pursuit, or because of such activity. Investigators must seek out the details of the dispute in assault cases in order to cast some light on the reason for the attack and the roles of both the victim and the assailant.

Sometimes in the preliminary investigation of an assault case the investigating police charge both participants with assault or "disorderly conduct." A "fielder's choice" of responding police has often been to charge the apparent victim (the one most seriously injured) with "disturbing the peace" until it can be ascertained whether the victim was responsible for the attack upon himself.

Data in assault investigations are usually organized within the following major segments:

1. *The scene*—reconstruction of assault event.
2. *Dispute*—origin, place, time, participants, witnesses.
3. *Weapon or weapons*—existence or nonexistence, identified with user (attacker, victim), recovered at scene, recovered elsewhere.
4. *Negative evidence*—whether lawful resistance, victim armed, victim in prior fear of attacker (state of mind).

PROBLEMS OF PROOF

The major problem of proof in criminal homicide cases is the lack of eyewitnesses who could testify to the fact that the defendant caused the death of the deceased victim. A collateral problem area is in showing that the defendant is criminally responsible for the killing.

Unless the police–prosecutor team has unearthed a "smoking gun" witness ("I saw the defendant standing over the deceased and he had a gun in his hand . . ."), who can testify to an act done in a close-up time frame to the killing, they must depend on less compelling evidence to prove this vital element of criminal homicide. Circumstantial evidence may appear to be compelling, but its impact on the jury in the case may be minimal.

Justification, excuse, diminished capacity, and insanity are all claims intended to overcome the defendant's criminal responsibility for the killing. When placed in evidence by the defense, the prosecution's problem is to disprove or foreclose this defense claim.

Insofar as the range from capital murder to manslaughter, the burden on the prosecutor is to explain the theory of his or her case and to relate the law to the facts in a manner that the jurors can understand—and that will serve to guide them in their decision as to the degree of crime.

Defense counsel in serial murder cases now ask judicial approval under "discovery" procedure for an order to the prosecutor to search out and report on all murder cases similar to the criminal homicides charged against his or her client. As a result, it is no longer the prosecutor who determines "similar" murders for court review; the defense can now present similar-but-different murders to establish doubt in the minds of jurors.

The prosecution's burden of proof initially in assault cases is to identify the defendant as the aggressor. Second, when a claim of self-defense and/or provocation is made, the prosecution must overcome this claim or foreclose its credibility.

Selected References

1. KENNETH M. WELLS AND PAUL B. WESTON, *Criminal Law* (Santa Monica, Calif.: Goodyear Publishing, 1978), pp. 178–80.
2. *Ibid.,* pp. 182–94.
3. WILLIAM F. KESSLER AND PAUL B. WESTON, *The Detection of Murder* (New York: Arco Publishing, 1961), pp. 1–9.
4. LARRY MILLER et al., *Human Evidence in Criminal Justice* (Cincinnati, Ohio: Anderson Publishing, 1983), pp. 115–46.
5. EDWARD A. DIECKMANN, SR., *Practical Homicide Investigation* (Springfield, Ill.: Charles C Thomas, Publisher, 1961), pp. 23–25.
6. PAUL B. WESTON, *The Police Traffic Control Function,* 2d. ed. (Springfield, Ill.: Charles C Thomas, Publisher, 1968), pp. 210–11.
7. DONALD JOHN GEISE, *The Carol Thompson Murder Case* (New York: Scope Reports, 1969), pp. 5–20, 38–56.
8. DARCY O'BRIEN, *Two of a Kind—The Hillside Stranglers* (New York: New American Library, 1985), pp. xxii–xxiii, *passim.*
9. GARY TERRY AND MICHAEL P. MALONE, "The Bobby Joe Long Serial Murder Case: A Study in Cooperation," *FBI Law Enforcement Bulletin,* LVI, No. 11 (November 1987), pp. 12–18; No. 12 (December 1987), pp. 7–13.
10. JAMES B. HOWLETT, KENNETH A. HANFLAND, AND ROBERT K. RESSLER, "The Violent Criminal Apprehension Program—VICAP: A Progress Report," *FBI Law Enforcement Bulletin,* LV, No. 12 (December 1986), pp. 14–22.
11. ROBERT D. KEPPEL AND JOSEPH G. WEIS, "Improving the Investigation of Violent Crime: The Homicide Investigation and Tracking System," in *Research in Brief* (National Institute of Justice), August 1993.
12. R. M. HOLMES, "Stalking in America: Types and Methods of Criminal Stalkers," *Contemporary Criminal Justice,* 8, No. 4 (December 1993), pp. 318–26.

Chapter Review

Discussion Questions

1. Define a criminal homicide.
2. What is the role of the medical examiner (autopsy surgeon) in evaluating suspicious deaths?
3. List and describe the common patterns in criminal homicides. What patterns in criminal homicide are often related?
4. What are the possible routes (techniques) for identifying victims in suspicious deaths?
5. Why is the determination of the time of death of importance in the investigation of criminal homicide?
6. What procedures should be followed to protect the integrity of an autopsy in exhumation cases?
7. List five major segments of the on-the-scene phase of a criminal homicide investigation.
8. What are the similarities and differences between the investigation of criminal homicides and the investigation of criminal assaults?
9. How can a pattern of "serial murders" be established? Why are they difficult to close out with an arrest?
10. Describe the man-in-a-car serial murder *modus operandi*. At what points in these crimes is the murderer(s) most vulnerable?

Library Assignment

Research the killer–victim relationship in criminal homicides.

Workbook Project

Chart or diagram an outline of the investigation to be used when an investigator is confronted with a serial murder investigation.

CHAPTER
16

Forcible Rape

Forcible rape is an act of violence. It is not a crime of sexual desire, but rather an act of brutal violence as in murder-with-intent-and-malice. It should be investigated in the same manner as criminal homicides and just as thoroughly.

At common law, rape was termed the carnal knowledge (sexual intercourse) of a woman with force and without her consent. Consent induced by fear of violence is not consent, and it is against the woman's will if her male attacker uses an array of physical force to overcome the victim's mind so she dare not resist. Of necessity, since force or fear is an essential element of the crime of rape, evidence should be developed of the victim's resistance or that her resistance was overcome by force or that she was prevented from resisting by threats to her safety.[1]

The means used to overcome the will of the female victim is of major importance in rape investigations:

1. Force or the threat of the use of force.
2. Administering of drugs (includes alcoholic beverages).
3. Incapacity of the victim to consent (physical or mental condition, or age).

In the terminology of state legislatures, rape is said to be "aggravated" when the rapist is armed with a dangerous weapon, kidnaps the victim, inflicts bodily injury (assault), or is in a position of trust in regard to the victim: official authority (custody/control) or a familial relationship.

Date rape or "acquaintance rape" is male sexual aggression in which the female half of a twosome is forced to have sexual intercourse. Sexual coercion by dates or acquaintances is really rape. This is not the "blitz" rape without prior interaction between offender and victim and in which the offender immediately threatens or employs force to overcome his victim. In date or acquaintance rape, there has been a prior relationship between the offender and the victim, but the victim has been forced to have sex without her consent.

The prevalence of forced sex among dates and acquaintances may be increasing, but what is more likely is that victims are now more aware of their basic rights. This so-called "simple rape," after years of underreporting, is now being reported for what it is: forcible rape.[2]

INITIAL ACTION

The initial task of police upon receipt of a report of a forcible rape is to aid the victim (see Figure 16–1). Injuries may require immediate transportation to a local hospital providing emergency services; apparent "shock" should also warrant medical attention. Men and women taking these reports must do their best to avoid contributing to the victim's mental distress. The professional reporting officer realizes that the person reporting a forcible rape has just been through an emotionally shattering experience and acts accordingly.

Depending on the condition of the victim, the next step is the initial interview, in which the victim is asked about the circumstances of the crime and the identity of the rapist. If the victim requires medical attention or is in a state of shock, this should be very brief and limited to the facts of the crime, and a description of the rapist for a radio-broadcast alarm. If the victim can be questioned, this interview should probe all the circumstances of the crime and the identity of the rapist.

At the conclusion of this interview the victim should be told about the necessity of a physical examination. In the past few years great strides have been made in standardizing this examination. The victim should be informed that this is voluntary, but that her consent is vital to the collection and preservation of evidence that will reveal and corroborate the acts done to her and contribute to the identification of the rapist.[3]

A medical examination of a forcible rape victim may be conducted as part of the medical treatment of the victim, when hospitalized, or by special arrangement with the victim. The report of the examining physician becomes part of the record of the case. It is usually concerned with (1) bodily injuries of the victim, (2) evidence of force in relation to the rapist's sex act, (3) evidence of the completion of the sex act to the penetration required by rape statutes, and (4) evidence likely to identify the suspect.

The victim of a forcible rape may not know where she was raped, or may have been raped in the rapist's car—and the vehicle is not usually available until the rapist is arrested. If a crime scene has been located, however, it must be promptly secured until properly searched.

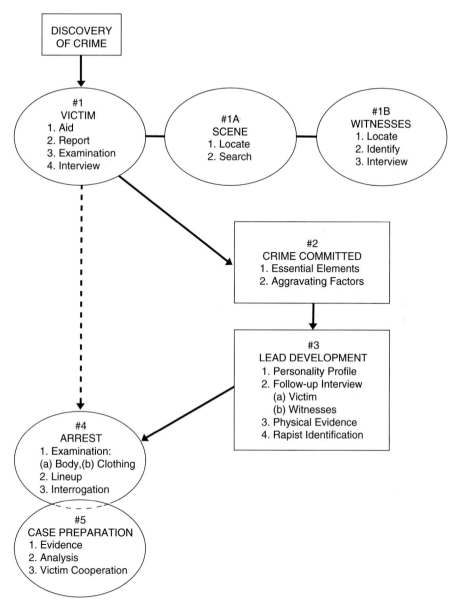

FIGURE 16–1 Investigation of forcible rape.

Correlated with the victim's detailing of what happened, who did it, and where it happened is the search for witnesses. Their identity and where they can be located is important at this time in the investigation; what they observed can be secured later.

When the reporting officer believes the circumstances of the attack spell out the elements of forcible rape (lack of consent, use of force/fear, resistance by the victim, and penetration), the case will be so classified and emphasis placed on identifying and apprehending the rapist.

When the victim identifies the suspect by name or as having been seen prior to the rape, the emphasis will be on locating this suspect. This is also true when the victim provides information as to the color, design, or license number of a vehicle used by the rapist.

Unless the rapist is promptly identified by information supplied by the victim (or witnesses), or arrested in the "hot pursuit" phase of the police apprehension process, discovering the identity of the rapist is likely to be the major problem in these investigations.

Identification of rapists is a problem because, as a general rule, informants are not helpful, *modus operandi* files do not supply any leads unless the rapist is a repeater (series rape cases), "benefit" and motive are common to all rapes, photographs of rape suspects are not usually available, and field interrogation reports are usually nonproductive.

Leads to the identity of an unknown rapist may be developed from the same areas as in criminal homicide investigations:

1. The victim's background.
2. Persons in contact with the victim and/or places visited by her in the hours immediately preceding the rape.
3. Weapons found at the scene.
4. Persons with "knowledge" or "opportunity"—access to the victim and scene of the crime, or actually at or near the scene at the time of the rape.
5. Injured suspects (when victim believes she scratched or otherwise injured the rapist).
6. Connect-ups with prior forcible rapes.

FOLLOW-UP INTERVIEW OF VICTIM

If a suspected rapist is arrested prior to this interview, the focus of this follow-up interview is identification that will be legally significant in court upon trial of the rapist.

Probing inquiries should concern just how the victim identifies her attacker. A lineup in which the suspect is placed among others to be viewed by the victim is warranted. All of the standard legal safeguards protecting this identification from suggestibility or other invalidating factors must be in operation.

When the victim is unable to identify the rapist at this lineup, but police believe they have arrested the right man, concentration is on other evidence of identity that will be compelling and will overcome this failure to positively identify the suspect in a lineup. Even when the victim does identify the rapist in a lineup, this other evidence of identity is important in the event that the lineup identification is attacked by defense counsel at trial.

If the rapist has not been identified, the focus of the interview is on what the victim can remember of the circumstances of the rape that will contribute to the rapist's identification.

What did the rapist look like? How was he dressed? Is a vehicle included in the circumstances of this rape? These and related questions should develop the physical characteristics of the rapist and how he was dressed at the time, and—perhaps—some vehicle identification. Investigators must probe the victim's recall of events to uncover any particular physical characteristics or article of clothing that is distinctive or unique. Even the most fragmentary description can be helpful.

Arrangements with a police artist or Identi-kit specialist may be indicated, with the victim cooperating and approving the final artwork as a reasonable illustration of the rapist.

Computer searches are now available in most state motor vehicle bureaus, and "possibles" may be obtained indicating vehicles matched to a fragment of a license number or a partial description, or both.

Extensive searches for unidentified multiple rapists ("series" rapists) by police in several urban jurisdictions have indicated the need for information on the rapist's behavior. Therefore, the victim should be questioned as to the rapist's "approach," how he exerted control of the situation, the sex acts attempted or committed, and whether or not the rapist made any effort to conceal his identity.

Was the approach friendly ("sweet-talking"), or brutal and surprising? What was the victim doing during this initial conduct? What had she been doing just prior to this contact? Where had she been? Who had she seen there? Who might have witnessed this initial approach? These are some of the questions that will give behavioral dimensions to the first contact of the rapist with his victim.

Rapists control their victims by some combination of the following:

1. Verbal activity, particularly threats.
2. Display of a weapon.
3. Physical force.

Threats and orders are the usual verbal activity, but some rapists are animated conversationalists. The essence of what was said and its pace are important aspects of the rapist's behavior.

What weapon was displayed? How does the victim describe it? What did the rapist do with it? The details of weapon display are also part of the rapist's behavior.

The use of physical force and its extent is one of the most important factors in defining the behavior of the rapist during the crime. A precise description of the force used should disclose whether it is minimal, excessive, or brutal. Another important factor is the rapist's reaction to resistance by the victim.

A problem area of these follow-up interviews of the rape victim may occur when the investigator seeks details of the sex acts attempted or committed by the rapist. Perhaps the best technique is to inform the victim that these queries are necessary to determine the behavioral pattern of the rapist, and—possibly—to connect him with other rapes.

This in-depth interview of the victim may be postponed because of her injuries, mental condition, the lack of a suitably private place, or a departmental ruling that such interviews should be conducted by specially trained personnel.[4]

FOLLOW-UP INTERVIEWS OF WITNESSES

The police officer accepting the report of a forcible rape has the duty of securing the names and addresses of possible witnesses, and—if time permits—of briefly interviewing them as to what they might have observed. Then, when the scene of the crime is located and the time of occurrence firmly fixed, investigators may interview or re-interview these witnesses.

Follow-up interviews of the person to whom the victim reported the rape, or from whom she initially sought help following the attack, are mandatory. These persons are primary witnesses to the victim's appearance and condition at the time. Of almost equal importance are witnesses who observed the victim and possibly the rapist just before the attack occurred.

Usually, rapists find some area in which they will not be observed to commit this assault upon their women victims. Therefore, investigators are unlikely to find witnesses to a rape. Of course, experienced investigators make every effort to find the chance onlooker who was a witness. Failing in this discovery, dependence is placed upon those individuals who observe the "before" and "after" phase of this crime.

The focus of these follow-up interviews of witnesses is to find evidence supportive and/or corroborative of the victim's report of the rape.[5]

PERSONALITY PROFILE: UNIDENTIFIED RAPIST

The victim's description of a rapist's behavior, upon analysis by competent personnel, reflects the personality of the rapist. From data secured in the follow-up interview of the victim, a criminal personality profile may be prepared. These profiles require the services of persons trained in the behavioral sciences who can review the manner in which the rapist behaved and portray the rapist as a person.[6]

The current history of the use of these criminal personality profiles in forcible rape cases indicates that this new tool of investigation has utility. Profiles have aided investigators to identify and arrest rapists. Experienced investigators believe that they are most useful in series-rape cases, but technicians in this field believe that they are equally useful in the investigation of any forcible rape.

There is a danger in working up a personality profile. Pretrial discovery procedures open to counsel for defendants in U.S. courts are likely to make this profile available to the defense.[7] A serious problem can develop for the prosecution when the defendant does not match the profile. Investigators must remember that the prosecution must show guilt beyond a reasonable doubt and that a defense attorney may use the discrepancies between a criminal personality profile and the defendant at trial to create this reasonable doubt.

ARREST OF SUSPECT RAPIST

Time is of the essence in arresting suspects in forcible rape cases. If the arrest is within a reasonable time from the time of the rape, a full body examination of the suspect should be conducted by medical personnel at a local hospital. Most hospitals with emergency treatment facilities have kits containing medical equipment and supplies used in these examinations. The report of the medical personnel conducting the examination becomes part of the total investigation report.

Since this is nontestimonial evidence, no legal problems should be encountered. Delays incidental to securing a court order could result in the destruction of evidence. If the arrestee consents to this examination, appropriate forms should be prepared for his signature.

Scratches, bites, bruises, and other wounds are searched for and reported; scars, moles, and tattoos are detailed; and physical evidence associated with the crime of rape should be secured. In addition, samples of the suspect's blood, urine, and hair (head and pubic) are taken.[8]

If there is reason to believe that clothing worn by the suspect at the time of arrest was worn at the time of the rape, it should be seized and sent to the forensic science laboratory for examination. If it is apparent that it is not the clothing worn at the time of the rape, a prompt search should be instituted for such clothing. A search warrant may be required. All suspect clothing should be promptly forwarded to the forensic science laboratory for examination. Reports of these examinations also become part of the investigation record.

The time of arrest is the time for investigators to search for associative evidence that will corroborate the testimony of the victim by placing the arrestee at the crime scene or in contact with the victim.

CASE PREPARATION

Investigators assigned to a forcible rape investigation must develop and hold the victim as a cooperative witness for the prosecution. The re-interviewing of a victim that is common in these cases, the time gap between arrest and trial, and the procedural safeguards protecting all accused persons would turn off most people—men and women—who had been victims of a serious, violent crime, and wanted the criminal punished.

Lack of victim cooperation may seriously complicate case preparation, and make it difficult or impossible to develop evidence proving the necessary elements of forcible rape. This aspect of forcible rape investigations, along with the humanitarian aspects of treating a rape victim decently and exhibiting a sincere concern for her well-being during the postrape period, should motivate an investigator to do his or her best to close out the case with an arrest and move it to trial without loss of time.

To overcome the common defenses of a forcible rape charge, the investigator must prepare a case in which the victim is cast as the most truthful witness in the trial, and confirming and compelling evidence must be available at the trial to depict the victim in this truthful-witness role.

PROBLEMS OF PROOF

When a defendant denies any involvement in a rape, the most common defense is mistaken identity plus an alibi for the time of the rape (a claim of being elsewhere at or about the time of the rape).

Identification of a defendant as the rapist is a major problem of proof. Some rapists pull a pillowcase over the victim's head or cover her face with an article of clothing; others wear gloves to avoid leaving conclusive physical evidence; and a few have been known to command their victim, "Don't look at me!" In recent years ski or stocking masks have become popular headgear for "blitz" rapists.

This problem can be overcome by a combination of the victim's identification of the defendant, the testimony about the initial meeting between victim and defendant (the rapist's "approach"), and "transfer" physical evidence linking the defendant to the victim or the scene of the rape.

An investigator must be innovative. In one recent New York case, the defendant was convicted primarily on a "voice lineup." The prosecution proved that this defendant wore a ski mask habitually, and the jurors apparently accepted the idea that the only possible identifier was his voice.

When a suspect admits to sexual intercourse with the victim, the usual defense is that of consent. This is an effective defense when the prosecution is unable to show that the victim's resistance was overcome by an overwhelming use of force or its immediate threat, or that the victim did resist and did attempt to flee from the defendant.

In cases involving date or acquaintance rape, the element of consent is likely to be a major problem. The fact of a prior relationship in these cases no longer implies such consent.

Problem-solving assistance is available from the Federal Bureau of Investigation's Investigative Support Unit (ISU). This is the unit of the FBI featured in the award-winning movie *Silence of the Lambs*. It offers profiles, assessments, and other support. The ISU may be able to take the details of the case under investigation and link them with multiple rapes elsewhere. Evidence from these "foreign" cases may provide a starting point for your case development.[9]

Sperm and blood are the common forms of evidence in rape cases. In fact, this has become such a given that many investigators have developed a "mental block" with regard to other physical evidence that may be as effective, if not more so, in proving guilt or innocence, and—possibly—penetration in rape cases.

As the use of condoms increases, it is likely that rapists will also use them with increasing frequency. Investigators aware of the potential for traces from condoms to associate a suspect with one or more rapes will find that many problems in investigating these sexual assaults will diminish and—possibly—disappear.*

This is because of the emerging forensic-science procedure for extracting condom lubricant traces from evidence items in sexual assault cases. If condom lubricant traces are to have significant evidentiary value, new collection procedures at crime scenes and in subsequent transport to a crime lab must be developed. This professional "how-to" is likely to include instructions for the doctor doing the medical examination, the investigator collecting crime-scene evidence, and the detective interviewing the victim and suspect.[10]

Selected References

1. Paul B. Weston and Kenneth M. Wells, *Criminal Law* (Santa Monica, Calif.: Goodyear Publishing, 1978), pp. 253–62.
2. Susan Estrich, *Real Rape* (Cambridge, Mass.: Harvard University Press, 1987), pp. 7–26.
3. Joseph A. Zeccardi and Diana Dickerman, "Medical Exam in the Live Sexual Assault Victim," in *Practical Aspects of Rape Investigation—A Multidisciplinary Approach,* Robert R. Hazelwood and Ann Wolbert Burgess (New York: Elsevier Science Publishing, 1987), pp. 315–25.
4. Lisa Brodyaga et al., *Rape and Its Victims: A Report for Citizens, Health Facilities, and Criminal Justice Agencies* (Washington, D.C.: U.S. Department of Justice, Law Enforcement Assistance Administration, 1975), pp. 37–42.
5. Jerry D. Moody and Vicki Ellen Hayes, "Responsible Reporting: The Initial Step," in *Rape and Sexual Assault: Management and Intervention,* ed. Carmen Germaine Warner (Rockville, Md.: Aspen Systems Corp., 1980), pp. 27–45.
6. Robert R. Hazelwood, "The Behavior-Oriented Interview of Rape Victims: The Key to Profiling," *FBI Law Enforcement Bulletin,* LII, No. 9 (September 1983), pp. 8–15.
7. Paul B. Weston and Kenneth M. Wells, *Criminal Evidence for Police,* 2d ed. (Englewood Cliffs, N.J.: Prentice Hall, 1976), pp. 314–17.
8. Richard Braen, "Examination of the Accused: The Heterosexual and Homosexual Rapists," in Warner's *Rape and Sexual Assault,* pp. 85–91.
9. C. R. Van Zandt and S. E. Ether, "Real Silence of the Lambs," *Police Chief,* 61, No. 4 (April 1994), pp. 45–52.
10. R. D. Blackledge, "Collection and Identification Guidelines for Traces from Latex Condoms in Sexual Abuse Cases," *Crime Laboratory Digest,* 21, No. 4 (October 1994), pp. 57–61.

Chapter Review

Discussion Questions

1. What is the major responsibility of police officers first on the scene of a forcible rape?
2. What are the "aggravating" factors in these cases?
3. Is the medical examination of a forcible rape victim necessary? When should it be conducted? What is its scope?
4. Outline the major factors to be covered by investigators during the follow-up victim interview.

*See Department of Justice Document 14 in Appendix C.

5. What is the focus of the follow-up interview of a witness in forcible rape cases?

6. Discuss the personality profile of a rapist. Have these professional evaluations utility? Is there a hazard to successful prosecution in these profiles? (Explain.)

7. What are the similarities and differences between the investigation of criminal homicides and forcible rape?

8. Does the prior relationship between victim and rapist in "date" rapes create a problem for the police–prosecutor team?

Library Assignment

Review available material on police–victim relations in forcible rape cases, and outline substandard police practices.

Workbook Project

Develop a list of all the items of evidence likely to contribute to the identification of a rapist. Divide this list into two segments: (1) evidence tending to identify the rapist prior to arrest, and (2) evidence tending to identify the arrested rapist as the person guilty of the rape or rapes under investigation.

CHAPTER
17

Abused, Sexually Exploited, and Missing Children

When children are the victims of criminal activity, they must be treated as persons to be helped (similar to victims of forcible rape). The shock of being a crime victim, particularly when it involves sex acts, is heightened by police inquiry into the circumstances of the crime. There must be prompt recognition by investigators that the child victim may require medical attention for possible injuries as well as the emotional shock of such a crime.

Investigators serve as the community's agent in redressing the harm done to the child victims of crime. The role of investigators in cases involving child abuse, sexual exploitation, or abduction is that common to all investigations: (1) reconstruct the event or events, (2) determine if a crime has been committed and—if so—what crime, (3) identify the person or persons responsible, and (4) take appropriate action. The investigator's role is not that of medical practitioner, social worker, counselor, or psychologist.

There is, however, a role carryover in these cases, and the investigator has the responsibility for referrals to professionals in any of the above disciplines whenever the investigation discloses that the child victim requires such help.

CHILD ABUSE

Child abuse is the intentional and deliberate assault upon a child in which serious bodily injury is inflicted by a parent, foster parent, babysitter, day-care worker, or a person in a nonparental relationship.

"Serious bodily injury" is a standard that excludes intervention by police in cases involving only minor assaults that could be described as corporal punishment incidental to disciplining a child.[1] In most areas of the United States, however, cases of child abuse brought to the attention of police—or discovered by them—are more properly classed as "child battering."

Signs of physical abuse, in the absence of a reasonable explanation for the injury, include:

1. Damage to the skin (burns, bruises, abrasions, lacerations, or swelling).
2. Brain damage (convulsions, coma, retardation).
3. Bone damage (pain on movement, deformity).
4. Internal injuries (shock, abdominal pain, signs of internal bleeding).[2]

When child abuse is suspected, the assigned investigator should take the child to a local hospital for examination by a physician. This examination and the physician's report will indicate the nature of the injuries and some age-dating, but the reporting physician may be reluctant to diagnose the case as child abuse.

Factors likely to influence physicians to link discovered injuries in a child with child abuse are:

1. Delays in seeking medical care.
2. Injuries not reported by parent or guardian.
3. Bruises or broken bones in an infant.
4. Age-dating of bruises indicate that they were sustained at different times.
5. Characteristic "wraparound" bruises caused by whipping with a belt, rope, or electrical cord.
6. Discrepancies in the story of parent or guardian as to how the injuries happened: the described circumstances are inconsistent with the nature of the injuries.

When the report of child abuse originates in a hospital, the examining physician may have been alerted by one or more of the above factors or simply because the parent or guardian bringing the child to the hospital were "hospital shoppers": bringing the child to a hospital outside their own community when a local hospital was readily available to them.

At this time, the investigator must make a decision as to whether or not to take the child victim into protective custody. The action taken should be in the best interest of the child. If a person in the home environment of a child is a suspect in the abuse, this is adequate cause to remove the child from this environment. (It also warrants action as to other children in the same household, if they have been abused or may be the subject of abuse.)

During the initial contact with a child victim, while present in the hospital, or following the physician's examination, the investigator must gather what facts he or she can from the child. This may be difficult when the child is very young (2 to 4 years old), or the child has been instructed by the person responsible for the injury not to talk to anyone about how it happened—or instructed to repeat a false story. Once a child realizes that the investigator is truly interested in finding out the truth, the details of the assault are usually forthcoming.

The when, where, and what-happened factors in these cases may cover a broad time period, several different locations, and different assaults. Once these factors have been correlated, the investigator can determine if a crime was committed, what crime, and the person or persons responsible for it (see Figure 17–1).

A prompt arrest and/or presentation of the case to the prosecutor for action will move the case to a court of competent jurisdiction. If warranted, after adjudication, the court can order a program for the child that will protect him or her from future serious injury or death.

CHILD SEXUAL ABUSE: INCEST

A person commits the crime of incest when he or she has sexual intercourse with a person known to be within the relationship of parent/child, brother/sister, uncle/aunt, or nephew/niece. Most state laws use a broad definition of incest: any sexual contact between family members who are not permitted such behavior by social norms.

So-called "psychological" incest is sexual activity between a child and a stepparent, foster parent, or a live-in boyfriend of the child's mother. It also includes such nonrelated family members as stepbrothers and stepuncles.[3]

This degrading form of child sexual abuse should be investigated along the same lines as physical child abuse: fact-gathering as to when, where, and what happened; and the identity of the adult involved and the adult's family relationship to the victim.

Some important validations of the fact that incest has been committed are:

1. The acts done were continuing and progressive.
2. The child's story of sexual abuse gives explicit detail in his or her own words.
3. Secrecy and the pressure to keep silent (gifts, threats, family disgrace).
4. Retraction of the accusation by the victim due to familial pressure.[4]

Child victims should be transported to a hospital for an examination similar to those conducted in cases of forcible rape. A similar examination of the suspect at the time of arrest may be warranted. Both examinations are oriented

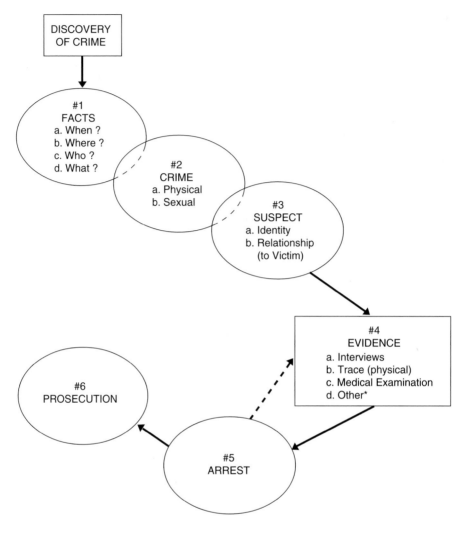

*Includes Network Development–Sex Abuse.

FIGURE 17–1 Investigation of physical and sexual child abuse.

to discovering and collecting evidence supportive of the victim's story of the sexual abuse.

CHILD SEXUAL ABUSE: PEDOPHILIA

Pedophilia is a sexual perversion in which children are the preferred sexual object. Pedophiles are child molesters whose sex acts against children run the full range of sex experience in all of its deviancy. Pedophiles may be male or female; heterosexual or homosexual.[5]

The Federal Bureau of Investigation suggests a two-part classification of child molesters: (1) situational and (2) preferential. Situational child molesters do not have a sexual preference for children but do molest them when the victim and the immediate environment encourage them. Preferential child molesters do have a strong sexual preference for children—their sexual fantasies include children. It is common to find child pornography in their home, office, and/or car at the time of arrest or in the postarrest period pursuant to a court-ordered search.[6]

Situational child molesters are sexually active only to the extent of the "targets of opportunity" encountered; preferential child molesters are usually sexually active, reusing old victims and seeking new ones. Investigators should assume that the offender in the case under investigation has committed the crime with some frequency, in various locations, and with other child victims. Diligent inquiry will disclose a network of other incidents, victims, and pedophiles. This "mushroom" factor links activity likely to identify a previously unknown child molester, and evidence available upon the arrest of a suspect (address book, identity of friends and associates) will often disclose the full details of a network of pedophiles and their victims. Common to this organization of pedophiles and child victims are registered sex offenders.[7]

Victims are good sources of information about these networks—particularly those boys or girls who have participated in this activity voluntarily, either because of friendship for the molester or because they were paid for their services. (Teenaged "runaways" of both sexes have admitted to this prostitution as a survival technique in a hostile environment.)

Many molesters operate in their home or business neighborhoods, sometimes using one victim to recruit others in the age group of the molester's sexual preference. Others gain access to children by seeking leadership positions in church and community programs centered on children. Name one organization for youths or an occupation providing contact with children and rest assured that some adult identified with it has been arrested for child sexual abuse. The *mushroom factor* in these cases takes little more than simple queries to develop: Who are the victim's friends in the neighborhood or what child group is involved?

Pedophiles (aka *chicken hawks)* now use computers and available online services to locate potential child victims. They pose as another youth and begin their conversations with teenage subjects (drugs, girls, school, parents), but as the friendship develops, they suggest a meeting. Child exploitation through computer bulletin boards and online information services is a rapidly growing problem.[8]

Investigators can learn more about this when they make their first arrest, questioning the offenders about their activities. When their acts do not imply guilt, but merely a displayed interest in the area, these offenders are likely to talk—and teach.

Sexual offenders who target children as their victims are not usually violent persons, but in the history of this crime in the United States there is considerable evidence of these offenders killing their child victims. Some of the serial murders uncovered in recent years have been committed by child molesters who killed with the frequency of their sexual attacks. Investigators should mentally red-tag any child abuse case: *Investigation may disclose a murderer!*

The discovery of the physical abuse of a child or familial child molesting depends on the reporting of a battered child or an incestuous relationship by a concerned adult or the victim. In the case of pedophilia, however, there is a great need for police investigators to detect and discover child sexual molesting. Detection may originate in a casual inquiry of a runaway child encountered in other police activity as to how they survived "on the street"; in the investigation of an unrelated crime; or in the willingness of a knowledgeable defendant in a case awaiting trial to reveal significant information as to child molestation in exchange for help with his or her plea negotiations.

A medical examination of the victim in these cases is more than warranted, as is a similar examination of the suspect upon arrest. This examination should be aligned with the reported sex abuse, and be focused on discovering urogenital or anal injuries, pain, or irritation; and whether there is evidence of a venereal disease or any illness related to child molestation.

Clothing worn by the victim at the time of the attack, and clothing belonging to the suspect seized by police as evidence at the time of arrest or in the post-arrest period, should be sent to the forensic science (crime) laboratory as physical evidence possibly containing trace evidence linking the suspect to the victim or place of occurrence of the attack, or evidence of the sexual contact or contacts.

When, where, what happened, and *who did it* are the classic queries indicating lines of inquiry likely to develop the circumstances of these crimes. If the collected evidence indicates child sexual molesting, the investigator should act promptly to identify and arrest the adult responsible. Then, from evidence developed by the investigator at the time of arrest or in the post-arrest period, the investigator works hard to link the suspect with other victims and other cases of child sexual abuse.

PSYCHOLOGICAL MALTREATMENT OF CHILDREN

Physical and sexual abuse of children by a parent or guardian are usually accompanied by psychological maltreatment: a pattern of psychically destructive adult conduct.

Psychological maltreatment is described as adult treatment of a child, such as:

1. Rejecting and ignoring the child as a person.
2. Isolating him or her from neighbors and friends.
3. Terrorizing a child with verbal threats.
4. "Mis-socializing" him or her by encouraging antisocial and delinquent behavior.[9]

Investigators should be alert for signs of this mistreatment when a parent or guardian is a suspect in a physical or sexual abuse case. Evidence of psychological maltreatment could be relevant and material to a case of parental (or a person in a substitute-parent relationship) child abuse. At the least, any significant evidence in this area should warrant a referral to local mental health, child welfare, and/or children's protective services.

THE CHILD AS VICTIM–WITNESS

Children may testify in court in a variety of cases, but they are most likely to be classed as "key witnesses" in child-abuse trials. It is in these cases that the child is not only the victim, but also the only eyewitness. Moreover, in these criminal proceedings there is a strong suspicion among police and court personnel that there is a special alertness about protecting the constitutional rights of the defendant(s). It isn't that the rights of the child victim–witness will be disregarded, but that the child's competence as a witness will be examined in depth, and the testimony given in court will be sharply scrutinized.*

Investigators usually operate on an assumption that the child is telling the truth, and this is desirable in any "first-line" agent: parent, teacher, neighbor, physician, or police officer. However, the assigned investigator must work beyond this assumption and critically appraise the story of the child during interviews and in post-interview periods when evidence supporting the child's story is sought. Linked to this appraisal is an ongoing demand that the investigator "carrying" the case offer an opinion as to the competency of the child victim as a future key witness.

Supporting evidence of a child's story of physical or sexual abuse should develop evidence in total at the "probable-cause" level along with basic leads likely to upgrade the case when fully developed. The investigator needs this for his or her decisions during the investigation; the child victim needs such support for his or her testimony in court.

In forming an opinion as to the child's competency, investigators should be mindful that the child must be observant, articulate, know truth as opposed to lies, and understand that a witness must testify truthfully.

California's McMartin preschool case was long and costly and a revelation to criminal investigators as to deficiencies in their inquiries. Police investigators attempted to jump-start their investigation by sending a letter to close to 400 parents of children enrolled in this school. This letter encouraged parents to question their children about any sexual abuse by teachers at the school. However, many parents promptly mentioned it to one or more of the suspect teachers, alerting them to the threat of an ongoing investigation. The case went on for several years to a very unsatisfactory conclusion: no one convicted; no truth of the accusations proved in court.[10]

Investigators need to learn the how-to of securing information from children. A nonsuggestive interview is likely to be more productive and have a basic integrity.

*See Department of Justice Document 5 in Appendix C.

The basic structure of this interview should contain several "don'ts": (1) don't suggest anything to the child—or to his or her parent(s)—or even appear to suggest; (2) don't reveal the allegations of other children involved in the same investigation; (3) don't use dolls of any kind until subsequent interviews, and then only with good reason; and (4) avoid news releases until the crime and its facts are clear and focused.

MISSING CHILDREN

Any young person under the legal adult age (unemancipated) who, without permission of parent or guardian, remains away from his or her home for twenty-four hours or more is generally termed a "runaway" by local police.

Police in large cities often field a "Diaper Squad" to patrol local bus stations and "gut" areas containing occupancies such as adult theaters and bookstores, massage establishments, the "stroll" section in which local prostitutes operate, and the "meat rack" frequented by boys and young men catering to homosexuals.

When runaways spend the funds they carried with them when they left home, they find difficulty replenishing the money through legitimate employment. "Hustling" is an aggressive reaction and is generally focused on sex-for-sale. Less aggressive runaways are picked up by pimps or sexual deviates and sometimes forced into prostitution.

Unfortunately, despite the work of police officers to locate missing children and return them to their parents or guardians, the number of runaway children in the United States provides pedophiles with recurring opportunities to find child victims.

The great number of runaways creates a major problem to searching for and finding a missing child. In addition, local police have to depend on police of other jurisdictions in this search-and-identify task. So-called "Runaway Programs" operated by various youth organizations are emerging as a new resource for runaways, getting them off the street and encouraging them to contact their parents or guardian. These programs may also become a resource for investigators seeking missing children, particularly when there is some evidence the child has fled to a particular city.

When some aspect of a child's disappearance indicates abduction, local police will generally make an effective and timely response. The 1982 Missing Children's Act placed federal resources at the service of local police. The National Crime Information Center's Missing Person File of the Federal Bureau of Investigation is being utilized in searching for missing children believed to have been abducted.

The first step in the investigation of child abduction is to make certain that the child has not been kidnapped by a parent or grandparent. Once it is certain that the child is not a pawn in a family dispute, every reasonable means should be used to broadcast the facts of the case and a description of the missing child. Since many of these victims are murdered, this description should contain the child's dental chart, medical information, and fingerprints—

if available. (Emerging programs by police to fingerprint local children is focused on providing the parents with the child's fingerprints in case he or she becomes a victim of an abductor.)

The investigation into an abduction generally follows the outline of any criminal homicide investigation. Since the victim is not available for interviewing, the investigator must concentrate on securing data about the victim's movements just before his or her disappearance. As facts are gathered, data are added to the published alarm.

Collaterally, investigators probe among registered sex offenders, suspected pedophiles disclosed as part of a network in child sexual abuse investigations, and suspect persons or vehicles seen in the neighborhood of the child's disappearance.

Investigators must move promptly along two general lines of inquiry: (1) find the child, and (2) identify and locate the suspect. One experienced detective has described this type of investigation as "frantic." And this is a graphic description of the fast-breaking and aggressive investigation likely to produce results in these cases.

PROBLEMS OF PROOF

One of the problem areas of great concern to the police–prosecutor team is the child victim as a witness. From the inception of the investigation the child victim has the burden of telling the humiliating and distasteful circumstances of the crime many times. Then, upon the trial of the offender, the child witness must testify under conditions that are bound to be stressful to the young boy or girl involved. A friendly, direct examination may lessen this stress, but there is undoubtedly an upward surge in the stress factor when defense counsel begins his or her cross-examination. Responses of a child witness under cross-examination can be disastrous to the prosecution's case.

Selected References

1. JOSEPH GOLDSTEIN, ANNA FREUD, AND ALBERT J. SOLNIT, *Before the Best Interests of the Child* (New York: The Free Press—Macmillan Publishing Company, 1979), pp. 72–77.
2. *Child Abuse Prevention Handbook* (Sacramento, Calif.: California Department of Justice, 1982), pp. 7–9.
3. ROBERT J. BARRY, "Incest: The Last Taboo," *FBI Law Enforcement Bulletin,* LIII, No. 1 (January 1984), pp. 2–9.
4. MARVIN R. JANSSEN, "Incest: Exploitive Child Abuse," *The Police Chief,* LI, No. 2 (February 1984), pp. 46–47.
5. SETH L. GOLDSTEIN, "Investigating Child Sexual Exploitation: Law Enforcement's Role," *FBI Law Enforcement Bulletin,* LIII, No. 1 (January 1984), pp. 22–30.
6. B. D. MCILWAINE, "Interrogating Child Molesters," *FBI Law Enforcement Bulletin,* 63, No. 6 (June 1994), pp. 1–4.
7. VINCENT DEFRANCIS, *Protecting the Child Victim of Sex Crimes Committed by Adults* (Denver, Colo.: The American Humane Association, 1969), pp. 1–2.
8. JAMES GARBARINO, EDNA GUTTMAN AND JANIS WILSON SEELEY, *The Psychologically Battered Child—Strategies for Identification, Assessment, and Intervention* (San Francisco: Jossey-Bass, Inc., Publishers, 1986), pp. 1–29.

9. Nancy Walker Perry and Lawrence S. Wrightsman, *The Child Witness: Legal Issues and Dilemmas* (Newbury Park, Calif.: Sage Publications, 1991), pp. 2–10.

10. T. M. Dees, "Cyberchip Chickenhawks: A Mix of Kids, Computers, and Pedophiles," *Law Enforcement Technology*, 21, No. 10 (October 1994), pp. 52–55.

Chapter Review

Discussion Questions

1. What is the role of the investigator when investigating physical child abuse? When investigating sexual child abuse?
2. What circumstances are likely to indicate physical child abuse?
3. What is "psychological" incest?
4. Describe "network" development in child sexual abuse cases.
5. Can police detect child sexual abuse? How?
6. What is "psychological maltreatment" of children?
7. Outline the reasons for the medical examination of victims in child abuse cases.
8. What is the relationship between "runaways" and abducted children?
9. How do child molesters use computers to find potential victims?

Library Assignment

Prepare a selective bibliography of at least five references in the following areas: (1) child battering, (2) incest, and (3) missing children.

Workbook Project

Prepare a checklist of action to be taken by an assigned investigator when a child under the age of 7 is reported missing.

CHAPTER
18

Robbery

To substantiate charging a suspect with robbery, the investigation must uncover legally significant evidence that a crime was committed, that this crime was robbery, and that the defendant committed it. In such investigations the basic evidence must range through each of the essential elements of the crime of robbery. These essential elements are:

1. Taking of personal property from the person or presence of a possessor.
2. Against the possessor's will.
3. By force or fear.

Taking "from the person" means from the victim's body or his or her clothing, and "from the presence of possessor" means within sight or hearing of the victim. It is in the nature of robbery that an offender not only takes personal property with intent to steal, but also carries it away. A taking of a possession away from the victim and into the control of the robber is sufficient. Control by the robber rather than the distance moved is the issue in asportation. "Against the will of the possessor" is implied in the force and fear element of robbery. This force or fear must be adequate to frighten the victim and make the victim part with his or her property against his or her will.

Robbery is generally divided into degrees to express the legislative intent that armed robberies are more serious than unarmed robberies:

1. First degree—robbery while armed with a dangerous or deadly weapon (likely to cause death/serious wounding).
2. Second degree—robbery accomplished by physical force or its threat, but without a weapon; includes purse-snatching.[1]

Robbery is a felony-level crime likely to result in a convicted robber receiving a lengthy sentence and may be aggravated (leading to a longer sentence) when the robber has an armed crime partner at the scene, and either of them inflicts serious bodily injury against victim and/or witness(es).

Related crimes, such as kidnapping, must be substantiated in a similar manner. However, larceny and assault merge with the robbery. Kidnapping, on the other hand, may not merge with the robbery. In 1969, the top court in California repudiated the doctrine that any movement of the robbery victim amounted to kidnapping. In *People* v. *Timmons,* 482 F. 2d 648 (1971), the court held that the true test was whether the movement of the victim(s) substantially increased the risk of harm beyond that inherent in robberies. If it did, kidnapping would be added to the charges against the robber or robbers; if not, the "movement" is part of the robbery activity.

During the robbery investigation, the investigator need not make the decision as to whether these crimes join with the robbery or are separate crimes; the investigator's role is simply to collect all available evidence and develop the existence of related crimes from the array of collected evidence.

Another area of concern is the difference between robbery and extortion. One of the essentials of robbery is consent resulting from force or fear); in extortion, the victim consents more willingly. Consent may be induced by persuasive threats that are related to future harm or disgrace rather than here-and-now harm. A close call for investigators is a scam described in 1890 by Chief of Detectives James Byrnes of the NYPD as the *"Badger Game."* This is an extortion scheme in which a woman places a selected victim in a comprising position (nude, in bed, in a hotel room) and then victimizes him by demanding money, when her male accomplice breaks in and pretends to be an outraged husband threatening violence, scandal, or the like.

The harassment of the victim is the key to the success of this scheme. It has been successful over the years with only minor changes, as evidenced in 1995 in Ventura, California:

A 71-year-old wealthy man is the victim; a 30-year-old "stripper" is "the woman." One night, in a developing friendship in the mind of the victim, he was invited to the woman's home. At some point thereafter a gunman entered and threatened the stripper unless the victim paid him $80,000. Victim negotiates for a $40,000 payment when the banks opened that morning. Fortunately for the victim, a suspicious teller double-talked him and called the police. Investigators arrested the stripper and her male accomplice, charged them with attempted extortion, and trial is pending.

The identification in an armed robbery case often relates to the tactics or style of the robbery. Robbery has been categorized as having three styles:

(1) the ambush, (2) the selective raid, and (3) the planned operation. The ambush robbery is the least planned of all and is based on the element of surprise. The selective-raid robbery involves a minimum of planning but some "casing" of the robbery scene. The planned-operation robbery is carefully structured, and the robbery group examines all aspects of the situation and plans for all foreseeable contingencies; in fact "dry runs" may be engaged in by the robbery gang in this style of robbery.

Crime partners in a robbery group form a loose partnership, providing the skills for the various tasks necessary to carry out different types of robberies. They participate in the planning of robberies as well as the basic decision as to whether or not a certain target can be successfully robbed. Crime partners usually are associates from spontaneous play groups in the underworld, such as persons who live in or frequent the same neighborhood, who purchase drugs from the same source, or who have served sentences in juvenile or adult institutions together.

New York's notorious "Robert's Lounge Gang" was composed of customers frequenting a small bar near the cargo area of John F. Kennedy Airport. This was a gang of varying size, depending on the availability of targets, but in total its membership was drawn from the spontaneous play group that assembled daily in this popular drinking place. Seven members of this gang carried out a robbery at the Lufthansa Air Cargo terminal at Kennedy Airport. Their loot totaled $8 million in cash, jewels, and gold. Investigators were frustrated in their probing until one of the suspects led them to Robert's Lounge and his gang associates.[2]

Investigators assigned a single robbery or series of robberies to investigate should search for "link-ups" or "connect-ups" that will indicate the operations of a group. In many instances a gang of two to six robbers will not allow more than two robbers to "surface" on the scene of a robbery.

A Chicago robber, whose robbery group specialized in ambushing lone pedestrians late at night in streets and alleys, explained this switching of the group's membership in various robberies: "Now we never did nothing with the four of us together, always two. I'd be with George when we'd get one guy, and next I'd be with Percy."[3]

Linking or connecting several robberies may develop the identification of four or five members of a gang, and such data may lead the investigator to some clues about the style of a particular robbery gang.

The fact that a robbery mob may be concerned in a robbery or series of robberies may be developed by the investigator through investigation of the manner in which information was secured about the robbery (if it was a selective raid or a planned operation), whether a "wheel man" aided the robbery, and whether a "backup" man was present at the scene.

Inquiry may develop data identifying one or two persons (not similar in description to the armed robber or robbers who committed the crime) as loitering about the premises and inquiring about employment, or making other inquiries that would permit them access to the premises and that would allow them to scan the scene of the crime prior to the robbery (*casing* the robbery).

The presence of a wheel man may be established from witnesses who can offer data as to how the robber or robbers who committed the actual robbery fled the crime scene. A *wheel man* is a driver specialist who remains in the escape vehicle until the robbers have completed the robbery, then picks them up and flees the scene.

A *backup man* is a member of the gang who remains in the background unnoticed, and in case of trouble supports the members of the gang who are actually committing the robbery. The presence of a backup man may be more difficult to discover as the backup man often does not flee from the scene in the same car as the armed robber or robbers. Because he has not been identified with the crime, he may stay at the scene for some time, and he may walk from the scene and meet with his crime partners at some prearranged location. The role of backup man in modern robbery gangs is to protect his crime partners from the unexpected. He is "buried" in the store (when customers are not the victims), or outside the robbery scene, where he can view the crime scene and its approaches. His job is to fight off police who might chance on the scene or respond to a silent alarm.

There are some *signature* aspects to robberies. These so-called trademarks are part of the *modus operandi* of a crime and distinguish it as work of a specific robber or robbery group who have committed previous crimes in which the same identifying circumstances occur. The investigating officers pick out from the *modus operandi* the most likely identifying "signature" characteristic and develop their investigation to lead to the identity of the robber group. For instance, the "paper bag robber" was a robber who carried a brown paper bag to the scene of the robbery and told the victims to put their money and valuables in the bag. The "lovers-lane robber" frequented lovers lanes and his victims were always a boy and girl. The "Mutt and Jeff" team of robbers were always described as a tall man and a short man.

Traditionally, weapons indicate violence, but violence is used in robberies only as a tool of the robber in carrying out the robbery itself. Only in recent years has a new measure of violence in robberies indicated some hostility on the part of the robber, and such hostility can serve as a "signature" characteristic to identify suspects because it is unusual among robbers. Most robbers view the employment of violence to overcome resistance only as a "self-defense" measure. But today there is an increase in the number of wanton pistol-whippings or shootings of victims. This is the use of force beyond that necessary to control the robbery victim or victims. As one convicted robber expressed it: "The last thing you want is trouble. If you gotta shoot somebody you gotta run, and you don't get any money. The thing is to get in and get what you are after and get out with the least trouble possible."[4]

The use of addicting and dangerous drugs by a robber is indicated when the *modus operandi* reveals restricted drugs are part of the proceeds of a robbery. Even when restricted drugs are not part of the proceeds of a robbery, an investigator can identify the robberies of a drug addict by the time span between robberies and the proceeds of each crime. This assumption is based on: (1) other *modus operandi* information identifying a "series" of robberies as the work of one or more robbers, (2) the amount of money stolen, and (3) the date of the next robbery of the robber or robbers under investigation. The time gap between the robberies is extended when a good "score" allows the robber(s) to buy sufficient drugs for a specific habituation level ($100-a-day habit; $200-a-day habit). A characteristic of the addict–robber is that robberies are not committed when the addict is on a drug "high," but rather when he or she needs money for drugs.

In the investigation of robberies, investigators must realize the potential for conflict between data contained in police reports and the testimony of witnesses in court. Accuracy in recording the statements of witnesses is primary. Investigators should not encourage a witness to guess, or record a guess as a fact; they should not suggest facts to a witness who is unsure. Let the witness describe the person, car, weapon, clothes, disguise, marks, hair, speech, and the like in his or her own terms, and record the description in the witness's terms and not in interpretive terms. There will be normal mistakes of description, but the investigator should not compound the mistakes by adding to or interpreting the witness's descriptions.

THE TARGET IN ROBBERIES

The determination of a criminally oriented person to rob a specific and predetermined person or place, and when and how to do it, or whether he or she cruises to find a place to rob are mental processes of considerable interest to an investigator. The selection of a target in robberies offers clues to who did it. In planned robberies the acts done in planning before the crime can suggest suspects or indicate persons in the suspect group who are unlikely suspects. In the unplanned robberies of the cruising criminal, an investigator can develop some theory as to who did it solely on the target selection.

In planned robberies the offender considers not only the victim of the robbery but also such operational facts as the number of accomplices necessary, the weapons selected, the number of persons likely to be present during the robbery, and the escape route. In unplanned robberies the offender acts on impulse, generally selects a weapon on its availability, and cruises an area with no specific victim in mind but in haphazard search of a victim.[5] Nevertheless, the "cruiser" does avoid victims likely to be armed or places that might be wired for a silent alarm that will alert police to a robbery in progress.

In using the target aspects of a crime to further an investigation, the investigator first attempts to determine if the robbery was planned or unplanned. Beginning with the victim and whether he was alone at the time of the crime, the investigator tries to evaluate the place of the crime and the need for precrime planning. The cruising robber seeks out victims who will present little or no operational problem (resistance or alarm operation). Lone victims are symptomatic of unplanned robberies, although the place of the robbery may offer more of a substantial clue to target selection and to the planning of the crime.

Residence *(home invasion)* robberies were always considered planned crimes until the advent in recent years of cruising robberies in above-average-income residential areas and secluded hotel rooms. Bank robberies also were considered planned until the emergence of the single-teller bank robbery in which persons armed with a note and some threat of force victimized only one teller. Off-street businesses are still the victims reserved for planned robberies, and residence and bank robberies can be placed in the same class when the residence victim has a local reputation for having large sums of cash at home or the bank robbery extends to more than one teller. Airport cargo areas are the targets of planned robberies, with information from dishonest air cargo employees indicating the best time for the robbers to strike for maximum profit.

Markets, liquor stores, and other retail establishments are a no-man's land between planned and unplanned robberies. A cruising robber will enter such premises and appraise their vulnerability in a few minutes of shopping or browsing and then make a decision.[6] Attendant circumstances may offer a meaningful clue illustrative of planning—a fast entry and an apparent knowledge of routine or personnel, or both, or timing to coincide with an unusual amount of cash on hand.

Automated Teller Machines (ATMs) are now a popular robbery target with younger and potentially violent robbers.

The robbery of service stations, taverns, ATMs, drive-in facilities, on-street victims, and victims in vehicles usually are the work of cruising robbers. The cruising of an area by a robber seeking victims appears to be a nocturnal activity, and these are the available targets. The lone service station attendant, the little-patronized drive-in or motel offer targets of opportunity, as does the isolated tavern or cafe. Pedestrians and victims in vehicles (who are accosted when stopped at a traffic signal, upon picking up a hitchhiker, accepting a taxi passenger, when operating a bus, or in response to a telephone order to deliver food) are victims by chance.

IDENTIFICATION EVIDENCE

In robberies in which the victim is not killed, identification is made through facial characteristics, identifying natural marks or tattoos, hair line and color, race, clothing, speech characteristics, and unusual habits or nervous spasms.

In robberies in which the victim is killed or unable to see the robber's face because of the use of a mask or other disguise, poor lighting, or other reason, identification is made, in addition to any of the factors noted above, by general physical build, fingerprints, footprints, type of disguise, recovery of the loot, means of escape (automobile license, type, or year if automobile is used), and type of weapon.

A sufficiently compelling combination of the factors noted above will succeed in convincing a court or jury of the identity of the robber. Facial characteristics, fingerprints, or an auto license may be sufficiently persuasive without additional factors.

Grounds for attacking the credibility of the identification evidence may be summed up as:

1. Suggestive use of photographs.
2. Failure to safeguard the rights of accused in placing a suspect or arrestee in a police lineup. (See Appendix A for Case Brief, *U.S.* v. *Wade.*)
3. Conflict between the physical description given by witnesses and the actual appearance of the defendant in court.
4. Conflict between the weapon described by witnesses, or "constructively described" by the nature of injuries inflicted on victim, and the weapon presented in court as the robbery weapon.
5. Conflict between the vehicle, if any, involved in the robbery as described by witnesses and the actual vehicle used in the robbery.

Fixed TV surveillance cameras have assumed an increasingly important role in the identification of robbers. This photographic surveillance frequently obtains identifiable photographs of persons engaged in a robbery. Such photographs are utilized in identifying suspects, in their apprehension, and as identification evidence at trial. Banks pioneered the use of overt, fixed surveillance cameras, but the rise in robberies of stores and other businesses has extended the use of these cameras in both overt and covert installations.[7]

CHECKLIST FOR THE INVESTIGATION OF ROBBERY

Prompt response by police to the scene of a robbery, a fast-breaking search for the robber or robbers, and a continuing investigation aimed at identifying the person or persons responsible are the basic routine for successful robbery investigations (see Figure 18–1).

The following is a checklist for the investigation of robbery:

1. Assume suspect is present, arrest.
2. Ascertain if suspect has left scene, how; description, vehicle.
3. Description of suspect to dispatcher; also:
   a. nature of offense
   b. weapon involved
   c. direction of flight
   d. description of vehicle
   e. loss, if any
4. Search for suspect:
   a. escape route
   b. refuges (theater, tavern)
   c. hide-ins (stairways, cellars, yards, trash bins)

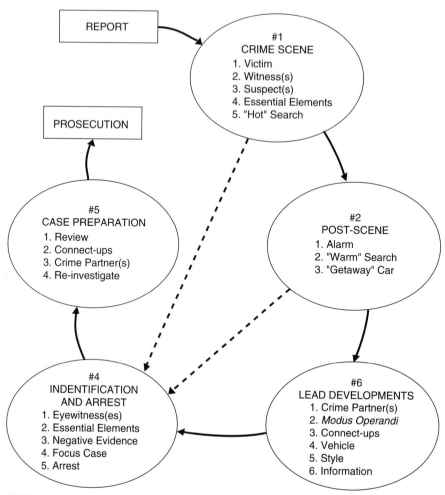

FIGURE 18–1 Investigation of robbery.

    d. prowler calls

    e. stolen cars

5. Scene—evidence:

    a. protect

    b. technician

    c. extend to "discard" area

6. Scene—witnesses:

    a. include latecomers, onlookers

    b. canvass view area, neighborhood

7. Advice to superior officer:

    a. details of offense

    b. identification of victim and witnesses

  c. personnel at scene and assignments

    d. progress of preliminary investigation

 8. Prepare report of preliminary investigation.

 9. Physical description of suspect(s) and vehicle, if any.

10. Crime partners—group.

11. *Modus operandi:*

    a. target

    b. bindings (tape, wire)

    c. weapon(s)

    d. plus rape

    e. plus kidnapping

    f. narcotics taken

    g. signature ("stripper," "rifle mob")

12. Informants.

13. Identification of robbery groups:

    a. number in group

    b. connect-ups

    c. spontaneous play groups:

      i. prison

      ii. neighborhood

      iii. same drug dealer

      iv. same teen center

    d. presence of "wheel man"

    e. presence of "backup" man

14. Identification by "style":

    a. ambush

    b. selective raid

    c. planned operation; "inside" information

15. Identification—other basic leads.

16. Identification of offender(s) and arrest.

17. Case preparation.

REPEAT-OFFENDER CASES

Career criminals are offenders who have had from one to ten previous arrests, have one to two cases pending in the local courts, and are on the street on some form of conditional release at the time of their latest arrest. While other violent serious crimes may be committed in a series of two or more, the "series" assailant and/or rapist is not usually a career criminal.

  Career criminals comprise a high percentage of armed robbers. Robbery is the violent crime favored by repeat offenders. As a result, many prosecutors have established special units to concentrate on the prosecution of recidivists, particularly armed robbers. From a crime-control standpoint, priority for such repeat-offender cases is now established as an appropriate strategy for prosecutors.

In the past, prosecutive effort was especially responsive to the strength of the evidence in a case, the probability of conviction, or the leverage of plea bargaining. More recently, prosecutors are realizing that repeat-offender cases are inherently more convictable. Witnesses are generally more cooperative in repeat-offender cases, and the factors leading to the frequent arrests of these robbers also contribute to the weight of evidence indicating guilt.[8]

Of course, investigators must make every effort to build a strong case against a repeat offender, to maximize the probability of conviction of such robbers, but they must also do so as rapidly as possible to get them off the street and into an effective corrections program.

PROBLEMS OF PROOF

The first major problem of proof in robbery cases concerns the defendant: identifying him or her as the robber. The second major problem is to show conclusively that the crime committed is a robbery in which the victim was separated from his or her valuables through force or against the victim's will.

The victim is expected to testify as a major identification witness. After all, the confrontation in robberies is between robber and victim. If a victim's testimony is weak and inconclusive, supporting witnesses need to be positive in their identification of the robber. Often, the defendant not only denies the act done, but claims mistaken identity and offers an alibi in support of this claim. If the alibi has strength and the identification evidence is weak, many jurors will think this constitutes a reasonable doubt.

The victim of a robbery is also mandated by the elements of the crime of robbery to testify that he or she handed over to the robber money and other valuables because the victim was afraid. Threats alone are not legally significant unless the victim testifies that he or she believed the robber had the intent to carry them out—and the apparent ability to do so promptly.

Selected References

1. Kenneth M. Wells and Paul B. Weston, *Criminal Law,* (Santa Monica, Calif.: Goodyear Publishing, 1978), pp. 200–11.

2. Ernest Volkman and John Cummings, *The Heist—How a Gang Stole $8,000,000 at Kennedy Airport and Lived to Regret It* (New York: Franklin Watts, Inc., 1986), pp. 1–27.

3. Henry Williamson; *Hustler* (New York: Doubleday & Company, 1965), p. 117.

4. John Bartlow Martin, *My Life in Crime: The Autobiography of a Professional Criminal* (New York: Harper & Brothers, 1952), p. 68.

5. Gerald D. Wolcott, "A Typology of Armed Robbers" (Master's thesis, Sacramento State College, 1968), p. 30.

6. Williamson, *Hustler,* pp. 188–206.

7. *Selection and Application Guide to Fixed Surveillance Cameras* (Washington, D.C.: U.S. Department of Justice, Law Enforcement Assistance Administration, 1974), pp. 1–5; United States v. McNair, 439 F. Supp. 103 (1977).

8. *Curbing the Repeat Offender: A Strategy for Prosecutors* (Washington, D.C.: U.S. Department of Justice, Law Enforcement Assistance Administration, 1977), pp. 16–17.

Chapter Review

Discussion Questions

1. What are the styles of robbery?
2. Relate the styles of robbery to robbery *targets*.
3. What are the essential elements of robbery that distinguish this crime from theft?
4. Describe the role of a *backup* man in a robbery.
5. What facts likely to be disclosed in a robbery investigation can serve as identification of a robber?
6. Why are ATMs a popular target in robberies?
7. Which of the basic leads should be used to develop evidence of identification in robbery investigations?
8. Discuss the groups from which robbers generally recruit crime partners.
9. What are the signature aspects of the *modus operandi* of robbers?
10. Why is it useful to determine whether a robbery suspect may be addicted to restricted drugs?
11. What is the role of fixed surveillance cameras in the investigation of robbery?
12. What are the similarities and differences between a "series rapist" and a repeat offender (robber)?
13. Is it a violation of a suspected robber's constitutional rights to give priority to the investigation and prosecution of career criminals (repeat offenders)?

Library Assignment

Locate and list at least five autobiographical writings by former robbers.

Workshop Project

Over a 30-day period, survey one or more of the local newspapers for news stories of (1) armed robberies, and (2) felony-murder robberies.

CHAPTER
19

Arson and Bombings

Fires set by arsonists and explosives placed to damage property and/or inflict death or injury upon people are crimes against both the person and property. Because great secrecy usually surrounds the fire-setting or the placing of explosives, these crimes create problems for investigators.

THE LAW OF ARSON

The great eighteenth-century British jurist Sir William Blackstone, in his *Commentaries on the Laws of England,* defined arson as the "malicious and willful burning of the house or outhouse of another man." In common law, arson was considered an offense against the home (habitation). It was defined as the malicious and willful burning of a dwelling (house or outhouse) of another, and extended to structures within the curtilage* of the dwelling.

Arson law in the United States has taken many twists depending on the individual state law examined. Arson may include the burning of buildings other than houses or outhouses, personal property, and crops; the law may distinguish between burning in the day or at night, and between vacant and occupied buildings; and arson, or the degree of arson, may depend on the value of the thing burned. Such laws generally make the burning of the cul-

---

*The space, usually enclosed, around a dwelling house.

prit's own insured property with intent to defraud a crime within the common name of arson. Common, however, to all arson or arson-type crime is the element of burning and the malicious intent of the person setting the fire.

The *corpus delicti* in arson cases requires that there be a burning as the result of a criminal agency, and that there be, in fact, actual burning—a consuming-type fire, although the fire need not in fact consume, for a charring is usually sufficient.[1] Thus, the things that must be proved in any prosecution for arson are:

1. That fire occurred—a burning, a charring.
2. That the burning was not accidental, that its origin was the result of a criminal agency.
3. That the person arrested, and who appears as a defendant in court in arson cases, is identified as the person who set the fire or caused it to be set, or otherwise acted in furtherance of a criminal plan for the fire-setting.

The term *aggravated arson* reflects public and legislative concern with arson as a crime against people as well as a crime against property. It is best described as any arson in which there is:

1. The use of explosives.
2. The presence of people, or people being placed in danger at the site.

Aggravation occurs when explosives are used to injure or harm people or property, or if at the time of fire or explosion a person other than the arsonist is within or upon the structure damaged. Inherent in the present or placed-in-danger element of aggravated arson is the fact that actual physical harm can result from the fire or explosion. Some states use aggravation as essential to first-degree arson; others cite it as adding to the seriousness of arson, and—if proven at trial—calling for additional years to be added to the sentence linked to basic arson.[2]

Although motive is an important element in the continuing phase of an arson investigation, it is not necessary to prove motive in an arson prosecution in order to convict the defendant, so long as the defendant can be identified as the fire-setter and his or her intent to set the fire is established.

THE SUSPICIOUS FIRE CONCEPT

In investigating a burning (see Figure 19–1) the investigator must *first* seek evidence to prove whether the fire was of natural or accidental origin. When little or no evidence can be secured to identify the fire as accidental, the *second* step is to seek evidence to eliminate all possible causes except incendiarism. The investigator must evaluate the possibility of persons smoking in bed, of spontaneous combustion, of a pilot light igniting fumes from flammable liquids, of electrical storms, or of faulty construction or maintenance of a building (electri-

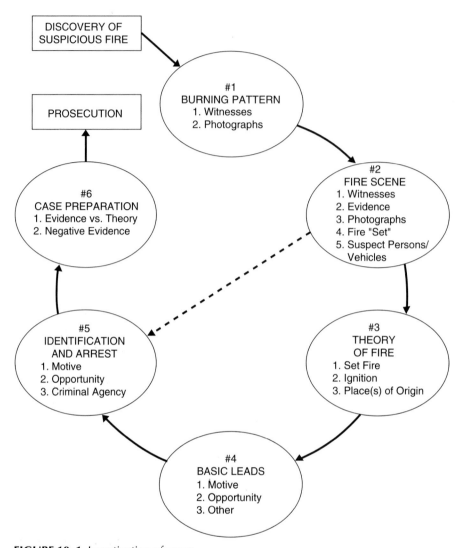

FIGURE 19–1 Investigation of arson.

cal wiring, motors, space heaters, furnaces, and flues). Also, he or she must review the possibility of small children, aged persons, intoxicated individuals, and the mentally ill being involved in a noncriminal incendiary fire through carelessness or misfortune.

The *third* step is to seek evidence that will prove the fire was of incendiary origin. Investigators seek such evidence as separate and distinct fires in different areas of the premises; the residue of inflammables; the odor of petroleum and like fire-starters; holes in plaster walls; windows and doors shaded and locked to prevent discovery and retard entry of firemen; removal of personal effects prior to a fire; owner or occupant not present, or absent when normally present; excessive insurance; and the presence of ignition devices or "fire-sets."

Once the suspicious nature of the fire has been revealed, the investigator attempts to classify the burning as a rationally or irrationally motivated fire. Rational motivation is based on either hate, profit, or the desire to conceal a crime. In rationally motivated fires the suspects are those people who would want the fire. Irrationally motivated arsonists are pathological fire-setters—pyromaniacs; fires set by such individuals offer no focal point for leads.[3]

Hate fires are based on some dispute. The work of the investigator is to question the victim as to his or her suspicions and any recent arguments. Landlords may not recall a dispute as such, but questioning may develop an unfulfilled tenant request. Employers may not recall an argument, but in response to queries about recently discharged employees or customers with complaints a few names may be recalled. Persons who set hate fires have some emotional problems, and the unimportant event to an average person may be overemphasized by these individuals and serve to trigger a spite or revenge fire. Religious, racial, and political disputes may be involved. Although the identity factor of the incendiary is not as apparent in these disputes, there is a potential for the discovery of suspects in the opposing group involved in the dispute if the investigator probes and pries.

Profit fire-setters are not difficult to expose once hate has been eliminated as motivation. The first step is a general inquiry as to the insurance company insuring the building and its contents and a more specific inquiry into the insurance and the record of the policyholder. Collaterally, a general inquiry as to the financial status of the insured and his or her business is appropriate and often rewards the investigator with information that the insured "needed" a fire.

Representatives of the national crime syndicate are being identified with arson with great frequency in recent years. They buy into a legitimate business and turn it into an illicit operation. The general procedure in these cases is for the new owners to manipulate the firm's operations to gain full control from the previous owners; to "milk" the business of its readily available assets in merchandise, services, and credit; and then to set a fire for the insurance money and possibly to conceal their raping of the legitimate business.[4]

A fire may have its origin in an attempt to conceal a major crime. This is not a difficult evaluation. What crime could be involved? Was there a human victim of the fire? Murder? Was there any hint of missing property? Robbery? Were the record books destroyed, found partially burned, or tented (spread half open with the bound edge up and the leaves spread out for burning)? Tax fraud? Embezzlement? Sometimes the seriousness of the basic crime does not appear to warrant arson, but people in trouble do strange things.

Pyromania is the obsessional impulse to set fires or a preference for arson as an instrument of damage. Pyromaniacs, the so-called "firebugs" who terrorize entire neighborhoods by their fire-setting activities, repeat their crimes unless they are apprehended and placed in a correctional setting oriented to their needs. These individuals may claim rational motivation, but they set fires for no practical reason and receive no material profit from their incendiarism.[5] "Motive" in these cases is some sensual satisfaction resembling the "irresistible" impulse, with the act of setting a fire solving the fire-setter's problems more efficiently and often more pleasurably than any other means available.[6]

The pathological fire-setter usually does not have any relationship to the victim or the place of burning. A "pyro" fire is similar to a "psycho" murder case in this respect. The fire-scene search may reveal a clue to personal identity, or the suspect may attract attention by his overt and suspicious conduct in a crowd watching a fire, for it is a tendency of these irrationally motivated incendiaries to act out the role of hero at the fire scene. In seeking a solution to these fires there is a possibility of developing suspects by a review of suspected juvenile vandals, sex psychopaths, known pyromaniacs, and others with a history of weird behavior or bizarre acts. When the fires occur in a series within reasonable geographic limits, the technique of working out the pattern of the fire-setter and organizing a surveillance for his or her apprehension is sometimes successful.

BURNING PATTERNS: STRUCTURE FIRES

Structural fires form a pattern that is determined chiefly by the physical layout of the building involved, the available combustible material, and ventilation. Simply stated, the fire burns upward from its original ignition in an inverted conical shape with the apex of the cone at the place of the origin—where the fire was ignited. Physical characteristics of a building may retard a fire or change its direction. Ventilation will cause a fire to spread away from this conical fire pattern: open doors, open windows, chimneylike physical characteristics (stairways or elevators), and holes in floor, wall, ceiling, or roof (either caused by the fire or some other means) contribute to the spread of a fire and its rate of burning (see Figure 19–2). Another variation from the classic fire pattern is caused when the fire encounters highly combustible materials which will burn more vigorously and radically modify the direction of a fire.[7]

Combustibility in structure fires usually is defined in terms of ignitability, rate of heat release, and total heat release, and is a function of the physical characteristics of the furnishings and building materials at the fire scene, their spatial relationships, and the structural features of the place of occurrence.[8] A little-known aspect of structure fires is room "flashover"—a rapid development of the fire that occurs when the volume of active fire becomes a significant portion of the room volume. At "flashover" all the previously uninvolved combustibles in a room suddenly ignite. At this time, the rate of the heat release is high and there usually is a flaming across the ceiling of the room.[9] A basic key to developing the pattern of a structure fire is to determine the approximate time between ignition and flashover in the room in which the fire originates.[10] A fire may be classified initially as suspicious when its pattern suggests more than one place of origin; when there is an inexplicable or unexplained deviation from a fire pattern common to the structural characteristics and ventilation of the place burned; or when a rapid buildup of a room fire is not in harmony with the known combustibility of the room and its contents.

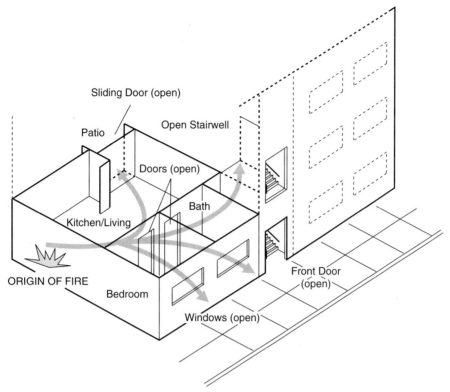

FIGURE 19–2 Normal fire path in structure fires. Arrows indicate spread of fire from origin in kitchen.

BURNING PATTERNS: NONSTRUCTURE FIRES

In outdoor fires in which a structure is not involved there is a predominant horizontal spread to the fire, rather than the typical cone pattern of structural fires. Factors that influence fire patterns in outdoor fires are the wind and the terrain. On level ground, in the absence of wind, a fire will spread from the point of origin in all directions. In the absence of a strong wind, the partial vacuum created by the fire which permits air to flow into the fire's base has a tendency to retard the spread of the fire. Wind spreads the fire in a fan shape with the apex of the fan being toward the source of the wind. On terrain with an uphill slope the fire will burn uphill from the point of origin. The combination of the two factors, wind and terrain, may produce a fire that burns uphill and is canted to the left or right because of the direction and velocity of the wind at the time of the fire. A strong wind sometimes can overcome the influence of terrain and cause a fire to burn laterally across a sloping hillside. In some cases, fires have been spread downhill by a very strong wind.[11]

A wind condition in southern California known as the "Santa Ana winds" contributes to the ignitability of forest-fire fuels. The Santa Ana winds, by their strong air flow associated with very low humidity, quickly dry out the forest fuels. When a fire is started, the increased ignitability of these fuels accounts for a rapid spread in all directions, with many spot fires ahead of the main fire because of the wind-driven embers. Under Santa Ana conditions fire can spread quickly and violently in any direction: a surge or slackening in the air flow or a sudden change in wind direction, rapid heat release, and the southern California mountainous terrain characterized by numerous canyons that act as chutes or chimneys all contribute to sudden changes in the pattern of the fire.[12]

IGNITION AND PLACE OF ORIGIN OF FIRE

One of the major differences between an accidental fire and an incendiary fire is that accidental fires frequently burn themselves out because of a lack of proper ventilation or availability of combustible material. On the other hand, the set fire is planned. The fire-setter places his or her fire so that it will burn vigorously after being ignited. He or she may use a fire accelerant, or may depend on ventilation and the combustible material normally at the fire scene.

Sparks, matches, mechanical lighters, friction, radiant heat, hot objects, and chemical reactions can cause fire. The primary source of ignition can be manual, as in striking a match; mechanical, as in some device such as a spark device used by welders; electrical, as faulty wiring or defective appliances; or chemical, as in spontaneous combustion.

When matches or other simple devices are used to set a fire, there is little evidence of the means of ignition. However, many arsonists seek a delay in the time of the fire and construct various mechanical devices to afford them a few hours in which they can establish an alibi of being elsewhere at the time the fire was started. Candles provide a delay factor for the arsonist, the time lag depending on the diameter and height of the candle above the "plant"— the fire-boosting material used to spread the fire. Alarm clocks are common mechanical devices to start fires. Both clocks and candles leave traces at the fire scene. When the debris and rubble at the fire scene are searched, some evidence of their use is often located. Electrical fire-starters often make a fire appear to be accidental, because faulty wiring and careless handling of electrical appliances often cause fires. Spontaneous combustion is often claimed as a cause of fire, but "oily rags" usually require ideal conditions to generate enough heat for self-ignition. In some industrial fires, however, spontaneous combustion might result from the chemical reaction of various oils with air.[13]

Where a fire was ignited is the place of origin. Fire-setters will set fires in more than one place to get a rapid buildup of the fire.

"Trailers" are often used to spread fires from a point of ignition, and because of this function they can be considered a secondary incendiary device, carrying the fire from the original place of ignition to other parts of the room or building. The trailer may be nothing more than a rope or a ropelike string of toilet paper, newspaper, or rags soaked in fire accelerant. Sometimes a fire accelerant is simply poured across the floor in a pattern similar to the spokes of a wheel, with each "trail" radiating outward from the original source of ignition.[14]

The major indication of a set fire is the fact that the source of ignition is such that the fire spreads rapidly, indicating a "trailer" and a fire accelerant, or that several different places give evidence of being the points of origin of the fire.

The investigator should investigate the lower regions of a fire for the place or places of origin. However, the place of origin may be higher than some of these burned portions of a building because the fire accelerant that was used as a source of initial fuel for the fire, or to spread the flames from the original place of ignition, might have dripped downward through holes or crevices in the floor (before the fire secured enough heat to change the fire accelerant from its liquid state).

THE FIRE SCENE

Happiness in arson investigation is when the investigator arrives at the fire scene while the fire is still in progress. All the fire fighters are still on the scene and occupants of the premises (or the owner of the land on which the fire started), onlookers, and other witnesses are also available at this time. The investigator, under these circumstances, can conduct on-the-scene interviews of persons knowledgeable about the fire and its circumstances. These interviews should point toward securing the following data:

1. Who reported the fire.
2. The color and volume of flames and smoke.
3. Whether anyone reported the odor of gasoline or other fire accelerant.
4. Where and when the fire started.
5. The movements of occupants and others involved in the fire.
6. Anything unusual at the fire scene.

After the fire is over and the investigator can enter the fire scene—which is when most investigators arrive at the fire scene—the onset of the fire and its circumstances can be reconstructed. Unfortunately, fire investigators usually are faced with various disturbances or changes in the original fire scene caused by the need of firefighters to "overhaul" after extinguishing a fire. *Overhauling* is the examination and search by firefighters for hidden flames or sparks that might rekindle the fire. To accomplish this overhauling, fire fighters often throw the contents of a room outside the building, and they frequently rip cabinets and paneling from walls to expose the space between the studs.

Tracing the root of a fire by examining the manner and direction of burning, from the point or points of origin, is the primary means of reconstructing the fire scene.[15] Basically, reconstruction of a fire scene requires the investigator to secure data on how a fire started, how it burned, and whether it was accelerated.

Once an investigator has reconstructed a fire, he or she can develop a theory about it. This theory may be backed up by various items of evidence, such as empty containers of flammable fluid found at the scene, traces of fire accelerants, or the remains of a fire-setting device in the rubble of a fire; but it is primarily concerned with the pattern of a fire: how it was ignited, the point of origin, and the source and direction of its burning.

Searching a fire scene is similar to searching any crime scene, with the exception that a lengthy period of "freezing" the scene is necessary to protect physical evidence until the searchers can find it among the rubble and debris of a fire. Although the fire-scene search is pointed toward discovery of the means of ignition and the point or points of origin of a fire, the searchers also look for anything unusual or foreign to the fire scene, evidence that will connect a suspect to the scene by revealing "presence" at the scene (the opportunity to set a fire), or clues to the motive of a fire-setter or evidence of the fire-setter's intent to set a fire (incendiarism).

Items of evidence suspected of containing volatile substances commonly used to accelerate fires (gasoline, kerosene, etc.) must be handled with some speed, not only in the finding of the evidence, but also in sealing it to prevent loss by evaporation. Such items must be transported to the crime laboratory in airtight containers.

Liquid fire accelerants (kerosene, gasoline, etc.) can and do survive fires. The areas most likely to contain residues of these accelerants are the low points at the fire scene: floors, carpets, or soil. When a suspect is arrested shortly after the fire at or near the scene, the suspect's outer clothing and shoes may contain residual traces if the fire-setter used a liquid fire accelerant. The human nose may detect the distinctive odor of a liquid fire accelerant at the scene of a fire, or upon a suspect, but it is best supplemented by flammable vapor detectors. These "sniffers" operate on several principles. The most common type operates on the catalytic combustion principle. However, the recovery and individualization of fire accelerant residues require the services of forensic scientists in a crime laboratory, and the use of solvent extraction devices.[16]

Recent advances in this field of fire debris analysis have resulted in the development of a new and unusual method for separating flammable and combustible liquid residues from fire debris. Results have demonstrated that multiple separations could be performed without jeopardizing the recovery and identification of volatile residues. This is an exploratory study of the non-destructive nature of passive headspace separation.[17]

Solvent extraction devices backstop the work of fire-scene searches by recovering flammable fluids from fire rubble (wood, cloth, and paper). The searchers find and recover the material suspected of containing residues of a fire accelerant, and transport it to the crime laboratory for processing by criminalists. Later, the report of these laboratory technicians may contribute to the development of the case, and their expert evidence in court upon the trial of the offender offers testimony in support of the prosecution's case.

FIRE SCENE: PHOTOGRAPHS

Fires and fire scenes are ideal subjects for photo "essays" that communicate otherwise undetectable facts about a fire, its origin, and its pattern of burning.

In-progress photos are seldom taken by assigned investigators, but they are taken by the news media, fire personnel, and amateur photographers, and can be secured by investigators. Such in-progress photographs, particularly when in color, identify the location of a fire, reveal its spread and intensity, and detail the mixture of smoke and flames. In addition, such photographs sometimes reveal the presence of a suspect at the fire scene, identify one or more vehicles parked at the scene or entering or exiting from the scene, and reveal signs of forced entry, attempts to bar firefighters from the structure, or methods used to prevent prompt discovery of the fire.

Investigators and assisting personnel assigned to process the scene of a suspicious fire should take both color and black-and-white photographs of the fire scene and of items of evidence found at the scene. Inasmuch as the *corpus delicti* of arson is the burning (charring) of a portion of a structure, this burning should be photographed from its place of origin to wherever the fire caused damage to the structure or its contents, both in overall views and in close-ups. Overall pictures reveal a fire's patterns and offer some clues to its ignition and origin, but it is the close-up photography in the area or areas of the origin of the fire that is of particular importance in revealing any ignition device, and the use of a "fire-set" with "trailers" and fire accelerants. Although the device itself may have been consumed in the fire, mute evidence of its use to set the fire may be developed from such photographs.

Photographs taken during the postfire processing of the scene of a suspicious fire may exonerate innocent suspects or serve as the only corroboration of an investigator's testimony as to things found (or not found) at the fire scene and their application to the prosecution's theory of the fire, the criminal agency, and the identity of the defendant on trial as the fire-setter.

THE CONTINUING ARSON INVESTIGATION

The preliminary investigation of a suspicious fire is complete when the fire-scene examination is recorded, the theory of an incendiary fire has been developed, and it can be proved by available evidence that the fire was not accidental.

The investigator assigned to the continuing investigation uses the following lines of inquiry as to motive and opportunity (presence at crime scene): (1) Who would want or benefit from the fire? and (2) Who would have the opportunity to set the fire?

The specific lines of inquiry suggested by the basic investigative leads are not exhausted until the dual inquiry as to motive and opportunity is fully developed.

The specific areas of inquiry in the continuing investigation of an arson case depend on the individual characteristics of each case, but the following major areas of inquiry should be explored in developing an arson investigation:

1. Burning pattern (whether in harmony with structure and contents).
2. Fire scene:
   a. examination for source of ignition

b. determination of place or places of origin

c. physical evidence

3. Witnesses:

   a. person discovering fire

   b. fire personnel

   c. eyewitnesses

   d. occupants (and owner of premises or place)

   e. others (onlookers, neighbors, and relatives of person discovering fire)

4. Suspicious persons:

   a. at fire scene

   b. at fire scene, but left before arrival of investigators (children playing; strangers in area; transients or homeless persons; former occupants; discharged employees; etc.)

5. Suspicious vehicles:

   a. at fire scene

   b. usually parked at fire scene, but not present

   c. at fire scene, but departed prior to arrival of investigators

6. Theory of fire:

   a. Rationally motivated:

      i. hate

      ii. profit

      iii. conceal crime

   b. Pathological fire-setter:

      i. lack of rational motive

      ii. fire in series

      iii. neighborhood involved

      iv. known "pyros"

   c. Criminal agency:

      i. not caused by accident

      ii. means of ignition

      iii. place of origin(s)

      iv. proof fire was set:

         (a) physical evidence

         (b) witnesses

         (c) other (motive, opportunity)

7. Identification of fire-setter:

   a. scene

   b. witnesses

   c. suspicious person or vehicle

   d. inquiries—basic leads

8. Review of evidence disclosed by:
   a. burning pattern
   b. examination of fire scene
   c. witnesses
   d. suspicious persons and vehicles
   e. basic leads
9. Compatibility of evidence—identifying fire-setter:
   a. burning pattern
   b. evidence at fire scene
   c. testimony of witnesses
   d. results of investigation
10. Case preparation: Compatibility of identification of fire-setter with theory of fire:
    a. criminal agency
    b. motive (rational; irrational)
    c. review of negative evidence (block common defense of accident, alibi, mistaken identification, or lack of motive)

THE INVESTIGATION OF BOMBINGS

Many fires result from explosions. Criminal investigation techniques used in arson investigation can be applied to bombings, despite the fact that a fire may not result from the explosion.

There are six stages to the investigation of bombings:

1. Determination of criminal cause—accidental origin, such as gas explosions or those resulting from the misuse of chemicals, must be eliminated as the cause of the explosion.
2. Pattern of explosion determined—high or low explosive; approximate amount used (damage).
3. The bombing scene is processed by police (responding officers and bomb squad personnel, if available) to locate and interview witnesses and victims, to find and preserve physical evidence, and to identify any suspicious persons or vehicles.
4. Case building—investigator develops a theory of the bombing: target, opportunity, motive, technical know-how.
5. Inquiries are initiated to exploit any basic leads, police intelligence, and other clues and traces (scene investigation and processing; case building) likely to result in the identification and arrest of the person or persons responsible for the bombing.
6. Case preparation—immediately following arrest of bomber and any associates (see Figure 19–3).

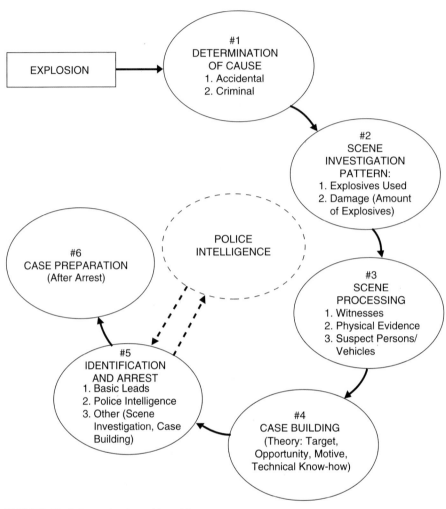

FIGURE 19–3 Investigation of bombings.

Because the nature of an explosion destroys traces of the explosives used, explosive "tagging" offers future promise that the scene investigation of a bombing will hold identifiable traces of the explosives used. An explosives tagging program developed at federal levels involves the addition of coded microparticles or "taggants" to explosives during their manufacture. The taggants survive detonation, can be recovered at the bombing scene, and can be decoded by crime laboratory examination to show where and when the explosives were made.

The use of police intelligence reports may be the most important factor contributing to the success of a bombing investigation. These reports have a capability of providing information that will link suspects to prior bombings and provide data on the associates and possible whereabouts of suspects and associates. In addition, a police intelligence unit may initiate preventive intelligence operations to disclose the identity of persons involved in the planning of future bombings (see Chapter 11).

Individuals or groups who use explosives as the ultimate weapon against persons and/or property may be linked to:

1. Politically motivated groups (extremists; radicals) (see Chapter 20).
2. Organized crime (bombings involving known criminals, informants for police, and witnesses or potential witnesses against members of crime syndicates).
3. Mentally ill persons (including bombers motivated by hate, anger, and revenge).

PROBLEMS OF PROOF

Two common defenses create problems of proof in prosecuting arson cases: (1) a claim that the fire resulted from accident, misfortune, or natural causes, and (2) if the fire did result from a criminal agency, the defendant was not that agent.

To prove that a criminal agency was responsible for the fire, the police–prosecutor team must foreclose all possibilities that the fire resulted from any other cause (accident, misfortune, natural cause) by a strong showing of evidence linking the fire to a single cause: someone set it.

Identifying the defendant as the fire-setter is a problem that is generally attacked along the dual lines of motive and opportunity. The prosecution must, at the least, produce evidence showing that the defendant "wanted" the fire or would "benefit" from it, and that he or she not only had the opportunity to set the fire, but did so by his or her presence at the fire scene or by the defendant "contracting" with a crime partner to set the fire.

While cases involving explosive devices may be linked to fires, their investigation is hampered by the fact that the explosion usually destroys most of the physical evidence at the bombing scene. When these cases are prosecuted, the "motive" and "opportunity" factors are important. In political bombings, anyone proven to be a member of a terrorist group is assumed to have a motive for bombings of that group.

Selected References

1. KENNETH M. WELLS AND PAUL B. WESTON, *Criminal Law,* (Santa Monica, Calif.: Goodyear Publishing, 1978), pp. 221–28.
2. Kehoe v. Commonwealth, 149 Ky. 400 (1912).
3. BRENDAN P. BATTLE AND PAUL B. WESTON, *Arson: Detection and Investigation* (New York: Arco Publishing, 1978), pp. 30–42.
4. Fire Marshalls on Duty—The Intelligence Unit in Fire Investigation," *The Fire Journal,* LXIV (September 1970), pp. 92–93.
5. NOLAN D. C. LEWIS AND HELEN YARNELL, *Pathological Firesetting—Pyromania* (New York: Nervous and Mental Disease Monographs, 1951), pp. 86–134.

6. W. Hurley and T. M. Monahan, "Arson: The Criminal and the Crime," *British Journal of Criminology,* IX (1969), pp. 4–21.

7. Paul Kirk, *Fire Investigation* (New York: John Wiley & Sons, 1969), pp. 71–81.

8. Edwin E. Smith, "An Experimental Determination of Combustibility," *Fire Technology,* VII, No. 2 (May 1971), pp. 109–19.

9. T. E. Waterman, "Room Flashover—Criteria and Synthesis," *Fire Technology,* IV, No. 1 (February 1968), pp. 25–31.

10. T. E. Waterman and W. J. Christian, "Characteristics of Full-Scale Fires in Various Occupancies," *Fire Technology,* VII, No. 3 (August 1971), pp. 205–17; "Fire Behavior of Interior Finish Materials," *Fire Technology,* VI, No. 3 (August 1970), pp. 165–78.

11. Kirk, *Fire Investigation,* pp. 82–88.

12. C. M. Countryman, M. A. Fosberg, R. C. Rothernel, and M. J. Schroeder, "Fire Weather and Fire Behavior in the 1966 Loop Fire," *Fire Technology,* IV, No. 2 (May 1968), pp. 126–41.

13. Bruce V. Etting and Mark F. Adams, "Spontaneous Combustion of Linseed Oil and Sawdust," *Fire Technology,* VII, No. 3 (August 1971), pp. 225–36.

14. Battle and Weston, *Arson,* pp. 17–29.

15. Richard D. Fitch and Edward A. Porter, *Accidental or Incendiary* (Springfield, Ill.: Charles C Thomas, Publisher, 1968), pp. 3–26; John J. O'Connor, *Practical Fire and Arson Investigation* (New York: Elsevier, Nov. 1987), pp. 81–105.

16. John F. Boudreau, Quon Y. Kwan, William E. Faragher, and Genevieve C. Denault, *Arson and Arson Investigation: A Survey and Assessment* (Washington, D.C.: U.S. Department of Justice, Law Enforcement Assistance Administration, 1977), pp. 77–89.

17. L. V. Waters and L. A. Palmer, "Multiple Analysis of Fire Debris Samples Using Passive Headspace Concentration," *Journal of Forensic Sciences,* 18, No. 1 (January 1993), pp. 165–83.

Chapter Review

Discussion Questions

1. Define a suspicious fire.

2. How does the burning pattern in structure fires differ from the burning pattern of nonstructure (field and forest) fires?

3. What is a *fire-set?* A fire *trailer?* A fire *accelerant?*

4. What basic factors should be considered in investigating fires set because of hate (revenge or jealousy), for profit, or to conceal a crime?

5. What are the basic characteristics of fires set by pyromaniacs?

6. What are the similarities and differences between arson and bombings?

7. Define combustibility.

8. What information is sought by investigators in on-the-scene interviewing of witnesses in the investigation of a suspicious fire?

9. How is the ignition and spread of a fire reconstructed at the crime scene? What is the primary objective of this reconstruction?

10. What special care must be taken with evidence suspected of containing residues of a fire accelerant?

11. Outline the major phases of the continuing investigation in arson cases.

12. What are the six stages of a bombing investigation?

13. What are the essential elements of Stage No. 3 in the investigation of a bombing (Scene)? Stage No. 4 (Case Building)?

14. What individuals or groups may be involved in a bombing?

15. What is explosives "tagging"?

Library Assignment

Update the references in this chapter concerned with burning patterns and the ignition of fires by incendiaries.

Workshop Project

Over a 30-day period, survey one or more of the local newspapers for news stories of (1) arson cases, and (2) bombings.

CHAPTER
20

Terrorist Activity

Terrorist violence aimed at achieving radical changes in society, capitulation to specific demands, or the weakening of an established government gives a new dimension to violent crimes such as arson, bombing, robbery, kidnapping, and murder.

The major role of criminal investigation is to conduct continuing investigations, either as the criminal conspiracy is being organized or subsequent to a criminal act by one or more members of a terrorist group. Police intelligence is the first line of defense against terrorism, trying to stop it before it starts; and police operations units have the major responsibility for containing the acts of terrorists while they are threatened or in progress (see Figure 20–1).

The political terrorist differs from other individuals who commit violent crimes. Persons who endanger life and property by fire, explosives, weapons, and other violent means usually are motivated by profit; the anger–hate–revenge complex; the need to eliminate or silence competitors, associates, or witnesses for the state; or some irrational motivation common to psychotics and other disturbed persons. Political terrorists, on the other hand, are motivated by their ideological convictions.

The rationale for crimes of violence by political terrorists is the major reason to modify basic investigative techniques, in order to track down and prosecute these "convictional" criminals. The basic techniques for investigating violent crimes are unchanged, the modifications reflect the characteristics of

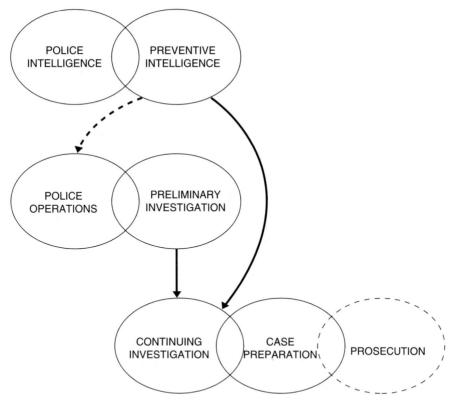

FIGURE 20–1 Investigation of terrorist activity.

political terrorists as members of a group believing in the philosophy that power comes out of the barrel of a gun; as persons who are trained and schooled to act in furtherance of group objectives; as persons who are monitored closely by other members of the group, and subjected to severe disciplinary measures for any breach of the group's code of conduct.

KIDNAPPING

The federal statute on kidnapping was a response to a vicious series of kidnappings for ransom in the years following the repeal of the Eighteenth Amendment (Prohibition). Rival gangs struggled for new sources of income to replace the former profits from making and selling beer and whiskey, seized other members of the underworld, and held them until five- and six-figure ransoms were paid. In many of these "snatches" (as they were termed at the time by news media), victims were seized in one state and held in another. These seizures were followed by similar kidnappings by others of members of rich and wealthy families, and ransom demands went up.

The kidnapping for ransom and brutal murder of the child of Charles Lindbergh, contemporary hero because of his solo trans-Atlantic flight, pinpointed the need for a federal statute. The child was seized in New Jersey, but most of the ransom negotiations were conducted in other states. Since there was no effective kidnap law, Bruno Hauptmann was tried and convicted for first-degree murder, the murder being committed during a burglary. After this notorious case, Congress enacted suitable legislation that was originally known as the "Lindbergh Law." (The ensuing state kidnapping statutes were nicknamed "little Lindbergh laws.") The Federal Bureau of Investigation (FBI) was authorized by the new law to enforce its provision against interstate kidnapping.

The present provisions of federal legislation on interstate kidnapping are:

(a) Whoever knowingly transports in interstate or foreign commerce, any person who has been unlawfully seized, confined, inveigled, decoyed, kidnaped, abducted, or carried away and held for ransom or reward or otherwise, except, in the case of a minor, by a parent thereof, shall be punished (1) by death if the kidnapped person has not been liberated unharmed, and if the verdict of the jury shall so recommend, or (2) by imprisonment for any term of years or for life, if the death penalty is not imposed.

(b) The failure to release the victim within twenty-four hours, after he shall have been unlawfully seized, confined, inveigled, decoyed, kidnaped, abducted, or carried away shall create a rebuttable presumption that such person has been transported in interstate or foreign commerce.

(c) If two or more persons conspire to violate this section and one or more of such persons do any overt act to effect the object of the conspiracy, each shall be punishable as provided in subsection (a). (Title 18, U.S. Code, Section 1201)

Under the statute barring interstate kidnapping, a major essential element is the transportation of the victim across state boundaries.

The aggravation factor in the statute is the harm to the victim. The legislation does not require harm to the victim as an essential element of the crime of kidnapping; the harm factor relates only to the degree of punishment. Additional punishment is imposed where the simple kidnapping or unlawful seizure and secret detention or asportation is aggravated by the purpose of extortion of ransom.

Ransom is a price, money, or other consideration paid or demanded for the release of the victim. The additional punishment has often been death for this form of kidnapping.

The state laws in this area were revised after the Congress enacted its legislation against interstate kidnapping. Except for the interstate element (transportation across state lines), the state statutes are similar to the federal legislation.

The broad elements of state kidnapping statutes include:

1. Seizing of another without his or her consent.

2. Transportation (asportation).

3. Unlawful confinement.

Some asportation or movement of the victim from one place to another is essential to distinguish kidnapping from lesser crimes.[1]

CONSPIRACY

Putting together a conspiracy case is difficult: the existence of a conspiracy must be detected; the essential elements of a crime of conspiracy under the law must be studied; and the circumstances of the conspiracy must be investigated so that significant and compelling evidence is developed.

For two or more individuals to combine to commit or cause a violation of the criminal laws is an offense of the gravest character, sometimes outweighing the contemplated crime in potential public injury. Conspiracy involves deliberate plotting to subvert the laws, educating and preparing the conspirators for further and habitual criminal practices. In addition, conspiracy is characterized by secrecy, rendering it difficult to detect, requiring more time for its discovery, and adding to the importance of punishing it when discovered.

A combination of persons to accomplish an unlawful purpose or to unlawfully accomplish a lawful purpose is a conspiracy. The essential elements of a criminal conspiracy are:

1. An agreement (two or more co-conspirators) to cause the performance of criminal conduct.

2. To have a specific criminal intent.

3. An overt act in the furtherance of the agreement.

When an agreement to commit one or more crimes is evidenced by an overt act, the precise nature and extent of the conspiracy is usually determined by reference to the agreement which embraces and defines its objects. Proof of specific intent is usually linked to the agreement and the overt act: "Intent to accomplish an object cannot be alleged more clearly than by stating that parties conspired to accomplish it" (see Figure 20–2).

Uncovering the existence of a conspiracy is the first step in assembling a conspiracy case. Since the crime of conspiracy is an illegitimate and punishable agreement, disclosure of the agreement is the most important aspect of detecting a conspiracy case. The agreement need not be a formal transaction, but it must indicate a knowing concert of action among two or more persons, a working together for the accomplishment of the common purpose.

A conspirator is a party to an agreement to commit an unlawful act at the time the conspiracy is in existence, and who understands and commits himself or herself to the basics of the agreement. It is the agreement that is the crucial fact, not the form or manner in which the agreement is made.

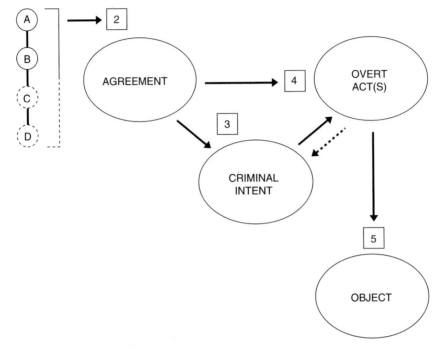

FIGURE 20–2 Anatomy of criminal conspiracy.

TERRORIST GROUPS

The broad goals of political terrorists have been summed up by Carlos Marighella, author of a how-to text on urban guerilla warfare:

1. To show the general public that police and military authorities are impotent to protect themselves from political terrorists—and thus powerless to protect the public.
2. To provide, by acts of terror, an overreaction by police and/or military authorities in order to "radicalize" many members of the general public and develop sympathizers for the political (revolutionary) aims of the terrorist group.
3. Ultimately, to overthrow the established government.

"Blind date" bombings are the acts of terrorist groups to gain publicity and public recognition. Any act of frightening violence is an attention-getter, particularly when the human victims are individuals who just happen to be in the vicinity at the time a bomb explodes.

"Target Blue" ambush slayings of police officers are in the same category of mindless violence. The police victims are also randomly selected, not because of who they are, but because of what they represent. The attention-getter is the willingness of the terrorist group to kill the armed representatives of law and order.[2]

Hostage taking is a theatrical way of gaining attention. If the demands of the terrorists are not met, hostages may be killed. While the hostages are the on-site victims, this type of terrorism is aimed at the people who learn of the event through the news media. A dramatic hostage situation forces the police (government; military authorities) into a confrontation in which they must bring all of the hostages out alive and terminate the situation by the surrender of hostage-takers.

Terrorism to punish is a carefully structured three-act play presented to the public with the terrorist group cast as the "good guys" and some representative of government or corporate life as the "bad guy." The first act concerns the kidnapping and taking away of the hostage and is quite frequently highlighted by the brutality of the seizure—the killing of bodyguards or casual passersby, for instance. The second act is devoted to identification of the terrorist group and delineation of their role as representatives of the "people" or the "revolution." The third act begins with the victim's body being discovered along with reports from the terrorist group to the news media that they had "executed" the victim after an alleged fair trial, and ends with the police hue and cry in pursuit of the terrorists.

A variation of this punishment theme is (1) assassination of political or corporate leaders, or their "knee-capping"—a technique developed by the Irish Republican Army to cripple rather than kill informers; and (2) execution of a disloyal member of the terrorist group or of a person who has infiltrated the group (police informant; police undercover agent).

In these deliberate dramas, the news media not only details the event and its circumstances, but also the assignment of guilt to the terrorists' victims and the terrorists' belief in the righteousness of their cause.

Armed robbery by terrorists is a basic means of gaining funds to support the terrorist group's activities. To avoid a total public rejection of the group and this activity, the terrorist group attempts to put a Robin Hood twist on this crime of violence by concentrating their attacks on banks and other lending institutions: taking money from those who have a great deal of it, rather than robbing the poor.

Kidnapping for ransom has become a profitable activity for terrorists. Primarily aimed at executives of multinational corporations, it is characterized by ransom demands in the millions. Although this crime is not common in the United States, there is a likelihood of its occurrence. When terrorists attack in kidnappings it is a planned assault upon a chosen target, and unless rescued or ransomed, the victim is usually killed.[3]

Any contemporary terrorist group has its hardcore "operations" personnel, and a larger group of people who aid and abet their activities by providing moral, political, and financial support. The operations personnel are usually divided into small "cells" of six to ten individuals for internal security purposes. Membership identity is a closely guarded secret. Cell members are only aware of the identity of each other and possibly one or two liaison persons whose function it is to provide communications between cells or with supporters.

The names of transnational terrorist groups usually have some connection with the nation of origin of the terrorists, the nation against whom their activities are directed, or to some key event in the history of the group. Home-grown terrorist groups usually have names linked to the objectives of the group, but the linkage is often tenuous. "The Weathermen" or "Weather Underground" certainly does not indicate a group whose membership are young and dedicated to violent revolutionary action; nor does the name "Symbionese Liberation Army" indicate a group of white radicals whose politicalization and radicalization of prison inmates developed a larger group of terrorists led by the radicals and in which the former prison inmates were "soldiers."[4]

Between 1960 and 1990, the majority of terrorists were people who were college-educated, well-trained, urban, multilingual, well-traveled, and sophisticated. Since then, particularly in the Middle East, terrorists are more likely to be from a large family, rural, unskilled and unemployable, illiterate, undisciplined, and poorly trained. When terrorists succeed today, there is a strong suspicion that the success was not because they were well trained and disciplined, but because someone (airport security, intelligence, investigation), somewhere, did not perform as well as expected.[5]

PREVENTIVE INTELLIGENCE

Preventive intelligence is an indispensable element in the investigation of terrorist activity. Federal, state, and urban-area police agencies usually provide local police agencies with intelligence data on persons and groups having a serious potential for future criminal involvement in acts of terrorism. Current intelligence material on political terrorism at local levels is the responsibility of the local police agency.

Preventive intelligence is focused inquiry. Intelligence operations may include informants (paid and unpaid), police undercover agents, and various techniques of surveillance.

Legal standards must be considered before preventive intelligence operations can be initiated. The nature of the existing grounds for suspicion must be examined in relation to the anticipated or past terrorist activity. Any secret agent (informant or undercover police agent) has an "agency" relationship to the employing police agency. Once police encourage an agent to collect information, they assume some responsibility for the agent's actions.

The U.S. Supreme Court is reluctant to place constitutional barriers on the use of informants or infiltrating agents by the police. In 1966, the U.S. Supreme Court dealt with the question of "whether evidence obtained by the government by means of deceptively placing a secret informer in the quarters and councils of a defendant during one criminal trial so violates the defendant's Fourth, Fifth, and Sixth Amendment rights that suppression of such evidence is required at a subsequent trial of the same defendant on a different charge." The Court answered this question with an opinion that said there was no legitimate interest protected by the constitution which protected a "wrongdoer's misplaced belief that a person to whom he voluntarily confides his wrongdoing will not reveal it . . . The use of secret informers is not *per se* unconstitutional . . . nor does it follow that his [secret informant; confidant] testimony was constitutionally inadmissible."

Preventive intelligence is not "counterterrorism." There is an awareness that any war on terrorism is difficult, but it is concerned with collecting intelligence, not interrogation. Therefore, police investigators are not confronted with the need to supplant intelligence gathering to the immediacy of interrogation and the dilemma that a breach of law is required to avert a greater harm—the "necessity defense."

Police deception in order to gather evidence for a criminal prosecution is not yet hindered by constitutional barriers. For instance, police investigators purchasing narcotics (a "buy") from drug sellers must conceal their true identity and occupation.

It is apparent that for the present a defendant cannot claim constitutional privacy if he or she voluntarily reveals his or her criminal plans to someone believed to be a confederate or a confidant. Even the use of electronic recording equipment by the pseudo-confederate or confidant has not yet been constitutionally criticized. The U.S. Supreme Court has even praised the use of recording equipment in these "misplaced confidence" situations because of its accuracy and reliability over human memory, and has allowed the recording as evidence in the absence of the informer/agent at the trial as a witness.

ROLE OF POLICE OPERATIONS UNITS

Operations units of a police agency have the responsibility for controlling the acts of terrorists once they are threatened or in progress. Patrol units are the first line of defense in these instances, with specialists available to them. Specialists in threat analysis will pass on the credibility and potential of the threat; bomb detection and disposal specialists will direct the search for explosives and incendiary devices, and effect their disposal if found; and hostage negotiators will establish communications with terrorists in hostage-kidnapping cases, and conduct negotiations leading to termination of the event.

The commanding officer of the operational units also has the responsibility of the preliminary investigation:

A. Threats

1. Date and time of threat, how received, and who received it.
2. Nature of act threatened, including target, time element, and weapon (fire, bomb, etc.)
3. Demands or grievances accompanying threat.
4. Stated political or organizational affiliation of threat-maker, including any claims of responsibility for prior terrorist threats or acts.

5. Other data such as background noises (telephone threat), speech characteristics, and apparent personal characteristics of threat-maker.

B. Events

1. Arrest any terrorist at scene; identify; collect data and prepare "alarm" for terrorists who have fled scene.
2. Assign personnel to interview victims and witnesses, and to search scene for evidence likely to identify the terrorists and their *modus operandi.*
3. Assign personnel to protect the scene until qualified personnel can assist in the search for physical evidence.
4. Assign a sworn officer or supervisor to collate all collected information and evidence, and to prepare the preliminary report.

ROLE OF THE CRIMINAL INVESTIGATOR

The role of a criminal investigator in relation to terrorist acts can be summed up:

1. Identification of responsible parties—co-conspirators.
2. Re-interview victims and witnesses, get statements, check stories; follow up on physical evidence and laboratory examinations.
3. Identification of aiders and abettors—individuals on the fringes of the crime or criminal conspiracy.
4. Pursuit of unapprehended terrorists, co-conspirators, and aiders and abettors.
5. In kidnapping cases, immediate organization of pursuit in the attempt to locate victim and terrorists; immediate action seeking the identity of the terrorists and the hideout in which their captive is held; participating in rescue planning; and—if ransom is paid—probing for clues to the kidnappers during ransom negotiations and the ransom payment, and upon release of the person kidnapped.
6. Apprehension of all persons wanted in connection with the terrorist act or conspiracy.
7. Investigation of all arrestees to disclose associations, past history, and potential for cooperation: (a) to serve out a role of accomplice–witness, and (b) to provide information.
8. Upgrading of preventive intelligence surveillance to secure more information on suspects.
9. Case preparation highlighting the relevancy and probative value of various items of evidence in relation to prosecution for a specific crime or crimes.

An investigation should be considered incomplete until evidence, direct or circumstantial, has been secured of an overt act that constitutes a "substantial step" in furtherance of the conspiracy. Forming or planning a conspiracy is not a true overt act, nor are acts done merely cementing the agreement.

A social network analysis is useful in investigating terrorism. This is a linking of known members of a group (or "cell") with suspected members, or just a linking of suspects believed to be joined in a group. First, the individual suspects are linked to each other, then to the group, and then to incidents and their scenes.[6]

Another network analysis is how the terrorists secured reliable information about the targets of their attacks, particularly the targets to be killed or kidnapped. The link-up here relates to who was the source of information: members, sympathizers, collaborators, dissidents, or whatever. The names of these individuals should be worked into the social network analysis for development of connections between known members of a group and sources of information.[7]

Investigators assigned to the activities of terrorists require all of the standard skills of criminal investigators plus a high level of integrity and an appreciation for the legal significance of collected evidence. One guarantees against illegal shortcuts that may ruin evidence; the other is a safeguard against building a case on evidence of little relevance or probative value.

The process of identifying perpetrators involved in the World Trade Center bombing was quicker than investigators anticipated. Investigators from the New York City Police Department, the Federal Bureau of Investigation, and the Bureau of Alcohol, Tobacco, and Firearms conducted an exhaustive initial search that produced the first clues. They determined that because the blast took place in the garage, the explosive device was probably a car bomb. The recovered vehicle identification number was quickly traced to a Ford Econoline van that had been rented to Mohammad Salameh. Once in custody, Salameh's clothing and the rental agreement he signed for the van were tested for traces of explosives. Investigative work subsequently led to other suspects, although the evidence against Salameh helped most in the investigation.

The more investigators looked into Salameh's activities, the more they became convinced he was part of a conspiracy. The case against another defendant, Nidal Ayyad, was almost as solid as that against Salameh but was developed using more technological methods. The cases against two other defendants, Mahmud Abouhalima and Ahmad Ajaj, were relatively weak. Evidence surrounding another suspect, Ahmed Yosef, helped solidify the cases against the others.[8]

Apparently, the prosecution in the World Trade Center bombing did avoid illegal short-cuts and built its case on relevant evidence with a high evidentiary value. The defendants were convicted as charged.

COMMUNITY THREAT GROUPS

Community threat groups are organizations of people who engage in antisocial and illegal behavior and who pose a danger to agents of criminal justice and the general public. To this definition, add that the hate violence is commonly directed at African Americans, Asians, Hispanics, Jews—and even the U.S. government itself (for example, the Oklahoma City bombing).

Organized crime mobs are not associated with hate groups in any fashion. They make money in prostitution, illegal gambling, labor rackets, and like activity.

Street gangs are usually among the "despised people" of hate groups. Any alliance between them is highly unlikely. Gangs are usually more concerned with shooting one another and drug selling and its profits.

Motorcycle, Asian, and Jamaican gangs do not share any of the hate; their focus is on drug making and selling.

The hate groups are organizations such as the *Ku Klux Klan (KKK)*, *Aryan Nation*, and the youngsters termed *Skinheads*. In some locales, various *militias* may demonstrate against the government for a specific reason.[9]

Alan Berg, a controversial talk-show host, was shot dead not far from his home on the outskirts of Denver. His killers were members of a Neo-Nazi group aligned with the Aryan Nation. He was Jewish and openly challenged Neo-Nazi and other hate groups.

Berg's killing was murder, but also a hate crime—he was killed because he was "different" in the eyes of his murderers.

A *hate crime* is not usually so closely identified with a community threat group. It is usually a single-offender case, with the offender acting out his or her particular hate. Arson is common and often fires occur in a series a few days apart. The motivation is irrational, but suspects can be found and evidence developed for a trial.

Cults range from those groups preaching revolution or resistance to taxation, or similar governmental activity, to those who preach the Bible and perform good works among the sick and the poor.

These groups may have other problems linked, for example, to the children of the group or the lifestyle of the group; some cults have been targeted for allegations of mind control—using undue influence and unethical means to recruit and retain members.

However negative the public perception of groups labeled as "cults," police investigators must remember that the United States has a longtime commitment to religious tolerance and freedom. Investigators should not probe and pry into any such group unless a crime has been reported or discovered, and unless there is strong probable cause to warrant police action.[10]

PROBLEMS OF PROOF

Most of the recent trials of terrorists in the United States have survived or perished on the issue of the legality or illegality of the means used by investigators to gather evidence. Electronic eavesdropping evidence has been attacked as an unreasonable and broad invasion of privacy; undercover agents described as partisan witnesses unworthy of belief; and informants (and the rare accomplice–witness) as persons of no credibility intent on getting some benefit from the prosecution for their testimony. Unless the police–prosecutor team can overcome the damage wrought by these attacks, many jurors will downgrade the legal significance of the prosecution's evidence in these areas and conclude there is a reasonable doubt of guilt.

Selected References

1. KENNETH M. WELLS AND PAUL B. WESTON, *Criminal Law* (Santa Monica, Ca.: Goodyear Pub., 1978), pp. 213–18.

2. See ROBERT DALEY, *Target Blue* (New York: Delacorte Press, 1973); and *Ambush Attacks: A Risk Reduction Manual for Police* (Gaithersburg, Md.: International Association of Chiefs of Police, 1974).

3. CHARLES A. RUSSELL, "Businesses Becoming Increasing Targets," in *Managing Terrorism: Strategies for the Corporate Executive,* ed. Patrick J. Montana and George S. Roukis (Westport, Conn.: Quorum Books, 1983), pp. 55–71.

4. National Advisory Commission on Criminal Justice Standards and Goals, *Report on Disorders and Terrorism* (Washington, D.C.: U.S. Department of Justice, Law Enforcement Assistance Administration, 1976), pp. 517–21.

5. THOMAS STRENTZ, "A Terrorist Psychosocial Profile: Past and Present," *FBI Law Enforcement Bulletin,* LVII, No. 4 (April 1988), pp. 13–19.

6. CHRISTOPHER A. HERTIG, "The Investigation of Terrorist Activity," in *Critical Issues in Criminal Investigation,* Michael J. Palmiotto (Cincinnati, Ohio: Anderson Publishing Company, 1988), pp. 235–45.

7. WALTER LAQUEUR, *The Age of Terrorism* (Boston: Little, Brown and Company, 1987), pp. 109–11.

8. D. MARTIN, "Cracking the World Trade Center Bombing (And Proving the Case Against the Perpetrators)", *Law Enforcement Technology,* 21, No. 8 (August 1994), pp. 36, 38, 40, 60–61.

9. JACK LEVIN AND JACK McDEVITT, *HATE Crimes—The Rising Tide of Bigotry and Bloodshed* (New York: Plenum Press, 1993), pp. 1–5.

10. HAMES D. TABOR AND EUGENE V. GALLAGHER, *Why Waco? Cults and the Battle for Religious Freedom in America* (Los Angeles: University of California Press, 1995), pp. 147–48.

Chapter Review

CASE STUDY: BASIC LEAD IN LANGLEY/CIA SHOOTING

This study concerns an inadequate follow-up on a lead to a suspect in this shooting, allowing the suspect to flee the United States.

Background

On Monday, January 25, 1993, a gunman shot two Central Intelligence Agency (CIA) employees to death and wounded three others at an employee entrance of the CIA headquarters compound in Langley, Virginia. According to witnesses, a man fired several gun shots at CIA employees arriving for work and then drove away.

The incident occurred about 100 feet from CIA property in Fairfax County, Virginia, in an area over which the Fairfax County Police Department has authority to investigate criminal activity. Immediately following the shooting, the Fairfax County Police Department set up an investigative task force that included the Federal Bureau of Investigation (FBI) and the CIA Langley Security Protective Service.

Because of BATF's (Bureau of Alcohol, Tobacco, and Firearms) expertise in firearms, the Special Agent-in-Charge of the BATF Washington Field Office offered assistance to the task force. BATF agents joined the task force operation on January

26, 1993, and on the next day, January 27, began contacting the largest gun dealerships in the Washington, D.C., metropolitan area. BATF management instructed the special agents assigned to the BATF Washington Field Office to examine firearm sales records at the dealerships to identify purchasers of the 11 or more types of firearms capable of chambering 7.62 × 39 caliber ammunition. Such ammunition was consistent with the shell casings found at the crime scene.

Alleged Identification Of Suspect

A BATF agent involved in the investigation of the shooting incident collected firearm sales records, including those of the suspected gunman, from a gun store in Northern Virginia and handled them in accordance with BATF regulations. The store manager and gunsmith claim that the gunsmith informed the BATF agent that a composite sketch (see Figure 20–3) of the suspected gunman looked like the individual who, a few days previously, had purchased an AK-47 assault rifle from the store. Although the evidence developed during our investigation tends to support the statements of the gunsmith and the store manager, the BATF agent involved denies that the gunsmith provided any identification of the composite.

FAIRFAX COUNTY POLICE
COMPOSITE SKETCH
Composite Number 1163
Date of Sketch 1-23-93

FIGURE 20–3
Composite sketch of suspect.

According to the gunsmith, the manager informed him that the agent was from BATF and was investigating the Langley shooting. The manager showed the wanted poster with the composite sketch to the gunsmith. According to the gunsmith and the manager, the gunsmith told the manager that he recognized the composite of the suspect and identified it as the man who had picked up an AK-47 a few days before. He recalled the man vividly because on the day the gun was delivered, according to the gunsmith, he helped the customer reassemble the weapon after the customer had dismantled it and could not put it back together. He also provided instruction to the customer on how to load and unload the weapon properly. The gunsmith told us that, at the time, he wondered why a person would purchase such a firearm if he did not have sufficient knowledge to handle it correctly.

According to the gunsmith and the manager, the gunsmith walked to the opposite side of the counter and faced the agent, held the composite up at eye level, pointed to it, and told the agent, "[This] looks like the guy who was here last week and picked up an AK-47 assault rifle." The gunsmith said that when the agent looked at him and did not respond, he repeated his statement and added, "This really looks like the guy." The manager told us that he asked the gunsmith, in the agent's presence, if he was talking about the AK-47 sold the previous week and the gunsmith confirmed that point.

Although the initial discussion between the BATF agent and the store manager is not in dispute, the agent provided us a different account of his discussions with the gunsmith. The BATF agent told us that he showed the composite to the gunsmith and asked if he recognized the suspect. The gunsmith said that he did not. According to the agent, no one at any time identified the suspect's composite or related the Kansi file to the composite. When we described the gunsmith's and manager's account of his visit, the agent said, "It did not happen."

Insisting that he be allowed to clarify BATF's position in this matter, the Special Agent-in-Charge of the BATF Washington Field Office made the following comments. He told us that he believes the gun store employees are being untruthful and that they made their statements in response to media pressure. He noted that the employees did not make public statements until after Kansi had been publicly identified as a suspect in the shooting. Further, the Special Agent-in-Charge believed that the gunsmith had not identified Kansi as the man to whom he had sold an AK-47 assault weapon a few days before the January 25 shooting. The Special Agent-in-Charge also raised the issue that the gun store owner, to protect himself from liability in the shootings, had fabricated the story about the BATF agent's ignoring the gunsmith's identification of the composite. The Special Agent-in-Charge told us that BATF officials strongly believe that the agent acted properly in his actions in this matter.

Identification Of Suspect

As the task force received information from its various sources, each document was sequentially numbered; listed on a chronological, handwritten log; and entered into a computer database. On February 6, 1993, an investigative analyst identified Mr. Kansi (Mir Aimal Kansi, aka Mir Aimal Kasi) as a suspect when the analyst linked the Kansi/weapon-purchase files submitted by both BATF and the gun store owner, through the Fairfax investigator, and a missing-person report filed by Mr. Kansi's roommate. However, Mr. Kansi was one of several suspects identified through such linkages at this level of the investigation.

On February 9, 1993, an arrest warrant was issued for Mr. Kansi on the charge of capital murder, based on forensic identification of the AK-47 found in Mr. Kansi's apartment as the weapon used in the Langley shooting. On February 10, 1993, the task force confirmed that Mr. Kansi had left the country on January 26, 1993.

Chronology Of Events

01/10/93	Kansi purchased AR-15 and Makarov 9mm handgun at gun store. (He returned with the AR-15 in 1 hour because a round had jammed in the chamber.)
01/16/93	Kansi picked up two handguns at gun store.
01/21/93	Kansi returned AR-15 to gun store.
01/22/93	Kansi picked up a previously ordered AK-47 assault rifle at gun store, trading in the AR-15 for this weapon. Kansi also bought three 50-round boxes of ammunition capable of being chambered in an AK-47. Gunsmith aided Kansi.
01/25/93	Langley shooting occurred. Fairfax County Police Department created and led a task force. CIA Langley Security Protective Service and FBI assisted.
	BATF contacted Fairfax County Police Department to offer assistance.
	First task force meeting held, and agency responsibilities established. (Established hotlines, including a 24-hour Task Force Hotline; a procedure for tracking follow-up information; the mechanical aspects of investigation, including daily briefings; communications with local and federal agencies; and a lead-tracking database system. Discussed investigative follow-up and addressed staffing needs.)
	Kansi purchased airline ticket. (5:00 P.M.)
01/26/93	Task force met with BATF to discuss assistance. (10:00 A.M.)
	Kansi boarded flight to New York at Dulles International Airport. (5:30 P.M.) In New York, he boarded a flight to Pakistan.
01/27/93	BATF agent reviewed weapon-purchase files at gun store and retained copies of Kansi's and other files. (10:00 A.M.–1:00 P.M.)
	Gunsmith faxed Kansi's file (firearm purchase receipt) to Falls Church sheriff; sheriff passed file to Falls Church investigator; investigator telephoned Fairfax County investigator and faxed file; Fairfax County investigator prepared report and faxed it with file to task force. (Beginning approximately 4:00 P.M.)

Second BATF agent visited the gun store to review files and was told by the store manager that an agent had previously been there. Second agent left without further discussion. (Approximately 5:00 P.M.)

01/28/93   Kansi's roommate reported Kansi missing by filing a missing-person report with the Fairfax County Police Department.

Kansi arrived in Pakistan.

Source: "Handling of Suspect Lead in Langley/CIA Headquarters Shooting Incident." Washington, D.C.: U.S. General Accounting Office, No. 94-11, 1994.

Discussion Questions

1. What is the major difference between political terrorists and other violent criminals?
2. What are "blind date" bombings? "Target Blue" ambush killings?
3. Describe "terrorism to punish."
4. Define "preventive intelligence." Define "misplaced confidence" situations.
5. Describe social network analysis. What is its basic utility in criminal investigation?
6. What information should be contained in the preliminary investigation report of a bomb threat? An actual bombing?
7. When is a conspiracy investigation considered complete?
8. Discuss the case study as a possible conspiracy. Think about what happened: Man buys assault rifle and ammunition for it, lies in wait on the edge of a high-security area, kills two CIA employees and wounds three or four more while in their cars on the way to work in broad daylight, drives off, and takes a commercial airliner out of the country.
9. What possible reason could the shooter have for this unusual crime?
10. What can be learned about terrorism from this case study? About crime investigation?

Library Assignment

Search available literature for at least five references to the organizational structure of terrorist groups or the psychosocial characteristics of members.

Workbook Project

Prepare a list of things to do from an investigator's viewpoint when assigned to (1) a bomb threat, (2) a bombing, and (3) a bombing followed by a fire.

Dangerous Drugs and Narcotics Cases

The possession of dangerous and restricted drugs or narcotics is prohibited. Exceptions are made when such dangerous drugs or narcotics are possessed through a lawful medical prescription. Previous conviction of one or more offenses related to possession of dangerous drugs or narcotics generally adds to the basic penalty imposed upon conviction; and many jurisdictions specify that a convicted offender not be eligible for release on parole, or on any other basis, until he or she has served a stated minimum number of years in prison. The basic law prohibits the unlawful possession of drugs and narcotics, transporting, importing, selling, furnishing, administering, or giving away of a dangerous drug or narcotic.

The word "possession," in statutes forbidding the possession of drugs and narcotics, means an immediate and exclusive possession under dominion and control with intent to exercise control; and such persons having such control must have knowledge of the presence of drugs or narcotics, and such knowledge must precede the intent to exercise, or the exercise of, such control. Knowledge is a basic element of crimes related to illegal drugs and narcotics. This also means that a knowledge of the character of the substance is essential to the offense of possession of narcotics.

In a prosecution for possession of dangerous drugs and narcotics, the burden is on the prosecution to prove knowledge of the presence of the drugs or narcotics; and the prosecution must show that a defendant charged with possession of illegal drugs and narcotics knew that the objects in his or her possession were drugs and narcotics. However, the burden of proof may be satisfied by facts that infer such knowledge (circumstantial evidence).

The events leading up to a suspect's arrest should show a state of facts amply sufficient to constitute reasonable cause for arrest (see Figure 21–1). Reasonable and probable cause for an arrest without warrant, on justified belief that a suspect has committed a violation of illegal drugs and narcotics laws, can be based on an officer's past experience, knowledge of the suspect, and observation of suspicious and furtive conduct.

The following instances are illustrative of evidence sufficient to arrest:

1. Where investigators knew of a suspect's previous arrest and conviction for possession of narcotics; learned from the manager of suspect's apartment building that a good deal of suspicious traffic had been going in and out of suspect's apartment; and overhead occupants' references to funnels, used in preparation of narcotics, and balloons, commonly used as containers for narcotics, the officers had reasonable cause for belief that occupants were committing a felony, and an arrest without warrant was proper.

2. In a prosecution for possession of heroin, the evidence, including evidence that the arresting officer had known the informant for approxi-

FIGURE 21–1 Investigation of illegal drugs and narcotics.

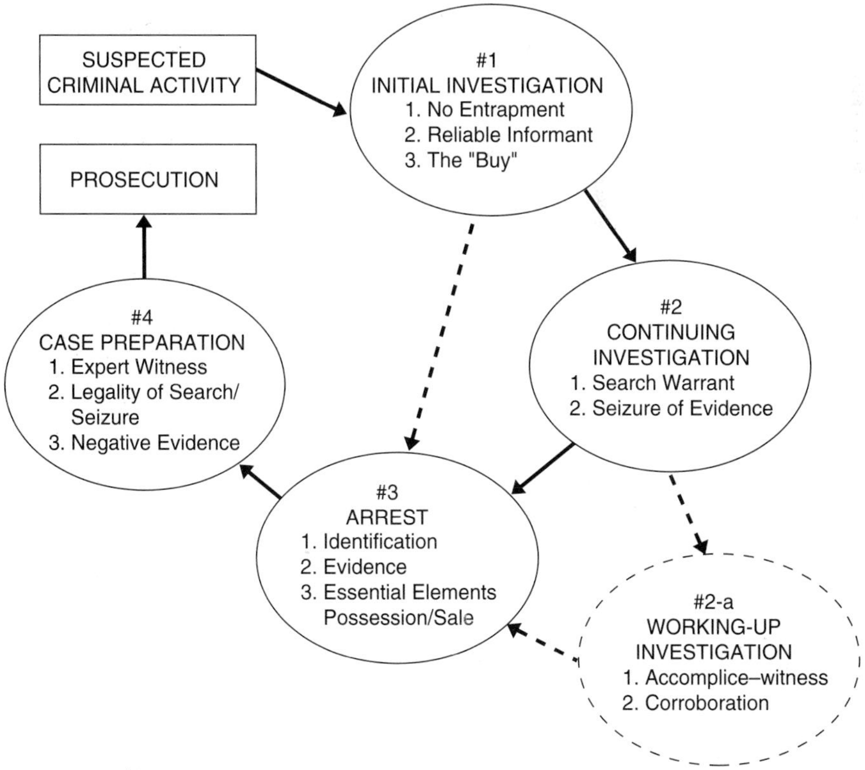

mately one year and that the informant had given information of a detailed nature and a complete description of the defendant and his or her *modus operandi* and that such information had been independently verified in substantial part, was reasonable cause to arrest the defendant without warrant.

Being a drug addict, a "user" of drugs, does not justify an arrest. In *Robinson* v. *California,* 370 U.S. 660 (1962), the U.S. Supreme Court ruled that drug addiction is an illness, drug addicts are sick people, and their capacity to form the necessary criminal intent is diminished. Prior to this case, California had a law that allowed police to arrest drug addicts just for being addicted—for a condition rather than commission of an act. In *Robinson,* the Court ruled the California law to be unconstitutional.

ENTRAPMENT

Any conviction for the possession (or sale, transport, etc.) of illegal drugs should be for a wrongful act voluntarily committed and not for an act induced by the investigator or his or her "special employee," and which would not have occurred without such urging. It is not simple to determine whether, in a particular case, facts suggest the unlawful entrapment of an individual who might otherwise have gone through life without an arrest.

For instance, one defendant charged with the possession for sale of narcotics was not a user; there was no evidence that he was regularly engaged in the traffic of narcotics, and he did not have a prior arrest of any kind. The sale of illegal narcotics, which was admitted, was consummated only after constant urging by a federal agent over a period of three months.

To avoid a defense claim of entrapment, no more pressure or persuasion can be exerted than that ordinarily occurring between willing buyer and willing seller. However, a defense of entrapment is not available to persons charged with possession of heroin where a suspect suggested to the police investigator that he could obtain illegal drugs or narcotics, and where no persuasion or allurement had been used by the officer, who had merely furnished an opportunity for the suspect to acquire illegal drugs or narcotics to sell to the undercover investigator. It is not the purpose of the law to prevent the unwary criminal from being trapped in a crime; it is instead the purpose of the law to prevent the police officer from manufacturing crime—that is, from seducing the unwary innocent person into a career of crime.

THE DRUG SCENE

There is a wide variety of restricted drugs and narcotics, from marijuana to heroin, being used by millions of people. The most common drugs that have a potential for drug dependence or addiction fall into four major groups:

1. *Narcotics.* Drugs with a depressant effect on the central nervous system. They usually lead quickly to both psychological and physical dependence.

2. *Sedatives.* These drugs, like the narcotics, cause both psychological and physical dependence, but dependence develops more slowly. They are also central nervous system depressants.

3. *Stimulants.* The amphetamines and methamphetamines are in this group. These drugs cause a rapid buildup of tolerance, so that additional quantities are needed to achieve the same stimulating effects, and quickly lead to psychological dependence.

4. *Hallucinogens.* These drugs cause sensory distortions and result in illusions and delusions. They are the psychedelic, or "mind-expanding" drugs. Abuse of these drugs leads to psychological dependence.

Descriptions of, and data about, drugs that may be encountered on the drug scene are detailed in Appendix B, Drugs.

Crack (the poor man's cocaine), "speed" or "meth" (methamphetamine), and marijuana ("pot") are currently the illegal drugs of choice across the country. They are reasonably priced; crack houses are local; meth can be snorted, smoked, or injected; and pot is a maintenance drug for the carryover between "hits."

Since 1992, two events have occurred on the drug scene: (1) sellers are now known or make themselves known, and (2) both sellers and users are younger—teenagers are almost a majority as both users and sellers. Most high schools and some junior highs have a resident dealer, sometimes more than one—known to most students.

The cottage-industry nature of both crack and meth accounts for some of these changes. "Cookers" swap know-how on innovative changes in manufacturing crack from its original cocaine powder, and they seek recipes for processing ephedrine (a legal drug) to "meth." When these amateur chemists were roadblocked by drug agents from the Drug Enforcement Agency (DEA), in obtaining ephedrine, they successfully switched to another legal substance, pseudoephedrine.

Clandestine meth laboratories are dangerous places to work or raid. Explosions, leaking toxic fluids and gases, and fires have killed and maimed cookers and are a continuing threat to police raiding one of these labs.

In addition, normally law-abiding teenage girls desperate to lose weight buy meth, and boys of like age, apparently equally desperate, buy drugs as aphrodisiacs. They are appetite killers, but their enhancement of sex is debatable. As a result, detectives are likely to find this class of users hostile to police inquiries and frequently part-time sellers to support their new habit.

DRUG-SELLING ORGANIZATIONS

Knowledge of the organizational setup of criminal organizations engaged in selling illicit drugs is important to investigators working on the drug scene. The traditional sales-marketing pyramid of manufacturer, importer (source of supply), distributors, wholesalers and jobbers, and retailers (peddling mobs, "pushers") has not changed a great deal in the last quarter-century.[1] "The boss" is still at the top of the pyramid, whether he or she is a major dealer or importer, or both. There are now a few more levels in the distribution network, generally based on the size of their sales (multi-kilo, kilo, fractional kilo), and the lowest level of street dealers has been augmented by lookouts and runners. One role is to warn of any police presence; another is to transport small quantities of drugs from the "stash" of the dealer to wherever the drugs are being sold (see Figure 21–2).

Twenty-five years ago, most of these sales-marketing pyramids were headed by the leaders of Italian crime "families" or their "under bosses," and importation into the United States was mainly in the hands of Europeans (French, Corsicans, Italians). Now, criminal organizations have expanded and importation routes originate in South America, Central America, and Mexico. Cocaine and its derivative crack are immensely popular in the United States, and both are readily sold at high profits. In addition, the pyramid networks have become more sophisticated in their sales marketing—and in avoidance of police interference with their daily sales. Currently, known criminal organizations engaged in major dealings in illicit drugs are:

1. Mafia (La Cosa Nostra) crime families.
2. Colombians.
3. Jamaican ("posses").

FIGURE 21–2 The marketing pyramid—illegal drugs and narcotics. Drug dealers, from sub-wholesaler levels up, depend on their anonymity to avoid arrest.

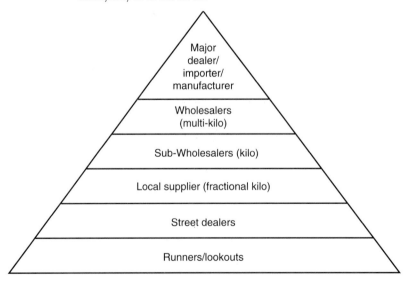

4. Asian (Chinese, Vietnamese, Korean).*
5. Bikers (Hell's Angels, Outlaws, etc.).**
6. Prison gangs.
7. Street gangs (Crips, Bloods, African-American, Hispanic).

Both the Mafia and Colombians are generally organized along "family" lines, with roles in the sales-marketing pyramid resulting from recommendations from internal sources.

The Jamaican "posses" are sophisticated crime mobs dealing primarily in "crack" in major cities across the country. Personnel are recruited from Jamaica and other countries in the Caribbean basin. They are a hard-ball organization characterized by ruthless and extensive violence.[2]

Oriental criminal organizations have kept a low profile. Not much is known about the extent of their operations, but a great deal is suspected. Because they operate in their own ethnic neighborhoods, investigators have had little success in developing informants or making buys. Youth gangs are often the source of personnel for these networks.

Motorcycle gangs have been into general misbehavior and traffic in firearms for some time. In recent years they have developed tightly organized drug-selling networks.[3] The Hell's Angels and the Pagans are nationwide groups with major dealers in most of the large urban centers. They are disciplined groups, with murder a common form of punishment for violations of gang rules.

Prison gangs originated in prisons, selling drugs to inmates. Released members of these gangs were soon employed as street dealers in illicit drugs. In the Southwest, the Mexican Mafia is a major prison gang selling drugs both inside prison walls and on the outside. Various prison gangs (Neo-Nazis, Aryan Brotherhood, etc.) operate in other areas of the United States.

Street gangs are a new addition to the drug-selling field. They do not usually buy as a gang, but rather as individual members or small groups of gang members. They do "sling dope," but their manner of purchasing drugs and selling them usually reflects the loose organizational structure of these street gangs.[4]

These drug-selling gangs commit murder as a business technique to (1) eliminate competition, (2) protect their territory from the competition of rival gangs, (3) discipline suspected informants, and (4) protect their cash and illicit drugs from rip-offs by armed robbers.

PICKUP ARRESTS

In warrantless arrests for the possession of dangerous drugs or narcotics, or both, the investigator must act within the legal image of a "reasonable man." The test is: Would the facts from which the arresting officer acted warrant a

*See Department of Justice Documents 6–9 in Appendix C.
**See Department of Justice Document 10 in Appendix C.

man of reasonable caution to believe that a crime was committed? The court usually takes into consideration police expertise from training or experience in determining whether the arrest was reasonable. An important case in this area of pickup arrests is *Draper* v. *United States,* 358 U.S. 307 (1959). In *Draper,* a federal narcotic agent of considerable experience (Marsh) had been informed by a special employee (Hereford), an informant, who had always been found to be accurate and reliable, that Draper was peddling narcotics and that he had gone to Chicago and would return by train with 3 ounces of heroin on the morning of September 8 or 9. The informant gave a physical description of Draper, said that he would be carrying a "tan zipper bag," and that he habitually "walked real fast." The agent kept the incoming trains from Chicago under surveillance, and on the morning of September 9 observed a person fitting the description given by the informant, walking "fast" toward an exit, and carrying a tan zipper bag. This person was Draper, and he was then arrested by the officer.

The information given to narcotic agent Marsh by "special employee" Hereford about Draper may have been hearsay to Marsh, but coming from one employed for that purpose and whose information had always been found accurate and reliable, it is clear that Marsh would have been derelict in his duties had he not pursued it. And when, in pursuing that information, he saw a man, having the exact physical attributes and wearing the precise clothing and carrying the tan zipper bag that Hereford had described, alight from one of the very trains from the very place stated by Hereford, and start to walk away at a "fast" pace toward the station, Marsh had personally verified every facet of the information given him by Hereford except whether petitioner had accomplished his mission and had the 3 ounces of heroin on his person or in his bag. And surely, with every other bit of Hereford's information being thus personally verified, Marsh had "reasonable grounds" to believe that the remaining unverified bit of Hereford's information—that Draper would have heroin with him—was likewise true.

In some instances officers discover contraband in the form of illegal drugs or narcotics in searches incidental to an arrest, or in the normal course of executing a search warrant. In such cases, the legality of the basic arrest and search or the search under the authority of a warrant, must be demonstrated and supported by evidence before the illegal drugs or narcotics case can be developed for prosecution.

ARRESTS BASED ON "BUYS"

The investigation of cases involving the possession and/or sale of dangerous drugs or narcotics usually is developed by one or more "buys" of these illegal substances. An undercover police investigator (sworn officer) or an informant ("special employee") buys a quantity of dangerous drugs or narcotics from a suspect; the transaction often is witnessed by officers conducting a surveillance of the undercover agent or special employee and of the suspect. The integrity of the informant's buy is preserved by a pre-transaction and post-transaction search of the informant; compelling evidence often is secured by prior registration by the investigators of the serial numbers of the money used for the "buy." The substance purchased is marked for identification and transported to a local police (or state) narcotic laboratory for examination and identification, and is retained as evidence of the sale of drugs or a narcotic substance to the informant or employee.

The informant, under supervision, sets up the "buy." The suspect may be identified by police and the informant asked to develop a case, or the informant may identify a suspect known to him or her as a drug seller to police. After the "buy," the informant details the circumstances of the transaction to his or her police associates, turns over the substance purchased, and returns any unused money advanced for the "buy."

The usual procedure in making a "buy" is:

1. The informant is advised to avoid any taint of entrapment.
2. The informant, under police supervision, makes contact with the subject and arranges the "buy."
3. The police arrange a surveillance of the informant, and possibly the suspect.
4. The police search the informant to make certain that he or she is not carrying any drugs or any substantial amount of money, and provide him or her with "state" money (serial numbers recorded) for the "buy."
5. The police maintain contact with the informant to the scene of transaction.
6. The police watch the transaction as closely as possible.
7. When the informant returns to his or her police associates he or she informs them of the transaction, turns over the purchase and any unspent funds, and is again searched (to allow police investigators to testify that the informant had none of the funds given him or her, or any other drugs).
8. The purchased substance is marked as evidence and transported to a laboratory.
9. A laboratory analysis is sought to confirm the illegal nature of the substance as drugs or narcotics, the kind, and the amount.
10. The case is prepared for (a) an arrest warrant, (b) an arrest (with or without warrant) on subsequent "buy," and (c) an application for a search warrant.

When an undercover police agent participates in a "buy," he or she conceals his or her identity as a police officer. A crewcut police recruit can become a long-haired participant in the search for drug sellers in a few weeks. The ability to act out his or her new identity without revealing police employment by use of police slang, or other misfortune, ensures continuation in this undercover role until the officer must reveal his or her identity as the investigation is terminated.

Successful undercover police operations in the drug scene usually require that an informant introduce and vouch for the undercover agent. The undercover agent's identity is revealed only when the agent has developed cases against a number of sellers of narcotics and the department decides to make all the appropriate arrests simultaneously.

SEARCH WARRANTS: DRUG INVESTIGATIONS

A "buy" is a normal prelude to an application for a search warrant in illegal drug and narcotic cases. The purpose of the search warrant is to gain judicial authorization to enter a place in which the suspect from whom the "buy" was made has his or her *stash* of drugs, to seize these drugs, and to arrest the suspect.

The past criminal record of a suspected person, his or her association with known narcotics users, and the fact that another person (usually the informant) was found to be in possession of a narcotic after leaving the premises of a suspected drug seller may be taken into account in determining whether probable cause exists for issuance of a search warrant. (See Figure 21–3.)

In many instances, the report of an informant in relation to his or her purchase of drugs will identify a specific room, or portion of a room, from which the drug seller procured the drugs. This allows the application for the search warrant to have the necessary particularity as to the place or places to be searched.

To be constitutionally sufficient, an affidavit (accompanying an application for a search warrant) based solely on an unnamed informant's tip must set forth some underlying circumstances which reveal the source of the informant's information pertaining to the criminal activity and must present sufficient objective evidence to enable the magistrate to conclude that the unnamed informant is credible or that his or her information is reliable.[5] The report of the chemist examining the substance purchased can be used to establish the fact that prior to the transaction or transactions ("buys") the suspect had possessed illegal drugs or narcotics.

Unlike an application for search warrants in burglary and theft cases, where specific articles of stolen property must be identified in the application, drugs may be described in general terms as contraband and by common names. Although returns to the issuing magistrate must contain a specific inventory of the drugs and narcotics seized under the authority of the search warrant, there is no need to "match" the drugs or narcotics seized with the drugs or narcotics in the application for the warrant.

An outline of the usual procedure in this major type of investigation is:

1. The case against the suspect is developed by one or more "buys" and information from a reliable informant.
2. The investigator makes observations supporting the transaction(s) and information, as evidence of the suspect's criminal behavior, and is prepared to show the reliability of the informant.
3. Application is made to the magistrate for a search warrant, naming the suspect and the place or places to be searched, and citing dangerous drugs or narcotics, or both, as the object of the search.

4. A warrant is executed, the suspect is arrested, and the "return" is made to the magistrate.

5. The substances are seized and analyzed; and the fact that the substances are illegal drugs or narcotics, or both, is revealed and reported to the magistrate in a supplementary "return."

6. The case is prepared against the arrestee for presentation to the prosecutor.

In the investigation of a major drug seller, the "buy" is the preliminary investigation. With this transaction, and any subsequent "buys," accumulating evidence is likely to support an application for a search warrant. In preparing and executing the search warrant, investigators are conducting a continuing investigation which will identify the drug seller as the person in possession of a quantity of drugs and/or narcotics.

WARRANTLESS SEARCHES: DRUG INVESTIGATIONS

Reasonableness is the constitutional test of any warrantless search. Exigent circumstances are often present in drug cases. Drug possession for the purpose of sale is an ongoing crime; drug sellers do not suspend their activity while police do the necessary paperwork involved with obtaining a search warrant. Evidence that might be sufficient to convict them may be destroyed if police do not take prompt action.

An example of this reasonableness is a case[6] in which a police officer observed a crime in progress inside a building (narcotics "cutting" and packaging operation; a "factory") and contraband (drugs) in plain view. An appellate court ruled that the police were fully authorized under these circumstances to enter the premises, make arrests, and seek out contraband. The police officer in this case, acting on an anonymous tip, went to a certain address, looked through a basement window, and saw the major narcotics-packaging operation in progress. He then sought the aid of other police officers. With this additional help, the officer subsequently (within 30 to 40 minutes) entered and searched the premises without a warrant. Searching officers found the "cutting" mirror (used for mixing the illegal drugs with cheaper adulterants) on a table, along with plastic bags and measuring spoons and pans. Nearby, the officers found a large quantity of narcotics packaged for distribution. Four persons found on the premises were arrested.

"WORKING UP" INVESTIGATIONS

Working up the drug-selling marketing pyramid utilizes both buy-and-bust arrests, and arrests and seizures under the authority of a search warrant. An arrest is first made at the base of the pyramid (see Figure 21–2), the street seller of illicit drugs. Then the supplier of this dealer is arrested, and onward

No.___

STATE OF CALIFORNIA – COUNTY OF SACRAMENTO

SEARCH WARRANT AND AFFIDAVIT
(AFFIDAVIT)

JIMMY ███ , being sworn, says that on the basis of the information contained within this Search Warrant and Affidavit and the attached and incorporated Statement of Probable Cause, comprising a total of __14__ pages, he/she has probable cause to believe and does believe that the property described below is lawfully seizable pursuant to Penal Code Section 1524, as indicated below, and is now located at the location(s) set forth below. Wherefore, affiant requests that this Search Warrant be issued.

Night Search Requested YES ███ NO [ ]   (Justification on page(s) (9))

Reviewed by _____ *Michael A. ███* _____
(Deputy District Attorney)

_____
(Signature of Affiant – after having been sworn)

(SEARCH WARRANT)

THE PEOPLE OF THE STATE OF CALIFORNIA TO ANY SHERIFF, POLICEMAN OR PEACE OFFICER IN THE COUNTY OF SACRAMENTO:

proof by affidavit having been made before me by JIMMY ███ , that there is probable cause to believe that the property described herein may be found at the locations set forth herein and that it is lawfully seizable pursuant to Penal Code Section 1524 as indicated below by "x" (s) in that it:

```
_____    was stolen or embezzled
__X__    was used as the means of committing a felony
__X__    is possessed by a person with the intent to use it as means of committing a public offense or is possessed by another to
         whom he or she may have delivered it for the purpose of concealing it or preventing its discovery.
__X__    tends to show that a felony has been committed or that a particular person has committed a felony.
```

YOU ARE THEREFORE COMMANDED TO SEARCH:

███ Arcade Boulevard located in the City and County of Sacramento. It is a single story, single family residence, beige in color with brown trim and a brown composition roof. The numbers ███ are affixed to the front of the residence and are visible from the street. The single car attached garage is to the right (west) of the residence and the house is on the south side of Arcade Boulevard, between Colfax Street and Edgewater Road. Also to include all attics, basements, rooms, garages, outbuildings, storage sheds, inoperative vehicles, garbage cans and containers located with in the property boundaries.

FOR THE PERSON(S) OF:

███ , Dennis Michael aka Dennis Michael ███ , DOB: 10-4-54.

306

FOR THE FOLLOWING VEHICLE(S):

A white with blue trim motor home, California license ███ and also request authorization to search the 1978 Datsun Pickup, California license ███, registered to ███

FOR THE FOLLOWING PROPERTY:

Methamphetamine and paraphernalia associated with its use, sales, transportation and manufacture, including; measuring and weighing devices, milk sugar, baggies, paper bindles, funnels, syringes, bent spoons, chemical formulas, phenylacetic acid, phenyl-2-propanone, methylamine, benzyl chloride, acetaldehyde, formamide, ephedrine, ether, acetone, lye, mercuric chloride, magnesium filings, sulfuric and hydrochloric acid, sodium acetate, chloroform, methanol, ethanol, red phosphorus, palladium black, and acetic anhydride, funnels, flasks, distillation flasks, various types of heaters and heating mantles, hot plates, various types of crystallizing dishes, desiccators, distilling apparatuses, extractors, vacuum dryers, beakers, jars, condensers, graduated cylinders, vacuum pumps, shakers and stirrers, thermometers, transformers, ovens, regulators, glass tubing, hoses, scales, filter papers, PH papers, plastic containers, gloves, masks, fans, air conditioners, generators, bills, receipts, ledgers, maps, charts, buyers lists, seller lists and recordation of sales, personal telephone books, address books, telephone bills, papers and documents containing lists of names, addresses and phone numbers, utility company receipts, rent receipts, addressed envelopes, keys and photographs. Searching officers are directed to answer the phone and converse with callers who appear to be calling in regard to drug/narcotic sales and note and record the conversation without revealing their true identity. They are also directed to note and record phone numbers or other messages received on telephonic pagers for the purpose of calling those persons paging the suspect(s) to determine if the page was regarding an intended purchase or delivery of drugs/narcotics.

AND TO SEIZE IT IF FOUND and bring it forthwith before me, or this court, at the courthouse of this court. This Search Warrant and Incorporated Affidavit was sworn to and subscribed before me this ___5___ day of _January_ , 19_89_ , at 10:25 A.M./P.M. Wherefore, I find probable cause for the issuance of this Search Warrant and do issue it.

_____
(Signature of Magistrate)

Night Search Approved YES [✗] NO [ ]
(Magistrates Initials)

Judge of the Superior Court [✗] Municipal Court-Sacramento Judicial District [ ].

Date ___1.5.89___ Hr. _10:45 P.M._

Executed by _____

FIGURE 21-3 Search warrant issued by a California court in an illegal drug case. The request for this warrant totaled 14 pages. Magistrates are aware of their responsibility for this prior approval of police action and scan these requests with great care. If they do not understand or believe it is accurate, they will deny the request.

and upward until a major supplier or importer is arrested. Informants in these working-up investigations are arrestees who have agreed to cooperate in revealing their suppliers in return for leniency in drafting the indictment or at the time of sentencing.

This is often termed "working off a beef." However, investigators must be cautious in these cases, as many arrestees make a deal with the arresting officer (and prosecutor) but have no intention of informing on their true source of supply. They engage in "lateral snitching." They inform only on drug sellers who are equal or lower to their own level in the drug-marketing pyramid. In this fashion, an arrestee manipulates an investigator, informing primarily on his or her competition.[7]

Lengthy investigations probing upward in a drug-marketing network can develop a case against a manufacturer, a major dealer, and/or an importer. To be successful, such investigations require (1) a criminal associate of the "targeted" major manufacturer/dealer/importer, and (2) evidence corroborating the expected testimony of the accomplice–witness.

Arrestees situated above the street-dealer level in a drug-marketing pyramid are more difficult to "turn" than are lesser network members. When a man or woman close to a major manufacturer/dealer/importer is arrested, the "boss" commonly provides legal counsel, bail, and other assistance pending trial. In addition, the past-performance record of informants being murdered while in prison or out on bail is an ongoing deterrent to cooperating with the police. As a result, an investigator needs a strong case against an arrestee to entertain any hope of turning him or her into an accomplice–witness.[8]

When an accomplice–witness can provide data as to the date and time of a future delivery of drugs, an arrest and seizure based on this information and involving the major dealer/importer are most compelling evidence.

Usually, corroboration results from an investigator collecting bits and pieces of information from such techniques as:

1. Physical and electronic surveillance.
2. Tally analysis of telephone records of outgoing calls from a "suspect" telephone.
3. A survey of car rental contracts, credit card purchases, hotel/motel registrations, and major cash purchases.
4. Tracing "laundered" cash.

Corroborating the expected testimony of an accomplice–witness against a major manufacturer/dealer/importer is a "paper chase" more or less. Ideally, the observations made by investigators of the activities of the suspect will reveal the linkage between others in the drug-marketing network. These observations are supported by these persons contacting the suspect from time to time by telephone. Renting cars, registering in hotels, and buying items, from gasoline to mansions, tend to place the suspect in various locations on specific dates. Finally, money can be traced.

The Bank Records and Foreign Transactions Act requires bank officials to report transactions (deposits/withdrawals) over $10,000. It is difficult to conceal millions of dollars in drug-selling profits.

It is a long and difficult investigation when a major manufacturer/dealer/importer is targeted for arrest and prosecution. Suspected informants are promptly murdered, both to negate their services to police and to build up a past-performance record of "death to the informer"—a long-time creed of organized crime. Confidential police files and operations are compromised by bribery—corrupting public employees in order to learn what evidence the police have to date and the scope of their existing plans.[9]

RAIDS

A raid in drug-law enforcement is an entry into a building for the purpose of seizing illicit drugs and arresting the occupants: one or more drug dealers and associates. Entry may be gained by subterfuge (a "tale" to gain entry without force), or by the use of force (sledge hammer, battering ram, feet).

Commonly, raids are no longer the combined effort of several investigators. They are now a major action of the investigating unit with a superior officer designated as the overall commanding officer. In fact, the expectation of a shoot-out during a raid has been integrated with raid planning: Special Weapons Teams are frequently assigned to back up the investigators, particularly when the place to be raided is a "rock house" from which crack is sold, as these premises are heavily armored and automatic-weapons fire from the premises being raided is more than a possibility. Most departments now require all members of a raiding party to wear bulletproof vests.

There is a great deal of responsibility in the leadership of a raid on the drug scene. There is fear of "hitting the wrong door," of having a member of the raiding party injured or killed, of failing to identify the major suspect among the occupants, of not finding any drugs at all (or only a small amount), and of not finding the "trap" containing the major "stash." (Traps are built-in hiding places usually constructed by a skilled carpenter.)

Legally, the authority for a raid is a search warrant authorizing police officers to enter a specific premises to seize illicit drugs believed to be in the described premises. These warrants and/or local laws will provide for a "no-knock" entry. In past years the notice-and-demand factor slowed up the raiding party to such an extent that drug sellers and associates had time to get rid of the incriminating evidence (usually flushing the illicit drugs down the toilet). Today, aware jurists and legislators have recognized the police need of speedy entry.

Armoring the place from which drugs are sold is the drug seller's response to this capability of police to gain speedy entry and to seize drugs before they can be destroyed. Sheet steel panels are screwed or bolted to entry doors, and windows are covered with steel panels and heavy iron gratings. Drug sellers claim that this armoring is necessary to protect them from rip-offs, but it has a valuable side action in preventing speedy entry by police.

Once entry is made and the occupants have been placed under control—and disarmed if carrying weapons—the commanding officer of the raiding party supervises a methodical search for illicit drugs and weapons, and a thorough scanning of the identity of the occupants.

PROBLEMS OF PROOF

The classic defense claim in drug-selling cases is entrapment: the investigator and/or police agent (special employee, informant) urged and persuaded the defendant to sell the drugs, and that the sale itself was solely to recover the cost of the drugs to the defendant. There are many variations of this entrapment defense, but it has been successful in many jury trials. It is likely to continue as a successful defense unless prosecutors can affirmatively show that there was no coercive persuasion or allurement used on the defendant.

In cases involving only a small amount of illicit drugs, a defendant may claim that he or she was "flaked" by the police investigator and/or his informant partner. This is a claim that the illicit drugs were planted by the informant or the arresting officer. Unfortunately for the prosecution in these trials, one or more jurors may have heard of "flaking" as a police practice in their home or business neighborhood and give greater credence to the claim than to the denial.

The compulsion of immunized testimony by an accomplice–witness is an in-court problem of credibility. This is not a sympathetic witness to whom jurors might relate, but a person who has turned state's witness to save his or her own skin. The problem is that many jurors are ready to believe that such a witness is prone to lie, and they are told this time and again by defense counsel.

Undercover investigators appear to many jurors as individuals who have used friendship, deceit, and persuasion in making arrests. Defense attorneys' allegations of entrapment—that their client did no more than "accommodate" a friend by getting him or her illicit drugs—cater to this conscious or subliminal belief.

The legal significance of most of the evidence may rest on the prosecutor's ability to somehow insert a "victim" into the case, but this is difficult, as drug selling is one of the so-called "victimless" crimes.

Selected References

1. Paul B. Weston, "The Illicit Traffic in Drugs," in *Narcotics, U.S.A.* (New York: Greenberg Publisher, 1952), pp. 127–40.
2. Phillip C. McGuire, "Jamaican Posses: A Call for Cooperation among Law Enforcement Agencies," *The Police Chief,* LV, No. 1 (January 1988); pp. 20–27.
3. William D. Hyatt, "Investigation of Major Drug Distribution Cartels," in *Critical Issues in Criminal Investigation,* 2nd ed. (Cincinnati, Ohio: Anderson Publishing Company, 1988), pp. 113–39.
4. Scott H. Decker and Barrik Van Winkle, "Sling Dope: The Role of Gang Members in Drug Sales," *Justice Quarterly,* 11, No. 4 (December 1994), pp. 583–604.

5. Aguilar v. Texas, 378 U.S. 108 (1964); Spinelli v. United States, 393 U.S. 410 (1969); United States v. Garrett, 565 F. 2nd 1065 (1977).

6. United States v. Johnson, 561 F. 2nd 832 (1977).

7. PETER K. MANNING, *The Narcs' Game—Organizational and Informational Limits on Drug Law Enforcement* (Cambridge, Mass.: The MIT Press, 1980), p. 161.

8. MARK HARRISON MOORE, *Buy and Bust* (Lexington, Mass.: D. C. Heath and Company, 1977), p. 135.

9. JAMES MILLS, *The Underground Empire—Where Crime and Government Embrace* (New York: Doubleday & Company, 1986), pp. 72–113, 283–394, 520–618.

Chapter Review

Discussion Questions

1. What drugs are common on the "drug scene"?

2. What is the primary motivation of drug sellers?

3. Briefly describe the drug-marketing pyramid (network).

4. What are the differences and similarities between major drug-selling criminal organizations?

5. Under what circumstances of investigation is a pickup arrest justified?

6. Name and describe the participants in a "buy" of illegal drugs.

7. Specify the facts that must be established to secure a search warrant after a "buy" has been made.

8. In working-up investigations, what investigative techniques have proven useful in discovering evidence to corroborate the testimony of an accomplice–witness?

9. What is the responsibility of the leader of a raiding party under the authority of a search warrant for the seizure of illicit drugs?

Library Assignment

Secure and list at least five references to writings describing drugs, their appearance, and effects.

Workshop Project

Prepare a chart or diagram of procedure in making "buys."

CHAPTER
22

Theft

In common law, larceny was defined as a trespassory taking and carrying away of personal property belonging to another with an intent to deprive the owner of such property permanently. Currently, larceny (theft) is defined in most states as the unlawful taking or stealing of property or articles without the use of force or violence. It includes shoplifting, pocket-picking, purse snatching without "strongarm" tactics, thefts of and from vehicles, and property or cash taken from a home.

New terms used in criminal justice statistics describe the scope of common larceny:

1. *Household larceny*—theft or attempted theft of property or cash from a residence or the immediate vicinity of the residence. The thief must have a legal right to be in the house—as a guest, maid, for example.
2. *Personal crimes of theft* (personal larceny)—theft or attempted theft of property or cash by stealth, either:
   a. with contact, but without force or threat of force; or
   b. without direct contact between the victim and the offender.
3. Personal larceny with contact—theft or attempted theft of property or cash directly from the victim by stealth, not force or the threat of force.[1]

Thieves steal money, vehicles, and other property from rightful owners. They sell it to individuals (bargain seekers) or criminal receivers of stolen goods (fences). The profit motive in thefts is too general to offer any promising leads. The solution of these crimes begins with a prompt alarm for the stolen property and an examination of the crime scene to determine the circumstances of the crime and to search for and collect physical evidence. Victims are interviewed to develop suspects, and witnesses to some preparatory or postcrime activity are sought and their help solicited. Extensive *modus operandi* comparisons are made. Information about the work of known thieves suspected of operating locally is correlated with the facts known about the crime being investigated. Thieves can be traced when the proceeds of the crime are sold and recovered by police. Persons who buy stolen property quite frequently reveal the identity of the thief. However, thefts are difficult to solve because of the lack of eyewitnesses. They generally are unknown identity investigations characterized by the absence of a named suspect (see Figure 22–1).

Prior to the recovery of the stolen property, investigators attempt to identify the perpetrator by seeking a characteristic signature in the *modus operandi*

FIGURE 22–1 Investigation of thefts.

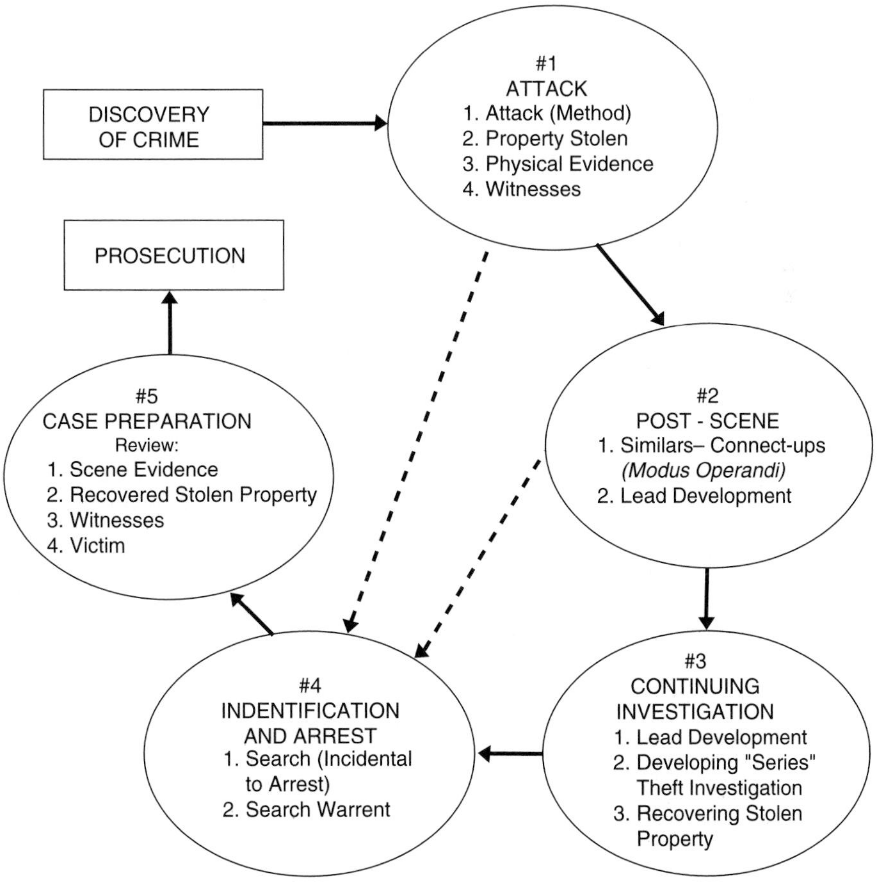

of the crime or a basic lead from field interview reports and tips from underworld sources of information. The value of physical evidence found and collected at the scenes of thefts has a growing importance. It is not likely that such scientific evidence will serve to name a suspect, but it can serve as an identifier when the foregoing techniques bring together a group of persons all about equally suspect.

Most investigations of thefts involve past thefts. The police patrol force sometimes detects a thief at work or responds to a theft-in-progress call; quite often in investigating prowler calls the responding officers discover a thief. But usually the victims of these crimes do not discover them until after the crime has been attempted or is completed. One of the unfortunate aspects of thefts is that police have to bracket the occurrence between the time of discovery and the time at which the stolen property was last seen or otherwise noticed.

Time is likely to favor a criminal. It may blur the focus of an investigation and can aid escape and safe disposal of stolen property. The time element in the past crimes does not encourage the assigned investigator and probably serves as a passive means of discouragement. Crimes of violence have an inherent motivation for any investigator; in thefts the investigator must seek motivation within his or her personal occupational goals for effective work.

THE ATTACK

Money and valuable property are usually safeguarded. To steal either, or both, requires planning, direction, and operating skills. This is the attack of the thief. To be considered are the premises attacked, the methodology of the attack itself, and the means used to dispose of the proceeds of the crime, the loot or swag. In fact, the proceeds of a crime are the objective of the attack, and they are an important highlight in viewing the attack as an event.

The property stolen is a major clue. The broadcast and Teletype alarms that announce to all cooperating law enforcement agencies the fact of the crime and identifying data on the property taken begin the tracing that often leads to recovery of the property and a backtracking to the thief. The stolen property is listed by quantity, kind, material, physical description, serial numbers, and value. Many investigators at crime scenes have discovered that victims cannot describe the stolen property; therefore, investigators often must question the victim about the stolen property item by item—what each item was used for, what it is made of, whether it is a man's or woman's item, what marks are on it, and its value (cost and estimated current value).

The characteristics of the property stolen have long been used as part of *modus operandi* searches, but they are gaining new significance as indicative of the routine decision making of a particular thief. The property stolen is being recognized as part of the attack event that can serve to name a suspect. It is a part of the criteria used to evaluate a target. Some thieves steal money only, which is not grossly incriminating even minutes after a theft. Other thieves consider a proposed theft and reject it because of the difficulty of disposing of the property that will be the proceeds of the crime. Some thieves having an established disposal route, with customers such as housewives, employees of gas stations and drive-ins along a highway, and small merchants in nearby towns and villages, reject all proposals unless the property is suitable for their customers. Other thieves use the wholesalers of the underworld, the fences, and tend to specialize in property that can be legitimized by removing all identifying marks. A few professional thieves have the friendships among members of the organized crime syndicate necessary to dispose of jewelry, furs, bonds, color television sets, and other merchandise with retail values in excess of $20,000 to $30,000.

MODUS OPERANDI SEARCHES

Modus operandi searches are rewarding in theft investigations. Thieves are known as single-pattern offenders.

Modus operandi searching will identify a group of suspects as persons actively engaged in committing property crimes and will produce a number of suspects for the crime being investigated. Computerized record searches allow the scanning of a huge number of past crimes for the purpose of *modus operandi* identification.

There is a great deal of personal satisfaction in solving a theft in the early stages of a continuing investigation *before* the proceeds of the crime have been recovered and the process of tracing back has been initiated. It is a possibility that is not being exploited to its fullest extent; the lack of a named suspect often relegates a theft investigation to a category of "no results possible" until there is some feedback about the stolen property being recovered.

The key to an early break in property crime investigation is the expanded *modus operandi* search to include the decision-making processes exhibited by the criminal in his or her operations. By developing an understanding of how thieves make decisions and the nature of the thought processes that underlie this decision making, an aware investigator can learn a great deal about these criminals. Interpreting selected *modus operandi* data of a theft under investigation provides clues about a thief's decision routines for dealing with each of the components of the overall task. Then it is the role of the investigator to develop an "identifier" from the thought streams of individual thieves. There is a pattern to a person's decision making because each person learns how to deal with a particular aspect of any task in an individual way. The investigator's use of this decision pattern may disclose the who, the when, the where, or the how, making it possible to identify, trap, or find the thief before or at his or her next crime.

THE UNIVERSE OF SUSPECTS

Each member of a criminal-investigation division should be able to recognize information that is of importance to all the members of the division, and to advise co-workers of possible suspects in current or future crimes. In solving thefts, unlike the pursuit of a named suspect in crimes of violence, one must engage in a battle for information, and every investigator needs the help of associates. Although mainly concerned with general information about individuals who are suspected of earning the major portion of their incomes from criminal operations, this information can sometimes isolate a number of persons as suspects in a specific crime.

Field interview reports may place into police records systems meaningful data about persons and vehicles stopped and questioned by police officers on patrol, but a great deal of data about people living and working in a patrol sector is stored in the minds of the officers working the sector with some regularity. This is useful information at times, but it never gets into the police records system. At one time local police supplied federal agents with this type of information; uniformed police supplied local detectives with similar data about persons coming to their attention and considered suspects because of their activity. The demands of federal service and local investigative responsibilities may have precluded giving appropriate credit. In any event, the upward supply of information from local levels has been noticeable in its absence in recent years. An investigator must work to correct this situation, allocating time on a daily basis to developing liaison with local sources of information among fellow police officers, to finding out the names and descriptions of persons known to be well supplied with money but without a known source of income, to noting the automobile make and license number of a newly arrived hoodlum or a recently released felony parolee, to learning the consensus in regard to a merchant suspected of buying and selling stolen property, and to hearing about a host of seemingly unimportant items given in friendship and appreciation of mutual occupational objectives.

Work also must be devoted to remedying current practices about credit and reward for information received. Entries should be made in the service records of the helping officers when such leads assist in breaking a case. More important, such fellow workers may be assisted in a normal ambition to step up into investigative work. Willingness to help an investigator is a good recommendation as to a man's basic worth for this type of duty.

Investigators also must allocate time regularly to frequent the haunts of known thieves. Taxi drivers, waitresses, cocktail hostesses, bartenders, and tavern owners in such areas are potential sources of information about persons new to the area and apparently well supplied with money. Persons in these occupations are less reluctant to talk about thieves than they are about people who rob and are assaultive. Underworld informants interviewed clandestinely can give supplementary information for a better understanding of data already collected; they can assist in interpreting information; and they can offer leads which may be developed by inquiries in the known hangouts of these criminals. This is necessarily a discreet inquiry in order not to compromise any ongoing investigation. The investigator's relations with such sources of information are guarded ones, quite different from the friendships necessary to develop information from among local police officers.

When a frightened spouse accused her husband of a thirteen-year-old homicide of a police officer it was discovered that inability to tie together stray bits of information about the basic burglary involved in this unfortunate killing had led to the classification of this case as unsolved for thirteen years. After the wife of the criminal disclosed his identity, an electronic surveillance resulted in compelling evidence against him. The case illustrates the need for collating the bits and pieces of information from the underworld and from investigative inquiries, and until electronic data processing and computer technology take over, this is the job of police officers assigned as investigators.

Learning to appreciate the significance of an apparently minor item of information is a developed skill. However, it is a learned skill that will enhance the value of other information collected during an investigation. It will also increase the universe of suspects and the probability that the group of suspects will contain the person responsible for the crime under investigation. Because of the lack of eyewitnesses in crimes against property, the ability to solve a crime is likely to rest on the necessary information getting into the police system without loss or distortion and being used to the best advantage.[2]

CRIMINAL RECEIVERS OF STOLEN PROPERTY

Theft investigators would be seriously handicapped if the proceeds of all thefts were cash or its equivalent. Most thefts are of various goods and merchandise. Unfortunately, there is a stable and continuing market for stolen property.

The real success in stealing is not the completion of the crime itself but the disposal of the stolen property at a profit without leaving the trace that so often identifies the perpetrators of these crimes. Criminals who commit property crimes are repeaters; and it may be they are fatalistic about this Achilles' heel of property crimes and consider it a permanent occupational hazard, but not many of them blithely pawn their loot or sell it to someone likely to identify them to police.

Initially, the receiver of stolen property insulates the thief from identification and arrest. As soon as the property transfer is made, the thief can no longer be caught with the stolen property in his or her possession. However, when police detect and apprehend a receiver with stolen property, the potential for tracing back to the thief is always present. This tracing from receiver to thief is an effective theft investigative technique. It is the only method to use when a thief does not leave any fingerprints or "signature" *(modus operandi)* at the crime scene, when the thief is not observed or apprehended while the crime is in progress, or while the thief is in possession of recently stolen property.

When the stolen property is purchased by an individual seeking a bargain, this tracing is relatively easy. The receiver is informed of the possible criminal implications of possessing stolen property. Usually, the price and the circumstances of purchase create a reasonably probable cause to assume the purchaser knew the property was stolen. In disclaiming any criminal responsibility, this type of receiver either identifies the seller/thief or gives sufficient information about the purchase to enable the investigator to identify the thief.

When the stolen property is purchased by a professional receiver (a fence), tracing from receiver to thief becomes a problem. Fences with long-standing business dealings with a thief are unlikely to reveal the circumstances of how they received the stolen property.

Fences are the intermediaries of larceny. They buy and sell stolen property regularly. They are in direct contact with thieves and with possible purchasers. Most of them have acquired a reputation on both sides of this business loop, and depend on this "goodwill" for third-party referrals of new business. This "rep" is that the fence will not, under any circumstances, inform police of the identity of a thief or a purchaser of stolen property.[3]

The storefront or "sting" technique is an investigative technique in property crimes aimed at the wholesale identification and apprehension of thieves. Police investigators pose as fences for the purpose of "buying" stolen property.[4] Since the prices paid to thieves by a real fence are copied by the police, the cost of this technique is not a real problem. The problem is whether such police activity may encourage local thieves to take more and more—as long as they have a readily available market.

AUTO THEFT

The theft of passenger cars, trucks, and motorcycles is common throughout the United States. "Auto theft" is the term generally used by police in describing this form of larceny. The universe of auto thieves is comprised of both amateurs and professionals:

1. *The joyriding juvenile.* This thief is usually host to several other juveniles, and they abandon the vehicle when it runs out of gas or they tire of it.

2. *The transportation thief.* This is the person who "borrows" a car for transportation, sometimes to cross state lines or for a lengthy period. The vehicle is abandoned when it has served the thief's purpose.

3. *The use-in-crime thief.* These thieves steal a car for the sole purpose of using it in the commission of another crime, such as a robbery. Again, the vehicle is abandoned when it has served its purpose.

4. *Insurance fraud swindlers.* Automobiles are abandoned in ghetto areas where the owner knows it will be stripped promptly for its parts, or the owner will have it dismantled or "squished" in a junkyard, or arrange for its burning. The owner claims—and usually receives—the current blue-book value of the vehicle from the insurance company.

   In a spin-off of this fraud the swindler registers and insures a "paper" car (forged title to a nonexistent vehicle), reports it stolen, and puts in a claim to the insurance carrier for the current blue-book value of the phantom car.

5. *Strippers and dismantlers.* *Strippers* usually attack a parked car, taking a variety of parts readily disposed of on the local black market. Radios, tape decks, batteries, bucket seats, transmissions, rear ends, generators, wheels and tires, and even motors have been stripped from automobiles in public places. *Dismantlers* steal a car, tow or drive it to a "chop shop," and cut

it up for most of its parts. The stolen car's body (sometimes even minus fenders, doors, headlights, front grill, and motor hood) is abandoned some distance from the shop, usually in a remote area. These thieves work fast; a parked car can be stripped in place in less than an hour, and dismantlers can chop up a car, dispose of the leftover body, and move the parts to be sold to another location all within an hour or so.

6. *Professional auto thieves.* The "pro" in this field steals late-model automobiles and resells them. Sometimes the stolen car is transported to another state and registered in that state with forged or fraudulent papers prior to resale. A contemporary practice is to ship the stolen car out of the country (Mexico and South America are favorite areas) and sell it on arrival. Some of these professional thieves have developed a new trade: stealing cars to order for "chop shops."

Many of the auto thieves described above now use weapons to gain possession of a car. "Carjacking" is the armed robbery of a person in possession of an automobile or other motor vehicle. One or more thieves confront a car's driver with a gun, knife, or other weapon and demand the car's keys, then drive off.

While the amateur car thieves (joyriders and transportation thieves) sometimes seek automobiles with the keys in the lock or the car doors unlocked, the pro uses tools such as a "dent puller" and "slide hammer" or a set of master keys to enter a locked car and to defeat the ignition lock. Of course, many amateur thieves are as skilled at hot-wiring a car's ignition as are the professionals.

An auto theft investigation has the following stages:

1. *Preliminary investigation.* The preliminary investigator accepts the report of a stolen vehicle from the owner or his or her representative. The report must contain the name, address, and telephone of the owner; a full description of the vehicle, including registration number and public and other identification numbers; the time and place of the theft and the location of the vehicle when stolen; and that the vehicle was not repossessed by a finance company or other legal owner. Anything distinctive about the stolen vehicle (design, color, damage, etc.) will be entered on this report to aid in its location as promptly as possible.

2. *Alarm.* Information from the preliminary investigation report, particularly distinctive characteristics of the stolen vehicle, is transmitted to all members of the police agency, and sent to cooperating agencies by Teletype or other means, and reported to state and national computerized records systems.

3. *Recovery.* Auto thefts for convenience or joyriding are usually identified by prompt recovery of the stolen auto without any evidence of stripping. This is also true of the use-in-crime theft, with the time of recovery usually within a short time after the crime. Citizens often notice these parked vehicles and assist the patrol force in locating them.

The recovery of a stripped or "chopped" vehicle identifies the work of strippers and dismantlers; and the nonrecovery of the stolen vehicle tends to identify the other types of auto thieves.

4. *Continuing investigation.* Probing into the circumstances of an auto theft is usually *reactive* to the arrest of an auto thief while in possession of the stolen vehicle, or to its recovery. The probing is *proactive* when the vehicle is not recovered within a reasonable time, with investigators prowling auto accessory and salvage yards, and body and fender shops (local laws usually require the proprietors to allow police inspection) to locate stolen vehicles.

5. *Case preparation.* Cases involving the theft of a single vehicle closed-out by arrest are simple: the appropriation of another's property to the thief's own use without permission of the owner. Cases involving multivehicle thefts require extensive evidence not only to show the larceny, but possibly to assemble a conspiracy case against all offenders involved. In either event, inquiries along the basic leads common in property crimes give initial direction to any continuing investigation of auto theft.

The reality of auto theft is that the current high prices for vehicle accessories and components contribute to the growth of "hot parts" dealers. This ready market for the proceeds of their crime assures strippers and dismantlers of better-than-average prices in comparison with thieves stealing other goods and merchandise. In fact, the "growth market" factor in this area has attracted many segments of the national crime syndicate to this lucrative field.

In preliminary or continuing investigations of auto theft, primary identification of a stolen vehicle is made by the public vehicle identification number (PVIN), motor number, and confidential vehicle identification number (CVIN) at various hidden locations on the vehicle. (Vehicle manufacturers and the National Automobile Theft Bureau supply police agencies with information as to the location of such numbers on passenger cars, trucks, and motorcycles.)

In the future, two innovations in police science are likely to be significant for investigators in identifying and arresting auto thieves. These are: (1) new methods for developing latent fingerprints, and (2) automated fingerprint search systems. Upon recovery, the stolen car could be safeguarded until processed for latents. With an identity linked to the car, investigators are in a position to focus their investigation. Possibly among the new procedures for recovering latents will be the capability of selecting "new" prints: time dating[1] in some fashion to avoid prints older than the date the car was stolen.

PROBLEMS OF PROOF

Problems of proof in theft crimes are as broad as the scope of theft crimes. Larceny is taking property and carrying it away from its rightful owner under circumstances indicating intent to steal. Larceny is an offense against lawful possession. Grand theft occurs when the property exceeds a stated value (varies from state to state); petty theft occurs when the property taken is below that baseline. Grand larceny is a felony; petty theft is a misdemeanor.

Cases are usually solved by police through experience—working many theft cases sharpens basic skills. They send cases to the prosecutor on the basis of the suspect's identity as the thief and the property as the true "loot" of the crime.

Selected References

1. Department of Justice, *Criminal Victimization in the United States, 1992,* Washington, D.C., U.S. Department of Justice, 1994, pp. 154–55.

2. M. A. P. WILLMER, "Criminal Investigation from the Small Town to the Large Urban Conurbation," *British Journal of Criminology,* VIII, No. 3 (July 1968), pp. 259–74.

3. DARREL J. STEFFENSMEIER, *The Fence—In the Shadow of Two Worlds* (Totowa, N.J.: Rowman & Littlefield, Publishers, 1986), pp. 13–35, 157–86.

4. *Strategies for Combating the Criminal Receiver of Stolen Goods: An Antifencing Manual for Law Enforcement Agencies* (Washington, D.C.: U.S. Department of Justice, Law Enforcement Assistance Administration, 1976), pp. 89–97. See RON SHAFFER and KEVIN KLOSE (with Alfred R. Lewis), *Surprise! Surprise! How the Lawmen Conned the Thieves* (New York: The Viking Press, 1977).

Chapter Review

Discussion Questions

1. Why does motive offer very little promise as a basic lead in thefts?

2. Why do the proceeds of thefts offer substantial promise as a basic lead?

3. Because a study of *modus operandi* and a search of police *modus operandi* files cannot be used in the same manner in thefts as in investigations of crimes of violence, cite the potential of such study and search in this area.

4. Discuss the motivation of investigators when assigned to different types of crimes. How can investigators be motivated to work at high levels of efficiency on any investigation?

5. Is the use of *attack* as the theme of fact seeking at theft scenes poorly conceived and, possibly, better adapted to fact seeking at the scenes of crimes of violence?

6. Explain the "Achilles' heel" of stealing and the bland acceptance of this occupational hazard by thieves.

7. What are the implications of the concept of a universe of suspects?

8. What circumstances may induce a receiver of stolen property to reveal the true circumstances of its purchase?

9. What are the advantages of a storefront or "sting" program to recover stolen property? The disadvantages?

10. What is a "chop shop"?

11. Are fingerprints useful in identification of auto thieves?

12. What type of auto theft is most difficult to investigate and close out with results?

Library Assignment

Review the available literature in criminal investigation and develop a 500- to 1,000-word profile of thieves. Conclude this paper with a selected bibliography of references utilized in its preparation.

Workbook Project

Prepare a reference listing possible sources of information that will develop and expand a group of suspects in a theft investigation.

CHAPTER
23

Burglary

In the past, conviction of common-law burglary required the proof of six essential elements.[1]

1. A breaking.
2. An entry.
3. In the nighttime.
4. Of a dwelling house.
5. Belonging to another.
6. An intent to commit a felony.

In most jurisdictions today, conviction for burglary requires only three basic or essential elements:[2]

1. Entry.
2. Of a building (or other structure, place, or thing described by the particular Penal Code section).
3. With intent to steal or commit another felony.

Burglary is usually separated into first-, second-, and possibly third-degree burglary. Some of the old essential elements of common-law burglary are used to divide the modern crime of burglary into degrees. The division into degrees may be based on whether the crime occurs in a dwelling house; whether such a dwelling is inhabited by a person actually present at the time; whether it is entered in the nighttime; or whether the act is committed by a person who is armed with a deadly weapon or who, while in the commission of a burglary, arms him- or herself with such a deadly weapon, or who, while in the commission of such burglary, assaults any person. Any of the facts above or various combinations may determine the seriousness (degree) of the burglary, depending upon the state in which the crime is committed. In recent years, the use of explosives has increased the degree of burglary.[3]

The allied misdemeanor offense of possession of burglar tools assists police in apprehending burglars and in preventing burglaries. Any person who has on his or her person or in his or her possession a picklock or other instrument with intent to feloniously break into or enter any building is guilty of a misdemeanor in California. So is any person who knowingly makes or alters any picklock or other instrument so that it can be used to open the lock of any building without the specific consent of a person having control of such building.[4]

Burglary is a crime of opportunity, a crime of *easy* opportunity. Although many burglars limit their activities to a certain area and thus reduce the scope of their burglaries, every area has many easy opportunities.

Investigators should try to develop some insight into how a burglar selects a site for his or her crime. Why the choice of one area? Why the selection of one house as opposed to a neighboring house? The probability of profit and safety are perhaps at the core of this site-selection process, with burglars having a large "awareness" space in which they evaluate (by search) the opportunity for a successful burglary.[5] If this insight can be developed, a roving stakeout of an area may be successful in apprehending the burglar.

Burglary is usually a passive crime, in that the burglar normally tries to avoid contact with victims. The chances of getting caught in an unoccupied structure are lower than the chances of being apprehended in an occupied structure. Persons who are not present at the scene of a burglary can never be eyewitnesses to the identity of a burglar and later identify him or her in court as the criminal they viewed at the scene of the crime. When there is no alarm to police of a crime "in progress" there can be no "hot" search. In the more public crimes, when a criminal has fled the scene of the crime shortly before the arrival of police, the victim may give the police a physical description of the criminal, of a vehicle, and of the direction of flight, thus giving the police the opportunity for a "warm" search. This is not possible when the victim does not even know his or her premises have been burglarized until some time after the burglar has fled the scene. This must restrict the police apprehension process to the "cold" portion of this crime-solving process, commonly termed the investigative phase of the apprehension process. In other words, burglars usually are not apprehended at the scene of their crime, or in flight, but must be apprehended as a result of an investigative process (see Figure 23–1).

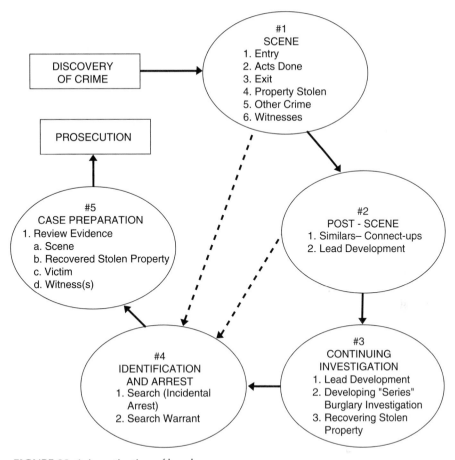

FIGURE 23–1 Investigation of burglary.

The objective of burglars may be something other than theft. It may be sex, usually rape. Sometimes theft and sex are joint goals. Both larceny and rape or any other crime involved is investigated along with the basic burglary. The investigator must be alert to obtain evidence of each essential element of the additional crimes, as well as the essential element of the burglary.

TYPES OF BURGLARS

For years police schools have taught that there are two general types of burglars: (1) the amateur, and (2) the professional. Professional burglars were described as those persons who worked at burglary as a "trade," making their living by burglary and larceny alone and having no other means of income. Other burglars are loosely grouped beneath this plateau of "professionalism." The amateur group includes the burglar who commits crimes primarily to secure money for drugs.

Because burglary is probably the most common serious crime in the United States, it is timely to reconstruct a typology of burglars that will encompass skill levels. This typology categorizes the skills of a burglar on two levels:

1. The ability to gain entry to a premises.
2. The business sense of the burglar in regard to the selection of loot and the method of disposing of the proceeds of the crime (i.e., selling the stolen property).

The skill required to gain entry to a premises may be limited to forcing a door or window open, but it can extend to the use of "lock-picking" tools, which keeps pace with the art of the locksmith in providing security against thieves, and to the skill that opens locked containers such as safes.

The business sense of a burglar depends on his or her ability to distinguish between valuable and worthless items at the time of the burglary, the burglar's contacts with "receivers" of stolen property, and whether he or she is in "panic" need (common with drug addicts) to sell the stolen property.

This new typology of burglars describes a burglar as being in one of the following categories:

1. Unskilled.
2. Semiskilled.
3. Professional.

The fact that such a typology of burglars exists does not mean that investigators should discount the classic *modus operandi* items used to describe various types of burglars. These items have served as a working typology for many years. They are:

1. Type of premises entered.
2. Means of entry.
3. Type of loot (stolen property).
4. Time of operation.
5. Presence of crime partners.[6]

It does mean, however, that these basic items of *modus operandi* information should be reviewed from the viewpoint of discovering the skills demonstrated in gaining entry to the premises, and the "business sense" demonstrated to some extent by the nature of the property taken at the time of the burglary, its quantity and value.

The "means of entry" differ in various burglaries and are related to the skill of a burglar. The various known means of entry are:

1. *The open door or window entry.* The burglar roams residence areas, apartments, and hotels looking for open doors or windows.

2. *The "jimmy" entry.* The burglar forces a door or window with an iron tool such as a tire iron, screwdriver, or small crowbar or box opener.

3. *The celluloid entry.* The burglar forces open a door's spring lock with a small piece of celluloid.

4. *The stepover or human fly entry.* The burglar is an aerialist; the "stepover" burglar steps from a fire escape, balcony, or other building to a nearby window; the "human fly" burglar can progress upward or downward on the sides of a building to a selected point of entry.

5. *Roof entry.* The burglar breaks into a premises through a skylight or air-conditioning duct on the roof, or by cutting a hole in the roof of a building.

6. *The hide-in entry.* The burglar hides in a commercial premises until all employees have left, and then breaks out with the stolen property.

7. *The cut-in entry.* The burglar uses tools of various kinds to cut through the floor, ceiling, or wall of a store or office to another store or office.

8. *Hit-and-run entry (smash and grab).* The burglar breaks a window of a ground-floor store and takes property from a window or nearby portions of the premises, and flees before police can be alerted to the crime.

9. *Key entry.* The burglar uses a key; the key may be given to him or her by an informant ("finger-man"), it may be stolen, or the burglar may obtain a duplicate or master key by various means.

It is apparent that most unskilled or semiskilled burglars are prowlers who enter a residence and search very rapidly for cash or property easily transported and quickly converted into cash. Whether or not they succeed in finding it, they will leave without any loss of time, taking with them the "portable wealth" of the householder—usually radios, television sets, portable typewriters, and other items that are easily disposed of to individuals seeking bargains or to persons who deal in and sell drugs and are willing to exchange the drugs for the stolen merchandise.

The semiskilled and the professional burglars also deal in articles of value, but articles that are not as easily converted into cash and that generally require the services of a "fence"—a receiver of stolen property. The loot of such thievery ranges through jewelry, furs, clothing, liquor, tobacco, meat, and textiles.

BURGLARY AS A BEHAVIORAL CONCEPT

Burglarizing is the behavior of committing a burglary, and—most likely—another and another and another. Burglaries usually are crimes in a series.

Like all behavior, burglary involves needs and the opportunity to satisfy these needs. It also involves a common decision as to whether or not to take advantage of opportunities. The behavior cycle in burglary is:

1. Needs.
2. Opportunities.

3. Means (skills).

4. Satisfactions.

5. Choice.

To understand the elements in this burglary cycle is to understand the behavior of burglars. Among burglars whose goals are theft (profit), the economic needs are met through successful burglaries, the successful taking away of stolen property, and its profitable disposition. The opportunity to commit a burglary is perceived; the burglary and its profit will meet the needs of the burglar; the burglar has the necessary "technology" to enter a premises successfully, to take away the proceeds of a crime, and to sell it. The individual with these needs who makes a choice of burglary over other possible activities to meet unmet needs not only receives satisfaction from the work but also a reinforcement of this behavior, thus increasing the probability of the recurrence of this behavior—more burglaries and theft.[7]

Many years ago burglars stole primarily for economic reasons. Today, the same economic reasons may be complicated by an addiction to drugs. Although the need for funds to buy drugs is an economic need, there is a more urgent compulsion related to the need for the drugs and their effect on the drug user.

Rape-burglars exhibit needs to satisfy their sex drive in an act associated with force. These burglars are abnormal in selecting forcible rape as a sex outlet, but they follow the burglar's "normal" cycle of behavior—and each successful crime is reinforcement for continuing this pattern of behavior.

SAFE BURGLARS

Burglars often demonstrate skill at opening locked desks, file cabinets, safes, and other containers. It may be that such entry to locked containers will be made by basic tools such as a jimmy or screwdriver, or tools picked up in the premises and utilized by the burglars. Most safe burglars, however, will bring to the crime scene whatever special tools they need: torch, sectional crowbar, and so on.

Force used to attack safes generally follows one of the following patterns:

1. *Punching.* In this manner of entry a sledge hammer and a drift punch are used to knock the combination dial from the safe and drive the spindle back into the safe. This makes the release mechanism of the lock accessible and allows the safe to be opened.

2. *Pulling.* A device similar to a gear or wheel puller is used to pull the dial or spindle completely out of the safe door, and thus allow the safe to be opened (as when the spindle is punched or driven back into a safe).

3. *Peeling.* This means of entry involves the prying off of the outer surface of the safe door so that the locking mechanism of the safe is exposed and can be pried open, allowing entry to the safe.

4. *Ripping.* This is a battering of the top, bottom, or sides of a safe with a chisel or other metal cutter, such as a ripping bar (burglar's tool) or the hydraulic ramming device used in a body-and-fender shop.

5. *Drilling.* One or more holes are drilled in the door of the safe to expose the lock mechanism allowing the safe-breaker to align the lock tumblers manually and open the door of the safe.

6. *Burning.* The safe is attacked by an oxygen-acetylene torch, and a section of the safe is burned out to allow entry. A variation of this burning technique, when bank vaults are involved, is the use of a thermal burning bar which makes the original oxygen-acetylene torch much more efficient so that it is possible to burn through 6-inch tempered steel in 15 to 20 seconds.

7. *Blasting.* The use of explosives against safes. This means of entry may be more common in the future because of the fact that many persons on the drug scene are knowledgeable in the use of explosives as a result of their activities related to civil unrest.

8. *Carrying away.* The burglar will remove a safe in order to open it at a more convenient location.

Intruders often open a safe without force, by means of its combination. It may be that the burglar found the safe open, but when no physical force is used to open a safe, investigators assume it was opened by using the combination. In such cases, the burglar may have found the combination written on the side of a drawer in a nearby desk, in an account book, or other convenient place; or he or she may have been given it by a dishonest employee.

THE BURGLARY SCENE INVESTIGATION

The purpose of the burglary scene investigation is to ascertain what clues or traces at the scene may identify the burglar and crime partner(s). The burglary scene investigation has three major phases:

1. The means of gaining entry.
2. What the burglar did while in the premises.
3. How the burglar exited the premises.

The place of entry and toolmarks are the classic identifying characteristics found at the scene of burglaries. If the burglar broke into any locked containers at the scene of the burglary, this is also a demonstration of a skill in the use of tools, and various identifying toolmarks may be discovered.

Acts done while at the crime scene may be no more than necessary to accomplish a theft. On the other hand, the acts of a rapist–burglar spell out the essential elements of a second major crime. In addition, some acts done may aid in identifying the burglars. The property stolen is another useful factor in identifying the burglar.

The means of exit rounds out what can be gleaned from a burglary scene by investigators. This may be no more than the fact that the burglar exited from a rear door, after a roof entry, but in the course of determining this fact investigators may find significant clues or traces in and about the place of exit.

However, none of the evidence likely to be found at burglary scenes will actually identify a burglar—that is, by name, or as a person. One or more factors related to the burglar's *modus operandi* may contribute to developing one or more suspects, so that this on-the-scene evidence should be preserved for future use. When one or more suspects are uncovered, the clues and traces can be related to these suspects by the investigator.

If the investigator has good reason to believe that a suspect is still in possession of stolen property from one or more recent burglaries, and the investigator can secure reliable information describing this stolen property and where it is located, such data can be tied in with the victim's reports of what was stolen and developed into an application for a search warrant. The execution of the search warrant and the recovery of the stolen property in premises controlled by the suspect will support other evidence identifying him or her as the burglar.

THE POST-SCENE INVESTIGATION

The post-scene investigation is the development of leads from connect-ups and a comparison of *modus operandi* with other crimes either solved or unsolved which tends to identify one or more suspects as the offender in a series of crimes of which the burglary being investigated is the latest. It often involves the use of informants or identification through recovery of the stolen property and a tracing back to the burglar.

Although connect-ups and the use of informants are classic avenues of investigation to identify suspects in burglary investigations, they offer little or no admissible prosecution evidence that a particular suspect committed the particular burglary under investigation.

The identification of the seller of stolen property through a questioning of the receiver of stolen property has a more promising potential as evidence. When a person is known to be in possession of stolen property, a search warrant can be secured. The resultant seizure of stolen property is lawful, and such evidence can be used in court against the receiver or against the person who sold the stolen goods to him or her—if there is testimony or other evidence that connects the seller to the stolen property.

KNOWN BURGLARS

When an investigator has developed a suspect known to police to be a burglar but is unable to develop evidence likely to serve as probable cause for an arrest, then he or she must continue the connecting-up of subsequent burglaries until sufficient evidence is accumulated to supply probable cause for the arrest of the suspect.

Innovative surveillance procedures have been used in recent years in many police departments to clear burglary cases when a "known" burglar is identified as the suspect in a series of burglaries. An "around-the-clock" surveillance of the known burglar (and usually a crime partner or partners) is established and continued until such time as the burglar enters a building under circumstances that indicate intent to commit a crime. This type of arrest is opportune and timely.

CASE PREPARATION

Case preparation in burglary cases connects up the clues and traces found at the scene of burglaries with the suspect, together with any activities of the suspect while under police surveillance, or any of the suspect's actions taken to dispose of the stolen property. Any testimony of witnesses is correlated with these basic segments of a burglary investigation. In rape-burglaries the victim can be, at the least, an effective witness to acts done. It is desirable that the investigator's case preparation be concerned mainly with bringing together the evidence that will prove that the crime of burglary was committed and that the person arrested can be identified as the burglar. Second, case preparation may be concerned with developing evidence that will prove that a secondary crime (larceny or rape) has been committed and that the arrestee is guilty of this crime (or crimes).

OVERCOMING INVESTIGATOR'S APATHY/INDIFFERENCE

Personal crimes of contact are considered more serious than household crimes. Investigators commonly react promptly and meaningfully when assigned to homicides, rapes, robberies, and assaults; they tend to respond with less enthusiasm when they "catch" a burglary or solve other property crimes.

About one-half of theft cases and one-third of burglary cases are not reported to police. Victims report these crimes primarily because they are told to do so by an insurer—to have a loss substantiated by a police record. The formula becomes: uninterested victim, disinterested investigator.

Victims who are enthusiastic about their chances of police finding their stolen property and returning it to them are in short supply. This cynicism is based on public knowledge of the police track record on recovery. The subconscious impact of this lack of faith is an equal lack of confidence by investigators.

The unfortunate aspect of this apathy and indifference is that it is possible to successfully investigate property-only crimes, particularly burglary. There are basic leads, clues, and traces that can lead to arrest, and recovery of the proceeds of not one crime, but perhaps a whole garage full of stolen property.

The dollar value of stolen property probably exerts the greatest effect on the time spent on these investigations.[8]

Another form of incentive occurs when a burglary in progress turns out well. (For example: a pair of suspected burglars are caught fleeing the scene of an attempted ATM burglary; sledgehammers, chisels, and crowbars are found at the scene; a car registered to one of the burglars is outside the bank; and they made numerous phone calls from the motel room in which they spent the evening before the attempt.) Of course, the war against apathy and indifference is won when the suspects are arraigned and the judge sets bail at a high sum.

THE COMPLETE BURGLARY INVESTIGATOR

The complete burglary investigator is a person who can:

1. Accumulate clues and traces at the scene of a crime that will serve to identify the offender.
2. Develop informants in the local underworld who are aware of the activity of burglars, particularly the activity of the semiskilled and unskilled groups (usually the addict-burglars).
3. Conduct a surveillance of likely receivers of stolen property, and uncover and trace back stolen property from its receiver to the burglar–offender.
4. Conduct surveillances of known burglars to ascertain if they are presently committing burglaries.
5. Learn all about the various types of burglars, and become knowledgeable about as many of the "known" burglars as possible—whether they are in or out of prison, whether they are "active," where they live, and other personal information.

The complete burglary investigator also has the analytical ability to develop the identification of suspects. This identification may be on an intuitive basis when the first connect-up is made, but the investigator's ability to link burglaries and burglars must extend to developing a structure of legally significant evidence in support of this identification.

Finally, the complete burglary investigator is a person who has learned the great need for evidence in support of every essential element of the crime or crimes charged, and the equal need for negative evidence to block common defenses such as alibi or mistake.

PROBLEMS OF PROOF

The major problem of proof in prosecuting burglars is linking a defendant to the scene of the burglary. Burglars try to be unobserved as they break into and enter a building for the purpose of stealing, and they are usually successful.

Sometimes the police–prosecutor team patch together physical evidence at the scene to connect the defendant with the place of occurrence of the crime. Fingerprints of the defendant at the scene, even partial prints, overcome this problem, but most of the physical evidence is much less conclusive than fingerprints. Toolmarks at the scene matching a tool found in the defendant's possession are only as legally significant as can be established by the expert witness who explains to the jury how the comparison was developed. Footprints tend to link up a defendant to the crime scene, but again, their legal significance depends on the quality of the expert-witness testimony about them. Tire impressions with unique characteristics of identity can identify a specific vehicle as being at the crime scene, but the defendant must be linked to this vehicle.

Defense counsel have often blasted the conclusive evidence of a *sting* in which police employees have purchased from a defendant property stolen in burglaries, claiming that the "sting" does no more than show that the defendant sold property to persons he or she now knows to be police officers. A collateral claim is that the defendant did not know that the property was stolen (it was "found" or purchased in good faith from an unknown seller).

Selected References

1. State v. Wiley, 173 Maryland 119 (1937).
2. California Penal Code, Section 459.
3. *Ibid.,* Section 461.
4. *Ibid.,* Section 459.
5. GEORGE RENGERT and JOHN WASILCHICK, *Surburban Burglary—A Time and a Place for Everything* (Springfield, Ill.: Charles C Thomas, Publisher, 1985), pp. 53–75.
6. MAURICE J. FITZGERALD, *Handbook of Criminal Investigation* (New York: Arco Publishing, 1960), p. 131.
7. HARRY A. SCARR et al., *Patterns of Burglary* (Washington, D.C.: U.S. Department of Justice, Law Enforcement Assistance Administration, National Institute of Law Enforcement and Criminal Justice, 1972), pp. 4–5.
8. S. G. BRANDL, "Impact of Case Characteristics on Detectives' Decision Making," *JQ Justice Quarterly,* 10, No. 3 (September 1993), pp. 395–415.

Chapter Review

Discussion Questions

1. Are burglars arrested, as a general rule, in the "hot," "cold," or "warm" phase of the police apprehension process? Explain.
2. What skills or "technology" should be taken into account in classifying burglars?
3. What are the characteristics of semiskilled burglars?
4. List and describe five means of entry common to burglars.
5. Describe the behavior cycle in burglaries.
6. List and describe five means of entry used by burglars to open and enter safes.

7. What is the primary purpose in on-the-scene investigation of burglaries?
8. Is the around-the-clock surveillance of known burglars unethical?
9. Describe the characteristics and/or capabilities desirable in a burglary investigator.
10. Describe the five stages of a burglary investigation.
11. What are the essential elements of Stage #1 (Scene)? Stage #2 (Post-Scene)?

Library Assignment

List five references to recent magazine articles concerned with physical evidence likely to be found at burglary scenes.

Workshop Project

Prepare a checklist of things to do in burglary investigations and case preparations.

CHAPTER
24

Fraud: Bunco to White-Collar Crime

Fraud is not new. It is defined as a nonviolent crime involving elements of intentional deceit, concealment, corruption, misrepresentation, and abuse of trust to gain the property of another, and is often facilitated by the willing cooperation of unaware or unknowing victims.

The guile, deception, and trickery common to frauds often silence the victim. Either the victim does not realize a theft has occurred or is unwilling to report it because of fear of being involved in a crime or of publicly admitting to being a "sucker" who has been duped. In addition, police frequently fail to discover unreported frauds because fraud is a covert scheme with a lower profile than overt thefts or violent crimes.

Fraud in the United States is on the increase. Swindlers use simple bunco or complex *"con" (confidence) games* to rip off unknowing victims. Fraudulent-check writers menace the integrity of banks. White-collar criminals operating in both the marketplace and the workplace abuse the trust common to merchant–customer and employee–employer relations.

Fraud investigations usually begin with a citizen's complaint or a police probe. A preliminary investigation should disclose whether the act or acts done to further the objective of the fraud are a crime under state laws. Such investigation should spell out the time, place, and *modus operandi* of the fraud, along with data on the victim, property lost, witnesses, and suspects.

Continuing investigations are the action phase in which suspects are identified, pursued, and apprehended, and the case prepared for criminal prosecution.

When a fraud case reveals substantial economic loss to a victim, but cannot be developed for criminal prosecution, it is best referred to state or federal regulatory agencies for possible civil action, a cease-and-desist order, or other appropriate remedial action (see Figure 24–1).

Fraud auditing is a new occupational specialty in commercial and industrial employment. Fraud "auditors" are assigned the task of detecting and preventing frauds in commercial transactions. Job descriptions in this role call for skills of a well-trained auditor and an experienced criminal investigator. Fraud auditors examine the covert aspect of employee behavior and the barriers established to prevent fraud. Can the barriers be breached? When? How? By whom?[1]

ELEMENTS OF FRAUD

Investigators must seek evidence of four common characteristics of fraud:

1. Criminal intent *(mens rea)*.
2. Wrongful objective (deprive true owner of property).
3. Disguise or concealment of objective (wrongful).
4. Reliance on victim's cupidity, carelessness, compassion.

The criminal intent is to achieve the wrongful objective of the scheme. The act or acts done to implement the scheme spell out the disguise or concealment of the scheme's unlawful objective. Thieves who profit from fraudulent schemes must induce the victim to part voluntarily with his or her property. This may be the signing of a contract, or the actual payment of money or transfer of property ownership.

BUNCO AND CON GAMES

Bunco schemes and con games are frauds based on promises of unusual returns: something for nothing, double your money, or income for life. The false hopes of the victim are fostered by assurances that the risk is minimal. The scheme is usually described as a "sure thing."

Some of the more common swindles classed as bunco or con games are (1) pigeon drop, (2) payoff, and (3) carnival bunco. The *pigeon drop* or *pocketbook drop* is street bunco that requires a minimum number of "props": pocketbook or envelope, and a sizable amount of cash. The pigeon is the victim, and no more than two or three swindlers participate in this crime. This is a scheme in which a victim is "conned" into withdrawing a large sum of money from a bank account to show financial responsibility. In the presence of the

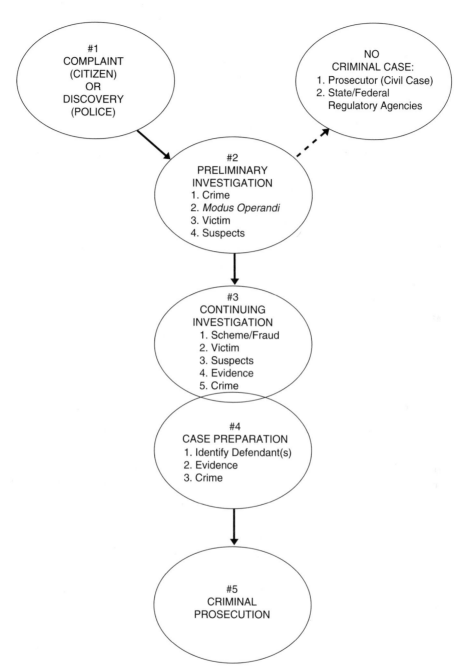

FIGURE 24–1 Investigation of fraud.

potential victim, one of the swindlers apparently "finds" a pocketbook or envelope filled with money (from $500 to $2,500 usually). The approach to the victim is disarming, combining happiness at finding the money along with the query, "What do I do now?" As the victim starts to discuss the swindler's apparent good fortune, the second swindler shows up. Assuming the role of a stranger who just happened to witness the "find," and wants to be part of it, the second swindler joins in the "spiel" that makes the victim a partner in a plan to withhold the money from its owner until the origin of this amount of cash can be determined. Since this will take time, the two swindlers team up to convince the victim that he or she should hold the find, but to assure them of the victim's "good faith," they ask the victim to "show" cash equal to the amount found (or close to it). Faced with the possible loss of one-third of the found money, the gullible victim goes to a bank, gets the cash, and reveals it to the swindlers. They go through the motions of counting it, advising the victim of their satisfaction, and bundling the found money with the victim's cash and arranging to meet again with the victim the next day. Sometime after this parting, the natural curiosity of the victim leads to an examination of the bundle of money. It turns out to be paper cut to size. The swindlers switched the bundle just before they parted from the victim.[2]

The *charity switch* is a variation of the *pigeon drop* used by swindlers who have a potential victim unlikely to be motivated by greed. The "pitch" in the charity switch is to a victim's compassion. The swindlers convince the victim (often a clergyman or nurse) to hold money ($500 to $2,500) for a sick or dying person. If the owner of the money does not recover, the victim can use the money for his or her favorite charity. However, to show "good faith" the victim is asked to show financial responsibility. At this point, the routine of the pigeon drop occurs, with the swindlers taking off with all of the money.[3]

The *payoff* is a swindle in which the swindler claims to have access to information regarding fixed horse races. In its simple, street bunco form, the swindler acts out the role of tout. Three or four bettor-victims place large bets on horses the swindler believes will win a selected race. If one of the swindler's horses wins, the winning bettor shares the winnings with the swindler. In its more elaborate form, victims are identified by "ropers" and put in contact with "inside men" who pose as representatives of the fixed-race conspiracy. Another "inside man" is the manager of the bogus horse-room used in this swindle. In a carefully orchestrated scheme, the "sucker" or "mark" is allowed to win at first, but he or she loses the final large bet. In breaking away with their loot, the swindlers "cool" the victim by implying that he or she is equally guilty of violating federal or state communications laws and/or participating in a criminal conspiracy.[4]

Carnival bunco is street bunco in which each victim may only be "taken" for small amounts of money, but the overall profit to these swindlers is huge. Customers pay a 10- to 50-cent fee to play these games, hoping to win one or more of the better-quality prizes exhibited, but they cannot win the better prizes. Customers are encouraged to try and try again by allowing them to win minor prizes (cheap merchandise) and *fast-counting* their scores: operators total up a customer's score above what has been achieved to convince the victim that he or she is really close to winning a better prize. Of course, the games are rigged so that these scores can never be attained. Trick balls, weighted dolls, underinflated balloons, and oversized marbles are some of the mechanical aids used to defraud gullible carnival goers.

THE BANK EXAMINER FRAUD

The bank examiner fraud is an ego-building swindle based on the hidden desire of many people to serve as a secret agent for the police. Victims are located through telephone books or pseudosurveys. The first telephone call to the victim is double-talk, alleging some problem with their account at the local bank. The next call is allegedly from an officer of the bank. The "spiel" is that one of the bank's employees has been tampering with accounts of depositors, they want to catch him, and they need the victim's help to do so. Cooperative victims are then informed they should go to the bank, withdraw a specific sum (usually just short of the victim's total deposited funds), and bring it home. The victim is assured that the withdrawal will be secretly watched by an armed agent who will follow the victim home to make certain the money is safe. A few moments after arrival at home with the money, the victim is visited by the swindler posing as the "armed agent." After some double-talk, the swindler counts the victim's money, gives him or her a signed deposit slip, and takes the money. Hours, days, and even weeks later, the victim finds out that the name on the deposit slip is fictitious, the bank knows nothing of any dishonest employee, and the money given to the swindler is a total loss.

FRAUDULENT CHECKS

"Passers" of forged checks have always been the concern of police forgery squads. However, it is the unusual fraudulent-check writer who attempts to pass off a signature as genuine. It is true that they sign names other than their own, but this is just the first step in a fraud that also involves (1) false or stolen identification cards; (2) a "spiel" that overcomes a merchant's reluctance to cash a check upon minimal identification; and (3) a bunco or a con artist's sense of the right time, place, and victim to conclude this fraud successfully. Fortunately, the *modus operandi* of these check passers identifies them to investigators. Sometimes, a victim will assist in identification, but since the identification documents are spurious and the contact at the time of check cashing is short, victims have recall problems.

NSF (Not Sufficient Funds) check writers are overt thieves, signing their name to a worthless check and cashing it. Willingness to repay the loss to the victim, and an active checking account can overcome the perception of fraud. So-called "occasional" fraudulent-check writers can postpone criminal prosecution on a promise of restitution. The true fraud investigation in this area is of the "chronic" fraudulent-check writer, and the extent of his or her theft when more than one NSF check has been cashed.

CREDIT CARD FRAUDS

Credit card fraud is emerging as a popular form of theft. Fraudulent use of credit cards provides the thief with various goods and services, and credit cards can easily be converted into cash by sale "in the street"—the illegal marketplace. Thieves obtain credit cards by theft (from mail, the person to whom the card belongs, a residence, an auto, a place of business, a hotel, or other location); by fraudulent application to the issuing firm; or by counterfeiting. Credit cards stolen from the mail, intercepted en route to the legitimate receivers, are sought on the illegal market because they have not been reported as lost or stolen; and if it is a card requiring a "signature," the illegal owner can sign the card in the name of the legitimate card owner and in a style he or she can readily replicate (despite disguising the handwriting).

Credit card thieves may be discovered upon the complaint of merchants who call for an authorization because of the amount of a purchase, who discover that the card is on the "hot card list," or who become suspicious because of alterations on the card itself; during legal searches; and in the course of other investigations. In one Los Angeles case, the investigation of a group forging motor vehicle driver's licenses led to several credit card thieves who bought forged licenses to show additional identification when "running a card."

CONSUMER AND BUSINESS FRAUDS

Consumer and business frauds are marketplace swindles in which the buyer or investor is defrauded by the swindler's misrepresentations.[5]

Common consumer frauds are:

1. *Bait and switch.* Advertised merchandise bargains lure customers into a merchant's place of business. Sales personnel then run down the advertised merchandise and switch the customer to a higher-priced item of allegedly better quality.
2. *Repair fraud.* Overcharging for services performed; charging for services not performed and/or parts not replaced; failing to provide labor and materials as agreed; and charging for labor and/or materials not needed or discussed with the customer, or within the scope of the customer's agreement.
3. *Misrepresentation.* Failing to give the facts as to product performance, warranties, credit charges, or other hidden costs.

The Ponzi scheme, or kiting, is the base of all investment frauds; securities frauds are get-rich-quick schemes; land frauds have a similar scheme along with the promise of a future home in a desirable climate; and advance fee swindles offer assistance in securing huge loans to poor-risk credit applicants.

In a Ponzi scheme (named after its originator) the swindler uses money invested by new victims to pay a high interest on the investments of earlier victims—whose money the swindler has appropriated to his or her own use, rather than investing it as claimed in the "spiel" given the victim. A Ponzi scheme collapses when the swindler runs out of victims.

Securities frauds are based on promises to victims of rapid capital growth and a high and quick rate of returns in dividends, and special advantages such as tax shelters. Victims are selected on the basis of their liquid or convertible assets; high-income professionals and persons approaching the threshold of retirement are common victims.

Land-sales frauds are based on the swindler's misrepresentations as to the value and future development of worthless, unimproved land. Fraudulent land sales have involved the sale of property at inflated prices in which the swindler had no existing title or interest; and undeveloped property owned by the swindler, but without roads, water, or other improvements, but sold because of false statements of current or future development (roads, water, etc.) that does not exist and that the swindler has no intention of providing.

Advanced fee frauds victimize business men and women who are having problems securing loans from local banks or other lending institutions. The swindler claims to have access to loan officers or out-of-town banks, or the mortgage loan officials of a labor union pension fund. The advance fee is money "up front" to motivate the loan arranger (swindler) to arrange the loan. The swindler has no intention of performing as promised, but will make any misrepresentation to secure the victim's money. This is a common swindle in the United States because the reality of securing loans by poor-risk applicants is that money "up front" has been utilized to influence bank loan officers and officials of union pension funds.

Home improvement frauds victimize homeowners by false claims that the work is necessary, or the cost of the proposed work is much below its real worth and will add to the homeowner's basic investment. These frauds include one or more of the following characteristics:

1. Misrepresentation of the need for labor and/or materials.
2. Poor workmanship.
3. Substandard materials.
4. Gross overpricing.
5. Failure to provide labor and materials paid for.
6. Concealment of the cost of credit, as well as the fact that failure to pay will result in a lien on the victim's home.

Gangs of home-improvement swindlers move from town to town, transferring their accounts payable to a local bank at a discount, and moving to new areas.

Bankruptcy frauds involve false claims of insolvency. The planned bankruptcy or *scam* has been utilized by organized crime personnel to loot the assets of a business. In bankruptcy fraud the swindler conceals or diverts to friends and associates the major assets of a business so that they cannot be sold to pay off creditors, or uses previously established credit to secure huge amounts of merchandise and then conceals or converts such merchandise to his or her own use just prior to the bankruptcy—and without paying the supplier's bills.

Insurance frauds are not uncommon in the world of commerce and business. They are in a class by themselves because the swindler must be the insured, and the victim is the insurer. The swindler may have crime partners, but only the insured can profit from defrauding an insurance company. The filing of false claims is the fraud. In some fraudulent fire cases, "sham" mortgages are used to raise the value of a building fraudulently. As a result, insurance policies are issued in amounts far in excess of the true value of the insured building. An arson investigation into a series of fires in an urban ghetto area found that the insured owner had engaged in selling to friends and business associates a number of times, with little or no cash involved in the transfer of ownership. Each time, the seller took a new second mortgage to artificially inflate the building's value.[6]

WORKPLACE FRAUDS

Major frauds in the workplace are embezzlement and computer frauds. Investigations are usually initiated upon discovery of the fraud, with investigators following leads as to the identity of employees having the necessary access to the funds or the computer.

Embezzlement is the conversion of another's property over which the thief has custody or control. Victims are the employers of these dishonest employees, with the scope of the theft depending on the position held by the employee and his or her ability to conceal the theft or thefts.

Investigators should be alert for money losses reported as armed robberies to cover up embezzlement.*

The newest fraud in the workplace involves computers and has frightening potentials for victimization. The Equity Funding Insurance Company fraud is an example of a computer as an essential tool for accomplishing a theft that totaled a $100 million loss to customers, stockholders, and others. To sustain its image as a successful insurance company, the Equity Funding firm produced fake insurance policies which were recorded in the computer as new business and sold for cash to reinsurance firms. In this case, the computer was also programmed to conceal the fraud: a special code was used to skip the usual premium billing procedures on the fake policies. At least 75 employees served as accomplices and participants in this crime. So-called "creative" accounting covered up this fraud for many years until a fired employee talked about it.[7]

*See Department of Justice Document 11 in Appendix C.

AUTOMATED TELLER MACHINE (ATM) FRAUDS

Thieves find ATM cards in the wallets and pocketbooks of their victims, where they also find a driver's license, sometimes a checkbook, and—often—photographs or papers with the names of family members. In past years, all this material was worthless; today, it has become the "kit" for finding the Personal Identification Number (PIN) that validates the ATM card. ATM card holders seem to have a subliminal fear of forgetting their "secret" PIN numbers and use easily remembered numbers such as birthdate or anniversary date, a fore-and-aft series of numbers from their bank account or driver's license number, or a simple 1-2-3-4 code based on their name or the names of children or grandchildren, or a transition of a home or office telephone number.

Now, with the ATM card, the correct PIN number, and a little footwork, the thief tries to get to the machine before the rightful owner of the card contacts the bank and cancels his or her card. Withdrawing whatever the cash limit is for a single transaction, thieves have hit an ATM, walked away; come back for another withdrawal, until the account is empty or the card reported stolen and the machine retains the card.

Thieves are aware of the surveillance cameras at these machines, but knowingly discount any in-court identification at trial, and openly scoff at the possibility of arrest.

However, police and bank fraud investigators struggle with the "gotcha" problem in these cases: (1) They move fast upon stolen card cancellation notice, study the rhythm of the withdrawals by the thief from the ATM transaction record, and—as long as funds remain in the account—wait until the thief arrives to hit the machine again; (2) when credit cards from the same source have been used successfully, they interview salesclerks writing up the sale for a good physical description, knowledge of the suspect, and cooperation of one or two of these individuals to help in producing a composite sketch; (3) when forged checks begin to appear, they interview the endorser for help in identification of suspect; (4) they send cards and checks to crime lab for lifting latent fingerprints; and (5) if they have partial identity, they seek out ex-lovers, ex-spouses, and former friends or crime partners for help in making full identification from photos or a composite sketch. If any one of these individuals is in jail awaiting trial, the investigator may have the classic leverage to secure cooperation.

COMPUTER FRAUD

The chief executive officers (CEO) of large corporations and the managers and owners of smaller businesses have accepted the responsibility for denying access by unauthorized persons to their computer systems. Access codes are guarded zealously to prevent "hackers" from entering their computer system, and some of the ongoing sales talk from both hardware and software computer representatives is super safety that not only blocks access but also sets up an alarm mode when attempts are made—closing down any entry and promptly triggering a trace program to locate and identify the source of the attempted entry.

When someone does break into a system, the response is fast and oriented to damage control. Computer security personnel of the victim firm react to this crisis in its continued employment by joining with industry "reps" who fear this unfavorable publicity.

When personnel determine who did it, how it was done, and the identity of crime partners, they will terminate with prejudice if an employee of the victim firm is guilty, and they may report to the police.

When a computer fraud is reported to police, the person reporting should be considered the victim or an identified representative of the victim (corporation, firm), and a standard crime report should be filled out with the interviewing investigator as the reporting officer. In addition to the called-for information, the narrative of this form should include: (1) what was taken without permission, (2) an estimated amount of the loss, (3) how this successful "attack" on the victim's computer system was accomplished, and (4) background information on any person listed on the crime report as a suspect.

When the interview is over, and data secured are summarized, the expanded report should be filed/forwarded as required by agency rules, and a request made to the squad commander or other supervisor for a "let's talk" session. At this session, if assigned to continue the investigation, seek help. You are likely to need legal assistance (what crime has been committed or attempted; what are its essential elements) and a computer expert (agency or contract employee) who can help in the here-and-now of an investigation and later testify in court as an expert witness.

Then, if the case develops well, go to the prosecutor's office and seek help in case preparation. It takes a large support group headed by a Cyber-sleuth to build a case against clever Cyber-thieves. Tsutomu Shimomura, a computational physicist and computer security expert, was a leader of a support group comprised of FBI agents, local police, and telephone experts from the networked world. Their charge and mission was to identify, arrest, and assist in the prosecution of a world-class hacker who had outwitted authorities for over two years. In 1995, they caught up with this offender. After his arrest, both parties negotiated a deal that lowered the severe sentence likely on 23 counts of computer fraud and related crimes to less than a year in a county jail and gained the cooperation of this offender as a willing witness in the trials of his former crime partners, an important prosecutorial advantage.[8]

INVESTIGATION OF FRAUDS

Since crime scenes are usually nonexistent in fraud cases, the investigator must concentrate on securing facts about the crime from the victim and witnesses, and from the records or other documents prepared and used by one or more of the participants.

Collected evidence should be organized under the following major headings:

1. *Description of the offense.* How was the scheme conceived, what was its nature, where was it placed in operation, and what dates was it in operation?
2. *Victim.* How was the initial contact made? Subsequent contacts? Where? Who was involved? Who made what representations? What was the victim's reliance on such representations? Extent of loss? How paid to swindlers?
3. *Suspect–defendant.* Name, address, occupation, date and place of birth, physical descriptions, associates, and criminal history of suspect–defendant when available. Identification of suspect–defendant who may cooperate with the investigation, possibly serving as accomplice–witness in a criminal trial.
4. *Evidence.* Data as to witnesses, victim, documentary and other physical evidence, and how obtained.
5. *Crime.* A review of the essential elements of the crime or crimes that might be charged, along with (a) major misrepresentations, false pretenses, false promises used by the suspect–defendant in obtaining the victim's money; and (b) an arraying of evidence in support of the investigator's conclusion that such evidence supports a belief in the criminal intent of the suspect–defendant and sets out the fraud involved.

Identification should not be a major problem in fraud investigations once a suspect is located and apprehended. The pursuit and apprehension of swindlers are often handicapped by the inability of victims to properly describe the swindler and others involved, but once apprehended the victim can usually identify the swindler.

In the investigation of credit card frauds, there is a splendid opportunity to uncover more serious crimes and to apprehend crime partners. A credit card is unusual in that the issuing firm (the theft victim in extensive frauds) will aid the investigation by tracing and reporting the activities associated with the illegal use of the credit card. As a result, investigators may secure:

1. Samples of handwriting in the form of signed sales drafts and applications.
2. License plate numbers recorded on gasoline sales drafts at service stations.
3. Drivers' licenses on car rental contracts, or on sales drafts where further identification is requested.
4. The credit card imprint on copies of sales drafts, airline tickets, hotel bills, or car rental contracts.
5. The description of a rented auto the subject had in his or her possession at any particular time.
6. The description of merchandise on a sales slip (this could reveal the purchase of guns, knives, or items identifiable by serial numbers, as well as distinctive clothing and wigs).

"Decoy" vehicles and appliances have opened up new horizons for proactive as well as reactive investigations of consumer frauds. The decoy vehicle or appliance is in good working order except for some minor or easily discovered and repaired fault. When the repair personnel entrusted with the decoy vehicle or appliance lie about needed repairs, or charge for repairs not done or parts not supplied, the investigator can begin developing a fraud case.

PROBLEMS OF PROOF

Deception, lying, and cheating suggest the broad dimensions of fraud, but each "scam" has its own characteristics. The primary problem for a prosecutor is to develop in court by the testimony of witnesses a simple, clear, concise unfolding of the criminal scheme and how the defendant was a participant or prime mover. As in other theft crimes, the intent of the defendant must be shown and the innate greed of the victim downplayed.

When one or more crime partners are involved in a case, prosecutors have found that developing one of them as an accomplice–witness is an effective means of procuring testimony of just how the scheme operated to defraud the victim and the role of the defendant in the swindle.

Selected References

1. G. Jack Bologna and Robert J. Lindquist, *Fraud Auditing and Forensic Accounting—New Tools and Techniques* (New York: John Wiley & Sons, 1987), pp. 27–42.
2. Mary Carey and George Sherman, *A Compendium of Bunk, or How to Spot a Con Artist. A Handbook for Fraud Investigators, Bankers and Other Custodians of the Public Trust* (Springfield, Ill.: Charles C Thomas, Publisher, 1976), pp. 9–20.
3. *Ibid.,* pp. 28–38.
4. David W. Maurer, *The American Confidence Man* (Springfield, Ill.: Charles C Thomas, Publisher, 1974), pp. 30–47.
5. See Herbert Edelhertz, Ezra Stotland, Marilyn Walsh and Milton Weinberg, *The Investigation of White-Collar Crime: A Manual for Law Enforcement Agencies* (Washington, D.C.: U.S. Department of Justice, Law Enforcement Assistance Administration, 1977).
6. Brendan P. Battle and Paul B. Weston, *Arson: Detection and Investigation* (New York: Arco Publishing, 1979), p. 108.
7. Edelhertz et al., *The Investigation of White Collar Crime,* p. 200; Lee J. Seidler, Frederick Andrews, and Marc J. Epstein, *The Equity Funding Papers: The Anatomy of a Fraud* (New York: John Wiley & Sons, 1977), pp. 3–19.
8. Tsutomu Shimomura, *Takedown* (New York: Hyperion/New York Times Company, 1996), pp. 313–314.

Chapter Review

CASE STUDY: DELAYED DISCOVERY—HOUSEHOLD LARCENY _____

This is the theft of property from a residence by a guest (no unlawful or forcible entry).

Narrative (Closing segment of basic crime report)

Victim describes suspect as about 5'7", 125 to 150 lb, Caucasian, short black hair, brown eyes, 15 years old, named Wayne Smith, does not know home address. Yesterday, V noticed card (Shell CC) missing, searched without finding it, and called credit card company, and when she could not find her ATM card, called her bank. When both bank and CC company told her of unusual activity on both cards, V changed her report of lost cards to Stolen. Yesterday—about 3 P.M.—bank (Wells Fargo-Bway branch) called about two possibly forged checks on her account; V told WFB she did not write them, and stopped payment on the two other stolen checks.

V believes suspect, while a guest of her teenage daughter on the night of 10-14 or 10-15, found V's purse and took her Shell CC and Wells-Fargo ATM card and four blank checks from the back of her checkbook (bank gave V check numbers when V talked to them about forged checks).

V states her losses as: $900.00 checks, $800.00 ATM, and $1,000.00 CC, total of $2,700.00.

V promised to return to SO in a day or two with the full names of other boys and girls in the house on the nights V believes theft occurred.

Supplemental

Det. Phelps assigned—follow-up/

Discussion Questions

1. What information is missing from the narrative?
2. Assume the role of Detective Phelps. What would you do?
3. What are the four elements of fraud?
4. What is the difference between the "pigeon drop" and "charity switch" frauds?
5. What are the similarities between "carnival bunco" and the "payoff" swindles?
6. Describe the bank examiner fraud.
7. What are the characteristics of the chronic fraudulent-check writer? The "passers" of forged checks?
8. Describe two consumer frauds; five business frauds.
9. Define embezzlement.
10. Under what major headings should collected evidence in fraud cases be organized? Why?
11. How are swindlers identified?
12. What are decoy vehicles? Appliances?

Library Assignment

List at least five bibliographic references from national or local news sources that will support the belief that bunco and con games are an ongoing problem for police agencies.

Workbook Project

Prepare a list naming and describing the most common consumer and business frauds.

CHAPTER
25

Carjacking

Carjacking is armed robbery. It is a felony-level crime, the theft or attempted theft of a motor vehicle by force or threat of force from the person or the immediate presence of the victim.

Even when the carjacker has not displayed a weapon, the force and fear required for robberies is present (a forced entry of the driver's side door, followed by a rude command to leave the car). When the circumstances and conditions of the robbery lead to a reasonable belief in the victim's mind that he or she may suffer injury unless there is compliance with the robber's demand, the "fear" required in robbery is present. The fact that just less than half of the "no weapon" carjackings were completed from (1987 to 1992) is evidence that a representative sample of drivers confronted by a carjacker are frightened. (See Figure 25–1.) If this crime is committed with use of a pistol or revolver by an assailant in his twenties and a crime partner, a most common carjacking is described.[1]

Auto thieves, on the other hand, commit crimes of stealth, without violence, out of the presence of the owner, and when they no longer need the car, they abandon it.[2]

Therefore, it is grossly unfair to carjacking victims to link their experience with auto theft, to say that carjackings account for only 2 percent of the 1.9 million vehicle thefts nationwide, annually (National Crime Victimization Survey [NCVS]). It should be classified with murder, attempted murder, rape, and robbery. At least once a week, the nation's newspapers carry stories of carjacking victims being killed.

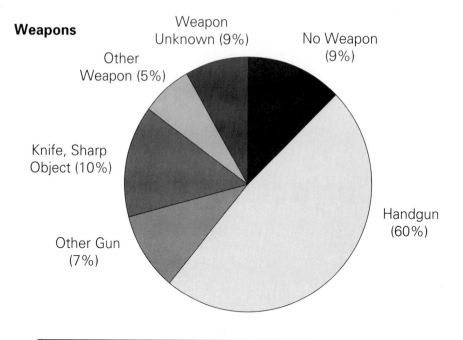

Weapons

Weapon Unknown (9%)

No Weapon (9%)

Other Weapon (5%)

Knife, Sharp Object (10%)

Other Gun (7%)

Handgun (60%)

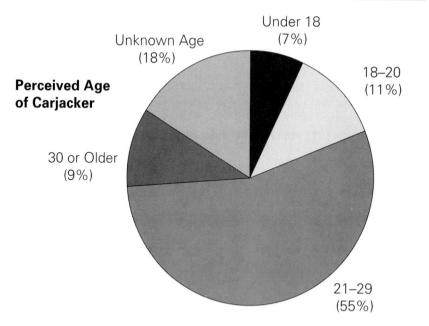

Unknown Age (18%)

Under 18 (7%)

Perceived Age of Carjacker

18–20 (11%)

30 or Older (9%)

21–29 (55%)

Note: Offender characteristics are based on victim's perceptions. For carjackings involving more than one offender, the age used is that of the oldest offender.

FIGURE 25–1 Weapons and age factors in completed carjackings— 1987–1992.(*Source:* Department of Justice Bureau of Justice Statistics, 1994.)

Investigators in police agencies must stop treating carjackings as they would auto theft (and closing out the case when the car is recovered) and consider them as crimes of violence, a crime primarily against the person, not against property.

OUTLINE OF CARJACKING INVESTIGATION

Most men and women with some experience in investigating crime develop an uncanny ability to project the "who" of a crime into their routines. After concluding an investigation into the perpetrator, an investigator will sum it up in his or her mind not as, "I knew it was this person," but rather, "This is what I figured."

The profile of a carjacker is a young man (women have not yet been identified as the "shooters" but may be crime partners in the role of drivers)— who wants to exhibit power to himself and/or others. If he has a pistol, revolver, or sawed-off rifle or shotgun, he probably senses the power of guns and the "high" of a successful encounter with this power. This aligns with the senseless violence of many carjackings, the unnecessary shooting of nonagressive victims.

The suggested outline is structured around a multiscene routine focused on using the recovery of the car to aid in the identification of the offender, not as a goal. Assuming that the offense runs true to form, the carjacking has taken place, the first officers and associates have secured a physical description of the carjacker from the victim along with data on his or her car, and the investigation is turned over to an assigned detective or detectives. The outline suggested is:

1. Scene of crime—standard for robbery (see Chapter 18), plus an expanded canvass for witnesses to the precrime activity of offender and crime partner, if any, vehicle used, conduct while selecting a victim.

2. In-progress "crime scene"—purchase of gasoline, traffic accidents, and when car found; if equipped with car phone, calls made.

3. Dump scene—prior notice to patrol units to secure car and "no touch;" ask finder to notify assigned detective or command; arrange for tow to crime lab and request top-class fingerprint examination of interior and exterior of car; note damage to car and other possible physical evidence.*

4. Pre-arrest scene—use *modus operandi* search for "similars" in past year and hourly scanning of incoming crime reports on carjackings, ATM heists, and robberies of fast-food spots. Arrange for composite sketch and photo "spreads," inquiries in line with relevant basic leads. (Use investigator's hunch as guide to home neighborhood of suspect, why crime-scene location selected, and suspect as former employee of fast-food restaurants in area of crime scene.)

*See Department of Justice Document 12 in Appendix C.

5. "Receiver scene"—trace car parts to buyers, seek identity of offender.
6. "Fraud scene"—if victim had a handbag in the car at the time of the crime, carjacker may use the victim's credit cards, pass them on to family or friends, or sell them "on the street." Trace each transaction for identity of offender.
7. Post-arrest—try to develop crime partner, if arrested with carjacker, receivers of car parts, abusers of credit cards, as witnesses against the carjacker at trial. (See Figure 25–2.)

This outline not only focuses on the identification of the carjacker, but also on "deals" with others involved to assure a successful prosecution.

Selected References

1. MICHAEL R. RAND, "CarJacking," *Crime Data Brief,* Washington, D.C.: DOJ, Bureau of Justice Statistics (March 1994) pp. 1–2.
2. ROBERT S. CHILIMIDOS, *Auto Theft Investigation,* (Los Angeles: Legal Book Corp., 1971), p. 17.

Chapter Review

CASE STUDY: THE YEAR MY LIFE WAS STOLEN* _____

It started in February. I came home about midnight, after an evening out with friends, only to see a sight that made my heart drop: There was the front door, wide open.

Someone had ransacked my house, strange hands pawing through my most private possessions. They stole jewelry, crystal, some electronics. They even took the oak night stand from beside my bed. A night stand!?

Then, two months after the burglary, things went from bad to horrific. It was 5 P.M., and I'd just gotten off work. There's a bar/restaurant on Broadway that I usually go to, and was just pulling up on a nearby side street when it happened.

As I turned off the ignition and started to open my door, I looked up to see a man—I couldn't tell if he was African-American or Hispanic—in a knit cap blocking my way. The first thing I noticed were his eyes. They were absolutely black. Black and cruel.

I started to tell him to back off, but he stopped me cold.

"I want your f***ing car," he hissed. "If you say another f***ing word, I'm going to blow your f***ing brains out."

Then he pulled back his coat to reveal a pistol tucked in the waistband of his pants.

I got the message.

Just then, two friends pulled up in front of us, and started walking toward me. And I was thinking "no, no, no," because from the look in that guy's eyes, I think he would have blown us all away and not thought twice.

So I jumped out and ran, yelling for my friends to "get away, get away, he's got a gun."

*Mari Brendel, *Sacramento NEWS AND REVIEW,* August 3, 1995. (Reprint of excerpts with permission.)

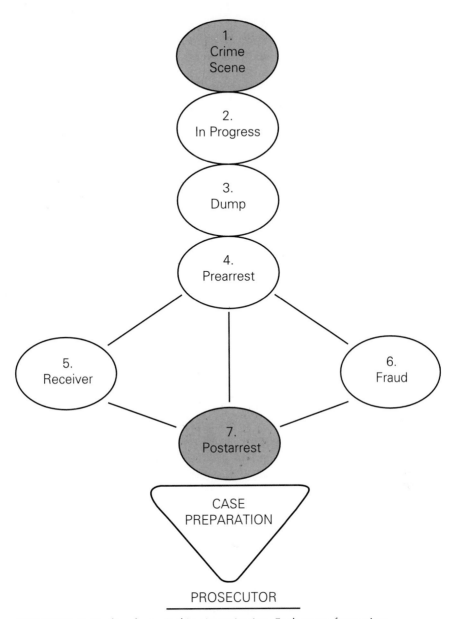

FIGURE 25–2 Outline for carjacking investigation. Each stage, from crime scene to postarrest, is of equal importance.

The police were there within minutes, but the carjacker was already long gone, burning rubber as he raced away. In *my* car. With *my* purse in the seat next to him.

I was numb, in a state of shock. But not too numb to hear one of my friends, a former policeman, tell the officers that he'd seen a gray Cadillac parked nearby with two men sitting inside. They'd been sitting there, waiting for more than a half hour.

Were they just looking for the right victim in the right car to come along, or were they waiting especially for me? The thought sent a chill through me.

It was the worst thing that had ever happened in my life, but as I was soon to learn, my problems were just beginning. Part of it was emotional. I was scared all the time. There were the nightmares, too—the carjacker's face, with those black, evil eyes filling my dreams night after night.

But it wasn't only at night that the incident came back to haunt me. Pretty soon, stores all over town were having checks from my account returned by my bank. Someone else, using my driver's license—yeah, that was in my purse, too—was writing checks like crazy. Hardware stores. Grocery stores. Clothing stores. Auto parts stores.

I wasn't held responsible—it was the stores' fault for not properly checking ID. But every time it happened, I had to deal with the store, provide them with police reports and things like that so that my credit wouldn't be affected. It was one hassle after another.

This was around Memorial Day, and by then I was getting pretty irritated by the Police Department, because as far as I could tell, it had done absolutely nothing. It wasn't like it didn't have some leads to work with. There was my cellular phone bill, for example. Even though I'd canceled within a half-hour of my car being stolen, the carjacker still made a few phone calls. When the bill came, those numbers were listed, but I don't know if the police ever did anything with the information.

They did find the car about three days after it was stolen. It had been abandoned alongside the road somewhere, the stereo and dashboard ripped out, the clutch blown and the body all banged up.

It cost about $7,000 to fix, and I never drove it again. Maybe if it had been stolen from my driveway or something, it wouldn't have been a problem. But the way it was, I was just too scared to ever get back in it. I was just about to make my very last payment on it, too, and I sure wasn't looking forward to all those new monthly payments. But I just couldn't get in my old car again, so I traded it in.

Discussion Questions

1. Discuss this case from the viewpoint of the investigating detective.
2. Is carjacking an armed robbery? Why?
3. Are latent fingerprints found on the hijacked car useful? How?
4. Discuss the "that figures" concept.
5. Why is the prompt solution of carjackings important to any community?

Library Assignment

Review recent print news on carjacking.

Workbook Project

Prepare a check list for a carjacking investigation.

Violent Crime,
and Kids with Guns

The proportion of violent crimes committed by juveniles is disproportionately high compared to their share of the U.S. population.

—U.S. Department of Justice

The violent crimes committed by "kids"—teenagers (age 13–19) and juveniles (under 16) include murder, attempted murder, felony murder, manslaughter, aggravated assault, and armed robbery. In addition, many state legislatures have enacted new laws to prevent street terrorism. Now, penal codes contain sections forbidding shooting at an inhabited dwelling or occupied motor vehicle; discharging or permitting the discharge of a firearm from a motor vehicle; carjacking; possession of a concealable handgun or sawed-off shotgun or rifle; and brandishing a weapon.

These young criminals generally seek out secluded areas for their crime when their motive is economic. Automated Teller Machines (ATM), pizza delivery people, and partly deserted highways or streets are preferred targets.

Some investigators believe the fear of police catching them while the robbery is in progress may encourage the shooting of their victims. Certainly, there was no reason to shoot and kill the British tourist in a Florida highway rest stop or Michael Jordan's father asleep in his car in a parking lot several hundred miles farther north—except the "license" inherent in seclusion.

Criminal homicides and other assaultive crimes committed for motives other than financial gain take place out in the open and numb the minds of reasonable persons. These interpersonal crimes are committed in home neighborhoods, and the victims are not wealthy tourists or people alone and asleep in expensive cars; they are the sons of neighbors. In Chicago, an 11-year-old shot and killed a 14-year old; in Miami, a 13-year-old was arrested in the shooting death of a 14-year-old high school classmate; and in Los Angeles, a 16-year-old fires several shots from a large-caliber pistol in a street not far from his home—police reported he fled the scene on a bicycle. These crimes also include *drive-by shootings.*

Many of these crimes are the result of gang membership, and gang members have expressed an unbelievably low regard for the value of human life: While in juvenile custody facilities, some members who participated have said they would kill "for the ——— of it" and would die "for the colors" of their gang.[1] (See Appendix D, Street Terrorism.)

THE GUNS

Guns are everywhere, and they are not the "Saturday Night Special" or the inexpensive small-caliber weapons of years past. They are large caliber, from .38 to .44, and usually in good working order. Most automatic pistols have super-magazines that hold from 14 to 32 cartridges.

Young burglars find guns during a household burglary and promptly sell them on the street—home neighborhoods—and they are often sold and resold. One young detective seeking to recover a "trophy" .357 Colt Python lost in a house burglary worked from one informant to another and found the gun had been resold four times in 24 hours (at escalating prices). This was excellent police work, as the gun was recovered from an ex-felon on parole. However, stolen guns are not usually recovered and returned to their owners.

Guns are also purchased at gun and sporting goods stores (even K-Mart) for the retail cost of several hundred dollars. Money is usually obtained from good "scores" in a burglary or from drug selling, and the gun purchased is most often a large-caliber automatic pistol with a large-capacity magazine, and, sometimes, with a full-automatic mode that will keep spewing bullets until the trigger is released or the gun is empty.[2]

"Discount" weapons in the underworld of gangs include rifles and shotguns with long barrels. These are frequently modified by cutting the barrel or barrels down short to concealable length. In New York, the work may be done by a high school student in the school's metal shop. In California, the job involves a simple hacksaw and duct tape to hold the shortened barrel and forearm to the rest of the gun. Assault rifles are not yet common in this young people's underworld market.

THE KIDS (TEENAGERS AND JUVENILES)

The kids do not have "rap" sheets. They are too young for that, but they usually have an extensive history of juvenile delinquency. However, juvenile courts restrict access to this information. Local detectives usually have a good idea of what's on these records, as the juveniles and their classmates and associates are often willing to talk to police investigators.

The beginning of a juvenile's entry into this life of crime is marked by stealing from parents, the parents of friends and neighbors; shoplifting; and selling drugs in school to classmates. Since most of them are drug users at this time, the drug selling is only to support their own habits.

The next step involves daytime household burglaries in their own neighborhood or nearby areas, daytime car "clouting" (stealing of merchandise from unlocked cars), and nocturnal thefts of batteries and radios from cars parked on the street or in driveways.

Upwardly mobile boys (girls are only distantly involved in this career path in crime) move on to purse snatching from elderly women in shopping malls, and this is a first sign of violence: Elderly victims are generally punched in the face with a clenched fist. Mugging—fists and feet robberies—may be next, or working into a local drug-selling group as hawker or puller-in for a crack house, a runner who carries drugs from the "stash" to the street vendors or an enforcer who collects drug debts.

By this time, young offenders have become drop-outs from school, runaways (or throw-aways) from family, who are living with and supporting a younger neighborhood girl, either pregnant or already a young mother. They always need money and usually own a gun.

JUVENILE DELINQUENCY

The investigation of an act that may result in a charge of juvenile delinquency must be investigated as a crime. In many cases, the investigation is in full swing before there is any indication that the guilty party, or one of them, is a juvenile. The investigator must continue as usual with the investigation, gathering all the evidence and preparing the case against the suspect as in any other case. When it is certain that a juvenile is the suspect the circumstances of any interrogation will be modified, and the prepared case will be presented to the juvenile court or the prosecutor's office—if the district attorney has assigned attorneys to the juvenile court.

The criminal investigation must remain an area of scientific inquiry and should not be otherwise influenced by the fact that one or more juveniles are among the suspects in a case.

In case preparation involving juveniles, custodial interrogation includes interrogation by police, juvenile authorities, or the probation officer; and the juvenile is entitled to all the procedural safeguards, including the *Miranda* warning. Police not only have their *Miranda* responsibility of advising juveniles of their right to silence and to legal counsel, but also have the added responsibility of determining whether the juvenile understands this warning and its application under all of the circumstances of the pending interrogation. The age of the child and the presence and competence of his or her parents, if present, are relevant factors in this decision-making process.

As a general rule, investigators should notify the parents of a juvenile prior to any interrogation. In addition, the parents must be fully informed of the circumstances of the offense and that it would be a crime if committed by an adult. Once parents, or a parent, has been informed as to the offense, they are in a position to give parental advice to the child. Just prior to the interrogation session, the parent(s) and the juvenile should be informed of the scope of the inquiry: that the juvenile will be asked to tell his or her story of any involvement in the offense committed in his or her own words. At this point, many investigators suggest the parent(s) and juvenile discuss the situation. After this brief discussion, the parents should be advised to allow the juvenile to tell his or her own story without interruption. Throughout the interrogation of a juvenile, the parent(s) should be required to act the role of silent participant–observer.

While the presence of one or both parents at an interrogation session will presently validate it, many investigators suggest the participation of legal counsel on behalf of the juvenile when the act done would be a serious crime if it had been committed by an adult (felony). The presence of counsel assures that any admission or statement of the juvenile is voluntary, not coerced or suggested, not the product of ignorance of rights, nor a result of childish fantasy or fear.

For many years police investigators believed the presence of parents was detrimental to interrogation sessions of juveniles. This is likely to be extended to the presence of legal counsel. However, the important fact that must now be considered is not whether the presence of one or the other is detrimental in any way, but that the absence of parents and/or counsel seriously jeopardizes the eventual usefulness of any information obtained during an interrogation.

The U.S. courts and various state courts continually remind investigators that juveniles are people and are protected by many of the same constitutional rights as are adults.

The controlling case in this area is *Gault*. Summary of this case is as follows:

In re Gault, 387 U.S. 1 (1962)

Facts: Gerald Gault, 15 years old, was confined as a juvenile for a period of his minority (six years) for an obscene telephone call. Complaint was made by a neighbor who received the call. Gerald was picked up while both his parents were at work, and no notice was given to them. The probation officer (also in charge of the Children's Detention Home) filed a petition with the court the next day, but none of the Gault family was notified of this filing or the contents of the petition. This petition stated only that the minor was under 18, was delinquent, and was in need of the protection of the court. It concluded with a request for a hearing and an order for the care and custody of the minor. At the hearing, no counsel was present for young Gault, no one was sworn in, no transcript was made (not even a substantive memorandum was made), and the complainant was not present. Two months later, when testimony was taken at a *habeas corpus* proceeding to secure the child's release, there was conflicting evidence as to the circumstances of this hearing.

Issue: Did the juvenile court infringe on Gerald Gault's constitutional rights?

Decision: A juvenile has the right to notice of charge, assistance of legal counsel, confrontation and cross-examination of witnesses, and the protection of the privilege against self-incrimination.

MAJOR CRIMES AND KIDS WITH GUNS—INVESTIGATION

The outline for investigating the major crime should include developing a major suspect and determining who is involved as crime partner.

If either the "shooter" or the crime partner is legally a juvenile, then the focus interview or custodial interrogation is conducted under proceedings for juvenile delinquents—advising the juvenile and parent(s) of all available legal protections.

Since juvenile crimes often involve more than a single offender, investigators should allow for the operation of the underworld's credo of "better him than me." Young people don't want to think of jail time, much less years in a state prison. The helper will often talk and be an in-court witness against the "boss," without any persuasion by the assigned detective (who cannot make promises on a "deal").

PROBLEMS OF PROOF

Evidence is usually compelling, particularly if the prosecutor bargains successfully with the crime partner(s) and secures an accomplice–witness at trial. Sometimes witnesses are reluctant to help in any fashion, but the district attorney can help in this area.[3]

Selected References

1. LEON BING, *Do or Die* (New York: Harper Perennial, 1992), p. 29–49.
2. ERIK LARSON, *Lethal Passage—The Story of a Gun* (New York: Vintage Books, 1995), *passim*.
3. CLAIRE JOHNSON, BARBARA WEBSTER, AND EDWARD CONNERS, *Prosecuting Gangs: A National Assessment* (Washington, D.C.: NIJ Research in Brief, February, 1995), pp. 1–10.

Chapter Review

Discussion Questions

1. Describe the growth of "wiseguys" to date.
2. Street gangs are armed. Explain their ready access to handguns.
3. Why are witnesses in gang-related crimes reluctant to accept the role?
4. What are the circumstances of a revenge/retaliation shooting?
5. Why should detectives investigating a gang-related crime make a special effort to build trust?
6. Should a 13-year-old murder suspect be tried as an adult? Justify your answer.

Library Assignment

Seek out any bibliographic references to wiseguys in organized crime.

Workbook Project

List briefly the legal rights of juveniles insofar as criminal accusation.

APPENDIX
A

Case Briefs

A. SEARCH AND SEIZURE

4TH AMENDMENT UNITED STATES CONSTITUTION

Mapp v. Ohio, 367 U.S. 643 (1961)

Facts: Miss Dolly Mapp was convicted of the possession of lewd and lascivious books, pictures, and photographs. At her trial, evidence seized during a forcible search of her home without a warrant was admitted into evidence and was the primary evidence leading to her conviction.

Issue: Can evidence seized during an illegal search be admitted as evidence to convict a defendant?

Decision: No evidence seized illegally may be admitted in evidence in any case.

Reason: The due-process clause of the Fourteenth Amendment guarantees that the right to privacy granted by the Fourth Amendment is enforceable against state and federal agents. For preservation of the right to freedom from unreasonable search and seizure, all evidence found by means of an illegal search must be excluded as evidence in any state or federal court. The exclusionary sanction is to deter the police from unlawful acts and preserve the integrity of the court.

Katz v. *United States,* 389 U.S. 347 (1967)

Facts: Charles Katz was convicted in a U.S. district court of transmitting wagering information by telephone. At his trial, the prosecution was permitted to introduce evidence of Katz's portion of telephone conversations, despite defense counsel's objection. Eavesdropping was by agents of the Federal Bureau of Investigation, who had attached an electronic eavesdropping and recording device to the outside of the public telephone booth used by Katz.

Issue: Was the evidence obtained through a legal surveillance (electronic eavesdropping)?

Decision: It was reversible error to admit such evidence, in view of the lack of prior judicial authorization (search warrant).

Reason: An electronic surveillance is a search. Antecedent judicial authorization (search warrant) is a constitutional precondition to the use of electronic surveillance equipment, unless authorized as provided for national-security cases. People, not places, are protected by the Fourth Amendment. Where the defendant has a reasonable expectation of privacy, he is protected from searches without a warrant.

Dalia v. *United States,* 99 S.Ct. 1682 (1979)

Facts: Pursuant to Title III of the Omnibus Crime Control and Safe Streets Act of 1968, the federal district court found probable cause and authorized the government to intercept all oral conversations taking place in the suspect's business office. Even though the court order did not specifically authorize entry of the suspect's business office by government agents, FBI agents did secretly enter the business office at midnight and install an electronic bug.

Issue: Was the secret entry of the specified office a violation of the Fourth Amendment or the federal statute?

Decision: Secret entry to install an electronic device pursuant to a lawful search warrant is not a violation of the Constitution or the statute.

Reason: The critical determination is whether there was a lawful warrant or court order to perform the search or the interception of conversations. The manner of execution of such warrant or order is within the discretion of the government agents. The review of the execution is to the issue of reasonableness. It is implied in an order to intercept conversations that there must be a secret entry to install the equipment.

Terry v. *Ohio,* 392 U.S. 1 (1968)

Facts: A revolver was introduced in evidence at the trial of John W. Terry for carrying a concealed weapon unlawfully (after failure of a pretrial motion to suppress). A police officer had observed unusual conduct by Terry and two other men, and—concluding that they were contemplating a robbery—he stopped and frisked them, discovering the weapon carried by Terry and seizing it.

Issue: Is the police stop-and-frisk procedure constitutional?

Decision: The police stop-and-frisk procedure does not violate the Fourth Amendment rights of Terry (under the circumstances of the case), and the revolver seized from Terry was properly admissible at his trial for carrying a concealed weapon unlawfully.

Reason: This was a reasonable search under the Fourth Amendment. The police officer reasonably concluded in the light of his police experience that these people might be armed and dangerous. This was no more than a reasonable measure for the officer's safety.

Chimel v. *California,* 395 U.S. 752 (1970)

Facts: Police officers armed with an arrest warrant but not a search warrant were admitted to Chimel's home by his wife in his absence. The officers awaited Chimel's arrival, and then arrested him when he entered his home. Chimel refused consent to the officers' search of his home (to "look around"). Despite this refusal, officers searched the entire home on a claim that the lawful arrest justified the search. Chimel was convicted on burglary charges, items taken from his home during the police search having been admitted into evidence despite defense counsel's objection on constitutional grounds.

Issue: What is the scope of a search incidental to a lawful arrest?

Decision: Under the circumstances of this case, the scope of the police search was unreasonable under the Fourth and Fourteenth Amendments.

Reason: No constitutional justification exists, in the absence of a search warrant, for extending a search incidental to a lawful arrest beyond the arrestee's person and the area from which he might obtain a weapon or destroy potentially adverse evidence.

Gustafson v. Florida, 414 U.S. 260 (1973)

Facts: James E. Gustafson was convicted for unlawful possession of marijuana, the state having introduced in evidence several marijuana cigarettes found in a box in his coat pocket when a municipal police officer conducted a full body search of Gustafson after a lawful arrest for driving an automobile without having his driver's license in his possession.

Issue: Was the scope of this search connected with a lawful traffic arrest reasonable?

Decision: The scope of the search was reasonable under the Fourth and Fourteenth Amendments of the Constitution.

B. INTERROGATION

5TH AMENDMENT UNITED STATES CONSTITUTION

6TH AMENDMENT UNITED STATES CONSTITUTION

14TH AMENDMENT UNITED STATES CONSTITUTION

Payne v. Arkansas, 356 U.S. 560 (1958)

Facts: The suspect confessed to murder, was convicted by this and other evidence of murder in the first degree, and was sentenced to death. Undisputed evidence in this case showed that Payne, a mentally dull 19-year-old youth, (1) was arrested without a warrant; (2) was denied a hearing before a magistrate, at which he would have been advised of his right to remain silent and of his right to counsel, as required by Arkansas statutes; (3) was not advised of his right to remain silent or of his right to counsel; (4) was held incommunicado for three days, without counsel, advisor, or friend, during which members of his family tried to see him but were turned away and he was refused permission to make even one telephone call; (5) was denied food for long periods; and finally, (6) was told by the chief of police "that there would be 30 or 40 people there in a few minutes that wanted to get him."

Issue: Did the acts and statements of the police deprive the suspect of due process of law?

Decision: The use in a state criminal trial of a defendant's confession obtained by coercion—whether physical or mental—is forbidden by the Fourteenth Amendment.

Reason: The totality of this course of conduct, culminating in the threat of mob violence, showed that the confession was not "an expression of free choice" (was coerced) and thus violated the due-process clause of the Fourteenth Amendment and should have been excluded from the trial. That Payne was not physically tortured affords no answer to the question whether the confession was coerced, for "(t)here is torture of mind as well as body; the will is as much affected by fear as by force. . . . A confession by which life becomes forfeit must be the expression of free choice."

Lego v. *Toomey,* 404 U.S. 477 (1972)

Facts: The suspect was arrested and made a confession to the police. There was conflicting evidence on the issue of voluntariness (coercion) of the confession. The trial court admitted the confession into evidence.

Issue: What is the burden of proof necessary to admit a confession into evidence? Who determines the *admissibility* of the confession?

Decision: "By a preponderance of the evidence" is a constitutionally permissible burden of proof. Admissibility of evidence is a determination for the court, not the jury.

Reason: There was no demonstration that the "preponderance of evidence" burden was unreliable or that the imposition of a higher standard of proof and expanded exclusionary rules would be sufficiently productive to outweigh the public interest in having probative evidence available to juries. The burden of proof for conviction remains "beyond a reasonable doubt." (See state constitutions, cases, and statutes for imposition of higher standards than the U.S. constitutional minimum standard.)

Miranda v. *Arizona,* 384 U.S. 436 (1966)

Facts: Ernesto A. Miranda was arrested by police for kidnapping and rape, and taken to an interrogation room in a police building. In response to police questioning, Miranda signed a confession containing a typed paragraph stating that the confession was made voluntarily with full knowledge of his legal rights and with the understanding that any statement he made therein might be used against him. This confession was admitted in evidence at his trial on kidnapping and rape charges, and Miranda was convicted as charged.

Issue: Were Miranda's constitutional rights to counsel and also against self-incrimination violated?

Decision: In the absence of intelligent waiver of the constitutional rights involved, confessions and other statements obtained by *custodial police inter-*

rogation are inadmissible in evidence, where the suspect (as Miranda) was not informed of his right to counsel, or of his right to be silent, or of the possible use of his statements as evidence against him. [Emphasis added.]

Reason: Custodial police interrogation is inherently threatening to criminal suspects and calls for procedures ensuring that the suspect is accorded his privilege against self-incrimination. Therefore, it is a constitutional prerequisite to the admissibility of any statements secured during a police custodial interrogation that the suspect must—in the absence of a clear, intelligent waiver of the constitutional rights involved—be warned prior to questioning that he or she has a right to remain silent, that any statement made may be used as adverse evidence, and that he or she has a right to the presence of a retained or appointed attorney. Interrogation is a "critical stage" of the proceeding and requires the presence of an attorney when not waived, after the suspect is advised of that right.

C. RIGHT TO AN ATTORNEY

6TH AMENDMENT UNITED STATES CONSTITUTION

Gideon v. *Wainwright,* 372 U.S. 335 (1963)

Facts: The defendant was charged and convicted of the felony of breaking and entering a poolroom with intent to commit a misdemeanor. The trial court denied defendant's request for an appointed attorney pursuant to Florida law, which allowed appointed attorneys for indigent defendants in capital cases only. The defendant proceeded to trial and was convicted without an attorney to represent him.

Issue: Does the Constitution require the appointment of an attorney for indigent defendants accused of crime?

Decision: The Sixth Amendment requires appointment of counsel unless waived for indigents accused of crime. The provision is obligatory on the states by the Fourteenth Amendment.

Reasons: "The right to be heard would be, in many cases, of little avail if it did not comprehend the right to be heard by counsel. Even the intelligent and educated layman has small and sometimes no skill in the science of law. If charged with crime, he is incapable, generally, of determining for himself whether the indictment is good or bad. He is unfamiliar with the rules of evidence. Left without the aid of counsel he may be put on trial without a proper charge.

United States v. Wade, 388 U.S. 218 (1967)

Facts: Several weeks after Wade's indictment for robbery of a federally insured bank and for conspiracy he was, without notice to his appointed counsel, placed in a lineup in which each person wore strips of tape on his face, as the robber allegedly had done, and on direction repeated words like those the robber allegedly had used. Two bank employees identified Wade as the robber. At the trial when asked if the robber was in the courtroom, they identified Wade. The prior lineup identifications were elicited on cross-examination. Urging that the conduct of the lineup violated his Fifth Amendment privilege against self-incrimination and his Sixth Amendment right to counsel, Wade filed a motion for judgment of acquittal or, alternatively, for a ruling to strike the courtroom identifications. The trial court denied the motions and Wade was convicted.

Issue: Are courtroom identifications of an accused at trial to be excluded from evidence because the accused was exhibited to the witnesses before trial at a post-indictment lineup conducted for identification purposes without notice to and in the absence of the accused's appointed counsel?

Conclusion: Since it appears that there is grave potential for prejudice, intentional or not, in the pretrial lineup, which may not be capable of reconstruction at trial, and since presence of counsel itself can often avert prejudice and assure a meaningful confrontation at trial, there can be little doubt that for Wade the post-indictment lineup was a critical stage of the prosecution at which he was as much entitled to such aid of counsel as at the trial itself. Thus both Wade and his counsel should have been notified of the impending lineup, and counsel's presence should have been a requisite to conduct of the lineup, absent an intelligent waiver. In-court identification by a witness to whom the accused was exhibited before trial in the absence of counsel must be excluded unless it can be established that such evidence had an independent origin or that error in its admission was harmless beyond a reasonable doubt.

APPENDIX
B

Drugs

Drugs commonly encountered on the "drug scene" are:

1. *Opium.* The coagulated juice of the poppy plant. It is a tarlike, dark-brown to black gum, with a texture varying from that of putty or soft tar to the hard, brittle quality of Bakelite.

2. *Morphine.* An active element of and derived from opium. It usually appears as a crystalline powder, and may feel like chalk. Color may range from white through ivory or tan or coffee brown. Morphine base also may be encountered in blocks about 4 inches by 3 inches by 1 inch weighing about 10 to 12 ounces. The blocks range in color from ivory white to fawn to coffee brown. Morphine also may be encountered in the form of Syrettes, capsules, tablets, cubes, or in solution.

3. *Codeine.* Derived from morphine, and may be encountered as odorless white crystals, crystalline powder, tablets, capsules, or in solution (as in cough medicines).

4. *Heroin.* Derived from morphine base to produce diacetylmorphine (the chemical name for heroin), which—when blended with hydrochloric acid—forms into a salt (heroin hydrochloride) which is easily soluble in water. It usually consists of crystals so small as to resemble powdered sugar or flour. Heroin ranges in color from white to ivory, to dull or brownish gray, to tan or brown.

5. *Cocaine.* A stimulant, usually derived from the leaves of the South American coca bush, but this bush also grows in the West Indies, Java, India, and Ceylon. The alkaloid is extracted from the leaves, treated with hydrochloric acid to form cocaine hydrochloride, a salt easily soluble in water. It is encountered as a fine fluffy white crystalline powder, and (depending on the degree of refinement) may resemble snowflakes, camphor, sugar, or epsom salts. It is sometimes found in tablet form.

6. *Crack.* A chemically altered form of cocaine hydrochloride. Crack is also known as "freebase cocaine," "hubba," and "rock." An off-white rocklike substance, crack is broken up into small chunks and placed in plastic containers or small glass vials for marketing. Crack is smoked in a pipe with a heat source. The user inhales the vapor as the crack is heated.

7. *Marijuana.* Consists of the leaves and flowering tops of the female hemp plant *(Cannabis sativa; Cannabis indica)* cultivated in many parts of the world (temperate zones). Crude marijuana contains parts of the leaves, tops, stems, and seeds (fruit) of the plant; "manicured" marijuana consists of smaller particles of the leaves and tops from which almost all the stems and seeds have been removed. Fresh marijuana is dark green in color and turns brown with age and exposure. It may be packaged in tobacco tins, cellophane, paper bags, tissue paper, or cigarettes. Bricks of crude marijuana are about 3 inches by 5 inches by 10 inches and weigh about 2 pounds.

8. *Hashish.* Resin containing cannabis from the leaves and flowering tops of the hemp plant *(Cannabis sativa* and *Cannabis indica).* When this resin is compressed it is hashish. It may be a liquid (hashish oil), a "cake" or "block" (compressed), or a powder. It ranges in color from light brown, to brown, to dark brown, to very dark green, to black. It may be packaged in cloth wrappers, plastic bags, waxed paper, butcher paper, cellophane, burlap bags, bottles, or any combination of these.

   Note: Tetrahydrocannabinol (THC) is the active ingredient in marijuana and hashish. The higher the THC content, the greater the potency of the drug.

9. *Peyote-mescaline.* Consists of the buttonlike tops of a small narcotic cactus *(Lophophora)* that grows in the Rio Grande region of the United States and Mexico. The "peyote" cactus contains eight alkaloids, the most important of which is mescaline. It may be encountered in seed pods, root tops, as seeds, ground into powder, or in capsule form.

10. *Dangerous drugs.* It is impracticable to list all of the vast number of dangerous drugs manufactured today. The most commonly used substances are:

Stimulants	Depressants
Amphetamine/methamphetamine	Amytal
Benzedrine	Nembutal
Dexedrine	Seconal
Dexamyl	Tuinal
Methadrine	

These drugs usually are encountered in tablet or capsule form; large quantities are packaged in plastic bags or bottles.

11. *LSD*. An odorless, colorless, tasteless, organic compound derived from lysergic acid and lysergic acid amide (chemically, LSD-25). It may be found as a powder or a liquid (it is highly soluble in water). The liquid may be applied to any absorbent substance such as sugar; the powder may be compressed in tablet form (with or without color added) or placed in capsules.

12. *PCP (phencyclidine)*. A hallucinogen known in the drug trade as "angel dust." Originally a tranquilizer for horses and other large animals, this compound has become popular among humans who abuse drugs. It is found as white or colored tablets, or in powder form (capsules and packets).

APPENDIX
C

U.S. Department of Justice Bibliographic Citations

The Department of Justice (DOJ) citations in this appendix were selected from several hundred received from the DOJ in response to orders for both topical and custom searches of the National Criminal Justice Reference Service (NCJRS) database by information analysts of the Bureau of Justice Statistics. These annotated references contain an abstract of the reported article or book that is more informative than any footnote and text comment. Figure A-1 is a key to publication data in these reports.

DOCUMENT 1 _____

ACCN: 146544
TITL: Reasonable Doubts
JCIT: ABA Journal, V 79 (December 1993), P 38-48
PAUT: Fricker, R L
PDTE: 1993   PAGE: 11 p   CLSS: article
ORIG: United States   LANG: English
TYPE: Histories/historical perspectives

ANNO: In an abduction-murder case, investigators have produced enough evidence to cast doubt on the conviction and death sentencing of an accused man.

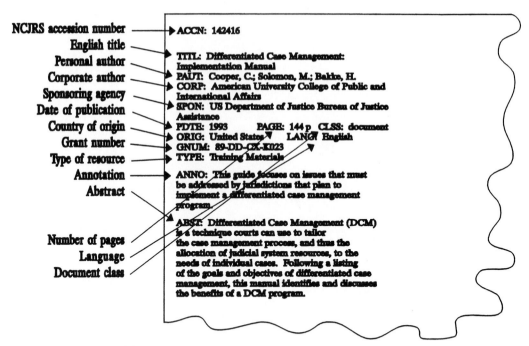

NCJRS accession number — ACCN: 142416

English title — TITL: Differentiated Case Management: Implementation Manual

Personal author — PAUT: Cooper, C.; Solomon, M.; Bakke, H.

Corporate author — CORP: American University College of Public and International Affairs

Sponsoring agency — SPON: US Department of Justice Bureau of Justice Assistance

Date of publication — PDTE: 1993   PAGE: 144 p CLSS: document

Country of origin — ORIG: United States   LANG: English

Grant number — GNUM: 89-DD-CX-K023

Type of resource — TYPE: Training Materials

Annotation — ANNO: This guide focuses on issues that must be addressed by jurisdictions that plan to implement a differentiated case management program.

Abstract — ABST: Differentiated Case Management (DCM) is a technique courts can use to tailor the case management process, and thus the allocation of judicial system resources, to the needs of individual cases. Following a listing of the goals and objectives of differentiated case management, this manual identifies and discusses the benefits of a DCM program.

Number of pages
Language
Document class

FIGURE A-1 Key to publication data on each Department of Justice biblio citation.

ABST: The author raises the question of whether the jury would have found the defendant guilty beyond a reasonable doubt if it had known certain facts that were later introduced. These facts include the following: (1) Three witnesses claimed to have seen another suspect and a vehicle near the scene of the crime, and no one claimed to have seen the accused there; (2) Local police steered lawyers away from a prime suspect, erroneously saying that the suspect had been in jail at the time of the murder; (3) The only on-site forensic evidence at trial had been produced under makeshift conditions, and findings amended to conform to the prosecution's theory; (4) A crime-scene photograph showed a bullet hole larger than the .22 caliber slug taken from the victim's body; (5) Photographs and measurements suggested a mismatch between the accused's vehicle and the one at the scene; and (6) Location of an article of clothing worn by the victim suggested that at least two perpetrators may have been involved. The condemned man now awaits a new trial.

DOCUMENT 2

ACCN: 153472
TITL: Evolution of the Crime Scene Diagram
JCIT: Journal of Forensic Identification, V 45, N 1 (January/February 1995), P 25-29
PAUT: Berg, E

PDTE: 1995   PAGE: 5 p   CLSS: article
ORIG: United States   LANG: English
TYPE: Technical reports

ANNO: Crime scene investigation methods have improved over the past 5 years with the use of forensic light sources, computerized fingerprint identification of suspects, and DNA technology, but actually diagramming the crime scene has not changed substantially.

ABST: In most cases, the crime scene diagram consists of a sketch depicting a room or a section of the street where the crime occurred. Various measurement methods are used to record the location of each piece of evidence. The baseline method involves establishing a line stretched between two reference points. The coordinate method identifies each reference point according to an X-Y axis. The triangulation method involves establishing two reference points; the distance between these two points is recorded and measurements are then made from the point of interest back to the reference points. Other crime scene measurement methods include angle and distance from a known point and computer-aided design (CAD). The CAD software market has expanded considerably over the past few years, but the defacto standard is Autocad. On the computer screen, Autocad looks like an updated version of a traditional drafting table. An Autocad drawing, however, is drawn to real world scale. Costs and benefits of CAD applications in crime scene investigations are noted. 1 figure

DOCUMENT 3

ACCN: 144691
TITL: Goldfinger: An Expert Computer System for the Determination of Fingerprint Detection Sequences
JCIT: Journal of Forensic Identification, V 43, N 5 (September/October 1993), P 468-480
PAUT: Ribaux, O; Lennard, C; Dugerdil, P; Margot, P
PDTE: 1993   PAGE: 13 p   CLSS: article
ORIG: United States   LANG: English
TYPE: Technical reports

ANNO: In order to detect latent fingerprints on a particular surface, fingerprint technicians must employ an appropriate sequence of physical or chemical techniques, and a computer program based on expert system technology has been developed to facilitate the choice of a particular fingerprint detection sequence.

ABST: The application of a logical and proven sequence of fingerprint detection techniques optimizes the chance of latent fingerprint detection on a given object. Certain steps are involved in elaborating an appropriate sequence of fingerprint detection techniques: determine the nature and state of the surface under investigation; select the relevant techniques for the surface; and construct a logical sequence from the chosen techniques. Known as Goldfinger, a computer program has been developed to help fingerprint technicians develop the best sequence of techniques for latent fingerprint detection. The program uses Microsoft Windows and requires at least a 386-based computer. It requires about 5 seconds to calculate detection sequences for a particular set of conditions and group techniques into three categories: high-priority (recommended), medium-priority, and low-priority (techniques with major disadvantages). Goldfinger serves as a valuable store of information on operating conditions, reagent formulations, and precautions. Experienced fingerprint technicians may not require such a system for routine casework, but Goldfinger may be a useful aid in difficult cases and in technician training. 6 references and 6 figures

DOCUMENT 4

ACCN: 140912
TITL: Detection of Trace Explosive Evidence by Ion Mobility Spectrometry
JCIT: Journal of Forensic Sciences, V 38, N 1 (January 1993), P 28-39
PAUT: Fetterolf, D D; Clark, T D
PDTE: 1993   PAGE: 12 p   CLSS: article
ORIG: United States   LANG: English
NOTE: Paper presented at the 44th Annual American Academy of Forensic Sciences meeting, 1992, New Orleans
TYPE: Technical reports

ANNO: The Federal Bureau of Investigation (FBI) has been evaluating various technologies for use in counterterrorism and counternarcotics investigations, and ion mobility spectrometry (IMS) may be a useful technique for explosives detection.

ABST: In the IMS technique, explosives residue is collected on a membrane filter by a special attachment on a household vacuum. Subsequent thermal desorption and analysis require 5 seconds. Experimental results indicate the limits of detection for most common explosives to be about 200 pg. The vacuum sampling method permitted the collection of trace physical evidence transferred to hands or surfaces through contact or postblast residue. Laboratory measurements of the sensitivity and specificity of IMS showed detection as low as 200 pg for common explosives. The demonstrated retention of explosives on hands and the contact transfer to other surfaces offer law enforcement investigators potential new sources for collecting trace physical evidence associated with suspected terrorism. The detection of postblast residue from improvised explosive devices can aid the investigator at a bomb scene by providing a rapid means of screening evidence for further laboratory evaluation. 15 references, 4 tables, and 7 figures

DOCUMENT 5 _____

ACCN: 152021
TITL: Child Witnesses: Fragile Voices in the American Legal System
PAUT: McGough, L S
SALE: Yale University Press 92a Yale Station New Haven, CT 06520; BK book.
PDTE: 1994   PAGE: 349 p
ORIG: United States   LANG: English
PNUM: ISBN 0-300-05748-2
TYPE: Issue overviews

ANNO: This book, written by a former social worker and current family law specialist, identifies problems inherent in the use of children as court witnesses and suggests a program of reform that would benefit both the children and the pursuit of justice.

ABST: The book first analyzes many actual trials that have featured the use of child witnesses, including the McMartin Preschool prosecution in California, the Morgan-Foretich custody and visitation controversy, and the five U.S. Supreme Court child sexual abuse cases. The analysis of these cases assesses how a child witness may be more prone to memory-fade, suggestibility, or fantasy than an adult witness. After assessing research on the cognitive capabilities of children and the emotional, social, and moral influences that might affect children's potential reliability, the author recommends three basic principles of reform. One recommendation is to videotape the child's testimony according to a strict set of rules that will ensure objectivity, thereby reducing both the unreliability and the trauma of giving in-court testimony. A second recommendation is to streamline the criminal investigation process so the child is not subject to numerous and harassing visits by therapists, detectives, and officers of the court. The third recommendation is to revise existing barriers to the receipt of out-of-court statements. Chapter footnotes, 437 references, and a subject index

DOCUMENT 6 _____

ACCN: 149213
TITL: Chinese Gangs and Tongs: An Exploratory Look at the Connection on the West Coast
PAUT: Joe, K
CORP: University of Hawaii Honolulu, HI 96822;
SPON: US Department of Health and Human Services National Institute on Drug Abuse Rockville, MD 20857;
PDTE: 1992   PAGE: 19 p   CLSS: document
ORIG: United States   LANG: English
NOTE: Paper prepared for presentation at the 44th Annual Meeting of the American Society of Criminology, New Orleans, La., November 4-7, 1992
TYPE: Surveys

ANNO: Based on quantitative and semistructured qualitative interviews with 73 Chinese gang members in the San Francisco area, this paper explores the connection between Chinese youth gangs and organized crime groups in Chinese communities in America as well as in Asia.

ABST: Over the last few years, policymakers and law enforcement officials have been concerned about youth gangs in general and the organization and activities of Asian gangs in particular. This study gathered information from two-stage interviews with 64 active and nine retired gang members. Participants were selected through a snowball sampling approach. Results revealed great variability in the composition, duration, and organization of the nine groups with which participants reported affiliation. Results suggest that Asian street gangs on the west coast are not entrenched in the heroin trafficking network, nor are they taking part in any organized way in illicit activities with tongs or triads. Instead, individual members of Asian gangs may establish loose informal connections with individual members of tongs or triads for specific legitimate or illegal purposes. At best, such groups provide the context for establishing connections between individuals. Nevertheless, heroin trafficking is taking place. However, this is a different reality from recent characterizations of the threat of Asian gangs and the Chinese Mafia in the United States. 32 references

DOCUMENT 7

ACCN: 148449
TITL: Asian Organized Crime: The New International Criminal—Hearings Before the Permanent Subcommittee on Investigations of the Committee on Governmental Affairs, 102nd Congress, 2nd Session, June 18 and August 4, 1992
CORP: US Congress Senate Committee on Government Affairs Permanent Subcommittee on Investigations Washington, DC 20510;
SALE: Superintendent of Documents GPO Washington, DC 20402; DO document. National Institute of Justice/National Criminal Justice Reference Service Paper Reproduction Sales, Box 6000, Department F, Rockville, MD 20850; DO Document.

PDTE: 1992	PAGE: 219 p
ORIG: United States	LANG: English

PNUM: ISBN 0-16-039794-4
TYPE: Legislative hearings/committee prints/reports

ANNO: As part of a series of hearings, this hearing focused on testimonies concerning crime organizations from Asia, their international operations, and their activities in the United States.

ABST: The opening statement by Senators Nunn and Roth emphasized the growing threat of Asian organized crime, especially of Hong Kong-based secret crime organizations which use latest technology to spread their activities to other countries. Witnesses who testified before the committee included a committee staff investigator, two detectives from the Metropolitan Toronto Police Department, and two convicted heroin smugglers who were also members of Hong Kong crime triads. A representative of Financial Crime Enforcement Network spoke on money laundering operations while an executive of VISA International explained how crime organizations use counterfeit credit cards to defraud credit card organizations. A member of the CIA discussed the role of organized crime groups in trafficking heroin from Southeast Asia to the United States. To conclude the hearing, a Japanese criminal described Japan's organized crime scene. The prepared statements of the witnesses in order of appearance as well as numerous exhibits are appended.

DOCUMENT 8

ACCN: 147234
TITL: Statement of Robert S. Mueller III, Assistant Attorney General, Criminal Division, United States Department of Justice, Before the Senate Permanent Subcommittee on Investigations, Committee on Governmental Affairs, United States Senate, Regarding Asian Organized Crime, November 6, 1991
PAUT: Mueller, R S
CORP: US Department of Justice Criminal Division Washington, DC 20530;
SALE: National Institute of Justice/National Criminal Justice Reference Service Paper Reproduction Sales, Box 6000, Department F, Rockville, MD 20850; DO Document. National Institute of Justice/NCJRS Microfiche Program Box 6000, Department F, Rockville, MD 20850; MF microfiche.
PDTE: 1991   PAGE: 52 p   CLSS: document
ORIG: United States   LANG: English
NOTE: Reprinted by National Youth Gang Information Center, Document Number D0097
TYPE: Speeches

ANNO: The speaker discusses the threat posed by Asian organized crime groups, and what the Department of Justice (DOJ) is doing about it.

ABST: DOJ has been expanding its efforts against Asian organized crime groups. In the last several years, it has developed a number of major criminal prosecutions, and enlarged and refined its planning and intelligence. The four major Asian organized crime groups are (1) Chinese groups, including triads, criminally influenced tongs, and street gangs; (2) the Japanese criminal society known as the Boryokudan or Yakuza; (3) Vietnamese groups, consisting largely of street gangs often affiliated with Viet Ching or Chinese groups; and (4) Korean gangs, some of which are closely associated with the Japanese Boryokudan. So far, Asian organized crime has been confined to certain urban areas with relatively large Asian populations. The speaker summarizes their activities in the following cities: Atlanta, Baltimore, Boston, Chicago, Dallas, Honolulu, Los Angeles, New Orleans, New York, Philadelphia, Portland (OR), Sacramento, and San Francisco.

He reviews two selected cases, and concludes his speech with descriptions of present and future DOJ initiatives.

DOCUMENT 9 _____

ACCN: 145163
TITL: Asian Organized Crime
JCIT: Police Chief, V 60, N 10 (October 1993), P 65-66, 68, 70, 72
PAUT: Mosquera, R
SALE: National Institute of Justice/NCJRS Microfiche Program Box 6000, Department F, Rockville, MD 20850.; MF microfiche.
PDTE: 1993   PAGE: 5 p   CLSS: article
ORIG: United States   LANG: English
TYPE: Training Materials

ANNO: This overview of Asian organized crime (AOC) in America discusses relevant law enforcement problems, the similarities between La Cosa Nostra (LCN) and AOC, and how prosecution techniques that are successful with LCN can be effective with AOC.

ABST: Triads are the oldest of the Chinese organized crime groups active in the United States. Triads evolved from secret societies originally formed as resistance groups to the Manchu dynasty. Most Triad societies participate in a wide range of criminal activities, including money laundering, drug trafficking, gambling, extortion, prostitution, loan sharking, pornography, alien smuggling, and various protection schemes. The author briefly describes the most active Triads in the United States. The Tongs, which originated from the Triad societies of China, are business and fraternal organizations active in many cities with large Chinese populations. Triads and Tongs are similarly organized and have many similar ceremonies and traditions. Vietnamese organized crime groups consist of two categories: roving bands and local groups. Roving bands travel from one Vietnamese community to another throughout North America and have a propensity for violence. Local groups establish their "turf" in particular Vietnamese communities and use violence to protect it. The Japanese organized crime group known as Yukuza or Boryokudan consists of over 3,000 groups with a membership of approximately 86,000 members. The primary law enforcement problems with AOC groups are cultural and language differences between police personnel and the residents of neighborhoods in which AOC operate.

DOCUMENT 10 _____

ACCN: 147691
TITL: Outlaw Motorcycle Gangs: USA Overview
PAUT: Richardson, A
CORP: California Department of Justice Organized Crime and Criminal Intelligence Branch Sacramento, CA 98153;

SALE: National Institute of Justice/National Criminal Justice Reference Service Paper Reproduction Sales, Box 6000, Department F, Rockville, MD 20850; DO Document. National Institute of Justice/NCJRS Microfiche Program Box 6000, Department F, Rockville, MD 20850; MF microfiche.
PDTE: 1991   PAGE: 37 p   CLSS: document
ORIG: United States   LANG: English
NOTE: This information was originally presented at the 36th Annual National LEIU Training Seminar in Albuquerque, N. Mex., in May 1991.
TYPE: Issue overviews

ANNO: This report provides a brief overview of the organized crime activities of outlaw motorcycle gangs in the United States.

ABST: Following a review of the evolution of motorcycle gangs, with an emphasis on the "Big Four," the overview provides an update on the activities of the five largest gangs. These are the Hells Angels, Pagans, Outlaws, Bandidos, and the Sons of Silence. Other dominant outlaw motorcycle gangs in the United States are then profiled. Associations between outlaw motorcycle gangs and other crime groups are then discussed. The other crime groups include white supremacy groups, prison gangs, and traditional organized crime. A section on the criminal activity of outlaw motorcycle gangs addresses motorcycle thefts, prostitution, money laundering, gang violence, illegal weapons, and narcotics. The report predicts that through the international networks established by outlaw motorcycle gangs, methamphetamine will become the drug of choice throughout the country. Outlaw motorcycle gangs will continue to move into legitimate businesses as they persuade the public of their "new image" and seek new ways to launder money. Wars and violence will continue as gangs try to expand their operations into new territories and law enforcement efforts continue to disrupt their operations. Attached maps of chapter locations

DOCUMENT 11

ACCN: 130032
TITL: Retail Theft Investigation: Embezzlement, Falsely Reported as an Armed Robbery
JCIT: Law and Order, V 39, N 4 (April 1991), P 81-83
PAUT: Chadd, G L
SALE: National Institute of Justice/National Criminal Justice Reference Service Microfiche Program, Box 6000, Department F, Rockville, MD 20850; MF Microfiche.; National Institute of Justice/National Criminal Justice Reference Service Paper Reproduction Sales, Box 6000, Department F, Rockville, MD 20850
PDTE: 1991   PAGE: 3 p
ORIG: United States   LANG: English
TYPE: Surveys

ANNO: Employee embezzlement is often covered up by reporting an armed robbery, and such dishonesty is often not detected because the crime is investigated as an outside theft instead of as an internal offense.

ABST: Employees have far more opportunity to steal than nonemployees. Employee embezzlement falsely reported as an armed robbery can often be identified by seven common characteristics: (1) timing—employees steal money at the most advantageous time; (2) suspect description—vague or changing suspect descriptions may indicate a poorly rehearsed cover story; (3) solitary witness—be suspicious if nobody but the victim saw the criminal; (4) suspicious injuries—superficial, possibly self-inflicted, injuries of a minor nature should be viewed with skepticism; (5) disguises—disguises are worn to keep from being identified or recognized; (6) defense victim—be wary if the witness-victim is defensive, perhaps opting for legal representation at an inappropriate stage of report taking; and (7) anything unusual—be aware of anything suspicious. The key to solving employee embezzlement is a thorough, timely investigation. Procedures to follow in obtaining statements, searching for the money, and prosecuting the crime are described.

DOCUMENT 12 _____

ACCN: 153471
TITL: Separation of Multiple Impressions Using a Four Color Proofing Process
JCIT: Journal of Forensic Identification, V 45, N 1 (January/February 1995), P 19-24
PAUT: Lonetree, L T
PDTE: 1995   PAGE: 6 p   CLSS: article
ORIG: United States   LANG: English
TYPE: Technical reports

ANNO: Color separation, either by electronic or photographic means, can facilitate the observation of fingerprint ridge detail when a known suspect's fingerprints are available and when some agreement of ridge detail has been discerned.

ABST: Instances in which developed latent fingerprints reveal superimposed multiple impressions occur frequently in criminal investigations. Computer-based image enhancement can be used to separate multiple impressions according to gray level density. While this method can be effective if a difference in density exists between different impressions, multiple impression—latent fingerprints developed with powders do not contain extensive density variations. Density values eliminated by computerized image enhancement remove all gray levels above or below specific thresholds, including part of the single impression being considered. Electronic image enhancement has also been employed successfully to separate multiple impressions with a color separation process that uses color scanners. As superimposed impressions are scanned, different red, green, and blue primary color channels can be electronically captured and enhanced independently. This same concept of color separation, but one that uses photographic instead of electronic procedures, can sometimes be beneficial when multiple impressions are involved. Color separation can be used to observe fingerprint ridge detail but may not be successful in all cases of multiple or superimposed latent fingerprints. When an identification is made using the color separation process, the use of film overlays provides a most convincing demonstration in court. 5 photographs

DOCUMENT 13 _____

ACCN: 146644
TITL: Likelihood Ratios for Deoxyribonucleic Acid (DNA) Typing in Criminal Cases
JCIT: Journal of Forensic Sciences, V 39, N 1 (January 1994), P 64-73
PAUT: Jarjoura, D; Jamison, J; Androulakakis, S
PDTE: 1994   PAGE: 10 P   CLSS: article
ORIG: United States   LANG: English
TYPE: Technical reports

ANNO: The likelihood ratio (LR) approach to DNA typing in criminal cases uses both size and pattern discrepancies between the crime scene profile of fragment lengths and the suspect profile for quantifying the strength of evidence.

ABST: The LR indicates evidence is stronger when a pair of profiles matches closely than when a pair barely meets statistical matching criteria. The LR also indicates evidence is stronger when a pair of profiles exhibits differences in the same sign for alleles than when a pair exhibits differences in opposite sign. The LR differs from the match binning approach in which size and pattern discrepancies are considered by experts in the match decision but match closeness is not quantified. In contrast to match binning, the LR avoids an initial decision about whether two profiles match. For DNA typing in criminal cases, the LR numerator is the likelihood of a model that assumes suspect and crime sample fragment length profiles are identical. The LR denominator is the likelihood of a model that does not assume identical profiles. LR's for pairs of profiles that meet published statistical criteria for matching show a wide range of values, including some that indicate evidence is strongly against identity. The theoretical foundation of LR's is somewhat complex for jurors, but their numerical values can be labeled with broad descriptions, such as "very strong evidence of identity." Descriptions should be followed by reports on the proportion of times such strong results have been obtained from two different persons. Effects on the LR value of choices for target populations and assumptions about measurement error distribution should also be provided. 24 references, 2 tables, and 1 figure

ACCN: 152183
TITL: Collection and Identification Guidelines for Traces From Latex Condoms in
Sexual Assault Cases
JCIT: Crime Laboratory Digest, V 21, N 4 (October 1994), P 57-61
PAUT: Blackledge, R D
SALE: National Institute of Justice/National Criminal Justice Reference Service
Paper Reproduction Sales, Box 6000, Department F, Rockville, MD 20850;
DO Document. National Institute of Justice/NCJRS Microfiche Program Box
6000, Department F, Rockville, MD 20850; MF microfiche.
PDTE: 1994   PAGE: 5 p   CLSS: article
ORIG: United States   LANG: English
TYPE: Technical reports

ANNO: Procedures for extracting condom lubricant traces from evidence items in
sexual assault cases have recently been reported, and evidence collection and
identification guidelines have been developed for analyzing latex condom traces.

ABST: In one sexual assault case, the assailant used a lubricated latex condom.
Microscopic examination of an internal vaginal swab from the victim identified
numerous core starch grains, and examination of the filtered extract by infrared
spectroscopy and mass spectrometry identified the presence of a silicone oil,
polydimethylsiloxane. The defense argued, however, that the corn starch could
have originated from gloves worn during the medical examination of the victim. In
another sexual assault case, the accused admitted to having sex with the victim but
claimed that it was consensual. He also claimed he wore a condom but that it
broke. Both claims were denied by the victim. In order for condom lubricant
traces to be reliable and have evidentiary value, a collection and identification
protocol must be developed. This protocol should include a medical examination
of the victim; the collection of physical evidence from the victim, any suspects,
and the crime scene; and inquiries about recent sexual activities of the victim. In
addition, the protocol should address the need to protect medical and investigative
personnel from bloodborne pathogens and other safety hazards. Guidelines are
proposed for developing a reliable protocol that covers the victim's medical
examination, crime scene, suspect interview, and laboratory procedures. The
guidelines recognize that, as habitual sex offenders increase their use of condoms
in criminal assaults, law enforcement personnel need to be aware of the potential
for traces from condoms to associate a suspect with a crime or series of crimes. 6
references and 2 illustrations

Street Terrorism Enforcement and Prevention Act (Step)
(California Penal Code, Chapter 11)

CHAPTER 11
STREET TERRORISM ENFORCEMENT
AND PREVENTION ACT

§§186.20-186.27: Enacted 1988. Repealed operative January 1, 1992, by their own provisions. 1988 ch. 1242.

Another Chapter 11 follows.

CHAPTER 11
STREET TERRORISM ENFORCEMENT
AND PREVENTION ACT

Chapter title. §186.20.

Findings and declarations. §186.21.

Criminal street gang activity—Punishment; definitions. §186.22.

Places used by street gang for commission of criminal conduct—Abatement as nuisance; confiscation of firearms used by street gang members. §186.22a.

Groups and activities not subject to chapter. §186.23.

Severability. §186.24.

Effect on local laws. §186.25.

Coercion of minor to participate in street gang a felony or misdemeanor; penalties. §186.26.

Repealer. §186.27.

Supplying or selling firearm used in criminal street gang activity—Punishment. §186.28.

§186.20. [Repealed January 1, 1997] Chapter Title:

This chapter shall be known and may be cited as the "California Street Terrorism Enforcement and Prevention Act." **Leg.H.** 1988 ch. 1256, effective September 23, 1988, repealed operative January 1, 1992, 1991 ch. 201 §2, repealed operative January 1, 1997 (repealing provision amended).

1988 Note: See §186.27 for repealer.

§186.21. [Repealed January 1, 1997] Findings and Declarations:

The Legislature hereby finds and declares that it is the right of every person, regardless of race, color, creed, religion, national origin, sex, age, sexual orientation, or handicap, to be secure and protected from fear, intimidation, and physical harm caused by the activities of violent groups and individuals. It is not the intent of this chapter to interfere with the exercise of the constitutionally protected rights of freedom of expression and association. The Legislature hereby recognizes the constitutional right of every citizen to harbor and express beliefs on any lawful subject whatsoever, to lawfully associate with others who share similar beliefs, to petition lawfully constituted authority for a redress of perceived grievances, and to participate in the electoral process.

The Legislature, however, further finds that the State of California is in a state of crisis which has been caused by violent street gangs whose members threaten, terrorize, and commit a multitude of crimes against the peaceful citizens of their neighborhoods. These activities, both individually and collectively, present a clear and present danger to public order and safety and are not constitutionally protected. The Legislature finds that there are nearly 600 criminal street gangs operating in California, and that the number of gang-related murders is increasing. The Legislature also finds that in Los Angeles County alone there were 328 gang-related murders in 1986, and that gang homicides in 1987 have increased 80 percent over 1986. It is the intent of the Legislature in enacting this chapter to seek the eradication of criminal activity by street gangs by focusing upon patterns of criminal gang activity and upon the organized nature of street gangs, which together, are the chief source of terror created by street gangs. The Legislature further finds that an effective means of punishing and deterring the criminal activities of street gangs is through forfeiture of the profits, proceeds, and instrumentalities acquired, accumulated, or used by street gangs. **Leg.H.** 1988 ch. 1256, effective September 23, 1988, repealed operative January 1, 1992, 1991 ch. 201 §2, repealed operative January 1, 1997 (repealing provision amended).

1988 Note: See §186.27 for repealer.

§186.22. Enacted 1988. Repealed operative January 1, 1993, by its own provisions. 1991 ch. 661 §1.
Another §186.22 follows.

§186.22. [Repealed January 1, 1997] Criminal Street Gang Activity—Punishment; Definitions:

(a) Any person who actively participates in any criminal street gang with knowledge that its members engage in or have engaged in a pattern of criminal gang activity, and who willfully promotes, furthers, or assists in any felonious criminal conduct by members of that gang, shall be punished by imprisonment in a county jail for a period not to exceed one year, or by imprisonment in the state prison for [1] **16 months, or 2 or 3** years.

(b) (1) Except as provided in paragraph (2), any person who is convicted of a felony [2] committed for the benefit of, at the direction of, or in association with any criminal street gang, with the specific intent to promote, further, or assist in any criminal conduct by gang members, shall, upon conviction of that felony, in addition and consecutive to the punishment prescribed for the felony or attempted felony of which he or she has been convicted, be punished by an additional term of one, two, or three years at the court's discretion. However, if the underlying felony is committed on the grounds of, or within 1,000 feet of, a public or private elementary, vocational, junior high, or high school, during hours in which the facility is open for classes or school related programs or when minors are using the facility, the additional term shall be two, three, or four years, at the court's discretion. The court shall order the imposition of the middle term of the sentence enhancement, unless there are circumstances in aggravation or mitigation. The court shall state the reasons for its choice of sentence enhancements on the record at the time of the sentencing.

(2) Any person who violates this subdivision in the commission of a felony punishable by imprisonment in the state prison for life, shall not be paroled until a minimum of 15 calendar years have been served.

(c) [3] If the court grants probation or suspends the execution of sentence imposed upon the defendant **for a violation of subdivision (a), or in cases involving a true finding of the enhancement enumerated in subdivision (b),** [4] **the court** shall require [5] that the defendant serve **a minimum of** 180 days in a county jail **as a condition thereof.**

(d) Notwithstanding any other [6] law, the court may strike the additional punishment for the enhancements provided in this section or refuse to impose the minimum jail sentence for misdemeanors in an unusual case where the interests of justice would best be served, if the court specifies on the record and enters into the minutes the circumstances indicating that the interests of justice would best be served by that disposition.

(e) As used in this chapter, "pattern of criminal gang activity" means the commission, attempted commission, or solicitation of two or more of the following offenses, provided at least one of those offenses occurred after the effective date of this chapter and the last of those offenses occurred within three years after a prior offense, and the offenses are committed on separate occasions, or by two or more persons:

(1) Assault with a deadly weapon or by means of force likely to produce great bodily injury, as defined in Section 245.

(2) Robbery, as defined in Chapter 4 (commencing with Section 211) of Title 8 of Part 1.

(3) Unlawful homicide or manslaughter, as defined in Chapter 1 (commencing with Section 187) of Title 8 of Part 1.

(4) The sale, possession for sale, transportation, manufacture, offer for sale, or offer to manufacture controlled substances as defined in Sections 11054, 11055, 11056, 11057, and 11058 of the Health and Safety Code.

(5) Shooting at an inhabited dwelling or occupied motor vehicle, as defined in Section 246.

(6) Discharging or permitting the discharge of a firearm from a motor vehicle, as defined in subdivisions (a) and (b) of Section 12034.

(7) Arson, as defined in Chapter 1 (commencing with Section 450) of Title 13.

[7] **(8)** The intimidation of witnesses and victims, as defined in Section 136.1.

[8] **(9) Grand theft, as defined in Section 487, when the value of the money, labor, or real or personal property taken exceeds ten thousand dollars ($10,000).**

(10) Grand theft of any vehicle, trailer, or vessel, as described in Section 487h.

(11) Burglary, as defined in Section 459.

(12) Rape, as defined in Section 261.

(13) Looting, as defined in Section 463.

(14) Moneylaundering, as defined in Section 186.10.

(15) Kidnapping, as defined in Section 207.

(16) Mayhem, as defined in Section 203.

(17) Aggravated mayhem, as defined in Section 205.

(18) Torture, as defined in Section 206.

(19) Felony extortion, as defined in Sections 518 and 520.

(20) Felony vandalism, as defined in paragraph (1) of subdivision (b) of Section 594.

(21) Carjacking, as defined in Section 215.

(22) The sale, delivery, or transfer of a firearm as described in Section 12072.

(23) Possession of a pistol, revolver, or other firearm capable of being concealed upon the person in violation of paragraph (1) of subdivision (a) of Section 12101.

(f) As used in this chapter, "criminal street gang" means any ongoing organization, association, or group of three or more persons, whether formal or informal, having as one of its primary activities the commission of one or more of the criminal acts enumerated in paragraphs (1) to [9] **(23),** inclusive, of subdivision (e), [10] **having** a common name or common identifying sign or symbol, **and** whose members individually or collectively engage in or have engaged in a pattern of criminal gang activity.

(g) This section shall remain in effect only until January 1, 1997, and on that date is repealed. **Leg.H.** 1989 ch. 930 §5.1, operative January 1, 1993, 1991 chs. 201, 661 §2, 1993 chs. 601, 610, 611, effective October 1, 1993, ch. 1125, effective October 11, 1993, 1994 ch. 47, effective April 19, 1994, ch. 451 §1.

§186.22. 1994 Deletes: [1] one, two, or three **[2]** which is **[3]** Any person who is convicted of a public offense punishable as a felony or a misdemeanor, which is committed for the benefit of, at the direction of, or in association with, any criminal street gang, with the specific intent to promote, further, or assist in any criminal conduct by gang members, shall be punished by imprisonment in a county jail not to exceed one year, or by imprisonment in the state prison for one, two, or three years, provided that any person sentenced to imprisonment in a county jail shall be imprisoned for a period not to exceed one year, but not less than 180 days, and shall not be eligible for release upon completion of sentence, parole, or any other basis, until he or she has served 180 days. **[4]** it **[5]** as a condition thereof **[6]** provision of **[7]** (7) **[8]** (8) **[9]** (8) **[10]** which has

Cross-References

Additional prison term for possession of firearm. Penal Code §12021.5.

Abatement of places used by street gangs. Penal Code §186.22a.

Confiscation of firearms. Penal Code §186.22a.

Effect on local laws. Penal Code §186.25.

Exempted groups and activities. Penal Code §186.23.

Repeal date of statute. Penal Code §186.27.

Severability of provisions. Penal Code §186.24.

"Willfully" defined. Penal Code §7.

Ref.: Cal. Crim. Def. Prac., Ch. 91, "Sentencing," Ch. 144, "Crimes Against Order."

§186.22a. [Repealed January 1, 1997] Places Used by Street Gang for Commission of Criminal Conduct—Abatement as Nuisance; Confiscation of Firearms Used by Street Gang Members:

(a) Every building or place used by members of a criminal street gang for the purpose of the commission of the offenses listed in subdivision (c) of Section 186.22 of any offense involving dangerous or deadly weapons, burglary, or rape, and every building or place wherein or upon which that criminal conduct by gang members takes place, is a nuisance which shall be enjoined, abated, and prevented, and for which damages may be recovered, whether it is a public or private nuisance.

(b) Any action for injunction or abatement filed pursuant to subdivision (a) shall proceed according to the provisions of Article 3 (commencing with Section 11570) of Chapter 10 of Division 10 of the Health and Safety Code, except that all of the following shall apply:

    (1) The court shall not assess a civil penalty against any person unless that person knew or should have known of the unlawful acts.

    (2) No order of eviction or closure may be entered.

    (3) All injunctions issued shall be limited to those necessary to protect the health and safety of the residents or the public or those necessary to prevent further criminal activity.

    (4) Suit may not be filed until 30-day notice of the unlawful use or criminal conduct has been provided to the owner by mail, return receipt requested, postage prepaid, to the last known address.

(c) No nonprofit or charitable organization which is conducting its affairs with ordinary care or skill, and no governmental entity, shall be abated pursuant to subdivisions (a) and (b).

(d) Nothing in this chapter shall preclude any aggrieved person from seeking any other remedy provided by law.

(e) (1) Any firearm, ammunition which may be used with the firearm, or any deadly or dangerous weapon which is owned or possessed by a member of a criminal street gang for the purpose of the commission of any of the offenses listed in subdivision (c) of Section 186.22, or the commission of any burglary or rape, may be confiscated by any law enforcement agency or peace officer.

    (2) In those cases where a law enforcement agency believes that the return of the firearm, ammunication, or deadly weapon confiscated pursuant to this subdivision, is or will be used in criminal street gang activity or that the return of the item would be likely to result in endangering the safety of others, the law enforcement agency shall initiate a petition in the superior court to determine if the item is confiscated should be returned or declared a nuisance.

(3) No firearm, ammunition, or deadly weapon shall be sold or destroyed unless reasonable notice is given to its lawful owner if his or her identity and address can be reasonably ascertained. The law enforcement agency shall inform the lawful owner, at that person's last known address by registered mail, that he or she has 30 days from the date of receipt of the notice to respond to the court clerk to confirm his or her desire for a hearing and that the failure to respond shall result in a default order forfeiting the confiscated firearm, ammunication or deadly weapon as a nuisance.

(4) If the person requests a hearing, the court clerk shall set a hearing no later than 30 days from receipt of that request. The court clerk shall notify the person, the law enforcement agency involved, and the district attorney of that date, time, and place of the hearing.

(5) At the hearing, the burden of proof is upon the law enforcement agency or peace officer to show by a preponderance of the evidence that the seized item is or will be used in criminal street gang activity or that return of the item would be likely to return in endangering the safety of others. All returns of firearms shall be subject to subdivision (d) of Section 12072.

(6) If the person does not request a hearing within 30 days of the notice or the lawful owner cannot be ascertained, the law enforcement agency may file a petition that the confiscated firearm, ammunition, or deadly weapon be declared a nuisance. If the items are declared to be a nuisance, the law enforcement agency shall dispose of the items as provided in Section 12028. **Leg.H.** 1988 ch. 1256, effective September 23, 1988, repealed operative January 1, 1992, 1990 ch. 223, 1991 ch. 201 §2, repealed operative January 1, 1997 (repealing provision amended), ch. 260.

1991 Note: See §186.27 for repealer.

Cross-References

Burglary. Penal Code §459.
Criminal street gang terrorism. Penal Code §186.22.
"Criminal street gang" defined. Penal Code §186.22.
"Deadly weapon" defined. Penal Code §3024.
"Firearm" defined. Penal Code §12001.
Rape. Penal Code §261 et seq.

186.23. [Repealed January 1, 1997] Groups and Activities Not Subject to Chapter: This chapter does not apply to employees engaged in concerted activities for their mutual aid and protection, or the activities of labor organizations or their members or agents. **Leg.H.** 1988 ch. 1256, effective September 23, 1988, repealed operative January 1, 1992, 1991 ch. 201 §2, repealed operative January 1, 1997 (repealing provision amended).

1988 Note: §186.27 for repealer.

Cross-References

Criminal street gang terrorism. Penal Code §186.22.

§186.24. [Repealed January 1, 1997] Severability: If any part or provision of this chapter, or the application thereof to any person or circumstance, is held invalid, the remainder of the chapter, including the application of that part or provision to other persons or circumstances, shall not be affected thereby and shall continue in full force and effect. To this end, the provisions of this chapter are severable. **Leg.H.** 1988 ch. 1256, effective September 23, 1988, repealed operative January 1, 1992, 1991 ch 201 §2, repealed operative January 1, 1997 (repealing provision amended).

1988 Note: See §186.27 for repealer.

Cross-References

Criminal street gang terrorism. Penal Code §186.22.

§186.25. [Repealed January 1, 1997] Effect on Local Laws: Nothing in this chapter shall prevent a local governing body from adopting and enforcing laws consistent with this chapter relating to gangs and gang violence. Where local laws duplicate or supplement this chapter, this chapter shall be construed as providing alternative remedies and not as preempting the field. **Leg.H.** 1988 ch. 1256, effective September 23, 1988, repealed operative January 1, 1992, 1991 ch. 201 §2 repealed operative January 1, 1997 (repealing provision amended).

1988 Note: See §186.27 for repealer.

Cross-References

Criminal street gang terrorism. Penal Code §186.22.

§186.26. [Repealed January 1, 1997] Coercion of Minor to Participate in Street Gang a Felony or Misdemeanor; Penalties:

(a) Any adult who utilizes physical violence to coerce, induce, or solicit another person who is under 18 years of age to actively participate in any criminal street gang, as defined in subdivision (f) of Section 186.22, the members of which engage in a pattern of criminal gang activity, as defined in subdivision (e) of Section 186.22, shall be punished by imprisonment in the state prison for one, two, or three years.

(b) Any adult who threatens a minor with physical violence on two or more separate occasions within any 30-day period with the intent to coerce, induce, or solicit the minor to actively participate in a criminal street gang, as defined in subdivision (f) of Section 186.22, the members of which engage in a pattern of criminal gang activity, as defined in subdivision (e) of Section 186.22, shall be punished by imprisonment in the state prison for one, two, or three years or in a county jail for up to one year.

(c) A minor who is 16 years of age or older who commits an offense described in subdivision (a) or (b) is guilty of a misdemeanor.

(d) Nothing in this section shall be construed to limit prosecution under any other provision of the law.

(e) No person shall be convicted of violating this section based upon speech alone, except upon a showing that the speech itself threatened violence against a specific person, that the defendant had the apparent ability to carry out the threat, and that physical harm was imminently likely to occur. **Leg.H.** 1993 ch. 557, repealed operative January 1, 1997.

1993 Note: See §186.27 for repealer.

§186.27. [Repealed January 1, 1997] Repealer: This chapter shall remain in effect only until January 1, 1997, and as of that date is repealed, unless a later enacted statute, which is chaptered before January 1, 1997, deletes or extends that date. **Leg.H.** 1988 ch. 1256, effective September 23, 1988, repealed operative January 1, 1992, 1991 ch. 201, repealed operative January 1, 1997 (repealing provision amended).

Cross-References

Criminal street gang terrorism. Penal Code §186.22.

§186.28. [Repealed January 1, 1997] Supplying or Selling Firearm Used in Criminal Street Gang Activity—Punishment:

(a) Any person, corporation, or firm who shall knowingly supply, sell, or give possession or control of any firearm to another shall be punished by imprisonment in the state prison, or in a county jail for a term not exceeding one year, or by a fine not exceeding one thousand dollars ($1,000), or by both that fine and imprisonment if all of the following apply:

(1) The person, corporation, or firm has actual knowledge that the person will use the firearm to commit a felony described in subdivision (e) of Section 186.22, while actively participating in any criminal street gang, as defined in subdivision (f) of Section 186.22, the members of which engage in a pattern of criminal activity, as defined in subdivision (e) of Section 186.22.

(2) The firearm is used to commit the felony.

(3) A conviction for the felony violation under subdivision (e) of Section 186.22 has first been obtained of the person to whom the firearm was supplied, sold, or given possession or control pursuant to this section.

(b) This section shall only be applicable where the person is not convicted as a principal to the felony offense committed by the person to whom the firearm was supplied, sold, or given possession or control pursuant to this section. **Leg.H.** 1992 ch. 370, repealed operative January 1, 1997.

1992 Note: See §186.27 for repealer.

Glossary*

Active Information Establishes a group of suspects. (7)

Aka Also known as, alias, nickname, street name. (12)

Back-up Man Shooter for a robbery gang. Mixes with bystanders as robbery is in progress; acts only when police or armed guard appear and threaten overt robbers. (18)

Badger Game Extortion Male offender with female crime partner operate a three-act scam: (1) victim (sucker) is placed in compromising position; (2) Offender discovers, claims to be husband or lover of female, screams and threatens, demands money; (3) goes to bank with victim to get cash. (18)

Better Him Than Me Crime partner agrees to testify for prosecution in return for a reduced charge or reduced sentence. (9)

Bugging Secret wiring of suspect's home, office, car with electronic eavesdropping device—bug. (11)

Bumper Beeper Electronic tracking device hidden on underside of suspect vehicle, monitored by receiver in police surveillance car, allows pursuit without fear of discovery. (11)

Canvass Systemic inquiry for witnesses in view, shopping, and neighborhood areas. (8)

Carjacking Vehicle taken from driver by force/fear; handgun most popular weapon; and—if handbag left in car, contents may be "bonus" loot. (25)

Chicken Hawk Pedophile, child molester; commonly an older man seeking out young boys as sexual partners. (17)

Community Threat Groups Organizations engaging in hate crimes and their advocacy (i.e., Klu Klux Klan, Skinheads, Aryan Nation). (20)

*Unusual words and phrases in crime investigation. Numbers in parentheses indicate chapter of first mention.

Con (Confidence) Game Fraud, rip-off, scam based on promise of high profit in a "sure thing." (24)

Corpus Delicti Body of a crime, essential elements. (4)

Crack Discount cocaine; crackheads are hopelessly addicted. (21)

Crank See Meth.

Crime Laboratory A facility equipped for the scientific examination of evidentiary material submitted by police evidence-gatherers, staffed by qualified forensic scientists/criminalisticians; and with a capacity to provide reports explaining what was discovered in the lab, by whom, relevancy to the issue of guilt or innocence, and whether examiner is qualified as—or can be—an expert witness in court in the scientific area of the examination. (6)

Criminalistics Individualization of physical evidence in a crime lab. Aka forensic science. (6)

Cryptography Ciphers and codes (cloak and dagger) used to protect the security of underworld communications; decoding. (6)

Cults An organization, group, or sect (not a gang) bound together by a charismatic leader and his or her "spin" on one or more segments of the Bible or areas of religious worship. Often accused of child abuse, unorthodox lifestyles, misuse of funds, and undue influence in recruiting members and mind-bending techniques to retain them. (20)

Date Rape Prior relationship betwen rapist and victim. (16)

DNA (Deoxyribonucleic Acid) Fingerprinting Identification by genetic code analysis in crime labs of blood samples and samples of other body fluids. Accuracy, reliability, and validity being established by in-court testimony of DNA experts in a growing number of cases. (6)

Drive-By Shooting One or more cars filled with members of a street gang and large-caliber, fast-firing assault rifles and handguns with large capacity magazines, drive by a house suspected of containing one or more members of a rival gang and open fire. This barrage of bullets threatens all occupants in the target as well as nearby yards and houses, and it is nondiscriminating—young/old, boy/girl, involved/uninvolved. (26)

Drugs, Narcotics (See Appendix B.)

Ethical Awareness An alertness to behavior that is wrong, immoral, unprincipled, substandard, and criminal. (2)

Firebug (See Pyromania.)

Fence Professional receiver of stolen property. (22)

Flipped Confronted with evidence of his/her guilt, suspect agrees to become accomplice–witness in return for reduced charge or lesser sentence. (10)

Forensic Science (See Criminalistics.)

Hate Crime Vandalism and violent crime motivated by apparent hate of victim's religion, race, ethnic heritage, or sexual orientation; may be linked to offender's membership in community threat group. (20)

Home Invasion (Robbery) A vicious and violent robbery of a family in their home. Pistol-whipping and threats to kill force victims into disclosing hiding place of cash, jewelry. Criminal homicides do occur. (18)

Jury Nullification Jury verdict apparently influenced by mistrust of police witnesses/testimony. (2)

Malice An offender's inexcusable, unjustified, unmitigated person-endangering state of mind. (15)

Match (Matching) Most favorable term in a crime-lab report of a comparison analysis of evidence submitted by police investigators. (6)

Meth (Methamphetamine) An illegal drug, a stimulant, popular because of "hit," low price, and availability. Usually made in clandestine labs or at home (kitchen lab) from legal substances. Aka crank, speed. (21)

Mushroom Factor Diligent investigation of child molester likely to lead to exposure of a network of these offenders. (17)

Passive Information Data are useful when a group of suspects is developed in a crime investigation. (7)

Physical Evidence Liquid to solid material amenable to scientic analysis by forensic science technicians in a crime lab. (5)

Pot (Marijuana) Most popular illegal drug in United States, and usually most available and inexpensive. (21)

Prima Facie On the face of, at first view, uncontradicted. (13)

Pyromania Obsessional impulse to set fires. "Pyro" is a fire bug, pyromaniac. (19)

Rigor Mortis Body appearance after death—stiffening. Factor in determining time of death in criminal homicides. (6)

Scam (See Con Games.)

Stakeout (Plant) Fixed visual surveillance. (11)

Stalking Aggressive and threatening pursuit of victim selected because of celebrity status, past relationship, or other irrational motive. Initial harrassing letters and telephone calls escalate to demands and threats and serious injury or fatal attack. (15)

Stash On drug scene, hiding place of a drug-seller's inventory of drugs; generally, hiding place of cash, weapons, stolen property. (21)

Sting Police-operated "fencing" operation to trap thieves as they sell their stolen property to undercover police, are videotaped and identified for future arrest at completion of operation. Also modified and used to trap graft-taking public officials, others. (23)

Selected Bibliography*

ABRAHAMS, PETER, *The Fan*. New York: McGraw-Hill, 1990.

ADLER, MORTIMORE J., *Desires: Right and Wrong—The Ethics of Enough*. New York: Macmillan Publishing, 1991.

ALLEN, BUD, and DIANA BOSTA, *Games Criminals Play—How You Can Profit by Knowing Them*. Sacramento, Calif.: Rae John Publishers, 1981.

BATTLE, BRENDON P., and PAUL B. WESTON, *Arson Detection and Investigation*. New York: Arco Publishing, 1979.

BING, LEON, *Do or Die*. New York: Harper Perennial (Harper Collins), 1993.

BIONDI, RAY, and WALT HECOX, *All His Father's Sins,* New York: Pocket Books, 1988.

BOLOGNA, JACK G., and ROBERT J. LINDQUIST, *Fraud Auditing and Forensic Accounting—New Tools and Techniques*. New York: John Wiley & Sons, 1987.

CAREY, MARY, and GEORGE SHERMAN, *Compendium of Bunk, or How to Spot a Con Artist: A Handbook for Fraud Investigators, Bankers and Other Custodians of the Public Trust*. Springfield, Ill.: Charles C Thomas, Publisher, 1976.

CLARKE, MICHAEL, *Business Crime: Its Nature and Control*. New York: St. Martin's Press, 1990.

CONWAY, JAMES P., *Evidential Documents*. Springfield, Ill.: Charles C Thomas, Publisher, 1959.

COOK, CLAUDE W., *A Practical Guide to the Basics of Physical Evidence*. Springfield, Ill.: Charles C Thomas, Publisher, 1984.

COUNT, E. W., *Cop Talk—True Detective Stories from the NYPD*. New York: Pocket Books, 1994.

CUOMO, GEORGE, *A Couple of Cops—On the Street, In the Crime Lab*. New York: Random House, 1995.

*See "Selected References" at the end of each chapter for other books and articles.

DALY, ROBERT, *Prince of the City—The True Story of a Cop Who Knew Too Much*. Boston: Houghton Mifflin, 1978.

DELATTRE, EDWIN J., *Character and Cops: Ethics in Policing*. Washington, D.C.: American Enterprise Institute for Public Policy Research, 1989.

DILNOT, GEORGE, *Great Detectives and Their Methods*. Boston: Houghton Mifflin, 1928.

ECK, JOHN E., *Solving Crimes—The Investigation of Burglary and Robbery*. Washington, D.C.: U.S. Department of Justice, National Institute of Justice, 1983.

ESTRICK, SUSAN, *Real Rape*. Cambridge, Mass.: Harvard University Press, 1987.

FARR, ROBERT, *The Electronic Criminals*. New York: McGraw-Hill, 1975.

GODDARD, DONALD, *Undercover—The Secret Lives of a Federal Agent*. New York: Times Books, 1988.

GRAYSMITH, ROBERT, *The Sleeping Lady—The Trailside Murders Above the Golden Gate*. New York: Onyx (Penguin Books, USA, Inc.), 1990.

GREEN, GARY S., *Occupational Crime*. Chicago: Nelson-Hall, 1990.

GROSS, HANS G. A., *Criminal Investigation,* trans. John Adam and J. Collyer Adam. Madras, India: Higginbotham, 1906; London, Specialist Press, 1907; 2nd ed., 1924; 3rd ed., rev. by Norman Kendal, London, Sweet & Maxwell Ltd., 1934; 4th ed., rev. by R. M. Howe, Sweet & Maxwell Ltd., 1950; 5th ed., rev. by R. L. Jackson, Sweet & Maxwell Ltd., 1962.

HAMMER, RICHARD, *The CBS Murders*. New York: William Morrow & Company, 1987.

HAZELWOOD, ROBERT R., and ANN WOLBERT BURGESS, *Practical Aspects of Rape Investigation—A Multidisciplinary Approach*. New York: Elsevier Science Publishing, 1987.

HIBBARD, WHITNEY S., and RAYMOND W. WORRING, *Forensic Hypnosis in Criminal Investigations*. Springfield, Ill.: Charles C Thomas, Publisher, 1987.

HICKEY, ERIC W., *Serial Murderers and Their Victims*. Pacific Grove, Calif.: Brooks/Cole Publishing, 1991.

KESSLER, WILLIAM F., and PAUL B. WESTON, *The Detection of Murder*. New York: Arco Publishing, 1961.

KIRK, PAUL, *Fire Investigation*. New York: John Wiley & Sons, 1969.

LARSEN, RICHARD W., *Bundy—The Deliberate Stranger*. Englewood Cliffs, N.J.: Prentice Hall, 1980.

LARSON, ERIK, *Lethal Passage*. New York: Viking Books, 1995.

LEVIN, JACK, and JACK MCDEVITT. *Hate Crimes—The Rising Tide of Bigotry and Bloodshed*. New York: Plenum Press, 1993.

LEVINE, MICHAEL, *Deep Cover—The Inside Story of How DEA Infighting, Incompetence, and Subterfuge Lost Us the Biggest Battle of the Drug War*. New York: Delacorte Press, 1990.

LOFTUS, ELIZABETH, and KATHERINE KETCHAM, *Witness for the Defense—The Accused, the Eyewitness, and the Expert Who Puts Memory on Trial*. New York: St. Martin's Press, 1991.

MAAS, PETER, *Serpico*. New York: The Viking Press, 1973.

MANNING, PETER K., *The Narcs' Game—Organizational and Informational Limits on Drug Law Enforcement*. Cambridge, Mass.: The MIT Press, 1980.

MAURER, DAVID W., *The American Confidence Man*. Springfield, Ill.: Charles C Thomas, Publisher, 1974.

MAUER, DAVID W., *Language of the Underworld*. Lexington: The University Press of Kentucky, 1981.

MCCARTHY BILL, and MIKE MALLOWE, *Vice Cop—My Twenty-Year Battle with New York's Dark Side*. New York: William Morrow & Co., 1991.

MCDONALD, PETER, *Tire Imprint Evidence*. New York: Elsevier, 1989.

MCGINNISS, JOE, *Cruel Doubts*. New York: Pocket Star Books (Simon & Schuster), 1991.

MOORE, MARK HARRISON, *Buy and Bust*. Lexington, Mass.: D.C. Heath and Company, 1977.

MURPHY, HARRY J., *Where's What: Sources of Information for Federal Investigators*. Washington, D.C.: The Brookings Institution, 1975.

NEFF, JAMES, *Mobbed Up—Jackie Presser's High-Wire Life in the Teamsters, the Mafia, and the FBI.* New York: Dell Publishing, 1989.

O'BRIEN, DARCY, *Two of a Kind—The Hillside Stranglers.* New York: New American Library, 1985.

O'CONNOR, JOHN, J., *Practical Fire and Arson Investigation.* New York: Elsevier-NDU, 1987.

PALMIOTTO, MICHAEL J., ed., *Critical Issues in Criminal Investigation.* Cincinnati, Ohio: Anderson Publishing, 1988.

POLLOCK-BYRNE, JOCELYN, *Ethics in Crime and Justice—Dilemmas and Decisions.* Pacific Grove, Calif.: Brooks/Cole Publishing, 1988.

RENGERT, GEORGE, and JOHN WASILCHICK, *Suburban Burglary—A Time and Place for Everything.* Springfield, Ill.: Charles C Thomas, Publisher, 1985.

ROBBINS, LOUISE, M., *Footprints—Collection, Analysis, and Interpretation.* Springfield, Ill.: Charles C Thomas, Publisher, 1985.

SAFERSTEIN, RICHARD, *Criminalistics: An Introduction to Forensic Science.* 5th ed., Englewood Cliffs, N.J.: Prentice Hall, 1975.

SCHMALLEGER, FRANK, *Ethics in Criminal Justice.* Bristol, Ind.: Wyndham Hall Press, 1990.

SHIMOMURA, TSUTOMU, *Takedown.* New York: Hyperion, 1996.

SIMON, DAVID, *Homicide—A Year on the Killing Streets.* Boston: Houghton Mifflin Company, 1991.

SLOAN, STEPHEN, *Simulating Terrorism.* Norman: University of Oklahoma Press, 1981.

THORNWALD, JURGEN, *Century of the Detective,* trans. Richard Winston and Clara Winston. New York: Harcourt Brace Jovanovich, 1965.

TOSI, OSCAR, *Voice Identification: Theory and Practice.* Baltimore: University Park Press, 1979.

WAKEFIELD, HOLLIDA, and RALPH UNDERWAGER. *Accusations of Child Sexual Abuse.* Springfield, Ill.: Charles C Thomas Publisher, 1988.

WALLS, H. J., *Forensic Science,* 2nd ed., New York: Praeger Publishers, 1974.

WAMBAUGH, JOSEPH, *The Blooding,* New York: Perigord Press (Bantam Books), 1989.

WARNER, CARMEN GERMAINE, ed., *Rape and Sexual Assault: Management and Intervention.* Rockville, Md.: Aspen Systems Corp., 1980.

WELLS, KENNETH M., and PAUL B. WESTON, *Criminal Procedure and Trial Practice.* Englewood Cliffs, N.J.: Prentice Hall, 1977.

WESTON, PAUL B., and KENNETH M. WELLS, *Criminal Law.* Santa Monica, Calif.: Goodyear Publishing, 1978.

WESTON, PAUL B., KENNETH M. WELLS, and MARLENE HERTOGHE, *Criminal Evidence for Police, Fourth Edition.* Upper Saddle River, N.J.: Prentice Hall, 1995.

WHITED, CHARLES, *The Decoy Man—The Extraordinary Adventures of an Undercover Cop.* Chicago: Playboy Press, 1973.

WILSON, JAMES Q., *The Moral Sense.* New York: The Free Press, 1993.

Index

Arson, burning patterns *(cont.)*
    structure fires, 268-69
  evidence of, 32, 265-66, 271-72, 277
  fire scene, 271-73
    photographs of, 272-73
  ignition and place of origin of fire, 270-71
  investigation of, 265-66, 273-75
  law of, 264-65
  motivations for, 267-68
  problems of proof in, 277
  suspicious fire concept, 265-68
Aryan Nation, 290
Asian gangs, 290
Asian organized crime, 301, 376-78
Asportation, 253
Assassination, 285
Assault(s), 229-30, 254
  aggravated, 229
  means of attack in, 34
  sexual. *See* Rape
Assessment, pre-employment, 10
ATMs (Automated Teller Machines), 258, 343
Audio surveillance, 167-70, 362
Audiotaping of suspect/witness, 143-44
Auditing, fraud, 336
Autopsy, 34-35, 80-82, 216-17
Autopsy report, 35, 81
Auto theft, 318-20. *See also* Carjacking
Ayyad, Nidal, 289

B

Backup man, 256
"Badger Game" (scam), 254
Bags, plastic, 66
Bait and switch, 340
Ballistics, defined, 22
Bank examiner fraud, 339
Bank Records and Foreign Transactions Act,
    309
Bank robberies, 258
Bankruptcy frauds, 342
Basic-lead informants, 151-52
Basic leads. *See* Lead(s)
Battering, child, 244
Beeper, bumper, 165-66
Benefit from crime, 96
Berg, Alan, 290
Bite wounds, 30
Blackstone, William, 264
"Blind date" bombings, 284
Blood, as evidence, 25-26, 78
  contaminated with infectious agent, 75
  hydrodynamics of drops and splashes, 27
  of rape, 240
  samples and swatches, 67, 68
  wall stains, 28
Bludgeons, as evidence, 76
Blunt instruments, as evidence, 25
Body fluids evidence, contaminated, 75
Body language, 208-9

Body substances evidence, packaging of, 67
Bombing(s), 275-77. *See also* Terrorist activity
  "blind date," 284
  World Trade Center, 289
Bones, identification of homicide victim
    through, 218
Boryokudan, 377, 378
Brief, legal, 193-94
Broadcast alarm, 180-81
"Bugging," 168
Bullet hole, cratering of, 32, 33
Bullets, as evidence, 24-25
Bumper beeper, 165-66
Bunco schemes, 336-39
Burglar tools, possession of, 324
Burglary(ies), 323-34. *See also* Theft
  as behavioral concept, 327-28
  case preparation, 331
  in common law, 323-24
  complete investigator of, 332
  conviction of, 323
  degrees of, 323-24
  evidence of, 329-31, 332, 333
  identification of suspect, 332
  investigation of, 325, 329-30
  investigator apathy/indifference to, 331-32
  known burglars, 330-31
  means of entry, 326-27, 329
  modus operandi of, 31, 326, 330
  problems of proof, 332-33
  rape and, 328, 329, 331
  of safes, 328-29
  site selection for, 324
  toolmarks at, 31
  types of burglars, 325-27
  witnesses to, 331
Business fraud, 340-42
Business sense of burglars, 326
Buyer-seller interactions, as leads, 106
Byrnes, James, 254

C

Camcorders, 50-51
Cameras
  Polaroid, 43
  surveillance, 259
Candles, as fire starters, 270
Career criminals, 261-62
Carjacking, 319, 349-54
  investigation of, 351-52
  offender characteristics, 350, 351
Carnival bunco, 338-39
Cartridges, as evidence, 22-23, 24
Case preparation, 190-203
  arraying evidence, 193
  for auto theft, 320
  for burglary, 331
  closing investigation, 195-96
  decision to charge, 194-95

Legal counsel. *See also* Case preparation;
    Defense counsel
  interrogation of juveniles in presence of, 358
  at lineups, 163-64
Lego v. *Toomey,* 365
"Lie box" capability, 161
Liebscher, William, Jr., 99
Lindbergh kidnapping, 282
Lineups, 162-64, 367
Linkage reports, 228
Locard, 61
Lock-picking tools, 326
Lovers, as leads, 106
LSD, 370

M

McCray v. *Illinois,* 158
McMartin preschool case, 249
Mafia (La Cosa Nostra), 300-301
Malice aforethought, 212-13, 214
Man-in-a-car pattern of serial murder, 226, 227
Manslaughter, 211, 214-16
  involuntary, 215
  vehicle, 215-16
  voluntary, 214
Mapp v. *Ohio,* 361-62
Maps of crime scene, 37
Margolies, Irwin, 155
Marighella, Carlos, 284
Marijuana, 299, 369
Measurements
  photography and, 44
  for sketches, 47
Medical examination
  of rape victim, 234
  of sexually abused child, 248
  of suspect rapist, 239
Medicolegal services, 73, 80-82
Merger doctrine, 214
Mescaline, 369
Meth (methamphetamine), 299
Micromomentaries, 146
Miller v. *Pate,* 82-83
Miranda v. *Arizona,* 70, 116, 132, 133, 186,
    365-66
Miranda warning, 133-36, 357
Misrepresentation, 340
Missing children, 250-51
Missing Children's Act (1982), 250
Mobile Crime Laboratory, 19
Mobs, 290
Modus operandi
  of burglary, 31, 326, 330
  of check passers, 339
  data on, 39
  leads from, 94, 102-3
  photographs to trace, 44
  of robbery, 256-57
  of theft, 313-14, 315, 317
Money, counterfeit, 65-66

Monitoring. *See* Surveillance
Morality, ethical awareness and, 9-10
Moral Sense, The (Wilson), 9-10
Morphine, 368
Motivation, extrinsic and intrinsic, 137
Motive(s), 93
  for arson, 267-68
  for murder, 225-26
Motorcycle gangs, 290, 301, 378-79
Motor number, 320
Motor vehicle bureaus, search for rapists
    through, 237
Motor vehicles, leads from, 93-94, 98-99
Moving surveillance (tail, shadow), 165
Mug shots, 103-4
Murder
  autopsy to detect, 216-17
  by drug-selling gangs, 301
  felony-murder rule, 214
  first-degree, 211, 213-14
  malice aforethought and, 212-13, 214
  motive for, 225-26
  second-degree, 211, 214
  serial murders, 226-28, 231, 247-48
Murder-suicide, 224
Mushroom factor in pedophilia, 247

N

Narcotics, 299
Narcotics cases. *See* Dangerous drugs and nar-
    cotics cases
Negative evidence, 192
Negligence, gross, 215
Neighborhood canvass, 119-20
Network analysis, 289
Neutron activation analysis (NAA), 86-87
New York City, detective selection in, 5
Nonverbal communication
  during interrogations, 146-47
  of investigator-witness, 208-9
NSF (Not Sufficient Funds) check writers, 339-40
Nullification, jury, 9

O

Observations by reporting officer, 42
Omnibus Crime Control and Safe Streets Acts
    of 1958, Title III of, 168
Operations units, police, 287-88
Opium, 368
Opportunity for crime, 93, 97
Organized crime mobs, 290
  arson by, 267
  Asian, 301, 376-78
  covert informants in, 153-54
  Mafia, 300-301
  recruiting defendant within, 154-55
Outrageous conduct by police, 10-11
Overhauling by firefighters, 271